The Chevalier
de Montmagny
(1601–1657)

"FRENCH AMERICA" COLLECTION

The "French America" collection publishes works pertaining to the various realities of the French in North America, in particular outside of Quebec: Ontario, the Maritimes, Western Canada, and the United States. In keeping with the University of Ottawa Press bilingual policy, this collection welcomes manuscripts in French or English.

Collection director :
Jean-Pierre Wallot, director of the Centre de recherche en civilisation canadienne-française (CRCCF)

Titles in the same collection:

Wallot, Jean-Pierre (ed.), *Le débat qui n'a pas eu lieu. La Commission Pepin-Robarts, quelque vingt ans après*, 2002.

Dennie, Donald, *À l'ombre de l'INCO. Étude de la transition d'une communauté canadienne-française de la région de Sudbury (1890-1972)*, 2001.

Huneault, Estelle, *Au fil des ans. L'Union catholique des fermières de la province d'Ontario, de 1936 à 1945*, 2000.

Blais, Suzelle, *Néologie canadienne, ou Dictionnaire des mots créés en Canada et maintenant en vogue de Jacques Viger*, 1998.

Farmer, Diane, *Artisans de la modernité. Les centres culturels en Ontario français*, 1996.

Martel, Marcel, *Le deuil d'un pays imaginé. Rêves, luttes et déroute du Canada français catholique des fermières de la province d'Ontario, de 1936 à 1945*, 1997.

Toupin, Robert, *Les écrits de Pierre Potier*, 1996.

Halford, Peter W., *Le français des Canadiens à la veille de la Conquête. Témoignage du père Pierre Philippe Potier, s.j.*, 1994.

Gaffield, Chad, *Aux origines de l'identité franco-ontarienne. Éducation, culture, économie*, 1993.

Jean-Claude Dubé

The Chevalier

de Montmagny

(1601–1657)

First Governor of New France

Translated by

Elizabeth Rapley

Collection
AMÉRIQUE
FRANÇAISE
N° 10

University
of Ottawa
Press

Library and Archives Canada Cataloguing in Publication

Dubé, Jean-Claude, 1925-
    The chevalier de Montmagny, 1601–1657: first governer of New France / Jean-Claude
Dubé; translated by Elizabeth Rapley.

(Collection Amérique française, ISSN 1480-4735; 10)
Translation of: Le chevalier de Montmagny.
Includes bibliographical references and index.
ISBN 0-7766-3028-8 (bound).–ISBN 0-7766-0559-3 (pbk.)

    1. Montmagny, Charles Huault de, 1583?-1653. 2. Canada–History–To 1663 (New
France) 3. Governors–Canada–Biography. 4. Knights of Malta–Biography. 5. Canada–
Biography. 6. France–Biography. I. Rapley, Elizabeth II. Title. III. Series.

FC341.M65D8214 2005   971.01'6'092   C2005-900388-X

University of Ottawa Press gratefully acknowledges the support extended to its publishing
program by the Canada Council and the University of Ottawa. We also acknowledge the
support of the Faculty of Arts of the University of Ottawa for the publication of this book.

We acknowledge the financial support of the Government of Canada through the Book
Publishing Industry Development Program (BPIDP) for our publishing activities.

Maps: Bruce Robin
Copy-editing: Carol Tobin
Proofreading: Stephanie VanderMeulen
Typesetting: Brad Horning

ISBN 0-7766-3028-8 (bound)   0-7766-0559-3 (pbk.)
ISSN 1480-4735

© University of Ottawa Press, 2005
542 King Edward Avenue, Ottawa, Ont. Canada K1N 6N5

press@uottawa.ca   http://www.uopress.uottawa.ca

Printed and bound in Canada

Table of Contents

List of Tables

List of Maps

List of Illustrations

Acknowledgements

I want first of all to thank sincerely all those who have helped me in the research, long and demanding, that I had to carry on to prepare this biography. I mention some of these people in the French version of the book. I just want to recall here the assistance that I received from the staff in charge of the rich collections of documents preserved in the National Library of Malta, and I mention in particular the name of Mr John De Bono, who took care of the notarial documents.

The advice and the suggestions that were given me by a French historian, Mr. Marc Perrichet, have been very important in the drawing-up of my work.

I also thank Mr. Bruce Robin, who prepared the maps in both French and English versions that illustrate the book.

Mrs. Francine Laramée was very helpful in typing the last version of the book and arranging the tables.

The production manager of the University of Ottawa Press, Mrs. Lynne Mackay, has given me good advice on the preparation of the present edition. I thank her most sincerely.

I should like to express my profound gratitude to my friend and colleague, Dr. Elizabeth Rapley. She has generously donated both her time and her expertise, as an historian and a translator, to bring this project to fruition.

I dedicate this book to her, with all my gratitude and my best regards.

Introduction

Charles [Huault], known as the chevalier de Montmagny, was received as a Knight of Malta on 3 August 1622. He commanded the galleys of the Order, and carried off a signal victory against the Bey of Rhodes on 6 August 1627; held the same command in 1630. Was named lieutenant general and commander for the King in Québec and throughout the Havre Saint Lawrence by the letter of 7 April 1639, was received as lieutenant general of the Order on 1 May 1652 and in this capacity made his entry to the island of Saint-Christophe, which then belonged to the Order of Malta, to replace Commander de Poincy.

This biographical notice, the first to be included in a published work, appears from 1725 on in the celebrated *Dictionnaire historique* of Louis Moreri.[1] It is very brief, since the mention of Charles is part of a genealogy of the Huault line. The essential elements in the life of the first official governor of New France are indicated, but the historic truth is somewhat mishandled. As to his becoming a Knight of Malta in 1622, and the maritime expeditions (in one of which he distinguished himself by a remarkable exploit), this much is true. But he never commanded the Order's galleys; he was indeed named lieutenant general and governor at Québec, but in 1636, not in 1639; he certainly ended his career in the Antilles, but he did not take the place of Commander de Poincy (who had been named governor in perpetuity), because he predeceased him by three years.

In fact, the editors of the dictionary had copied, uncritically and word for word (and what can "Havre Saint Lawrence" possibly mean?), what they found in the genealogy which members of the Huault family had had printed at the beginning of the eighteenth century, for the purpose of gaining both a certain notoriety and specific social advantages – of making sure, among other things, that their right to be buried in the choir of the church of Saint-Jean-en-Grève in Paris would not be taken from them.[2]

To this day, no complete biography of the chevalier de Montmagny has been written. On the Maltese and Caribbean periods of his life we find only scraps scattered here and there in the historiography. Only the Québec years have been the object of a fairly in-depth analysis. At the beginning of the twentieth century, J. Edmond Roy allowed him a fairly long article in two parts.[3] In the first he studied "his administration," and in the second, the "character" of the individual. Since these pages offer an initial attempt to discern the work and the personality of Charles Huault, it is fitting to give them a brief consideration.

Taking his inspiration from the *Relations* of the Jesuits – practically his only source – Roy, in describing Montmagny's government, concentrates on his action toward the Amerindians: on the one hand, his collaboration in the work of the colony's priests and nuns; on the other, his initiatives to counter the serious menace which the warlike activity of the Iroquois tribes was bringing to bear on the very existence of New France. According to Roy, the "incomprehensible inaction" of the *Compagnie des Cent-Associés* made this task exceedingly difficult. He then attempts to say what kind of a man Charles Huault was. For information on his family, he has consulted the *Dictionnaire* of the chevalier de Courcelles, which has not provided him with an accurate genealogy; thus the social origins are incorrectly presented.[4] To describe what he calls his "character," he has relied on the portrait that the Jesuits have left us of their one-time pupil: integrity, piety and charity, modesty, a healthy liking for entertainment.

This first look at the administration of the chevalier de Montmagny allows us to see the value in returning to the study, in order to make it more complete, more profound.[5] But the work should be expanded to include all of his life; indeed, this is a wish that has been expressed recently by Québecois researchers.[6] What is more, the 1725 notice, despite its inaccuracies, revealed an existence which can hardly be called ordinary, since this man, Parisian by birth, was called to work in three theatres of action that were all very distant and all very different from each other: the Mediterranean, the Saint Lawrence valley, and the Antilles.

It is essentially for two reasons that we have undertaken to fill this lacuna: the first has to do with the political domain – mainly the colonial administration; the second, with the vast field of investigation that constitutes social history.

Charles Huault arrived at a crucial moment in the history of the Canadian colony; he replaced the founder of Québec, Samuel de Champlain, who, for various reasons, had not been able to carry out most of the projects which he and others had conceived for New France. The task was extremely arduous. To understand the positions Montmagny took, and his actions, we need as far as possible to know his antecedents, his upbringing, his early activities. But the departure from Canada in 1648 did not put an end to his career as a colonizer; from 1649 onward he pursued it in another sector, the Antilles.

Furthermore, a man's life is not fully grasped unless it is placed in its social context. The reverse is also true: the study of a lineage, or of an individual career, always contributes interesting details to the understanding of a given society. Where the Knights of Malta are concerned, the case makes itself, so to speak: entry into the Order was allowed only after an inquiry into the antiquity of the candidate's nobility. Remember, too, that this reference to the religous world (the Order of Malta) does not take us far from the social domain – religion being an essential component of *ancien régime* society.

Given the aspects just mentioned, our research has had two major objectives. First we had to study Montmagny's active life in detail. Priority has been given, most certainly, to his Canadian administration; in Québec he was the representative of the king and of the *Compagnie de la Nouvelle-France*. This was the most important post entrusted to him, and it was here, we believe, that he gave his full measure. But we cannot pass over his first career – the struggle against the Turks in the Mediterranean – that shows how he lived up to the demands of his vocation as a Knight of Malta. It can be said that, with the exception of a few meetings at the Company's head office, which he probably attended, this experience was his only preparation for his work in Canada. In the years that followed his time in Québec, it was the colonies again. We have to explain why, after a relatively active period from 1649 to 1653, he was reduced to inactivity on the island of Saint-Christophe from 1653 to 1657, the date of his death.

Following this, it was necessary to reconstruct the social framework into which he was born and which conditioned a significant part of his life. His family (his close family, but also, to a lesser degree, the ancestors, the more distant kin, and those related by marriage), we have attempted to describe, by way of the professions they followed, the levels of fortune they attained, and the attitudes (intellectual or religious attitudes, for example) which the records have transmitted. Complementing the earliest formation received within the family was the education received in institutions such as, in his case, the college, the university, and the novitiate of his Order: this too we tried, as far as possible, to retrace. We have also attempted one comparison or another with certain people contemporary with our subject, thus allowing us a better understanding of the course of Montmagny's own life.

So this study is global in its intention – that is to say, open to all aspects of human activity, with its multiple points of contact. Hence the title: "The Chevalier de Montmagny," which has an undeniable connotation that is at the same time social, religious, and military – and thus political.

It is in this spirit that we have approached the rare sources which still survive. The administrative correspondence is lost; as well, Montmagny's reactions to each of the incidents which marked his time in Canada elude us. The Jesuits' writings (the *Relations*, above all) have enabled us to fill this void to a certain point. Though certainly the most complete and most voluminous source that we possess for the period of his time in New France, the highly detailed reports of these religious were drawn up with a very particular purpose: to alert French opinion to the urgency of the missionary project in Canada. They ought then to be used with all the necessary precautions.

Our work has been greatly facilitated by the consultation of the important works that have been written on this period of New France during the past fifty years (see the bibliography and the notes). To achieve a certain originality in this part of the work, we have constantly tried to identify the part that Montmagny took in the events of those years, which is a way of considering them from a new angle. The social origins of the chevalier and the first part of his life have been described with the help of the Parisian notarial archives. But there remain several question marks regarding his childhood and his years at college and university.

The same may be said for the Maltese period: by consulting the minutes of notaries in Valetta and Paris we have been able to reconstruct his privateering activities, but we know nothing of the five expeditions (known as caravans*) which he undertook on the ships of the Religion (as the Order of Malta was often called).

For the last part of his life, the years from 1649 to 1657, our information comes from documents held in Valetta and Paris.

Thus it has been possible, thanks to this documentation, to write the biography of the first official governor of New France, following him from birth to death, even though some stages in his life remain shadowy, due to the scarcity of sources.

Taking account of the various parameters we have defined and the availability of documents, we have divided our work in the following fashion.

In the first two chapters we seek to situate the Huaults de Montmagny on the social ladder of France at the opening of the modern epoch. Since a false version of things has circulated for a long time, only a patient investigation in the Parisian archives enabled us to know the true history of his lineage. A twofold approach was necessary: first, to present the corrected ancestry of the chevalier; second – and this because of the great importance that it exercised in his life – to examine the evolution of his immediate family (his mother, his two brothers, and his sister). A short epilogue will be added, permitting us to follow the Huault de Montmagny family until their extinction in 1699.

Following this, in Chapter 3, his years of formation are considered. All that is known for certain is the broad outline: his childhood at home, his eight years at college, his eight months at the faculty of law, his eleven months in Italy. By means of various cross-references we try to bring this period to life, so that we can imagine what Montmagny might have experienced during these years that were so important to the development of his personality.

Then begins his active life – we dare not speak of a professional life, as would have been the case if our man had become a magistrate or a military officer. Rather, we are dealing with three careers, realized in three different parts of the world, the only common element being his membership in the Order of Malta.

The first career, recounted in Chapter 4, comprises the Maltese years following his novitiate: the *corso** against the Turkish ships and the service aboard the ships of the Order.

The second concerns the years in Québec: this is the least poorly documented. For twelve years and in difficult conditions, the chevalier had to direct a struggling little colony, threatened by the Amerindians and practically abandoned by the mother country. Four chapters are devoted to this. The first, Chapter 5, serves as introduction, describing the New France of 1636. Chapters 6 and 7 describe the problems confronting the new administrator in two distinct domains: relations with the Amerindians; the colonization of the Saint Lawrence valley. In Chapter 8, by way of drawing conclusions about his time of service, we ask, where was Canada in 1648? An amusing digression accompanies this balance sheet: the portrayal of Montmagny in one of the most audacious tales of the time.

Finally, Chapter 9 deals with his third career, which lasted close to eight years. It coincides with the opening of the Maltese adventure in the Antilles, in which Montmagny was involved from 1649. He lived in these islands from 1653 until his death in 1657. These four years must have been frustrating; Father Du Tertre says politely that he exercised himself "in the practice of all the virtues," most of all patience, we can certainly add. During his time on the island of Saint-Christophe (which had been bought by the Order at his suggestion), he was named procurator general of the Grand Master and lieutenant of another knight who was the governor, but whose character traits and behaviour differed radically from his own.

So it is this adventurous life that we will try to recount. It is utterly representative of the times – has the title "baroque" not been applied to the years between 1560 and 1660, and even to the political domain?[6] Numerous comparisons could be brought up; but we shall limit ourselves to two examples. These are two contemporaries of Montmagny: the "chevalier Paul" (1598–1667), who was the terror of the Turks in the eastern Mediterranean before placing his tactical abilities at the service of the king of France in the western Mediterranean; and, in a completely different field (though he, also, succeeded in a little-known military exploit when he intervened, unarmed, between two armies about to confront each other), and Jules Mazarin (1602–1661), Italian by birth, diplomat, cardinal of the Holy Church, and great French man of state.

List of abbreviations used in the tables

a.l.	(*autres lieux*) other places
b.	born
bap.	(*baptisé*) baptized
c.r.	(*conseiller du roi*) Counsellor of the king (more often a title than a function)
ca.	(circa) around, about
capt.	(*capitaine*) captain, a military rank
cons.	(*conseil*) council, counsel
d.	died
extr.	extraordinary
G.c.	(*Grand Conseil*) Grand Council
gén	(*géneral*) general
gent.	gentleman or squire
inv.	post-mortem inventory
m.	married
me.	(*Maître*) Master
mil.	military
N....	woman whose first name is unknown
ord.	(*ordinaire*) ordinary
parl.	parlement
prés.	President
rep.	(*Représentant*) Representative
req.	(*requêtes*) requests (juridical term)
s.a.	(*sans alliance*) unmarried
s.r.	(*secrétaire du roi*) Secretary of the King (often a title, and not a function)
sgr.	(*Seigneur*) Lord (of an estate)
Sr.	(*Sieur*) a title not necessarily indicating nobility
X...	a man whose first name is unknown

List of abbreviations used in the notes

AC	Archives des colonies
AD	Archives départementales
ADIL	Archives départementales d'Indre-et-Loire
ADVO	Archives départementales du Val d'Oise
AE	Archives des affaires étrangères (Paris)
AESC	*Annales, Économie, Société, Civilisations*
AN	Archives nationales (Paris)
ANM	Notarial archives of Malta (Valetta)
AOM	Archives of the Order of Malta (Valetta)
ASQ	Archives du séminaire de Québec
BN	Bibliothèque nationale (Paris)
Cab. H.	Cabinet d'Hozier: a collection of manuscripts held in the BN (Paris)
Car. H.	Carrés d'Hozier, idem
D.B.	Dossiers bleus, idem
DBC	*Dictionnaire biographique du Canada*
DBF	*Dictionnaire de biographie française*
E.O.	*Édits, ordonnances royaux, déclarations et arrêts du conseil d'État du roi concernant le Canada* (Québec 1854–1856) 2 vols.
ICFS	*Inventaire des concessions en fief et seigneurie...* ed. P.G. Roy (Beauceville: L'Éclaireur 1927–1929) 6 vols.
JJ	*Le Journal des Jésuites* ed. C.H. Laverdière and H.R. Casgrain (Montréal 1892)
Libr	Library, a section of the AOM
MC	Minutier central de Paris: a section of the AN. The Roman numeral that follows MC indicates the number of the notarial office
MNF	*Monumenta Novae Franciae* ed. L. Campeau s.j.
Mss frs	Manuscrits français, a collection in the BN
M.T.	*Histoire de la Nouvelle-France* by Marcel Trudel, t. II or t. III, vol. 1 or 2

Nouv. H.	Nouveaux d'Hozier: a collection of mss in the BN
PO or P.O.	Pièces originales, idem
RHMC	*Revue d'histoire moderne et contemporaine*
RJ	*The Jesuit Relations and Allied Documents* ed. R.G. Thwaites. 73 vols.

The Chevalier de Montmagny

(1601–1657)

CHAPTER 1

The Ancestry of the Chevalier de Montmagny

If, in our search for the ancestry of the chevalier de Montmagny, we turn again to Moreri's *Dictionnaire*, this is what we read at the opening of the article devoted to the Huault name:

> Family originating in Touraine, close to Azay-le-Rideau, on the Indre River. The first of this name, who came to live in Paris in 1418, at the time of the seizure of Azay from the partisans of Jean Sans Peur by the dauphin Charles, was
>
> I. RAOUL, Sr de Huauldière in Touraine, who according to the proofs of nobility of the chevaliers of this name for the Order of Malta, was named Seigneur de la Roque and du Puy, by an act of faith and homage made to the baron de Montmorency in 1448. In 1440 he had married Marie Luillier, daughter of Jean Luillier, *avocat au Parlement*, and Marie Bethysi, by whom he had Jacques (the following)
>
> II. Jacques Huault Seigneur du Pui and, in part, of Montreuil by the Bois de Vincennes; he followed King Charles VIII to the conquest of Naples, and died there on 14 May 1495. In the year 1459, according to the order in council cited hereafter, he had married Alix de Villiers-l'Isle-Adam, of the Chettenville branch, who as his widow passed procuration on 29 April 1515, to Pierre Huault her son (the following).[1]

If we accept this version, we are in the presence of a family whose upward movement was already well-advanced by the middle of the fifteenth century, through military service to the king, through possession of seigneuries both in Touraine (La Huauldière, in particular, being a place name that apparently had links to the patronymic Huault)[2] and in the Parisian *banlieue;* and through marriage in 1459 into a lineage honoured by the sovereign since the previous century.[3] There is, however, much that is vague in this highly changeable account, for example the titles and the charges which are not specified. We are entitled to suspect an embroidering of the truth.

This chapter is intended, with the help of authentic documents, to lay out the true background of the Huaults de Montmagny, and to study their evolution up to 1610, a date which is important because it marks the death of the first Charles and, as well, the departure of his son Charles, the future chevalier, from his home in Paris for the college of La Flèche. So there will be an examination of the transformations which took place within the lineage – in terms of titles, charges, and fortune – during the century between approximately 1510 and 1610.

Some pages will also be devoted to the family of Antoinette Du Drac, Montmagny's mother. The maternal ancestry will be studied from more or less the same angle as the paternal ancestry, but with less detail, given the limits of this work.

Our first step will be to present and explain the process of mystification that led to the creation of a genealogy of impressive dimensions which, however, does not stand up to rigorous examination (it was already being contested in the eighteenth century,[4] though it can still be found in nineteenth-century dictionaries).[5]

In stage two, we shall establish the facts, present what the Parisian archives have told us, and lay out the true line of descent. Many obscurities remain, however, and we shall point them out in studying the career of Pierre Huault, the first Parisian member of the family for whom we have solid information.

The next generation brought novelty, both in the professions (the Robe,* the Church) and in the fact that two branches began then: those of Vayres and Montmagny. We specially need to emphasize the actions and deeds of Louis, the chevalier's grandfather. For example, the marriages of his son and his daughters into important Parisian Robe families are evidence of a definite upward movement of the lineage.

The man who followed the Robe tradition begun by Louis – his son Charles – will also receive our attention. The office of *maître des requêtes* * which he purchased was relatively distinguished; it was, indeed, the highest point that the Huault de Montmagny family achieved in the magistracy.

Finally, it remains for us to trace the evolution of the Du Drac family, whose social rise antedated that of the Huaults. Like them, they knew dramatic episodes at the end of the sixteenth century – a period which, we know, was extremely turbulent – and these also will be briefly addressed.

1. An invented origin

For the nobles of the *ancien régime*, the precise knowledge of antecedents was of great importance, to ensure that their status was not contested, that they would continue to be exempt from the taille,* and, if they could prove the antiquity of their nobility, that they could have their children enter an order of chivalry or a convent of canonesses. Hence the many genealogies stored in the archives. There was no hesitation, in the case of recently acquired nobility, in creating genealogical lists or notarized contracts out of thin air, and in taking advantage of like-sounding names.

Here are two examples of this practice.[6] The family of the intendant Jean Talon, posted to Québec in 1665, claimed in the seventeenth century to be descended from a Scottish noble who had come to live in France at the beginning of the previous century. It was necessary to conceal a peasant background, uncomfortable for the grand magistrates that Omer and Denis Talon had become. Also, attempts were frequently made to acquire an ancestor from the time of the Crusades. Thus the family of Gilles Hocquart, named intendant in 1731, maintained in the eighteenth century that among its ancestors there was an Irish knight by the name of O'Cart, who lived in the twelfth century. In fact, as late as 1600 Gilles's great-grandfather was still a bourgeois merchant in Fismes, a little city near Reims.

In the case of the Huaults, the fabrication was bound up with admission into the Order of Malta; thus it can be dated with a certain precision. This religious institute required aspirants to prove the nobility of their parents, their grandparents, and their great-grandparents – in other words, eight quarterings. In each case an inquiry took place. The first witness called up to the inquiry of 1622 affirmed without hesitation that Charles I Huault, father of the postulant Charles II, "was a gentleman by name and by arms, of an ancient and noble house, who, in his youth, and before and after he was given judicial office, bore arms for the King."[7] This witness, by name of Gilbert du Fillet, had had a military career; he was a chevalier in the orders of the king. What he said of Charles I indicated clearly that the nobility of his family was ancient. One word says it all: he was a "gentleman," even if his judicial office was awarded to him by the king. He found confirmation for his opinion in the fact that there was an illustrious family in the Huaults' ancestry: "He heard tell [it was whispered to him] that the Huaults were descendants of the house of Villiers Adams, from which there has sprung a most worshipful Grand Master of your Order." Philippe de Villiers de l'Isle-Adam[8] had just been elected head of the Order when, in 1522, the island of Rhodes which was then the property of the Knights was conquered by the Sultan of Istanbul, Soliman II; it was de Villiers who assured the success of the transition (1522–1530) and the transfer to Malta.

Thus the Lady Alix de Villiers, of whom we are informed by Moreri's *Dictionnaire*, would have been the mother of Pierre Huault and the great-grandmother of the chevalier. It is not impossible that there is a play here on the resemblance between Villiers and Badouvilliers, the surname of Pierre Huault's first wife. Then, in referring to the Huaults' place of origin, Azay-le-Rideau – where the place-name, La Huauldière, still exists – another mythical ancestor was unearthed: Raoul, whose mother belonged to the Argy family, known in Touraine since the twelfth century.[9] Jacques Huault died in 1495 in Naples, where, we are told, he had followed the king; here they had simply made use of a family memory, with the name of Jacques Huault substituted for that of Philippe de Billon: Louis Huault, Pierre's son, married Claire de Billon in 1547; her grandfather, Philippe de Billon, who was also a notary and *secrétaire du roi*,* was sent by the Duke of Bourbon to Naples, to the side of Charles VIII.[10]

But 1622 was not the first time that this strategy was used, since two cousins of Charles, whose mothers were Huaults de Montmagny, had preceded him into the Order of Malta: François Faucon de Ris in 1594, and Jean Anjorrant in 1613;[11] it would be used again in 1629, when Alexandre Huault de Vayres also decided to enter the Order.[12] In 1714, the Huaults de Bernay "the only remaining bearers of the name of Huault de Vayres et de Montmagny,"[13] again used it; this prestigious genealogy enabled them, as we have mentioned, to retain "their right to burial under the main altar of the Church of Saint-Jean-en-Grève," in Paris.

Table 1 groups together the information from Moreri's *Dictionnaire* and from the *Cabinet des Titres* of the *Bibliothèque Nationale* in Paris; it offers a fine example of genealogical fiction.

As can be seen, this schema follows up Moreri's genealogy, except for a few details, some of which are hardly significant: the mention of Gatien Huault, prior of Cormery – that is, superior of an abbey under the authority of the abbot (who in the majority of cases was absent during the *ancien régime*); or that of the Toupin-Le Maistre alliances, the importance of which escapes us. More revealing, however, is the fact that there are titles attached to the names of the three family heads, Raoul, Jacques, and Pierre. They are designated as *écuyers*. But in the first

TABLE 1

Fictitious Genealogy of the Huault Family

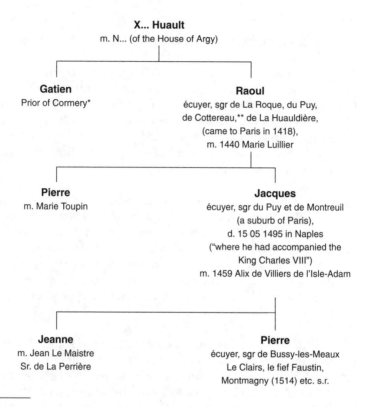

X... Huault
m. N... (of the House of Argy)

Gatien
Prior of Cormery*

Raoul
écuyer, sgr de La Roque, du Puy,
de Cottereau,** de La Huauldière,
(came to Paris in 1418),
m. 1440 Marie Luillier

Pierre
m. Marie Toupin

Jacques
écuyer, sgr du Puy et de Montreuil
(a suburb of Paris),
d. 15 05 1495 in Naples
("where he had accompanied the
King Charles VIII")
m. 1459 Alix de Villiers de l'Isle-Adam

Jeanne
m. Jean Le Maistre
Sr. de La Perrière

Pierre
écuyer, sgr de Bussy-les-Meaux
Le Clairs, le fief Faustin,
Montmagny (1514) etc. s.r.

---

*   Cormery is a city located near Tours, including inside of its walls an abbey.
** There existed a fief, named Cottereau-Villiers, which was under the jurisdiction of
    the castle of Amboise.

two cases, no function is mentioned; in the third, the charge of *secrétaire du roi* appears. Now, this reference is valuable because the purchase of this office was a convenient means frequently used by commoners in the *ancien régime* to enter the second order, the nobility. The fact that Pierre was *secrétaire du roi* is confirmed in a number of ways. Thus, we must put in doubt not only the nobility of his two forbears, but even their identity, and conclude that this genealogy is pure invention. And for an additional proof: the power of attorney given by Alix de Villiers to her son Pierre in 1515, reported by Moreri, is a fake.[14]

It is time to present the true version of things.

2.   Pierre Huault de Montmagny (d. 1534)

A notarized act of 19 May 1565 will put us on the trail of the true origin of the Huault family, and allow us to understand the career of this man, the founder of the Montmagny branch. On that day Louis Huault, seigneur of Montmagny, previously an auditor in the *chambre des comptes*,* made a gift to his cousin Étienne Victor, goldsmith and bourgeois of Paris, of a section of field located above the bridges of Azay-le-Rideau, and furthermore, of

> all the fruits and revenues of the said section of field fallen to him since the death of the late Jeanne Langloys previously widow of the late Mathurin Huault and mother of said M. Pierre Huault and grandmother of said donor. He also cedes all rights of succession which belong and may belong to him, to the chattels and real estate of the said late Mathurin and Jeanne Langloys and of the late Mathurin uncle of the donor, in his lifetime notary resident at Azay-le-Rideau.[15]

This document adds important details to our subject.[16] First of all, the recipient, the Victor cousin, is shown belonging to the world of artisans – certainly, as goldsmiths, the most highly regarded in Paris,[17] but still in a social level inferior to that of the officers, which the Huaults had just entered.[18] His father-in-law, Louis Guyot, had been a *maître maréchal*.[19] Étienne Victor immediately took advantage of the gift that Louis Huault had given him to make over the aforesaid section of field to his son, Étienne the Younger, "in order to support him in the schools while he studies and gets his degree."[20] Doubtless he wished to have him also attain an office after his university years.[21]

Already we note that the only representative of the Parisian Huault clan who has been found for this period belonged to the world of artisans. But there is much more. The true antecedents recorded here do not take us far from the social stratum of Étienne Victor.

So this was the ancestry of Pierre Huault for which we were seeking.[22] His father's Christian name was Mathurin, and Mathurin was the husband of Jeanne Langloys.[23] There are no details regarding place of residence or profession; however, we must presume that they lived in Azay, where they owned real estate and where a second son, also named Mathurin, kept a notary's study. Did Mathurin I practise the same profession? We cannot tell; but the fact remains that the notarial practice of Mathurin II, Pierre's brother, represented (as did the profession of barrister) an intermediate stage between the artisan or merchant world and that of royal offices.

Moreover, Pierre's career was relatively simple, but the model that it represents is very typical of the *ancien régime*, as we have already pointed out. He had the chance to enter the service of a *secrétaire du roi*, Thomas Thioust, who had practised in the chancery of the Palais[24] since at least 1489.[25] He served him as bookkeeper and clerk, which resembled to some degree the functions which his brother, Mathurin II, the notary of Azay, was performing.[26] However, fortune smiled upon him, allowing him to marry the widow of his patron, who died in 1497.[27] It was relatively easy for him to acquire the latter's office.[28] He resigned in favour of his son Jacques on 11 May 1534.[29]

The owner of this office of *secrétaire du roi** – the formation of which into a corporation had been recognized by the king in 1485[30] – was responsible for signing and sending off the letters coming out of the various chanceries of the kingdom. He enjoyed very considerable privileges: exemption from numerous taxes, for instance, and from the obligation to lodge men of war; but the principal advantage was access to the nobility. It marked the beginning of the emergence of the Huaults.

This simple and convenient manner of getting into the nobility gave rise to various commentaries – we think at once of the expression "savonette à vilain" (washing away the commoner) which was much in fashion. Certain individuals with a talent for satiric poetry did not hesitate to insist on the "mean and dirty" origins of one or another of these families, or to make even spicier suggestions. The Huaults and their kind did not escape – a *pasquil* of 1576 recalled it in amusing fashion. This is how Pierre de L'Estoile recorded it in his journal:

> Notwithstanding all these miseries [the wars of religion], they didn't stop making merry in Paris, or singing and dancing without a care, and making lampoons, among others the following very scandalous and defamatory one against most of the city's great families and houses, which was spread around everywhere in this month of February 1576.

Awake, Pasquil, great prophet of mankind,
The secret darling of the times, the years, the truth!
Fill up your lungs, take back your liberty,
To sing the secrets of this world of ours.

Hennequins, manikins, contemptible canaille,
Children of cobblers, counting-houses, stalls,
Raised from the dungheap and from poverty,
To fill our halls with cuckolds and with louts.

....

Huaud, if shamelessly your mistress raised
You up to be her master and her lord,
Boast not; the Times which make and then unmake
Can bring you once again to poverty.

And you, you tribe of cobblers, soiled with wax,
Little Bragelonnets, sons of Bragelonne,
Your cobbler father, mending his old shoes,
Could never teach you how to put on airs.[31]

So it was not forgotten, in the last quarter of the sixteenth century, that it was by marriage to his patron's widow that Pierre Huault had seized his future and his fortune. As for the Hennequins and the Bragelongnes, who were related by marriage to the Huaults, the reference to their artisan and merchant background was also made in a highly cutting manner.

Let us quickly examine the three marriages that Pierre Huault made in his lifetime. We have just mentioned the first; suffice it to add that Madeleine de Badouvilliers[32] was the daughter of Jean, who himself had also started as a *secrétaire du roi*.[33] She bore her husband a son, Jacques, born at the latest in 1509, since he had reached his majority by 1534 (the year of his father's death).

After becoming a widower, Pierre remarried on 31 August 1516,[34] but this time into the Parisian bourgeoisie. Isabeau Le Brest was the daughter of Mathurin, a cloth merchant. In fact, it was she who was the great-grandmother of the chevalier de Montmagny; and, contrary to the statements of proof of nobility presented in 1622, she was not noble.[35] She died on 21 February 1525.[36] She left two sons, Claude and Louis Huault, of whom there will be some mention later.

Before dealing with Pierre's third marriage, we should point out that Isabeau Le Brest, his second wife, had a sister, Jacqueline, who in about 1513 had married a cloth merchant, Claude Sanguin,[37] a member of a rich family which, like the Huaults, was beginning to invade the world of offices. Claude was elected alderman of the city of Paris; his brother André began as *lieutenant particulier des eaux et forêts,** before entering the parlement as a councillor. And it was the daughter of this André Sanguin, Jeanne, who in 1527 became Pierre Huault's third wife,[38] a childless marriage which ended in 1534 with the death of Huault. But note this coincidence: Étiennette Sanguin, Jeanne's first cousin, who married Simon Lallemand,[39] was the grandmother of Father Étienne Charlet, an important figure in the Society of Jesus, whom the Jesuit *Relations de la Nouvelle-France* designated as a relative of Montmagny.[40]

An additional indication of Pierre Huault's social success comes to us from the state of his fortune, even though the provenance of this fortune escapes us for the most part. It was quite considerable, but it cannot be precisely calculated, because the documents which would have allowed us to do so (the will, the inventory after death, and the distribution to the heirs) no longer exist.[41] Happily, an account of guardianship, dated 1545, has survived.[42] Threatened with a lawsuit by his younger brother, Jacques Huault gave the young man an account of the administration of his goods from the time of his father's death to his majority. This account tells us, in effect, that Jacques was alone in exercising the guardianship which, at his father's death, had been entrusted to him jointly with a son-in-law of Claude Sanguin, Étienne Le Picard, who was the young Louis's first cousin by marriage. By way of this account we can see how the father's goods were shared out at his death, and thus we can have an approximate idea of their total value, which is somewhere between 60,000 and 100,000 livres.

This is a fortune that can be considered solid and well-balanced. Real estate predominates, as the following description attests: two important properties, Montmagny and Montreuil-sous-le-Bois de Vincennes; two farms, one close to Saint-Denis (and thus to Montmagny) at Épinay-sur-Seine,[43] the other at Villenoy, close to Meaux; two houses in Paris, one of them on the rue des Blancs Manteaux, the other on the rue de la Grande Truanderie.[44] We can confidently state that these properties formed three quarters of all Pierre Huault's goods. Note again that his interest was not limited to the Paris region: in 1520 he again bought lands near Azay-le-Rideau.[45] It was also a diversified fortune; in addition to his real estate he possessed, at the time of his death, incomes and receivables

TABLE 2

The Huaults, from the mid-Fifteenth Century to the Early Seventeenth Century

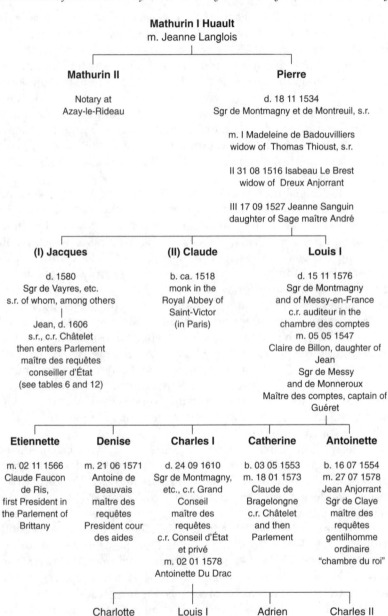

Mathurin I Huault
m. Jeanne Langlois

Mathurin II

Notary at
Azay-le-Rideau

Pierre

d. 18 11 1534
Sgr de Montmagny et de Montreuil, s.r.

m. I Madeleine de Badouvilliers
widow of Thomas Thioust, s.r.

II 31 08 1516 Isabeau Le Brest
widow of Dreux Anjorrant

III 17 09 1527 Jeanne Sanguin
daughter of Sage maître André

(I) Jacques

d. 1580
Sgr de Vayres, etc.
s.r. of whom, among others
|
Jean, d. 1606
s.r., c.r. Châtelet
then enters Parlement
maître des requêtes
conseiller d'État
(see tables 6 and 12)

(II) Claude

b. ca. 1518
monk in the
Royal Abbey of
Saint-Victor
(in Paris)

Louis I

d. 15 11 1576
Sgr de Montmagny
and of Messy-en-France
c.r. auditeur in the
chambre des comptes
m. 05 05 1547
Claire de Billon, daughter of
Jean
Sgr de Messy
and de Monneroux
Maître des comptes, captain of
Guéret

Etiennette

m. 02 11 1566
Claude Faucon
de Ris,
first President in
the Parlement of
Brittany

Denise

m. 21 06 1571
Antoine de
Beauvais
maître des
requêtes
President cour
des aides

Charles I

d. 24 09 1610
Sgr de Montmagny,
etc., c.r. Grand
Conseil
maître des
requêtes
c.r. Conseil d'État
et privé
m. 02 01 1578
Antoinette Du Drac

Catherine

b. 03 05 1553
m. 18 01 1573
Claude de
Bragelongne
c.r. Châtelet
and then
Parlement

Antoinette

b. 16 07 1554
m. 27 07 1578
Jean Anjorrant
Sgr de Claye
maître des
requêtes
gentilhomme
ordinaire
"chambre du roi"

Charlotte   Louis I   Adrien   Charles II worth more than 6,000 livres, and cash to the amount of 2,313L, 2S, 3D. His office of *secrétaire du roi* was valued at 4,000 livres. His chattels were worth close to 4,000 livres, with 2,153L, 14S, 9D of it in silverware.[46]

It is important, however, to emphasize that Pierre Huault's two most important acquisitions of land were Montreuil, which he gave to his older son Jacques, and Montmagny, which he gave to his younger son, Louis. The former, which we shall only mention, is situated today just outside the ring roads, and the *Mairie* of Montreuil is only some six kilometres from Notre-Dame – in other words, in the inner *banlieue*.[47] As for Montmagny, to which we shall often refer, it is important to give some details about it. Today it is an agreeable little town, fourteen kilometres from Notre-Dame, just north of Villetaneuse and not far from Saint-Denis. The date of Pierre Huault's purchase of the seigneurie is not known.[48] It was a dependent fief of the duchy of Montmorency,[49] for which he rendered homage no later than 1532.[50] Since 1184 the parish had been under the protection of Saint Thomas of Canterbury.[51] The medieval church was rebuilt around 1640; it stands today, and contains memories of the passing of the Huaults.[52] Did the town boast more than sixty households at the beginning of the sixteenth century? Probably not.[53] The lie of the land fitted it more for stock-raising and viticulture than for anything else – in notarized contracts most of the peasants called themselves vine-growers.[54] This seigneurie remained in the family until the last decade of the seventeenth century.

When Pierre died in November 1534, the Huault family was solidly established in the capital,[55] and its insertion into the world of offices was assured. We have, therefore, a double motive for presenting the second genealogical table, "The Huaults, from the mid-fifteenth to the early seventeenth century." First, it allows us to picture what we have just established regarding the true background of the chevalier de Montmagny; second, it shows how the professions evolved in the two generations that followed the founder, thus highlighting what remains to be addressed.

3. The three sons of Pierre Huault

The three sons of Pierre Huault would all move in different directions. The eldest, Jacques, would be a *secrétaire du roi* like his father. The second would opt for the religious life. The third, after his studies in the law, would enter the *chambre des comptes*.*

Jacques Huault practised first of all as a barrister.[56] From 1534 until his death in 1580,[57] he was generally designated as "Honorable homme Jacques Huault, notaire secrétaire du roi, seigneur de Vayres."[58] His father resigned this charge in his favour on 21 May 1534,[59] and it was, apparently, the only one that he ever occupied. He also participated in charitable organizations (unpaid, no doubt), since he appears in 1548[60] as "receiver of the common funds of the poor of the city of Paris."[61] Also, like his father, he was a church warden in his parish, Saint-Jean-en-Grève.[62]

He was well off financially, since in 1564 he could offer his daughter Marie a dowry of 14,000 livres.[63] He possessed several seigneuries, but he usually had his name followed by that of Vayres, which came to him from his wife, Philippe de Hacqueville.[64] It is because of this that we refer to the senior branch of the family as the Huaults de Vayres.

Of the descendants of Jacques Huault (see Genealogical Table 6, "The Huaults de Vayres family in the sixteenth century," in the appendix to this chapter) we shall give only the most salient features. His son-in-law and his two sons were magistrates. Only the career of the older son, Jean, will be described here; it makes us think of that of the chevalier's father, which we shall soon be studying. After a short time at the Châtelet, and then at the parlement, he turned up as a *maître des requêtes*, then a *président au Grand Conseil.** His loyalty to the king during the troubles of the League caused him problems; in fact, he was captured by the Leaguers, who burned his manor.[65] To save his life he was forced to pay out 4,000 écus; his house in Paris was pillaged.

He married into a family that belonged to the *grande robe*, the Piedefers.[66] In the middle of the fifteenth century, Robert de Piedefer had been *président à mortier** in the parlement of Paris. Of their alliances, some are of great interest to us: the Simons, and through them the Bocharts, the Briçonnets, the Bérulles (note two Piedefer-Bérulle cross-marriages), who were related to the Séguiers.

The descendants of Jean Huault de Vayres (apart from a few who entered the clergy) abandoned the robe for the sword. They did not return to service in the magistracy until the eighteenth century.

The older of the sons of Pierre's second marriage, Claude Huault, entered the canons regular of the royal abbey of Saint-Victor in Paris.[67] The members of this institution, founded in 1113, followed the Rule of Saint Augustine, but without being cloistered; they had a highly-developed liturgical life, but they also played a pastoral role.

Claude's entry into this order took place in 1535, shortly after his father's death; he must then have been about eighteen. By the act of 12

June 1535, by which he made a settlement of his goods to the convent of Saint-Victor, he donated the rest to his two brothers.[68] According to the guardianship account made in 1545 at the time of Louis's majority, there was an outlay of 362L, 15S, 8D for Claude's profession, clothing, and library, as well as for the costs of his first Mass.[69] As prior-curé, Claude served in Vaujours, a little parish situated east of Paris, about fourteen kilometres from the Porte de Pantin.[70] In 1547 he was elected claustral prior, that is to say the superior of the monastery in the absence of the abbot.[71] It was he[72] who, before 1556, drew up the *ordinarium*,[73] or liturgical customary, of the abbey.[74] Thus he was a priest of some standing who contributed to the administration of his convent and to its pastoral work, and who paid particular attention to the codification of its ritual.

A third person, also a son of Pierre, will now be considered: the grandfather of the chevalier, *noble homme maître* Louis Huault, seigneur de Montmagny.[75] He was born in 1520,[76] and died in 1576.[77] His life was active but relatively peaceful. It was he who spearheaded the entry of the Huaults de Montmagny into the magistracy, to which the family remained faithful until its extinction at the end of the seventeenth century.

What is truly unusual is that we possess details about his education. He studied law at Orléans.[78] So he was a barrister like his older brother, prepared, by his profession, for a magistrate's career. Once his studies were completed, he left for Italy (doubtless at the beginning of the 1540s, which would be three-quarters of a century before his grandson Charles).[79] We know nothing of his motives or of the details of his trip. It is probable that he wanted to round out his culture at a time when the Italian Renaissance dominated the European continent.

To our knowledge, he was the possessor of only one office, that of *conseiller du roi,** auditeur en sa chambre des comptes*, which he was granted officially on 15 November 1547.[80] This court of justice was responsible for the preservation of the royal domain and for the verification of the accounts of the king's fiscal agents.[81] It examined, and then registered, a number of official acts, among others the letters of ennoblement. The acquisition of this office followed closely on his marriage with Claire de Billon, the contract of which was signed on 8 May 1547.[82] There are two things to note here: the dowry of 6,500 livres,[83] which undoubtedly helped to pay for the office and the fact that the father-in-law, Jacques Billon, had himself been a *maître des comptes*.[84]

The social progress of this family closely resembled that of the Huaults.[85] Jean de Billon's father, Philippe, had started as a clerk to a *secrétaire des finances* before becoming *secrétaire du roi*. He passed on his office to his son between 1515 and 1518. As for the grandfather, he seems to have remained a clerk all his life. One of Jean's brothers, Charles, was a lieutenant in the compagnie de gendarmerie of Jean de Bourbon; he was also a captain of Guéret, capital of La Marche (Monneroux, a seigneurie owned by the family, was located in this province). Another brother, François, was a priest.

In the Billon line during the seventeenth century, we shall only note two things which coincided with the time of the chevalier de Montmagny: a military career, an important alliance.

Guillaume de Billon (ca. 1600–1662) knew a certain success in the army, since he became *maréchal de camp** in 1649;[86] in the previous year Mazarin, his patron, had signed his marriage contract.[87] Louis Huault's sister-in-law, Louise Billon, married Antoine de Barrillon,[88] also a *maître des comptes* who became a *maître des requêtes*. His nephew, Antoine de Barrillon de Morangis, member of the *Compagnie du Saint-Sacrement*, had close ties to Vincent de Paul; he drew two children of his brother, Jean-Jacques de Barrillon, into lives of devotion. The first was a canon in Paris and in Laon; the other, Henri, originally destined for the Order of Malta, preferred to enter the secular clergy. He became friendly with Rancé, the reformer of La Trappe; then in 1672 Louis XIV named him to the see of Luçon, where he led an edifying life, being assiduous in his functions, gentle and amiable in his relationships with all others, including Huguenots, and exemplary in his charity.[89]

But we return to Louis Huault, with a few more words on his fortune and the marriage of his daughters. His fortune undoubtedly outstripped that of his father; it stood, broadly speaking, at more than 100,000 livres.[90] It included seigneuries, numerous farms in the Paris environs, and *rentes* either on the Hôtel de Ville or on private persons. Louis paid close attention to his lands – for he seems to have rid himself quickly of his office[91] – and he bought a number of properties around Meaux [92] and Montmagny.[93]

This wealth permitted his daughters to make very good marriages. Étiennette married Claude Faucon de Ris, also of a Robe family;[94] in the contract, the future husband was designated a barrister; later he became *premier président* in the parlement of Brittany. The dowry was 12,000 livres in cash, of which 11,000 came from the father and 1,000 from the grandmother, Catherine Lescuyer. Then, on 21 June 1571, it was Denise's turn; she took for her husband Antoine de Beauvais, then *conseiller au parlement*, and later *maître des requêtes*; her dowry was 13,000 livres in cash.[95] As for Catherine, she made a marriage contract with Claude de Bragelongne, counsellor to the Châtelet of Paris, and later to the parlement;[96] and the fourth daughter, Antoinette, did the same on 27 July 1578, with Jean Anjorrant, who became *maître des requêtes*.[97]

Thus, though Louis Huault de Montmagny led an unglamorous life, a prudent and careful management of his wealth allowed him to marry his daughters into good families of the Parisian Robe, and it also assured his son, Charles, the father of the chevalier, a very fine alliance in the same milieu, and a career which can be qualified as more successful than his.

4. Charles Huault, father of the chevalier de Montmagny (1553–1610)

It is to be remarked that the years 1553–1610 that mark the lifespan of Charles, father of our chevalier, were also those of Henri IV, the monarch who personifies the restoration of order after the long period of religious wars. In the short description that we shall make of Charles's life there are three aspects to consider: the stages of his career, the nature of his fortune, and the marriage which he contracted in January 1578 with Antoinette Du Drac.

Like his father, Charles studied law and became a barrister; this was the title that he bore at the time he contracted his marriage.[98] The substantial dowry that he received (more than 27,000 livres) allowed him to enter a sovereign court. On 28 April of the same year, he received his letters of provisions of *conseiller du roi au Grand Conseil*.[99] This tribunal had jurisdiction over all the realm; it was authorized to pronounce on the conflicts which broke out among the other courts of justice, or on cases which the king decided should be removed from these (if there was a conflict of interest, for example). This is to say how important this office was.

However, his career was momentarily disturbed, as was the case with many magistrates, by the serious troubles that marked the beginning of Henri IV's reign. He took the king's part and participated in 1590 at the siege of Crépy-en-Valois and the blockade of Paris.[100] But he did not suffer anything like what his cousin, Jean Huault de Vayres, experienced at the hands of the Leaguers.

Even before the end of the civil wars, he obtained a new position: on 26 June 1592 he was awarded the office of *maître des requêtes de l'hôtel*.*[101] But because of the troubles he was only received in April 1594. The tribunal, which was then called the *requêtes de l'hôtel*, was attached to the court; certain cases were reserved to it, particularly those that were sent by the king's council.[102] The *maîtres des requêtes* could sit in the parlement. Special missions were entrusted to them, for two easily understandable reasons: their experience in the important affairs of the realm, and the proximity of the supreme power.

This is in fact what happened to Charles. The king sent him to Poitou in 1599, along with a member of the bureau of finances, Gaucher de Sainte-Marthe.[103] He had named them "commissioners ... for the regulation of the *tailles* and the reformation of abuses committed with regard to his finances in the generality of Poitou."[104] The activity of the two commissioners was to be of short duration and limited to a search for false nobles.[105]

An episode belongs here which, though certainly amusing, cannot be measured for importance or for impact. In 1600 a Parisian intellectual composed and circulated a satiric poem incriminating Charles Huault.[106] He was imprisoned for a time for this slur.[107]

INDIGNATIO VALERIANA
sive
Parisiensis Academiae Querimona
Ad virum amplissimum Carolum de
Mommagny Regi a secretioribus
consil[i]s et libellorum supplicû

We can translate the title of this poem as "Valerian Indignation, or the complaint of the Parisian Academy against the very distinguished Charles de Montmagny, representative of the king in the most secret counsels, and *maître des requêtes.*"[108]

Nicolas Bourbon (1574–1644),[109] the author of this poem, was teaching rhetoric in the college des Grassins in Paris when a judgment by parlement suppressed a fee which the professors had levied on their students since the Middle Ages.[110] It seems that Charles Huault was the scapegoat for the parlementary class in this protest by the professorial body, but we have not been able to find out why he was chosen.

The poem (in which there are recognizable virgilian accents) ends with a wild diatribe: the Academy (that is, the University) berates Montmagny, the personification of the venerable institution that was the parlement of Paris:

You, Montmagny, who most knowledgeably court the sisters of Mount Pierus [the Muses], and used to court them even more often in your first years;

Well, now you are thrusting away these Muses,
And those who publicly profess the study of poetry.
This is why your name has become hateful to me,
This great Charles once gave me his innermost life.
You, great one, take off your magistrate's robe; let another Charles
appear before me there – your son and worthy heir of your virtues –
and let him suitably guide the last years of his father.
The Academy, mournfully calling to mind these things,
Is torn from my eyes, and with the shadows fled away,
A purer Phoebus rises from the waves.

The end of Charles's career was peaceful, it seems. About 1605 the king conferred the title of *conseiller du roi en ses conseils d'État et privé* on him,[111] which seems to have been a purely honorary distinction, since he kept his office of *maître des requêtes* till his death.

Did this man, while so active in the public sphere, know how to manage his fortune adequately? Did he leave his wife and children the wherewithal for a comfortable life, in keeping with their social status? The answer to these questions is yes.

Two documents have enabled us to recreate his fortune, at least in a general way: the inventory after the death of his wife Antoinette Du Drac in 1618[112] and the division of goods which took place some months later.[113] (We are dealing with the joint fortune; Antoinette Du Drac, on her own account, possessed a seigneurie, La Baillie, close to Amiens). However, there is a gap in these texts: the value of the office that Charles held at the end of his life – that of *maître des requêtes* – is not specified, though we believe it to have been around 90,000 livres.[114] There were, apparently, no passive debts. Table 3 provides the known information.

The total amount is impressive. For the beginning of the seventeenth century, close to a half-million livres represents an important capital. It was clearly more than the total fortune of his father Louis I; and his son, Louis II, would be less rich at his death in 1646.

As for the composition of the goods, it can be established that half the fortune was in land, the surest value of the times, and that *rentes constituées* represented only 6 per cent of the total. The Parisian real estate accounted for 20 per cent, about the same as the offices. The sobriety of the furnishings is, perhaps, surprising; it is evidence that bourgeois habits lived on in the family. This impression is confirmed by an examination of two features of the inventory: the management of Montmagny and the purchase of the Hôtel de Baillet.

The "meubles meublants" (as they were then called) of the seigneurial manor amounted to only 363 livres, 8 sols; but there was

TABLE 3

The Presumed Fortune of Charles Huault I

Items		Amount	Subtotal	%
1. Furniture				
	in Paris	6 113		
	in Montmagny	7 570	13 638	3.1%
2. Houses in Paris				
	Hôtel de Baillet	53 000		
	4 houses in Saint-Antoine Street	37 000	90 500	20.2%
3. Estates				
	Montmagny and Goyencourt	121 000		
	Messy-en-France	93 000		
	Vignolles	9 600		
	Gonesse (some acres))	600	224 200	50.2%
4. Offices				
	two small offices of commissaire des tailles	2 300		
	office of maître des requêtes	ca. 90 000	ca. 92 300	20.7%
5. Annuities				
	6 constitutions	25 800	25 800	5.8%
Total amount			**ca. 446 483**	**100.0%**

wine to the tune of 374 livres, 10 sols.[115] The grain in the barns was worth 3,796 livres, much more than was required for the family's consumption, which supposes a commercialization of production. What was more, this was varied, since we also find oats, barley, vetch, and beans. Where horses, pigs, cattle, and fowl are concerned the stock was not unusual, but it was more significant in the matter of sheep: 324 head, estimated at a total value of 1,134 livres – in that respect also the commercial motivation is clear.

Further evidence of his spirit of initiative comes from the installation of his family in another sector of the Marais, which promised a brilliant future – a building which would later become one of the capital's high spots, under the name of Hôtel de Sully, in the parish of Saint-Paul.

For a while he was faithful to the parish of Saint-Jean-en-Grève; in 1581 he was sharing a lodging with his mother on the rue des Blancs Manteaux.[116] Afterwards he lived close by, on the rue des Haudriettes, but in a new parish, Saint-Nicolas-des-Champs; he was still there in March 1600.[117] Some months later he took up residence in the Hôtel de Baillet which he had just bought, on the rue Saint-Antoine, in Saint-Paul parish. It is to be noted that after moving into his new house, he continued to buy properties in the neighbourhood.[118]

Some detail is necessary here, because this was the place where the chevalier de Montmagny was born, and where he spent most of his childhood. The rue Saint-Antoine was, so to speak, the heart of the Marais; it was the longest street in the capital. The king possessed two properties close by: the Hôtel Saint-Pol on the south side and, on the north, the Hôtel des Tournelles, demolished in 1563, whose park was destined to become the centre of the Place Royale (today the Place des Vosges) which Henri IV decided to lay out in 1605. In 1580, the Jesuits built a convent on a property which had been offered to them by Cardinal Charles de Bourbon (of which only the present-day church of Saint-Paul-Saint-Louis remains). This property was close to the Hôtel de Baillet, on the other side of the rue Saint-Antoine and a hundred metres to the west.

The Hôtel de Baillet which Charles Huault was entering with his family already had quite a past – one in which the historians of the Hôtel de Sully have recently been taking an interest.[119] Since the middle of the fourteenth century, it consisted of a collection of buildings and lands that was called "the hôtel de la Moufle." Around 1477, the whole property was divided into two parts, the larger of which, located to the north and east, passed at the beginning of the sixteenth century into the hands of Charles de Villiers de l'Isle-Adam, bishop of Limoges, who turned it over to his niece, Louise de Villiers, widow of Jacques d'O, seigneur of Baillet. The d'O family owned it until 1600.

But its history did not end there. As already mentioned, in 1605 Henri IV, wishing to leave a tangible memory of his reign, ordered the opening of a square on the north side of the rue Saint-Antoine. In the interests of symmetry the neighbours were forced to cede him a part of their properties. It was thus that by decree of the Council in 1607 a piece of land measuring 1,239 ½ *toises* 5 feet[120] was chopped off the property of Charles Huault. In March 1611, Antoinette Du Drac and her son Louis received the sum of 20,110 livres as reimbursement for this expropriation.[121]

But now we are encroaching, almost for good, on the "post-Henri IV" and "post-Charles Huault" era which will be the subject of Chapter 2. Let us now examine the maternal background of the chevalier de Montmagny, by looking briefly at the marriage contracted in 1578, before starting on the Du Drac lineage.

Antoinette Du Drac, whom Charles Huault married in 1578,[122] was the daughter of a *maître des requêtes de l'hôtel*, the late Adrien, vicomte of Ay,[123] seigneur of several places. Two brothers signed the contract; one was, at this time, *conseiller au parlement*; the other, *maître des requêtes*. So their offices were at a level superior to that of the Huaults, and in fact the family's accession to the magistracy dated from further back.

As regards their economic situation, it seemed, in this last third of the sixteenth century, to be even more prosperous on the Du Drac side: the bride's dowry totalled 28,000 livres (18,000 in *rentes*, 10,000 in cash). This was quite a considerable sum, particularly if we take account of the fact that Antoinette was the youngest of the family, that four sisters had already made very good marriages,[124] and that her three brothers, Olivier, Jean, and Adrien, had succeeded in entering the sovereign courts.

This family will interest us on more than one account.

5. The Du Drac family

To begin the study of this lineage, let us go back to an event somewhat later than the 1578 marriage which we have just mentioned. At the beginning of 1585, Antoinette's oldest brother, Olivier Du Drac, contracted a second marriage.[125] His new wife was called Madeleine Le Charron. He swore "to be from now on a very faithful and loyal friend, husband and lawful spouse," a handsome formulation which contrasted with the usual dryness of these contracts,[126] but which was undertaken in a precise religious context:

> the two spouses have vowed to God and promised to one another that they will continue and persevere in the true religion, its exercise and open profession, in conformity with the word of God and following what is more fully contained and declared in the confession of faith of the reformed churches of France.

Both of them were members of the R.P.R., or "the religion claiming to be reformed," as Catholics of the period would say. We do not know how far back their conversion went, but the political and religious climate at this beginning of the year 1585 was particularly intense. The civil war had lasted almost twenty-five years; the death of the Duke of Anjou the previous year had opened the throne to the Protestant Henri of Navarre; the Holy League, formed in 1576 to extirpate the heresy of the kingdom of France, was becoming more radical. Protestants, especially those in the Paris region, felt themselves threatened. The marriage contract makes direct allusion to this:

> and should it happen that they cannot be secure in France because of the persecution that might break out (God forbid), they will leave and go together wherever the safety and tranquillity of the country will call them, even if by their absence they suffer a total and entire loss of all their goods.

The prospect of seeing their fortune disappear did not discourage them. This eventuality was not at all imaginary, since four years later, in 1589, as we have said, Jacques Huault de Vayres, a mere "political" Catholic and supporter of Henri IV, saw his manor burnt and his house in Paris sacked. We note further that a first cousin of Olivier, Guy Arbeleste (of whom more later) was despoiled of all his possessions after having abjured Catholicism.

But – and this demonstrates how full the period was of turnabouts – Olivier did not persevere in the religon that he seemed so ardently to have embraced, for he was buried in the church of Saint-Gervais in Paris.[127]

Olivier was a *maître des requêtes;* the office which his father had possessed had come down to him. Did he exercise it in these troubled times, and while he was living in his seigneurial manor at Beaulieu, several leagues from the capital? We cannot tell. His second wife was the widow of a councillor on the *Grand Conseil;* the Robe was also the occupation of her brothers and brothers-in-law.

Save for the (temporary) Protestant allegiance, Olivier was a typical representative of the Du Drac family, which had been members of the Robe for many generations, and had owned lands for a long time in Brie and Champagne. In fact, during the fourteenth and fifteenth centuries it had known a period of splendour, of which traces remained in the sixteenth. However, we shall concentrate on this last century, because the access to notarized documents permits cross-checking.

The earliest known Du Drac was Barthélemy; in the second half of the fourteenth century he was a *trésorier des guerres*.[128] His son, Jean I (d. 1423) was a barrister, who spent his life in the service of the Duke of Burgundy, and became his *maître des requêtes de l'hôtel* in 1385. He took a direct part in the Burgundian – Armagnac struggle during the Hundred Years War; he may have been one of the leaders of the popular movement of the Cabochiens (1411–1414), supported by Jean Sans Peur. It was at this time that he became *président* in the parlement of Paris.

He had married Jacqueline d'Ay, daughter of Jean d'Ay, a celebrated barrister of the period.[129] This alliance assured the Du Dracs of an entry into the parlementary circles to which they remained faithful for more than two centuries. His daughter Jeanne married Philippe de Morvilliers, who was president in the parlement of Burgundy, then in that of Paris. One of his sons, Jean I, was bishop of Meaux;[130] his grandson, Jean III, was elected mayor of the city of Paris.[131] (See the "Abbreviated genealogy of the Du Drac family, fourteenth and fifteenth centuries," Table 7, in the appendix to this chapter.)

Let us sum up what the end of the Middle Ages signified for the maternal ancestors of the chevalier de Montmagny. Socially speaking, their success was complete: high positions in the magistracy, in the administration of the city of Paris, and in the clergy. From the economic point of view they maintained a solid base of properties around the capital, the viscounty of Ay close to Reims,[132] and the seigneurie of Claye (which would later pass to the Anjorrants) close to Meaux.

Throughout the sixteenth century, it is in the magistracy that we find most of the Du Drac family members.[133] (See Table 8, "The Du Dracs in the sixteenth and seventeenth centuries" in the annex to this chapter.) From the beginning of the seventeenth century they began to move away from it, and we find honorific charges, theoretically attached to the king's household, and military careers. Equally, from the middle of the sixteenth century, the office of *bailli* of Melun (by now more honorific than anything else) was passed from father to son.

Nor was the service of the Church neglected: the family included a canon of Notre-Dame of Paris and treasurer of the Sainte-Chapelle, who died around 1554,[134] and two nuns. But worthy of special mention is the altogether special vocation of one of Adrien II's daughters – and, thus, Antoinette's own sister and an aunt to the chevalier de Montmagny. Marie Du Drac (born 27 January 1563), who had married Jacques Avrillot, *conseiller au parlement*, participated with enthusiasm in the Holy League. On her husband's death, she entered the Third Order of Minims, a community vowed to asceticism, founded by Francis of

Paula (1416–1507) and approved by Rome in 1474. She distinguished herself by her assiduous practice of the Christian virtues and died in the odour of sanctity in 1590. She was buried (and joined later by her disciple, Anne Lelieur) in the chapel of the convent of Nigeon, located close to the village of Chaillot.[135]

So we are in the presence of a family that is truly representative of the various political, social, and religious phenomena that marked the passing of the Middle Ages into the modern period.[136] A very brief examination of two other families which figure in the maternal ancestry of Charles II Huault – the Arbalestes and the Rappouels – will give us some other interesting examples.

Simon Arbeleste, the first of this line known to history, seems to have been the elected mayor of the city of Beaune; he had married Madeleine Bochart, a native of Vézelay.[137] Something often noted in this study is the large number of provincial nobles who cast covetous eyes upon Paris and the sovereign courts. Simon Arbeleste's son, Guy I, married the daughter of a *président* in the parlement of Paris; he swiftly entered the same court, rose to a presidency there, and later became *président* in the *chambre des comptes*. He was the great-great grandfather of the chevalier de Montmagny. Nicolas, one of Guy's sons, held the ecclesiastical offices of archdeacon in the diocese of Langres and apostolic protonotary.[138]

As was the case with many of the families studied here, the Arbalestes changed the course of their careers and left the magistracy at the turn of the seventeenth century, for charges in the king's household or service in the army. One of them even succeeded in contracting a marriage that can be qualified as truly exceptional. On 28 April 1636 Guy III Arbaleste married Marie de Montmorency, daughter of Pierre, chevalier and marquis of Thury.[139] By that act he entered one of the most ancient families of the high nobility. To understand what that meant, we have only to consider the impressive list of signatures on the contract, from both sides of the family. For the bride, it is not surprising to see the signatures, among others, of the wife of Condé, the first prince of the blood, and of her daughter Anne de Bourbon, both designated as cousins. And – which is surely one of the explanations of the marriage – among the witnesses for the bridegroom there appear Henri IV's one-time minister, Maximilien de Béthune, Duke of Sully, and his wife, Rachel de Cochefillet. This, his second wife, was the first cousin of Louis Arbaleste, Guy's father. Another signatory was the *surintendant des finances*,* Claude Bouthillier, whose wife, Marie de Bragelongne, was designated a cousin of the bridegroom. We should add that Guy's great-aunt, Marie de Bragelongne, was married in 1576 to Philippe Duplessis-Mornay, the celebrated Protestant writer, a much-trusted counsellor of Henri IV; and we recognize that this family had been able, by means of its alliances, to get near to the highest spheres of State and government. Again: let it be noted that we have just caught sight of two of the most prominent personalities of the Huguenot world, Duplessis-Mornay and Sully; this fact is to be linked to the conversion to protestantism of Guy II Arbaleste.[140] The former was his son-in-law; the latter had, for brother-in-law, another son-in-law, Jacques de Cochefillet.

In Charles Huault's maternal ancestry there remains one person (and one lineage) to consider: "Noble homme et saige maistre Thomas Rappouel, seigneur de Baudeville, conseiller notaire et secrétaire du roi et de sa chambre"; this is the title that he bore in 1549.[141] Thus he was, apparently, a commoner who had entered the second order; he later became *intendant des finances* and received the title of *conseiller du roi en ses conseils*.[142] However, to impress the inquisitors of Malta, a glorious genealogy was dreamed up there, too;[143] despite the fact that Thomas's father was actually a merchant bourgeois of Paris,[144] and his grandfather, a "bourgeois residing in Melun." Here is a situation that closely resembles the one that we have described for Pierre Huault, founder of the Parisian branch of his family, who, like Thomas Rappouel,[145] was one of the great-grandfathers of the chevalier de Montmagny. In both cases, the dynamism of the man would explain his access to the ennobling charge of *secrétaire du roi,* and the takeoff into social ascension.

To know Thomas a little better, we have been able to use two interesting documents: the inventory after his death and a donation which he made to his son-in-law.

The first document, though it contains very few figures, nevertheless shows us the essentials: a fine fortune; two houses, one of them in the Marais and the other in the inner *banlieue* – "situated in the village of La Chapelle;" two seigneuries which we have not been able to place, Bandeville and Vignolles; a rich interior, with pictures, silverplate, rings and jewels.[146] It should also be added that he had owned a seigneurie not far from Nangis (Beaulieu, Seine-et-Marne), which he gave to his son-in-law, Adrien II Du Drac.[147]

One thing seems to have been particularly dear to his heart: his house "on the rue de la Chapelle de Braque."[148] He gave it to his son-in-law in 1549.[149] The contract of donation is full of very precise details of the location ("between the said street and that of the four Aymond sons in one direction, and, in the other, between Christophe Luillier and the widow Michel Perrignon"), on the tax which it owed to the Grand Priory of France,[150] and of the various improvements which he had made to it. What he wished at all costs to prevent was that the house should be subdivided by the heirs. His preoccupations were sanitary and aesthetic: the cramped living spaces thus created would favour the spread of "dangerous and contagious illnesses;" furthermore, he had seen too many "beautiful old houses in the same city entirely deformed in a short time, and there remains no trace of the original beauty and appearance of the said houses" to accept that his own would be thus disfigured.

In addition to this, his château of Beaulieu had apparently been carefully fitted out. In the centre of the main body was a "Pavillon du Roy," preceded by a "grande Galerie Paincte"; a "galerie blanche" on the opposite side made up the pair, and, on the main floor, there was "une grande salle peincte" – of wall paintings, it seems.[151] In this line – interior decorating – Thomas Rappouel had a solid reputation; his competence was recognized by the king himself. Here is what François I wrote in 1535:

> For this purpose [the project of a monumental staircase for the Hôtel de Ville in Paris] I have decided to write to you, and the provost and the others who come with him will tell you at greater length, that having summoned Master Thomas Rappouel, secretary in my Chamber, and other persons whom you know to be knowledgeable and experienced in this, you should go together to the said spot to see, examine and look at the first and last drawings made for the said staircase, to advise which of the two seems to you the most appropriate.[152]

A man, then, who lacked neither ideas nor artistic sense, and whose competence was recognized in high places. We can understand why Canon Du Drac, the uncle of his son-in-law, chose him as one of the executors of his will.[153]

What strikes us in the examination of the Rappouel genealogy is the evolution of professions. This evolution stands in contrast with those that we have laid out for most of the families we have studied, where we have discovered a predominance of the magistracy and accession to important offices. Here we notice more variety, and the absence (except for one son-in-law or another) of elevated positions. Let us take a precise example: in the generation at the start of the seventeenth century – which corresponds chronologically to the career of the chevalier de Montmagny – we find Claude Rappouel, a *commissaire d'artillerie* (an office in the military administration), and Martin, a barrister; as for Olivier, he is a doctor and he will become "doctor regent," that is, professor at the faculty of medicine at the University of Paris. Among his brothers-in-law, two are of lower military rank and another is a steward of the house of Angoulème, whose job is to manage the fortune of a great noble household.

There are perhaps fewer churchmen than in the other families, but not a total absence, since we find a canon regular of the abbey of Saint-Victor (reminding us of Claude Huault, member of the same institution in the mid-sixteenth century) and a nun in the monastery of the Filles-Dieu.[154]

We lack details on the oldest alliances of the Rappouels. In the mid-sixteenth century, however, there was one with the Bragelongne family, a member of which would marry, soon after, a Montmagny girl. Still more worthy of note is the union sealed on 28 October 1571 between Catherine Rappouel, daughter of Jacques and Catherine Brangelongne, and Jean Boileau, *commissaire des guerres*.[155] Catherine Rappouel was to be the grandmother of Nicolas Boileau (1636–1711), the famous author of the *Satires* and of the *Art Poétique*.

The maternal lineage of Charles Huault differed very little from the paternal, in the aspects that interest us; there were several intersections in the marriages. The professions were similar, with the magistracy predominating; the positions were comparable: *maîtrise des requêtes du palais* or *de l'hôtel; présidence* in a sovereign court. Their wealth was of the same order: houses in Paris, and, indeed, in the Marais; seigneuries around the capital, though to the east, and further from the centre than were Montmagny or Montreuil. Religion certainly had a presence; only one nun, but a canon who seems to have been active,[156] and a bishop.[157] Above all, the contribution of the family to the Counter Reformation movement should be mentioned – their participation in the establishment of the Minims in Paris and in Reims. Two personalities seem to have been more dynamic than the others: Thomas Rappouel, a counterpart, so to speak, of Pierre Huault, at the end of the fifteenth and start of the sixteenth century; and, at the turn of the seventeenth century, a holy person, Marie Du Drac, aunt of the chevalier de Montmagny.

In order to research the ancestry of the chevalier de Montmagny, we have had to engage in a long and painstaking genealogical exercise – without being able to arrive in every case at full certitude. But this scene-setting was necessary to determine as exactly as possible what place his forbears occupied in French society at the beginning of the modern era.

Overall, one thing is very clear: the social rise of these families did not go back to a very ancient past. However, this is what the makers of these genealogies – which they created out of whole cloth – wanted to have believed; and what apparently learned books have perpetuated until the twentieth century. In reality, this promotion was linked to the modernization of the monarchic state, that is to say, to the formation of a class of "officers" – what we now call "civil servants" – and it was concomitant with the development of absolutism. As we can see in Table 5, of the four great-grandfathers of Charles, two were ennobled precisely by the acquisition of the office of *secrétaire du roi,* and it is interesting to note that the nobility of their spouses was pure invention. Remember, the eight quarterings of nobility were a minimum for entry into the Order of Malta.[158]

We have also been able to note how success in these careers coincided with relatively elevated fortunes – fortunes, moreover, which seem to us in the main to have been well-balanced and free from luxury, even if the location of the residences chosen by most of the families in our study, the Marais, was on the way to becoming one of the finest neighbourhoods of Paris.

The search for profitable marriages – whether from an economic point of view (dowries bringing property, cash, and investments) or from a professional point of view (that is to say, assistance in career advancement) – bore fruit in the case of the Huaults. Networks of alliances were set up, whose beneficial effects could still be observed in the seventeenth century.

Some personalities appear to us to have been out of the ordinary – for their intellectual or moral qualities, or for their business sense. We think of Pierre Huault, founder of the Parisian branch of the family; of Charles I and his cousin, Jean Huault de Vayres, directly involved in the troubles of the civil wars and in the subsequent reconstruction of the kingdom; of Thomas Rappouel, an intelligent and far-sighted man; and of the two figures in the incipient religious renewal, Claude Huault, the priest of the abbey of Saint-Victor, and Marie Du Drac, who entered the Third Order of the Minims.

TABLE 4

"The Tree of Consanguinuity," Model for the Preparation of Proofs of Nobility for the Knights of Malta

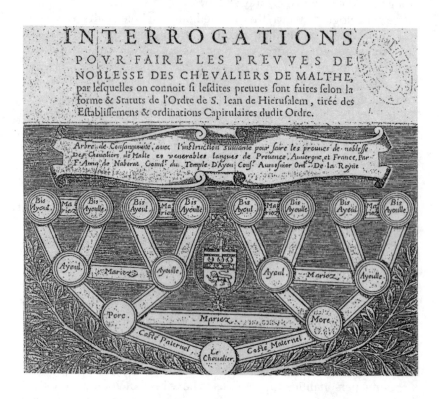

Taken from I. Baudoin, *Histoire de Malte avec les statuts et les Ordonnances de l'Ordre*, Paris, 1652, 163.

TABLE 5

The Eight Great-grandparents of Charles Huault

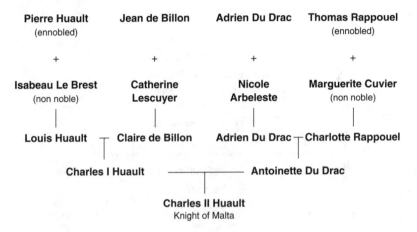

TABLE 6

The Huault de Vayres Family in the Sixteenth Century

(Pierre Huault)

|

Jacques I

Sgr de Vayres, Aubigny, Challemaison
Montreuil, Bussy-les-Meaux
s.r.

m. Philippe de Hacqueville
daughter of Nicolas, sgr de Vayres etc.

Jean I	**Guillaume**	**Marie**
b. 1539	b. 1543	b. 1545
d. 1606	s.r.	m. Jacques Petremol
sgr. de Vayres etc.	greffier au baillage	sgr de Bierville
s.r., c.r. Châtelet	de Troyes	c.r. Parlement
and then Parlement	marker in the	maître des requêtes
maître des requêtes	chambre des comptes	
president in the	of Paris	
Grand Conseil		
conseiller d'État		
		Philippe
m. 07 02 1569		
Anne de Piedefer		m. Nicolas Viole
daughter of late Robert		sgr d'Onzereaux
sgr de Goyencourt		
c.r. Parlement, and of		
Jeanne Briçonnet		**Isabeau**
		m. Sébastien de
		La Grange-Trianon

Jacques II

d. 08 02 1616
sgr de Vayres, Courcy, Bussy
etc.
gentilhomme ordinaire
de la chambre du roi
m. 19 09 1601
Anne de Maillard de Bernay
daughter of François
Knight of the orders of the King
gentilhomme ordinaire
de sa chambre
and of Madeleine Janvier
(daughter of Girard
and Marie Berangeon Dame de
Champrond)

TABLE 7

Abridged Genealogy of the Du Drac Family, Fourteenth and Fifteenth Centuries

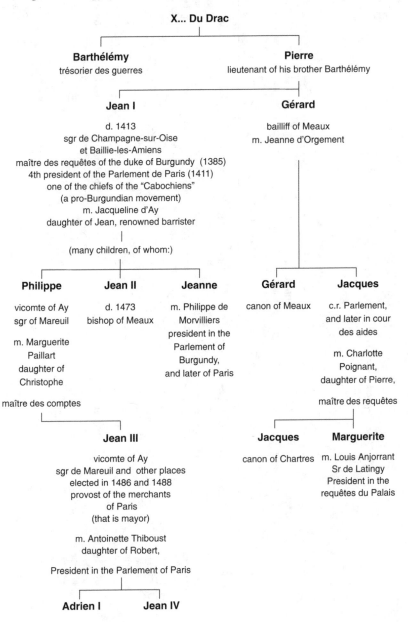

X... Du Drac

Barthélémy
trésorier des guerres

Pierre
lieutenant of his brother Barthélémy

Jean I
d. 1413
sgr de Champagne-sur-Oise
et Baillie-les-Amiens
maître des requêtes of the duke of Burgundy (1385)
4th president of the Parlement de Paris (1411)
one of the chiefs of the "Cabochiens"
(a pro-Burgundian movement)
m. Jacqueline d'Ay
daughter of Jean, renowned barrister

(many children, of whom:)

Gérard
bailliff of Meaux
m. Jeanne d'Orgement

Philippe
vicomte of Ay
sgr of Mareuil

m. Marguerite
Paillart
daughter of
Christophe

maître des comptes

Jean II
d. 1473
bishop of Meaux

Jeanne
m. Philippe de
Morvilliers
president in the
Parlement of
Burgundy,
and later of Paris

Gérard
canon of Meaux

Jacques
c.r. Parlement,
and later in cour
des aides

m. Charlotte
Poignant,
daughter of Pierre,

maître des requêtes

Jean III
vicomte of Ay
sgr de Mareuil and other places
elected in 1486 and 1488
provost of the merchants
of Paris
(that is mayor)

m. Antoinette Thiboust
daughter of Robert,

President in the Parlement of Paris

Jacques
canon of Chartres

Marguerite
m. Louis Anjorrant
Sr de Latingy
President in the
requêtes du Palais

Adrien I   **Jean IV**

TABLE 8

The Du Dracs in the Sixteenth and Seventeenth Centuries (abridged)

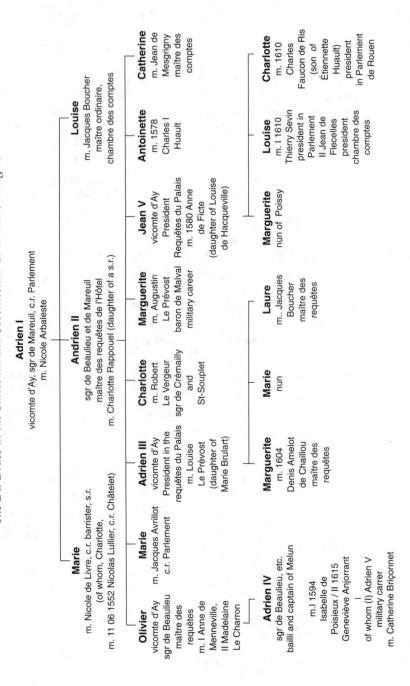

MAP 1

The Marais District of Paris in the Seventeenth Century

*(The Marais is the section of Paris where the Huault de
Montmagny lived during the 16th and 17th centuries)*

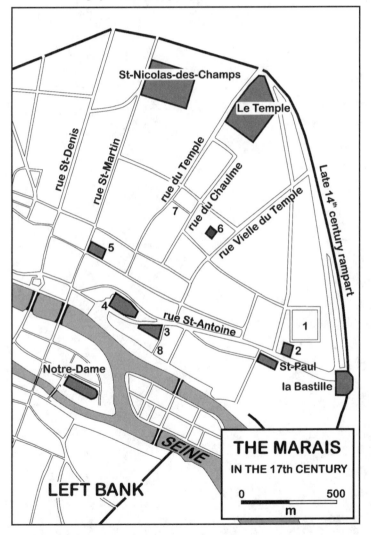

1. La Place Royale. 2. Hôtel de Baillet (later the Hôtel de Sully). 3. Saint-Gervais.
4. Saint-Jean-en-Grève. 5. Saint-Merri. 6. Les Blancs-Manteaux. 7. Rue de Braque.
8. Rue des Barres.

CHAPTER 2

The Huault de Montmagny Family
in the Seventeenth Century

On 19 November 1623,[1] Charles Huault, "received as a Knight of the Order of Saint John of Jerusalem presently in the Island of Malta,"[2] was on his way to Paris. He stayed with his brother Louis on the rue des Barres. The purpose of his journey, "before making the vows of religion in the aforesaid Order,"[3] was to come to an agreement with his brothers and his sister regarding the goods that he had inherited from his parents. In return for a life pension of 2,400 livres per annum, he left them his entire estate. He obtained from them a promise to pay up to 9,000 livres in ransom, in the event that he should become a prisoner of the enemy. He was even entitled to ask them for an advance on his pension of the sum of 15,000 livres, if an opportunity arose to purchase a boat – he was already thinking of becoming a privateer. "These present donations," it was added, "being made on account of the friendship that has always existed, and still exists, between the said Sr chevalier and the said Srs and lady, his brothers and sister."[4]

This agreement was profitable for the chevalier; it helped him finance his privateering expeditions. As well, it illustrates his relations with his immediate family, which certainly seem to have been good, even cordial – in keeping with the foremost recommendation of their mother on her deathbed.[5] Until the end of his life, his *pied à terre* in Paris was the residence of one or the other of his brothers. It was to them that he constantly entrusted the care of his interests during his absences, which, as we shall see, were lengthy. So it is important to try to know these persons who, as it were, remained close to him in spite of his distance. This will allow us to identify an evolution which will turn out to be very different from that which the family had experienced throughout the sixteenth century. Here we will focus on the first half of the seventeenth century (the period which corresponded to Charles's career), and give only a few facts about the second half, which saw the end of the Huault de Montmagny line.

We shall therefore concentrate above all on the immediate family, beginning with Montmagny's mother, Antoinette Du Drac, who survived her husband by eight years. She was greatly preoccupied with the future of her "two young ones," Adrien and Charles. These two brothers stayed in constant contact from their early childhood until the death of the chevalier in Saint-Christophe in 1657. Adrien died ten years later, and some pages are dedicated to him. About the older sister, Charlotte, who married a country nobleman, Anne-Antoine de Gouy, some explanations are also necessary. She left the family home when Charles was three, but continued her relations with her childhood home. Louis Huault became head of the family upon his father's death in 1610. There are some interesting observations to be made about his career, his numerous changes of residence, and his marriage to Catherine Lottin – an alliance which had decisive effects on Charles's career, since Jean de Lauson, the "intendant" (as the documents generally described him), or, rather, the director general of the *Compagnie de la Nouvelle-France*, was the son of Isabelle Lottin, Catherine's aunt. At the end of the chapter we shall touch very briefly on the descendants of Louis Huault. The last male bearing the Montmagny name died in 1699.

1.   The chevalier's mother, Antoinette Du Drac (1588–1618)

At the time of her marriage in January 1578, Antoinette Du Drac was not yet twenty. She had been baptized on 7 September 1558 in the chapel de Braque (her parents, as we have noted, lived on the street of the same chapel) by the curé of Saint-Nicolas-des-Champs. Her godfather was a priest, Antoine Le Cyrier, dean of the chapter of the cathedral of Paris.[6]

She had at least seven children, five of whom were baptized in Saint-Jean-en-Grève between 1579 and 1586.[7] Three of these died at an early age; the only survivors were Charlotte, baptized on 22 March 1583, and Louis, baptized on 31 January 1585. Apparently the births were then interrupted, to be resumed only on 2 June 1598 with Adrien;[8] they ended for good with Charles, baptized on 11 March 1601 in Saint-Paul.[9] Widowed in September 1610, Antoinette Du Drac was shortly afterwards named "the tutor having the noble guardianship of her underage children."[10]

Some months after her husband's death, Antoinette decided to lease her hôtel on the rue Saint-Antoine to two *écuyers*, Jean Langlois

and Harasse [Horace?] Morel, for four years at 1,300 livres a year.[11]
Perhaps she wanted to reduce her expenses, or simply to get away
from the construction taking place in the Place Royale, and to find
more tranquillity in another corner of the Marais. So she moved with
her three sons[12] and her domestics to the rue de Chaulme, close to the
tennis court of Tabarin, into a hôtel which belonged to a related family,
the Anjorrants.[13] This street corresponds to today's rue des Archives,
between the Francs Bourgeois and the Quatre Fils. The widow Huault
did not, however, cease to take an interest in her property on the rue
Saint-Antoine, since in 1612 she bought "a little place" situated at the
corner of the rue Saint-Antoine and the rue Royale (which opens into
the Place Royale).[14]

In fact they had acquired – she and her husband – five houses in
all on this rue Saint-Antoine: their residence, and four other properties
close by. These served as a guarantee for a *rente* constituted in 1615.[15]
In addition to the Hôtel de Baillet, we have been able to identify three
of the properties. First of all, "a little building with carriage entrance,
courtyard and garden," was leased at 800 livres in August 1614;[16]
another more modest house, containing "kitchen, little courtyard,
cellar, rooms and an attic," was leased in 1614 for 330 livres, though
the widow reserved the outer room of the principal chamber "to make
an entrance for her adjoining house, and for this reason deducting 15
livres per annum from the price";[17] and the last, leased at 900 livres in
1618 to a receiver general of finances, was more spacious, containing
"two buildings, a courtyard and a garden."[18]

There is little to say about the few properties and the *rentes*
constituted on individuals which she possessed.[19] For one thing, she
did not have to worry so much about the management of her goods,
since she could leave this to her son Louis and her son-in-law, Anne-
Antoine de Gouy.

More interesting and more revealing is the examination of the two
wills that she drew up, forty-two years apart: the first on 21 February
1576,[20] and the second on 1 September 1618.[21]

In the first she was seventeen years old, "sick in bed, though of
sound memory and understanding"; an illness from which she must
have recovered rapidly, since two years later she married Charles
Huault. The impression of wealth that her dowry has given us is
confirmed here. What, above all, characterizes this testament is the
expression of piety and of genuine charity, mixed, however, with a
childish desire for display. The funeral procession was to include the
priests of her parish, Saint-Nicolas-des-Champs, representatives of

the four mendicant orders of the city of Paris, some Minims and some Capuchins; to these were to be added children from three orphanages, some of them from the *hôpital des Enfants Rouges,* situated not far from her home.[22] She envisaged "three dozen torches" for this procession; 670 livres were to be distributed in alms of various kinds, including 300 livres for six poor girls "to help them marry or enter the religious life." Ten livres were to go to her confessor – so this was a devout household. For her deceased brother and sisters, she asked that three services be said for the soul of each, "as soon as possible after her decease."

The second testament, that of her maturity, appears to us more thoughtful and less flamboyant, though it, too, is characterized by devotion. In it we find religious and familial specifications.

The burial was to be simple: "[she] wishes that there should be no ceremony," but – and this is what counted most with her – "that every day for three consecutive years there should be said and celebrated in the aforesaid church of Saint-Jean [Saint-Jean-en-Grève, where she was to be buried] a low requiem Mass." She left 200 livres to the Jesuits, doubtless because they were responsible for the education of her sons. But there is, above all, the following highly significant clause:

> [she] begs the two young ones who are Adrien and Charles to honour and serve their older brother, and her older son, also, to continue to serve them and act as their father, to love them as his brothers and nevertheless not to raise them with vanity; if God calls them to the service of the Church, let him not dissuade them, considering them to be happy indeed if God calls them there.

This passage calls for a brief comment. First of all there is the charming expression "the two young ones" (they were, respectively, twenty and seventeen years old) which is a striking illustration not only of her motherly attention, but of the distance in their age from the two older children, Charlotte and Louis, who were thirty-five and thirty-three. Since the death of their father, it was Louis who represented the paternal authority, so important in this society. But this authority had to be tempered by an altogether fraternal charity, built out of reciprocal "service" – the word "serve" recurs three times. The "vanity" which should be banished from his life was the immoderate and ostentatious use of the goods of this world, contrary to the true Christian spirit. Above all, we should remark on the recommendation not to hinder the priestly or religious vocation, which seems to have been, in her own words ("considering them to be happy indeed"), the best thing that could happen to her two younger sons. Her wish would be realized in Charles's case, but not in Adrien's.

As to those specifications which I call familial, they rest on the following principles: first, a good relationship must at all costs be established; second, justice must be done to each according to his position as older or younger; third, service, as well as esteem, must be reciprocal. These rules would be followed, as the rest of this narrative will show. The other decisions were in keeping with the rest. Antoinette wished to be buried in Saint-Jean-en-Grève, in the Huault family crypt.[23] She asked her oldest son to remit to his co-heirs the sums which she had lent him to obtain his office of councillor in the *Grand Conseil*. Concerning the property of Goyencourt, which belonged to the *coutume* of Picardie, she had a page of recommendations to ensure that the law should be properly observed and all her heirs fairly treated.

Numerous points stand out in this testament: a penchant for devotion, a prudent sense of family realities – meticulous arrangements for the redistribution of the patrimony, for example; and a keen sense of justice – the attention to detail in matters of a material order proves this abundantly. And crowning everything else, a constant concern for balance: balance in devotion, in charity, and in the tone of her recommendations to the heirs. There, it seems to me, we have some of the personality traits of the mother of the chevalier de Montmagny.

This way of life, we may suppose, was equally shared by her husband; we may believe that she sought to inculcate it in her children.

2. Adrien Huault (1598–1667)

Among those near to him, it was assuredly with his brother Adrien that the chevalier maintained relations for the longest time. After his decease, Adrien was obliged, together with a member of the Order, to take over the matter of his succession. They had, however, followed totally different paths. Genealogies originating in the family endow Adrien with a military career as "captain of light horse."[24] This is an evident supposition.[25]

His life can be summed up in a few words. He did not found a family; however we must recognize that in the nobility (both of Robe and of Sword) celibacy was relatively frequent among younger children. If he followed studies in law, he never held the title of barrister. Thus,

TABLE 9

The Huaults de Montmagny in the Seventeenth Century

Charles I Huault

d. 1610
sgr de Montmagny, etc.
maître des requêtes, c.r. conseils d'État et privé
m. Antoinette Du Drac (d. 01 09 1618)

Charlotte	**(*)**	**Louis (II)**	**Adrien I**	**Charles II**
b. 22 03 1583		b. 31 01 1585	b. 02 06 1598	b. 11 03 1601
m. 21 02 1604		d. 06 02 1646	d. nov. 1667	d. 04 07 1657
Anne-Antoine de		sgr de Montmagny,	sgr de La Baillie	Knight of Malta 1622
Gouy		etc.	and of Messy in	Governor of
sgr d'Arsy et de		c.r. Grand Conseil	part,	Nouvelle-France
Cartigny		and then en ses	contrôleur gén.	1636
gentilhomme		conseils	extr.	Representative
ordinaire		m. 08 10 1614	des guerres	of the Order of
chambre du roi		Catherine Lottin		Malta in
c.r. Conseils d'État				Saint-Christophe,
et privé				1652–1657

Adrien II	**Charlotte**	**Louis (III)**	**Jacques**	**Jeanne**
b. 27 03 1620	b. 27 08 1618	b. 09 05 1621	b. 14 08 1627	b. 05 08 1629
d. 02 06 1699	nun 1637	d. 16 05 1691	d. 01 12 1662	m. I 01 03 1647
c.r. Grand Conseil		abbé of	sgr de Miremont	Louis Ribier
and Conseils d'État		Saint-Avric, etc.	m. 1654	sgr de Cottereau
et privé	Catherine	c.r. Parlement	Julle de Magy	c.r. Parlement
m. 03 02 1651	b. 04 12 1622			II 21 02 1660
Jeanne d'Espinoze	nun 1638			Robert Guérin de
				Berzeau
				military career

Michel-Louis	**Catherine**			**Pierre Guérin**
b. 23 10 1652	nun			military career
d. 06 10 1676	abbaye du Trésor			m. 26 01 1699
sgr de Richebourg	(near Gisors)			Anne-Geneviève
	juin 1676			Hatte
				daughter of
				Messire Nicolas,
				chevalier

(*) Three children died young: Claire, b. 1579, Claude, b. 1580, Anne, b. 1596.
Note that "b." in this table means "baptized."

apparently, he had no profession. All the same, he possessed three offices in military administration, though he kept none of them for long.[26] There was no continuity in the offices he occupied, and not much more stability in his places of residence; to our knowledge, he changed houses at least ten times.[27] But all the same, he remained faithful to the Marais where his ancestors had chosen to live since the beginning of the preceding century.

It has been possible to find some information on the state of his fortune that will allow us to verify if what he suggested in his will is true, when in effect he claimed this: "and [his nephews] will pardon the poverty of the aforesaid testator."[28]

The first of the offices that he acquired cost him 55,000 livres,[29] a considerable sum; the price of the other two must have been more or less of the same order.

For some time he owned half of the Hôtel de Baillet, the sale of which by his brother Louis brought him 29,333 livres.[30] This was the only residence which he owned. Until 1646, he lived with his brother Louis; after this date, he resorted to renting.

As to his lands, that is more complicated. He always bore the title of seigneur of "La Baillie," but this seigneurie never belonged to him, since after the death of his mother, to whom it belonged, Louis appropriated it while compensating his co-heirs.[31] The older brother also took over the property of Goyencourt, again with compensation to Adrien, Charles, and Charlotte.[32] In 1619, Adrien became co-proprietor, with Charles, of Messy-en-Brie; and a half of the latter's share fell to him in December 1623. He kept it for a long time, since on 22 December 1655, he farmed it out for the sum of 3,000 livres,[33] but from 1661, it does not appear after his name; doubtless he had sold or given away his share.

During the year 1663 he reached the age of sixty-five; he considered himself "very far gone[34] in age."[35] He then made several arrangements with a view to assuring a peaceful end. Between 2 March and 25 April, he bought a series of *rentes* for the total sum of 25,905 livres.[36] On 30 April, he made a gift of 10,800 livres to his two nephews, Louis and Adrien Huault, in exchange for an annual pension of 1,200 livres.[37] In July, he added a further 3,600 livres, for Louis alone, who in return promised to pay him 400 livres annually.[38] This last donation seems a little like a will, since he asked his nephew to have a hundred Masses said "on the day of his decease," and to begin distributing alms.

We recognize, all the same, that to hand out more than 40,000 livres "in cash" in the space of four months could not have been the act of a poor man. Furthermore, the two donations in question (14,400 livres altogether) resembled *rentes,* since the recipients had to provide him 1,600 livres a year for the rest of his life.[39] And in his will of July 1667, we learn that he enjoyed another pension of the same type, which brought him 2,000 livres.[40] Thus he was assured of a comfortable revenue, and the administration of his goods was greatly simplified. He had the wherewithal to pay his rent and the wages of his two domestics, and to follow a suitable lifestyle.

There is a suggestion of luxury in his lodging, from the silver dishes engraved with his arms, "two large mirrors with gilded frames," books,[41] a walnut cabinet, and, in the courtyard, two "chaises roulantes."[42]

There are some further details in his will: an invocation to his patron saint, and a reference to "Monsieur de Genève," that is to say, Saint François de Sales – a family devotion, it would seem.[43] Like his mother, he asked that a Mass should be celebrated daily for three years for the repose of his soul, and he wanted a burial in the "family crypt," "without any mourning ceremony." There was some charitable thought: money was left to two hospitals, principally to the Hôtel-Dieu, which was situated close to the Marais. Gratitude, also, is evident: gifts were made to his valet "in consideration of the good and agreeable services that he has rendered to the aforesaid testator during the thirty years that he lived with him in all possible fidelity."

Like many younger sons, Adrien Huault could not follow his father's example in either his lifestyle or his career. At first sight, it seems a colourless life, but it was precisely the flexibility which he enjoyed that allowed him to support his brother Charles in the various missions which the latter took on across the world.

3.   Charlotte Huault (1583–ca. 1650)

By her marriage with Anne-Antoine de Gouy, Charlotte Huault, the older sister of Charles, brought her family an unprecedented alliance. It was no longer a question, as before, of men of the Robe, but of a landed nobility.

The contract is dated 21 February 1604.[44] The dowry amounted to 30,000 livres.[45] As well, the husband-to-be received from his father, in anticipation of his inheritance from the succession of his late mother and also by way of a gift from a cousin, the vicomte d'Arsy, a series of properties and rights. This enlightens us as to the nature of his patrimony; two pages are devoted to them, and here is a short, most revealing, extract:

The land and seigneurie of Demaretz situated at Remy [close to Compiègne], consisting of twenty *muids* of arable land, eight to nine *arpents* of meadow, fifteen *arpents* of woods, twelve livres in *menus cens*, twelve capons, twelve *muids* of barley or twelve *mynes* of oats, and *rentes* and *cens*.

The young Parisienne was marrying a country gentleman.

It has not been possible to verify the antiquity of this family.[46] It is claimed that it originated in Flanders,[47] that Jacques de Gouy, husband of Catherine de Melun, was buried in the church of Sainte-Catherine of Brussels in 1492, and that the family then emigrated to France. The seigneurie of Arsy, near Compiègne, came to them around 1480 with the wife of Louis de Gouy, Jeanne de Villars, to whom it had been given by a cousin.

In reality, it is only from the time of Michel, Anne-Antoine's father, that we have positive information. In 1604, he is called "gentilhomme de la chambre du roi et chevalier de ses ordres."[48] In 1615, in his will, he is named "chevalier de l'Ordre de Saint-Michel."[49] This decoration came to him, perhaps, because of the role that he seems to have played during the wars of religion.[50] As for his son, Anne-Antoine, at the time of his marriage in 1604 he was qualified only as "Messire ... chevalier, Seigneur de Cartigny" (an estate situated close to Péronne). However we should note that he himself had doubtless also served the king, who rewarded him in 1594 and again in 1614 – which explains why, at the time of the marriage of Louis Huault, his brother-in-law, which took place in that year, his titles were more impressive: "Chevalier, conseiller du roi en ses conseils d'État et privé, gentilhomme ordinaire de la chambre du roi, sgr de Cartigny."[51] At his death his father left him other lands, including that of Arsy.[52] Like Marie Du Drac, his wife's aunt, he had interests at Nigeon.[53] On 21 July 1603, he passed a contract with a mason in Auteuil for "the construction of an oratory in the gardens of the convent of the Minim Friars of Nigeon-lez-Paris."[54] A tinge of devotion, at the very least.

In 1651 the son of Anne-Antoine, François, was designated as follows: "Me François de Gouy, chevalier, Marquis d'Arsy, Cartigny et autres lieux, conseiller du Roy en ses conseils, grand maître des eaux et forests en l'Île de France."[55] Through this last charge, François participated in one of the most important administrations in the kingdom, having under him the supervision of everything concerning hydrography and sylviculture.

An examination of the genealogy (Table 10) makes us aware, also, of the Church's part in this lineage: several nuns, including two canonesses

TABLE 10

Genealogy of the de Gouy Family

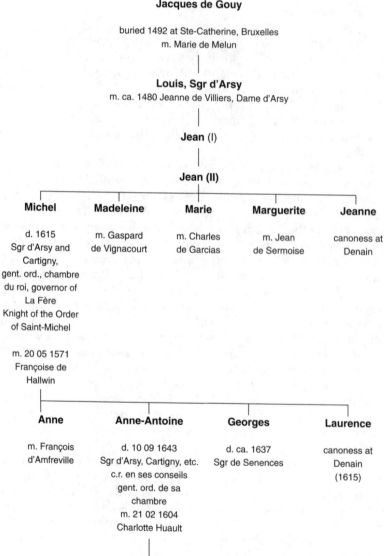

Jacques de Gouy

buried 1492 at Ste-Catherine, Bruxelles
m. Marie de Melun

Louis, Sgr d'Arsy
m. ca. 1480 Jeanne de Villiers, Dame d'Arsy

Jean (I)

Jean (II)

Michel	**Madeleine**	**Marie**	**Marguerite**	**Jeanne**
d. 1615 Sgr d'Arsy and Cartigny, gent. ord., chambre du roi, governor of La Fère Knight of the Order of Saint-Michel	m. Gaspard de Vignacourt	m. Charles de Garcias	m. Jean de Sermoise	canoness at Denain

m. 20 05 1571
Françoise de
Hallwin

Anne	**Anne-Antoine**	**Georges**	**Laurence**
m. François d'Amfreville	d. 10 09 1643 Sgr d'Arsy, Cartigny, etc. c.r. en ses conseils gent. ord. de sa chambre m. 21 02 1604 Charlotte Huault	d. ca. 1637 Sgr de Senences	canoness at Denain (1615)

9 or 10 children (see
following page)

TABLE 10

Genealogy of the de Gouy Family (cont'd)

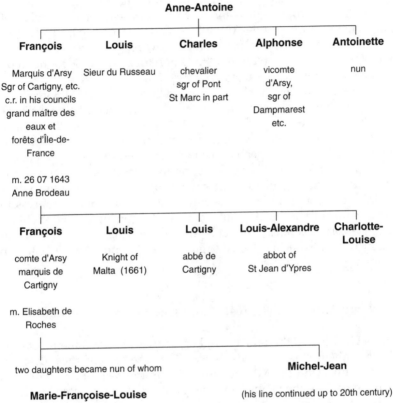

Anne-Antoine

François	**Louis**	**Charles**	**Alphonse**	**Antoinette**
Marquis d'Arsy Sgr of Cartigny, etc. c.r. in his councils grand maître des eaux et forêts d'Île-de-France	Sieur du Russeau	chevalier sgr of Pont St Marc in part	vicomte d'Arsy, sgr of Dampmarest etc.	nun

m. 26 07 1643
Anne Brodeau

François	**Louis**	**Louis**	**Louis-Alexandre**	**Charlotte-Louise**
comte d'Arsy marquis de Cartigny	Knight of Malta (1661)	abbé de Cartigny	abbot of St Jean d'Ypres	

m. Elisabeth de
Roches

two daughters became nun of whom   **Michel-Jean**

Marie-Françoise-Louise   (his line continued up to 20th century)

nun Saint-Cyr (Versailles)
proofs of nobility: sept. 1697

(an aunt and a sister of Anne-Antoine). The convents which received these "canonesses" had been established to bring together young ladies of noble blood (proofs of nobility were required there, as in the Order of Malta); the rule was inspired by that of Saint Augustine, exactly as was the case with the men – also canons regular – who entered the abbey of Saint-Victor. Among Anne-Antoine's grandchildren, we find a Knight of Malta[56] and two priests and, in the following generation, two nuns, one of whom was accepted into "the house of Saint Louis founded by the king at Saint-Cyr in the park of Versailles."[57]

Since this convent had been founded by Madame de Maintenon to come to the aid of young noblewomen of little fortune, one might think that the lineage was in decline. If so, this decline was short-lived, since until the twentieth century we find strong personalities in this family, who played a not-negligeable role in political and military spheres.[58]

The promotion of the de Gouy family went back, perhaps, to the fourteenth century; alliance with them could help the Huaults in their social ascension. The former family continued to make progress in the seventeenth and eighteenth centuries, acquiring titles of nobility (*vicomte, comte, marquis*); and high posts in the army – while the second family went into decline, then disappeared at the end of the seventeenth century.

4.   Louis Huault (1585–1646) and his wife, Catherine Lottin

Louis Huault was the fourth child of Charles and Antoinette. On the death of the first boy, Claude, born in 1580, he became the oldest son of the family and the Montmagny heir; on the death of his father in 1610 he became the head of the line. And in fact, even after the death of his mother in 1618, his house served as a residence for his brother Adrien, who remained a bachelor, and a *pied-à-terre* in Paris for both Charlotte, who lived on her lands close to Compiègne, and Charles who, as we have noted, returned constantly to the capital after his numerous distant wanderings. The reciprocal esteem and mutual service which the widow Huault recommended to her children on her deathbed seem to have been the norm in their relationships.

Louis's career was quite uneventful, compared to that of Charles; we shall only sketch it here. The management of his goods had some originality, which should be examined briefly. We shall emphasize the Lottin alliance, because of its effect on the life of the chevalier.

Louis Huault was baptized in Saint-Jean-en-Grève on 31 January 1585.[59] His career seems to have unfolded without problems, but it did not have the same dash as his father's. After having been a barrister for some years he, also, entered the *Grand Conseil* in 1612,[60] but he did not leave it. His only consolation was to become dean of the councillors of this court in 1641.[61] A 1633 document instructs us on one of the tasks confided to him: he was designated as "one of the judges of the chamber of justice established by the king in his château of the Arsenal and commissioner, and by this chamber charged with this task."[62] A chamber of justice was an extraordinary tribunal set up to judge special cases (scandals or frauds, for instance), of which one of the most frequent was the excessive enrichment, real or judged to be so, of financiers.[63]

Let us follow his successive changes of residence. Until about 1622 he lived in the houses bought by his parents. Then, in April 1624, when he was thirty-nine years old, he sold his hôtel on the rue Saint-Antoine to Mesmes Gallet for the sum of 64,000 livres.[64] As this Gallet[65] had the reputation of being an inveterate gambler – the one whom Boileau vilified in his eighth satire[66] – it has been claimed that Louis Huault was of the same stripe and that it was gambling that had lost him his hôtel.[67] Perhaps this is true, but for want of proof it remains a mere hypothesis.

In any case, in June 1622 (we do not know for how many months) he was living on the rue des Barres;[68] it is impossible to know if the property belonged to him or was only rented. On 9 April 1626, in return for some *rentes*, he acquired from his cousin Madelaine de Bragelongne a house on the rue du Chaulme, comprising two buildings separated by a courtyard.[69] He stayed there for eight years, and, in mid-February 1635, rented it out for seven years, at 1,200 livres per annum, to the great financier Thomas Bonneau.[70] The reason for this was that, two weeks before, he had paid 40,000 livres for a house on the rue Sainte-Avoye, in the parish of Saint-Merri, on the edge of the Marais.[71] It comprised several buildings with a courtyard and a garden, and a second entrance off the rue Neuve Saint-Médéric. He resold it on 2 May 1640 for the sum of 73,000 livres (a handsome profit!) to Messire Nicolas Faure, chevalier, seigneur de Berlize.[72] He then moved to the rue du Bourg-Tibourg, close to the Hôtel de Ville. He was still there in December 1643, when he borrowed the sum of 100,000 livres from his brother-in-law, François Lottin.[73] At the time he was intending to buy a large house on the rue Sainte-Croix de la Bretonnerie, which also had an entry off the rue du Plâtre; and this is what he did, some days later.[74] It was there that he died, in February 1646.

But is it in fact possible to know the state of his fortune, at the end of his life, for example? Some documents, scattered between January and March 1646 (he died on 6 February) allow us to make some interesting observations, but they do not contain sufficient precise figures to arrive at anything other than an approximation of the extent of his wealth.

On 29 January, a week before the drawing-up of his will, he effected two important transactions.[75] He borrowed 18,500 livres (against a *rente* of 925 livres per annum) from none other than Michel Le Tellier, "secrétaire d'Estat [de la guerre] et des commandements de Sa Majesté." He did this for the purpose of redeeming a *rente* of 1,077 livres, 15 sols, 4 deniers from Henri de Mesmes, with a payment of 19,400 livres. As a guarantee for the annual payment of 925 livres, four properties were mentioned: the large house where he was living (on the rue Sainte-Croix de Bretonnerie); another house on the rue du Chaulme "where the Sr Palleologo resides;" two estates, Montmagny and Goyencourt (near Roye in Picardie). Thus, he owned two houses in the Marais. To the two seigneuries must be added that of Messy, a quarter of which belonged to him, and which he mentioned elsewhere in his will,[76] and that of La Baillie, not far from Amiens. There is no further detail on the value of these lands or of these houses in the inventory drawn up on 26 January.[77] It is only concerning the office of *conseiller au Grand Conseil* that we have explicit information; on 15 March,[78] Louis's widow and three younger children sold the father's office to his oldest son, Adrien, for 107,000 livres.[79]

It is possible, then, to have at least an approximate idea of Louis Huault's assets. If to the value of the office (107,000 livres), we add the value of 110,000 livres for the four seigneuries,[80] 60,000 livres for the two houses in Paris, 10,000 livres for furnishings in Paris and Montmagny and 30,000 livres in *rentes constituées*, we arrive at the sum of 317,000 livres – let us say between 300,000 and 400,000 because of remaining uncertainties. But the debts? It is impossible to assess, though it is certain that there *were* debts, since in his will Louis ordered that all his debts be paid as soon as possible. Perhaps his fortune stood at around 300,000 livres.

Some additional information drawn from his will allows us to add a few touches to the portrait that we have just sketched.

Religion had a certain importance in his life; this came, without doubt, from his mother – there are similarities between her will, which we have studied,[81] and that of her son. Besides, one of his brothers, Charles, was a Knight of the Order of Saint John of Jerusalem, and he helped him in his undertakings, as we shall see later. Two of his daughters entered the religious life, and one of his sons embraced the ecclesiastical state. But let us return to his last wishes. The invocation to "Monsieur St François de Salles," not yet canonized (this only happened in 1665) but one of the most prestigious symbols of the French Counter-Reformation, was original. His charitable donations and the sums set aside for Masses totalled 2,537 livres.

Also evident in this document is the importance that he attached to family solidarity. He begged his brother Adrien, whom he named as one of the executors of his will, to "continue the good affections that he has always had for the aforesaid testator and his house, commanding his children most expressly to honour him and never depart from the obedience which they owe him." To his oldest son, Adrien, he recommended that he "never dispose of anything" without referring to his mother and his uncle.

Catherine Lottin, his "dearest and most loving wife" (the words used in the will), came from a Robe family whose nobility was more ancient than that of the Montmagnys. At the beginning of the seventeenth century its members maintained close connections, through the Acaries, with the spiritual milieux of France; through the Lausons, they were not slow in establishing the same ties with New France. A town situated close to the city of Québec bore for many years the name of Charny, the Lottins' principal seigneurie.

The marriage contract of 1614 was advantageous for the Huaults. The dowry was 60,000 livres, of which 20,000 entered the joint estate and the rest, which was reserved to the bride, was to be spent in the purchase of *rentes* and properties.[82] It was exactly the same sum that Guillaume Lottin had given in the previous year to his other daughter, Jeanne, who married Théodore Berzeau.[83]

Socially speaking, the families resembled each other. In 1614, Guillaume Lottin, the father of the bride, was "conseiller du roi au Parlement de Paris, president es enquestes d'icelle [cour]"; Charles Huault, as we have seen, had been a *maître des requêtes*. But the Lottins' entry into the magistracy took place earlier than that of the Huaults. The examination of the genealogy (Table 11) provides some interesting details.[84] It was in the second half of the fifteenth century that their entry into parlement took place. Robert Lottin, seigneur de Charny, was a clerk there before becoming councillor, then magistrate.[85] There was undoubtedly a relation between this accession to the sovereign court and his marriage with the daughter of a man who was himself a councillor there.

TABLE 11

Abridged Genealogy of the Lottin Family

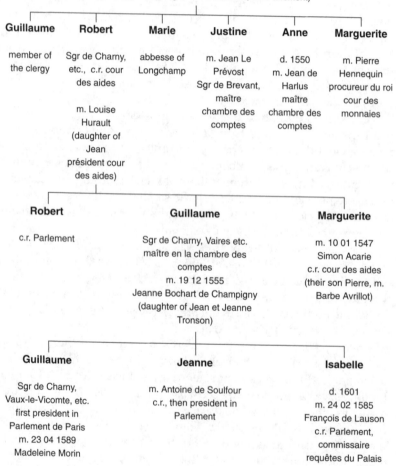

Robert Lottin

greffier des présentations, then (1480) c.r. Parlement

m. Marie Aguenin (daughter of Guillaume, c.r. Parlement)

Guillaume	**Robert**	**Marie**	**Justine**	**Anne**	**Marguerite**
member of the clergy	Sgr de Charny, etc., c.r. cour des aides	abbesse of Longchamp	m. Jean Le Prévost Sgr de Brevant, maître chambre des comptes	d. 1550 m. Jean de Harlus maître chambre des comptes	m. Pierre Hennequin procureur du roi cour des monnaies
	m. Louise Hurault (daughter of Jean président cour des aides)				

Robert	**Guillaume**	**Marguerite**
c.r. Parlement	Sgr de Charny, Vaires etc. maître en la chambre des comptes m. 19 12 1555 Jeanne Bochart de Champigny (daughter of Jean et Jeanne Tronson)	m. 10 01 1547 Simon Acarie c.r. cour des aides (their son Pierre, m. Barbe Avrillot)

Guillaume	**Jeanne**	**Isabelle**
Sgr de Charny, Vaux-le-Vicomte, etc. first president in Parlement de Paris m. 23 04 1589 Madeleine Morin	m. Antoine de Soulfour c.r., then president in Parlement	d. 1601 m. 24 02 1585 François de Lauson c.r. Parlement, commissaire requêtes du Palais

TABLE 11

Abridged Genealogy of the Lottin Family (cont'd)

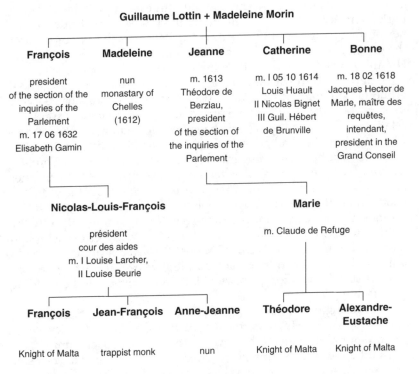

Guillaume Lottin + Madeleine Morin

François	**Madeleine**	**Jeanne**	**Catherine**	**Bonne**
president of the section of the inquiries of the Parlement m. 17 06 1632 Elisabeth Gamin	nun monastary of Chelles (1612)	m. 1613 Théodore de Berziau, president of the section of the inquiries of the Parlement	m. I 05 10 1614 Louis Huault II Nicolas Bignet III Guil. Hébert de Brunville	m. 18 02 1618 Jacques Hector de Marle, maître des requêtes, intendant, president in the Grand Conseil

Nicolas-Louis-François

président
cour des aides
m. I Louise Larcher,
II Louise Beurie

Marie

m. Claude de Refuge

François	**Jean-François**	**Anne-Jeanne**	**Théodore**	**Alexandre-Eustache**
Knight of Malta	trappist monk	nun	Knight of Malta	Knight of Malta

In the following two generations we observe a rather significant phenomenon of diversification that included the *cour des aides*, the *chambre des comptes*, the *cour des monnaies* – all three sovereign courts – and the Châtelet of Paris. Then, in the fifth case, a presidency in the *parlement* – and this was Guillaume, the father of the bride. As for her brothers, one would be *président aux enquêtes* in parlement, and the other, *maître des requêtes*. This evolution resembles that which the Huaults experienced, but with more important functions.

There is no question here of a detailed study of the Lottins' economic situation; if Guillaume was capable of giving 60,000 livres to each of his three girls who married, it is a sign that he possessed a relatively imposing capital. We have no information on the land of Charny, which they had possessed since the end of the fifteenth century, at least.[86] But here are some interesting facts about that of Vaux-le-Vicomte, acquired in 1600. This seigneurie was awarded to them, after an auction sale, for the sum of 16,630 écus, in June 1600 (the year, one should note, that Charles Huault bought the Hôtel de Baillet).[87] It had for most of a century belonged to the Soulfours, a family allied to the Lottins. It passed to Guillaume, then to his brother François, who sold it on 1 February 1641 to Nicolas Fouquet.[88] The latter decided to build a magnificent château there, surrounded with sumptuous gardens. The artists who worked there were later the foremen in the building of Versailles.

Returning to the genealogy, we note several important alliances: the Huraults, the Hennequins, the Bocharts, and the Acaries. More important for our inquiry, however, is that of the Lauson family.

Catherine Lottin's aunt had married François de Lauson.[89] Her son, Jean de Lauson, followed the classic career of provincial intendants, resembling that of Charles I Huault: councillor to the parlement, then to the *Grand Conseil*, then *maître des requêtes*, before leaving to be intendant in Dauphiné, then in Guyenne. After this he became governor of New France.

It is not known through exactly what connection Jean de Lauson became director-in-chief of the *Compagnie de la Nouvelle-France* in 1627, practically from the moment of its foundation.[90] One plausible hypothesis is that it came through his kinship with Richelieu. His grandmother, Jeanne Bochart de Champigny (Guillaume Lottin's wife) was a cousin of Suzanne de La Porte, the cardinal's mother.[91] In any case, the company had the last word in the administration of the colony, which means that Montmagny, as governor, found himself more or less under Jean de Lauson's orders. The latter ended up by going to Québec, where he was the second successor after Montmagny (from 1651 to 1657).

But the Lausons' Canadian adventure did not end there. Jean, the governor's son, who accompanied him in 1651, married in Canada, and died there tragically in 1661.[92] He had no doubt passed through the faculty of law, since his father awarded him the title of *grand sénéchal* and entrusted him with the task of organizing the justice system in the colony. Another son, Charles de Lauson, was interim governor for a few months, replacing his father, who had decided (because of discouragement, it was said)[93] to return to France earlier than planned. Undoubtedly this experience turned Charles, too, away from politics, for he decided to become a priest, served several years under Monseigneur de Laval, bishop of Québec, and returned to die in the mother country.

We may suppose that it was through his family's alliance with the Lottins and the Lausons that the chevalier de Montmagny entered the company of New France in 1632 and was named governor of Québec in 1636. A hypothesis, however, for which no hard evidence has yet confirmed.

5.   The end of the Huault de Montmagny family

To complete the family portrait that we have just drawn, it remains to give brief consideration to the end of the Huaults de Montmagny. This end can be dated precisely: "On this Thursday 4 June 1699 was buried in the choir of the church of this parish Messire Adrien Huault, chevalier, seigneur de Montmagny." This is written in the register of the parish of Saint-Thomas of Montmagny.[94] Adrien no longer had a male descendant, since his only son had died in 1676.

It is interesting from the viewpoint of social history to witness the end of a lineage that, from the mid-sixteenth century to the mid-seventeenth, had played a not unimportant role in the life of the kingdom of France and that had been involved in events which were anything but ordinary. Nothing of the same occurred in the second half of the seventeenth century; there is little to say about the children of Louis Huault, except for two persons who were rather unusual: Louis, the worldly priest, and Jeanne, twice a widow in tragic circumstances.

The oldest son, named Adrien, continued in the charge that his father had exercised, that of *conseiller au Grand Conseil*.[95] He obtained the title, which seemed in his case to have been purely honorific, of *conseiller du roi en ses conseils*.[96] He had contracted a very suitable marriage in 1651 with Jeanne d'Espinose, who was the daughter of a president in the parlement of Brittany.[97] She brought a dowry of 75,000 livres, an advance on her inheritance.

His fortune was certainly respectable, but at the end of his life, he made a gift of his seigneurie of Montmagny – all that remained to him of his landed property, it seems – in return for an annual pension and a place in the manor of the same seigneurie. The recipient went by the name of Nicolas de Malebranche;[98] a little later he also made him his universal heir.[99] According to the inventory after death, all that remained to Adrien was his furniture, estimated at 2,591 livres[100] – the remnant of a family fortune which in the good years at the start of the century totalled 400,000 livres.

The youngest of Louis Huault's sons, named Jacques, who lived from 1627 to 1662, did not, to our knowledge, possess any office. He married a commoner, Julle de Magy.[101] He seems to have lived on his *rentes*; he owned two little fiefs.[102] His life course contrasted with those that we have hitherto studied.

Louis's second son, also named Louis, had been baptized in Saint-Paul on 21 May 1621.[103] When he had reached the age of ten years, his parents presented him for admission into the Order of Malta.[104] We do not know why this presentation was not followed up. When we rediscover him later – in 1643[105] – he is twenty-two years old, a cleric in the diocese of Paris, and the holder of a priory in Normandy.[106] He was enrolled in the faculty of theology of the University of Paris,[107] but there is nothing to show that he finished his studies, or even that he entered the priesthood.

Over a period of some years he accumulated ecclesiastical benefices, and in 1664 he bought the office of *conseiller au parlement*,[108] which allows us to suppose that he had done studies in law.

He was a cultivated man. His library contained 471 books, among which the inventory after death identified only a dozen: the Bible, Plutarch, Seneca, Pliny, some juridical treatises, some history.[109] This short list gives the impression of a balanced culture. Continuing the examination of the inventory, we discover a certain refinement: among his numerous paintings was a large canvas by Bassano,[110] estimated at 30 livres, and another, of unknown provenance, "representing a woman and a cupid." There were tapestries, among them a set of six valued at 3,000 livres, and precious textiles – for example, three *pentes* of embroidery worth 2,000 livres.[111]

He seems to have loved society life – this is suggested by the agreement made with his brother Adrien in 1679, which allowed him, during his lifetime, "occupation and habitation in our château of

Montmagny, in addition to all the quarters that he occupies when he comes to Montmagny," as well as the use "of the great garden, in respect of using the walks only, both for himself and for his friends."[112]

But he did not know how to manage his fortune properly; after his death, his creditors formed a syndicate, entrusting the direction to four persons, among them Nicolas de Malebranche, of whom we have already spoken.[113] His goods were auctioned off to repay his debts.

A man altogether different from all the Huaults whom we have met so far, but, it seems to us, representative of a considerable part of the clergy of that time, who entered into ecclesiastical benefices to lighten the burden on the family fortunes.

The contrast that we observe in the circumstances of Louis Huault's three sons – the chevalier's nephews – continues with respect to his three daughters.

Charlotte Huault[114] entered, at the end of December 1637, "the professed religious of the Third Order of Saint Francis in their monastery of the Conception of the Virgin, newly established on the street and close to the Porte Saint-Honoré in Paris." She was nineteen years old and wished "to spend her life in the praise of God."[115] But it is not certain that she persevered in her vocation, for in the parish register of Montmagny, the presence is noted, on 29 September 1650, of "Dlle Charlotte Huault, daughter of the late Louis."[116]

Catherine, her younger sister,[117] chose another community, the convent of the Annunciades at Saint-Denis. This town, as we have already indicated, was situated close to Montmagny; within its walls it harboured several convents which clustered around the celebrated basilica containing the remains of Saint Louis and the other kings of France.

Jeanne was the youngest of the family. She did not experience her older siblings' peaceful life. In 1647, however, at the age of seventeen years,[118] she had contracted what seemed like a promising marriage.[119] She brought 30,000 livres to the joint estate – which lets us suppose a marriage settlement in the order of 100,000 livres.[120] Louis Ribier, seigneur de Cottereau, her husband, was a magistrate in the parlement of Paris. For his marriage, his father gave him the office of *conseiller*, valued at 120,000 livres, the house where he was living on the rue des Mauvaises Parolles in the parish of Saint-Germain l'Auxerrois, close to the Halles, worth 80,000 livres, and a rather remarkable library, "consisting of printed books, manuscripts, medals, pictures, globes and other things belonging to the said library in the state in which it is at present, according to the inventoried catalogue in the inventory taken after the decease of the said late Dame Ribier [...] and estimated at the sum of ten thousand livres."

A family very much at ease, cultivated, and in every way respectable – one of Jeanne's brothers-in-law entered the Fathers of Christian Doctrine.[121]

Ill fortune seems to have pursued the couple. This was their situation in 1656.[122] Louis Ribier was overwhelmed by debt; he had to sell his office of *conseiller au parlement.* A syndicate of his creditors had been formed to sell his furniture and his library. His wife had obtained a separation of goods, and one of the members of the syndicate, François Ménard, had been able to put aside a sum of 11,250 livres for her, which was handed over to her fifteen years later.[123] This was a ruined man. We have no way of knowing the cause of his troubles.

But the worst was still to come. He was murdered in March 1659 in the forest of Compiègne.[124] It appears that this event unleashed a most astonishing reaction on the part of the widow. Indeed, a rumour ran around Paris that she had "promised to marry the man who brought her her husband's assassin."[125] Pure gossip? We cannot say. The fact is that less than a year after the event in question she was remarried, and this time to a military man![126] Robert Guérin de Berzeaux, chevalier, seigneur de Tarnault and other places, was a captain of infantry in the regiment of Picardie. He would become a brigadier in the king's army.

To complete Jeanne's misfortune, he too was murdered, on 5 January 1678, just as the war with Holland was coming to an end.[127]

All the same, she had the consolation of witnessing[128] the brilliant career of her son, Pierre Guérin, seigneur de Goyencourt, La Baillie and other places – we recognize the seigneuries of the Huaults – who, at the time of his marriage in January 1699, was *maréchal des logis* in His Majesty's armies.[129]

Jeanne Huault was the last representative of the name of the Huaults of Montmagny; she died some years after her brother Adrien, the last male of the line. But the descendance continued through the women: the Guérins, the de Gouys, the Faucons, and other families which we have mentioned in passing.

The path taken by Charles Huault de Montmagny offers a striking contrast with the rest of his family, whose lives we have just followed through a hundred years. His vocation was military and religious – that was, in fact, the special character of the Order of Saint John of Jerusalem. But of these two domains there is hardly a trace to be found among his kin. No soldier appears – save, after 1660, the second husband of Jeanne Huault, Robert Guérin, the brigadier in the king's armies. The professions, such as there were, were juridical or administrative. Only women – Charles's two nieces and a great-niece – are found embracing the religious life. The abbé Louis, his nephew, seems to have been more a worldly cleric than a man profoundly marked by religious feeling. But above all, the difference lies in the career of the chevalier, characterized by movement, numerous travels (see Table 15 in Chapter 4), and infinite distances, while the others (apart from his brother Adrien, for a short time) spent their lives within a very narrow zone, scarcely larger than the triangle of Montmagny-Paris-Meaux (or Compiègne, for the de Gouys).

To find any similarities to Charles Huault's career, we would have to turn to the Huault de Vayres branch. From the end of the sixteenth century, these abandoned the pen for the sword (see Table 12). One of them, Philippe, took part in the Fronde, in the camp of the prince of Condé.[130] He died from the effects of a wound received in the famous battle of the faubourg Saint-Antoine (2 July 1652).

The presence of the Church was also relatively important in this branch. There were Alexandre, who entered the Order of Malta in 1629 and was killed at the siege of Dôle in 1636; two priests, one of whom refused a bishopric that was being offered him;[131] and five nuns.

This last fact has led us to consider the significance, quantitatively speaking, of the Church's place, both in the two branches of the Huault family and in a part of those allied to them, between the fifteenth and the end of the eighteenth century. We have drawn this up in Table 13. The bishops, canons, and diocesan priests appear first, then the religious men and women, and, finally, the members of the Order of Malta.

Charles Huault's entry into the Order of Malta was most certainly a personal choice; but there is reason to remark, all the same, that this vocation fitted well into the practice of the families with whom he was related, by blood or by marriage.

TABLE 12

Abridged Genealogy of the Huaults de Vayres,
Seventeenth and Eighteenth Centuries

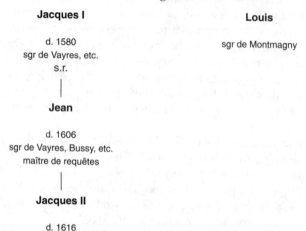

Jacques I   **Louis**

d. 1580   sgr de Montmagny
sgr de Vayres, etc.
s.r.

Jean

d. 1606
sgr de Vayres, Bussy, etc.
maître de requêtes

Jacques II

d. 1616
sgr de Vayres, Bussy, etc.
colonel régiment d'infanterie
m. Anne de Maillard, Dame de Bernay

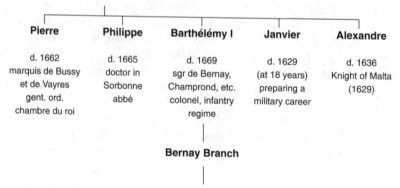

Pierre	**Philippe**	**Barthélémy I**	**Janvier**	**Alexandre**
d. 1662	d. 1665	d. 1669	d. 1629	d. 1636
marquis de Bussy	doctor in	sgr de Bernay,	(at 18 years)	Knight of Malta
et de Vayres	Sorbonne	Champrond, etc.	preparing a	(1629)
gent. ord.	abbé	colonel, infantry	military career	
chambre du roi		regime		

Bernay Branch

TABLE 12

Huaults de Vayres (con't)

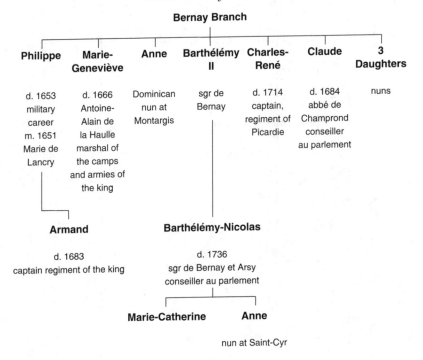

Bernay Branch

Philippe	Marie-Geneviève	Anne	Barthélémy II	Charles-René	Claude	3 Daughters
d. 1653 military career m. 1651 Marie de Lancry	d. 1666 Antoine-Alain de la Haulle marshal of the camps and armies of the king	Dominican nun at Montargis	sgr de Bernay	d. 1714 captain, regiment of Picardie	d. 1684 abbé de Champrond conseiller au parlement	nuns

Armand

d. 1683
captain regiment of the king

Barthélémy-Nicolas

d. 1736
sgr de Bernay et Arsy
conseiller au parlement

Marie-Catherine	Anne
	nun at Saint-Cyr

TABLE 13

The Huaults, Du Dracs, Some Allied Families, and the Church, Fifteenth to Eighteenth Centuries

Family	Bishop	Canon	Priest	Regular	Nun	Order of Malta	TOTAL
Huault de Montmagny			1	1	3	1	6
Huault de Vayres			2		5	1	8
Du Drac	* 1	** 3			2		6
Anjorrant		1	1		4	2	8
Bragelongne (de)	1	6	2	8	*** 11	3	31
Faucon	1	1	2	1	1	6	12
Gouy (de)			2		5	5	12
Lottin			1	1	3	1	6
Arbaleste				1			2
Hacqueville (de)	1	2	1	2	3	1	9
Piedefer						8	8
Ficte (de)			2		1	2	5
Rappouel				1	1		2
Bochart****	4		7	1	6	2	20
Hennequin****	3	3	3		3	5	17
TOTAL	11	16	24	16	47	37	152

* Lived in the 15th century

** One of the canons lived in the 15th century

*** Of whom one lived in the 15th century: Marie, abbess of the Abbey of Lys (near Melun).

**** They were allied of allied (or relatives of relatives); but it should be noted that Madeleine Bochart, spouse of Simon Arbaleste, figures among the ancestors of Charles Huault; and according to the method Stradonitz, she would have the number 53, and her husband, 54, in the genealogical tree.

CHAPTER 3

A First Direction: The Robe

When it was a question of choosing his life's direction, Charles Huault de Montmagny considered law first; family pressure, both from his father's and his mother's side, carried him in this direction. However, there remained an alternative solution, the Church; there, again, earlier examples were not lacking, as we have seen. He hesitated between the two.

We shall now retrace the story of his own life, beginning with his childhood and adolescence, the years from 1601 to 1622. Without a doubt, the salient fact is that his professional formation – Jesuit college, the faculty of law – turned him towards jurisprudence. But he had second thoughts, and, choosing to give himself some months of reflection, left for Italy. On his return he took the decision which established his future: to enter the Order of Malta.

At first sight, nothing would be simpler than an account of the life of a young Parisian, son of an influential magistrate. In reality it is not so easy, for a very commonplace reason: the sources are very thin. There remain no letters from him or from his family. Of the institutions he frequented, no register survives from the period; of the Italian trip, the journal (if he kept one) has not come down to us. Only a careful search through the Parisian notarial archives has enabled us to learn the essential outlines of this part of his life. We note, especially, the account of guardianship, closed in June 1622, that sketches the pattern of his activities between this date and November 1617.[1] Here is the use of time as it appears in this document:

1. from 25 November 1617 to 30 July 1618: the college of La Flèche;
2. from 31 July 1618 to 1 May 1619: Paris;
3. from 2 May 1619 to 25 March 1620: University of Orléans;
4. from 26 March to 8 September 1620: Paris;
5. from 8 September 1620 to 15 August 1621: voyage to Italy;
6. from 15 August 1621 to 11 June 1622: Paris.

He would have started his studies at the college of La Flèche in the summer or the autumn of 1610.[2] From his birth in March 1601 to this time, he lived with his family and received the education appropriate to people of his condition.

The dearth of sources forces us, for the study of the first part of his life, to adopt an indirect method; that is to say, to find what each of these stages might have meant through a series of cross-references: comparisons with other cases drawn from his social milieu, information on the life of students at La Flèche and Orléans, and on the experience of visitors to Italy at the beginning of the seventeenth century.

The chronological order will be observed; we shall address, in turn, the years in Paris, the formation under the Jesuits, the interlude in Orléans, and the journey to Italy.

1.   The earliest years (1601–1610)

Before leaving for the west of France to begin his years of study with the Jesuits, Charles Huault had lived to the rhythm of the family microcosm, the characteristics of which we know already; suffice it here to recall the persons who surrounded him and to reflect briefly on certain aspects of his childhood.

Until his death, Montmagny remained very much attached to his family, a sign no doubt that his early contacts had been good. His father's career was essentially Parisian; he had to go off to Poitou, as we have seen, but he does not appear to have stayed there long, and we do not know if he was given missions of the same kind to other regions. So he was present in the home during the years that preceded his son's departure for La Flèche. He could participate in some way in his early formation. However, it was the mother who had the responsibility – above all during his infancy – for her child's physical health and socialization. Louis, his older brother, who was received as a barrister around 1605 and who reached the age of twenty-five in 1610, was well placed to help and counsel his younger brother; he would become his tutor upon their mother's death in 1618. It was undoubtedly with Adrien, born two years and some months before him, that Charles was the most familiar; they went together to the college of La Flèche and the university in Orléans, and throughout their lives the contact remained unbroken. He could not have known his sister Charlotte well, since she married in February 1604 and went to live north of Paris. This marriage was without doubt the most important event of all those years in the family. It was also at this time that Louis ended his studies, at the college in about 1603,[3] and at the faculty of law around 1605.[4]

We remember, also, the milieu in which Charles's childhood was passed – in complete conformity with the ideal of the very best of the *noblesse de robe*. The Montmagny family lived in the Marais, in a residence which was still at that time known as the Hôtel de Baillet; a part of the property was sold to the king in 1607 to permit the construction of the Place Royale. It was an upscale quarter, as we have seen, but the Huaults' lifestyle was not marked by great luxury; we have been struck by the sobriety of Charles I's furniture.[5]

For some days or some weeks every year, the family went to the manor north of Paris, not far from Saint-Denis. There, again, an agreeable, comfortable atmosphere reigned. The inquisitors for the Order of Malta were impressed in 1622 by the château gardens when they went to Montmagny:

> the aforesaid Charles Huault's place of birth and extraction on the paternal side, where we have seen the aforesaid house and ancient château surrounded by gardens where there is a fountain, and a grand park in which there are tall trees and many fine walks which display a great antiquity.[6]

We do not know the frequency of the Huaults' stays there, but their presence is noted in the parish registers of Montmagny; thus, on 17 July 1613, continuing a practice current among his kin, "noble Charles Huault, Seigneur de Messy, *écuyer* to our lord the King," stood godfather to the son of a peasant.[7]

The socialization of a child of the nobility involved two critical years.[8] When he was about four years old, there would be an intensification in his training, first in good manners, principally table manners, and then in etiquette. The same went for religious rites, Christian vocabulary, and ways of thinking. But before reaching his seventh year, the child was seen as a being without reason; corporal punishments – the infamous birch rods – were the order of the day. Then, at seven, there began the so-called age of reason. The boy was detached from his governesses, to be taken in hand by men. According to his parents' financial means or their interests, masters of dance and riding, or tutors to introduce him to the things of the mind, were engaged. His clothes became resolutely masculine; the wearing of hat and sword were permitted. Physical exercises multiplied. It was possible to join in the games of adults, such as backgammon, chess, and others. This pattern would have applied to the Huault children.

Very soon, through the more or less biased viewpoint of his family, Charles would have been acquainted with the great affairs of the realm, politics first of all. It would have been from his father, who had been personally involved, that he received this first introduction.[9] Order and stability characterized the France of 1601–1610, in strong contrast with the last four decades of the previous century. The conversations must have recalled the roles of various members of the family – the broader family of which we have spoken in preceding chapters – in those troubled years, as in those of the reconstruction led by Sully, Henri IV's energetic minister.

Certain events were undoubtedly the subject of numerous commentaries: the rise of the Brulart family (with its many ties to their own), Nicolas becoming *garde des sceaux* in 1603, then chancellor in 1607; the foundation of Québec in 1608, which represented the renewal of the French colonizing effort in America; and, above all, not to be forgotten, the catastrophe which the king's assassination on 14 May 1610 represented for them.

As well, the Montmagnys were fairly closely involved in that dynamic current buffeting the Church of France, the Counter Reformation. Three persons, two of whom were part of their network of alliances, embodied this movement in the first decade of the century. François de Sales preached to the court in 1602 and, in 1608, published his masterpiece, the *Introduction to the Devout Life*. In reminiscence of this period, Louis Huault, in his testament of 1646,[10] invoked "saint" François de Sales, though at this date he had not yet been canonized by the Church,[11] and his brother Adrien did the same in 1667.[12] The other two, Bérulle[13] and Madame Acarie,[14] together introduced the Carmel into France in 1604, and the former founded the Oratory in 1611.

The Jesuits were readmitted into the kingdom in 1603. They then took back the buildings that they had occupied since 1580 in the Marais, close to the Hôtel de Baillet. More important still is the fact that they re-entered their houses of education, which had had such great success among the French elite. And then, in 1608, Father Étienne Charlet was named rector of a newly-founded college at La Flèche. All in all, this priest had a remarkable career, since he was twice provincial of France and, for many years, assistant to the general in Rome.[15] A bond of kinship joined Father Charlet to the Huault family.[16]

When there was a question of sending Charles to college, it was La Flèche that came to his parents' mind.

2. With the Jesuits of La Flèche (1610–1618)

On the eighth page of his account of guardianship of his brother, Louis Huault had this written:

> To the Jesuits of La Flèche for the terms begun the 25 November 1617 and for the pensions of Masters de la Baillie [Adrien] and Huault [Charles] until the end of the month of August 1618: six hundred livres, including twelve livres sixteen sols which the said masters owe to the Jesuits of Orléans, the costs of their clothing, and two écus for the valet who served them at La Flèche, altogether forty eight livres seven sols six deniers, total 600 L.

This rather prosaic and, at first sight, altogether banal statement is highly valuable: it establishes the presence of Charles and his brother at the college of La Flèche, and indicates the end of their pre-university studies. It is strange, by the way, that they were at exactly the same level, given the difference in their ages. Whatever the case, the fact that the two brothers were simultaneously in the same institution made for lower expenses – for the valet, for instance, or for their books. Since the duration of college studies was generally eight years, sometimes seven, there is every reason to conclude that their stay at La Flèche began in the autumn of 1610 or, at the latest, in 1611. Preparation for the following stage, the university, was made easier for them by the presence of the Jesuits in Orléans.[17]

It is important to explain here what the college of La Flèche represented in the second decade of the seventeenth century. After a few words on the college, we shall try to bring out the essential characteristics of Jesuit pedagogy. After that, the study of some individual cases – Montmagny's fellow students – will concretize this presentation of the intellectual and spiritual milieu in which he spent most of his adolescence.

It was in 1603, at the very time that he recalled the Jesuits to France,[18] that Henri IV decided to found a full-fledged university[19] at La Flèche and entrust it to them.[20] For this purpose he gave them the château that his grandfather had built there in 1540. He had a particular attachment to this place in which his mother had spent the greater part of her pregancy when she was expecting him. Furthermore, one of his favourites, Guillaume Fouquet de La Varenne, was born there. Finally, in 1607, the institution which had begun to function in 1604 took its final form; it was to be "a college of the first order, or general and universal seminary ... equal to the greatest of the Jesuits' colleges and universities";[21] that is to say that the course would be complete, from the so-called "sixth year" to "philosophy,"[22] and that theology would also be taught – a branch of learning that almost nobody followed except students who were already members of the Society. Considerable sums were spent on fitting out the buildings.[23] A number of priories and abbeys were granted to it in order to assure the regular financing of the establishment.

Success was immediate with more than 1000 students enrolled in the first year. In fact the king was responsible for this. He did not fail to publicize "his college," pressing the nobles to send their sons there,[24] and, for the benefit of the new institution, forbidding the reopening of the college of Clermont in Paris.[25]

However, this was not the only reason for its success. The Jesuits were in demand everywhere, above all for the fact that they had instituted remarkable teaching methods.

For more than fifty years,[26] and, at the beginning, under the direction of Loyola himself, the Fathers had striven for a profound renewal in an education system that had long grown decrepit. Their objective was to protect the fundamental principles derived from Christianity and Antiquity, while adapting to a rapidly changing clientele. It is, we believe, under these two headings that we should undertake our examination.

Let us start with the elements of a pedagogical character. The first is what was then called "accommodation," which is to say that the teacher, or master, had to "accommodate" or adapt himself, and so take account of the capacities, intellectual or otherwise, of the young people whose formation was confided to him. This meant, among other things, not pushing too hard, but accepting that the steps should be progressive, and the difficulties graduated.[27]

The second principle followed from the first: in a course of studies it was not only the material that mattered, but also, and just as much, its "ordering," organization, presentation; hence the famous Ratio studiorum, "the order of studies,"[28] a book that contained the essentials of this new method. It was published for the first time in 1582, but its final version dated from 1599. The putting into practice of the rules defined in it depended on an important innovation, the training of the masters. They had to be prepared for a task that had become very exacting.

And there is a third point to be made: the initial substratum for all culture is language; and this language, for the literate of the sixteenth century, was above all Latin, to which Greek was added naturally, but in second place. And the base of European culture was the civilization that we call "classical," which had been restored to a place of honour by the humanists. In this lay the pedagogical underpinning of Jesuit education.

We must, however, go further and discern the foundation of this renewed humanism. This time, what was at issue were universal rules, so to speak. To start with, this fact was basic: the values of Greco-Roman antiquity still maintained their authority, representing a summit in the history of humanity – as far as one could go without the light of faith. But it was in the Christian faith that they found all their meaning and knew their perfection.

Thus, Jesuit education aimed to form a complete man, a man of equilibrium, with an intelligence properly developed, a will directed toward the good – the good as Christ defined it – and a dignified behaviour in clothing, language, and deportment.

Certainly it was aiming to form an elite,[29] but in a fundamentally egalitarian context. Father de Dainville's conclusion on this subject is highly enlightening:

> In reaction against both the social prejudices of a dying feudal world and the growing influence of the two great modern forces, office and wealth, they [the Jesuits] affirmed, and made their students live, the eternal Christian newness. Excellence depends on neither the office nor the wealth nor the birth of a man; he attains the highest place who is entirely faithful to the responsibilities of his station, who knows how to live and to accomplish to the full his "métier d'homme."[30]

To reach this ideal, various techniques and procedures were developed. There was an effort, for example, to stimulate the interest of the students; emulation was aroused by competitions followed by rewards, by debates, and by contests; to a certain point "the class became a game." It was in this view that the art of theatre was cultivated to celebrate annual feast days with the lustre that they deserved; in great displays on the occasion of extraordinary events, such as the transfer of the heart of Henri IV to the chapel of La Flèche in June 1610. Undoubtedly Montmagny was present at the anniversary of this event in 1611, as well as at the visit of Louis XIII and his mother in 1614. The theatre had a great vogue in La Flèche; between 1608 and 1618, no less than fourteen pieces were staged, all composed by the Jesuits around historic themes (mainly Antiquity and the Middle Ages).[31]

Also characteristic of the Jesuits was that there was no relaxation in discipline, though this was tempered by the understanding of situations and attention to individual cases. We can easily infer that the care of the body was not neglected; it was considered that, for everybody, health was an important factor in achieving good results. For the boarders, meals were supervised and sleep well-regulated.

In return, what was expected from the student was docility – the fundamental virtue of his condition – and obedience. Submission of the spirit was the virtue proper to childhood, just as loyalty befitted the subjects of the king.[32]

In considering Montmagny's career, we cannot help seeing that he assimilated the essential points of this formation well. For the moment we confine ourselves to a few thoughts. The Jesuit system favoured emulation, justified rewards, incited the young to develop a sense of honour or, otherwise stated, "glory." "Glory! This is truly the last word, the soul of the Ratio Studiorum," writes Father de Dainville.[33] To accomplish honourable, glorious deeds: this was assuredly the motive that impelled our chevalier to fight against the "enemies of the faith" in the Mediterranean, then to cross the Atlantic to assist the missionaries in their work of evangelization. In addition, the Jesuits laid heavy emphasis on "the purity of intention," which should be "brought to the choice of a state of life."[34] But by purity of intention it was meant "to serve God first," not to think, for example, of the "benefices" which constituted one of the blemishes on the Church of the day. Montmagny was faithful to this spirit; he entered the Order of Malta "to serve God." He did not perform all his caravans straight away, he did not pronounce his formal vows until much later, he never had a commandery – even though commanderies were much sought-after by the chevaliers and their families because they assured the financial independence of their holders.

There is another dimension of Jesuit thought which we have not yet mentioned, and which was capital in the life of the chevalier – Italy. Rome, the capital of Christianity, was the residence of the Jesuit general and of the supreme pontiff. In addition to the three traditional vows, the Jesuits pronounced a fourth: obedience to the pope. This, in part, is what explains Montmagny's departure for Italy. But there is more. From very early days, the Jesuits took an interest in faraway worlds. Surely their students must often have heard them talk about them. François Xavier (1506–1552), one of Loyola's first companions, began what we may well call the Society's Asiatic saga. When Montmagny arrived at La Flèche in 1610, the Fathers had just inaugurated their famous Reductions in Paraguay.[35] In the following years, Fathers Biard and Massé commenced their apostolate in Acadia. Three years later (1614) Ennemond Massé,[36] chased out of Acadia by the English, returned to France, and his superiors sent him to the college, where he became bursar. This was doubtless the future governor's first contact with Canada. The missionary had magnificent tales to tell, of tangles with the Huguenots and with the Biencourt family, and experiences with the Indians which nearly ended in tragedy.

At the college Montmagny also met three religious who would later, on the other side of the Atlantic, have the closest of relations with him. Paul Le Jeune (the first author of the celebrated *Relations*)[37] did his training in philosophy from 1615 to 1618; they must have been fellow students for several months. It was Le Jeune who welcomed the new governor of Québec in June 1636, when, as superior of the Jesuits, he represented the ecclesiastical authority in the colony. Charles Lalemant (a member, like Charles Huault, of a Robe family) studied at the college from 1609 to 1612, and then from 1615 to 1619; he exercised a ministry at Québec from 1634 to 1638. Finally, Barthélemy Vimont trained in philosophy at the same institution from 1615 to 1618; they must have known each other. Twenty years later, on 1 August 1639, they found themselves on the banks of the Saint Lawrence. The arrival in the little settlement of an imposing number of religious (including Vimont, and also Poncet and Chaumonot)[38] and of nuns (among them Marie de l'Incarnation) was one of the important moments in the administration of the governor, and also in the history of New France.

And while we are on the subject of what might be called astonishing coincidences, it is fitting to mention the presence at La Flèche, during the years that Montmagny attended the college, of two remarkable personalities: Descartes and La Dauversière.

The author of the *Discours de la méthode* entered La Flèche at the age of ten years in 1606, and studied there until 1612.[39] It is useful to note that the regime which the Jesuits authorized for his constitution (which until then had been very fragile) had good results: his health came to flourish. He astounded his masters with his ingenious mind and his implacable logic; he himself, however critical he was of the learning he had received, boasted of having been "in one of the most celebrated schools of Europe." This is what he was saying in 1641, many years after he left the college:

> Because philosophy is the keystone of all the other sciences, I believe
> that it is useful to have studied the entire course of it as taught in the

schools of the Jesuits ... I must render this homage to our masters in saying that there is nowhere in the world where I consider it better taught than at La Flèche ... As there are numbers of young men from all quarters of France, they create a certain blend of humour by their conversation with each other, which teaches them the same thing as though they were travelling. Finally, the equality which the Jesuits build among them, by hardly treating the highest differently from the least, is an extremely good device for ridding them of the softness and the other faults which they could have acquired from the habit of being cossetted in their parents' house.[40]

His father had entered the parlement of Rennes after the death of his wife. A similar career was opening for René Descartes; he studied law at Poitiers. But it was not in this direction that he later directed his energies. He became a soldier, enlisting as a volunteer from 1616 to 1622, and served in Holland and Germany. But after 1622, he again changed direction: it was to study and philosophical reflection that he came to devote all his time, first at Paris, then, always in search of more calm and tranquillity, in the countryside, and later in various cities in Holland. He died in Sweden in 1650.

There were, we should note at once, interesting resemblances between Montmagny and Descartes: the college, the faculty of law, the war, and the journeys. But the occupations that finally absorbed them differed completely the one from the other.

As for Jérome Le Royer de La Dauversière (1597–1659), he too was at La Flèche; he entered the college at its opening in 1604.[41] We do not know if he passed through the faculty of law like Descartes and Montmagny, but in 1618 he succeeded his father in the office of *receveur des tailles* – a career which could have been very unexceptional. What was less unexceptional was his interest in religious affairs. First he undertook, layman though he was and father of six children, to found an institute of nursing sisters; then, following an inspiration which he said came to him from heaven, he decided to set up a society for the purpose of establishing a city in New France dedicated to the Virgin, whose first vocation would be the conversion of the native peoples. This was the origin of the *Société de Notre-Dame de Montréal*. The foundation of Ville-Marie in 1642 was one of the outstanding events of Montmagny's administration.[42]

We should also make mention here of another pupil of the Jesuits who was a contemporary of Montmagny. His name was Pierre Corneille (1606–1684).[43] He himself studied at the college of Rouen. His family also belonged to the Robe; the father was *maître des eaux et fôrets* in Normandy. The faculty of law was imposed upon the young Corneille; but from 1629 onward, the better part of his time was given to poetry and the theatre. The premiere of *Le Cid* in 1637 was a triumph. Less than ten years later, in December 1646, the piece was played in Québec – the first performance of this play in America – at the behest of none other than the governor of Québec, Charles Huault de Montmagny.[44]

There remains for our use here an interesting record that has survived the period, concerning a student who arrived in La Flèche in October 1611.[45] The two years which he had spent in Angers had done him little good. Once with the Jesuits, he entered the fifth year; he was thus Charles Huault's fellow student, if, as seems likely, the latter began his course in 1610. His name was Louis Thévenin.[46] He was the youngest in his family, and, on 14 May 1611, five months before sending him to La Flèche, his father had had him tonsured. He would then have been twelve years old.

These documents, coming from a private archival collection, are statements of account (twelve between October 1611 and October 1616) and letters (fifteen between 9 February 1612 and 6 May 1615); remnants of a series which, it seems, had been much fuller. But these pieces can serve our purpose, in that they give us a little glimpse of the life which the collegians of the early seventeenth century faced, and some of their reactions.

There are three sorts of accounts. First, those that came from Père Jacques Fournier, the procurator (or bursar) of the house, which deal with the necessities of student life – books, ink, pens, and candles. This last article reappears frequently; I point to a remark of the Jesuit: "Plenty of candles, but we go to bed late and we rise early in the morning." Remark, also, the notes that the priest sometimes adds, at the end of his accounts, on the boy's behaviour, such as: "I tell you that, thank God, he behaves very well and does his duty and gives all of us satisfaction. I hope that he will give you the same."[47] Then come the "costs of clothing" – the heaviest costs – and then the "costs of illnesses," which means the sums paid to the surgeon and the apothecary.

There are several things to draw from the correspondence, starting with the subjects discussed. These can be sorted under three headings. First – and it is the question which returns most often – the money which the youngster claims to need to buy clothes and books – above all books. Louis Thévenin was at the beginning of his adolescence (as also was Charles Huault); he had to replace suits and shoes that had become too small, and even to follow the fashions, as when he asked in 1613 that they buy him boots with spurs, because, according to him, "in the college there is no one however young who doesn't have them." Secondly, the state of his health, especially in 1613 and 1614 as the expense caused by his indispositions aroused reflections and explanations on his part. Thirdly, the state of his studies. He was most happy to announce, a few months after his arrival, that from being in the last place at the beginning, he had become "emperor," that is to say the first in the class. On the other hand, when he reached the second year – the "humanities" – he wrote to his father about how much the composition of poems bored him; and he even dreamed for a while of leaving the college. Then the Fathers made some adjustments and everything fell into place again.

There are also some questions of style to note. In 1612 he addresses, again to his father, and in the language of Cicero, a sort of epistle on the subject of reciprocity in father-son relations. The spelling and grammar are very respectable – but he may have had help. On 15 January 1614, he mentions that several letters which he has sent remained unanswered, and that one of them contains two epigrams, one addressed to the father, the other to the older brother. More interesting still is the letter he addresses to "Mademoiselle ma mère." He thanks her for the suit of clothes which she has arranged to have sent to him, and he promises her his obedience, especially where his studies were concerned. "I try to study the best I can, since I didn't promise you anything else while I was in La Roche, except to try to advance in my studies so that I can be finished with them."

Two events affecting his stay are mentioned, the epidemic of 1613 and the danger of civil war the following year. On two occasions (28 August and 18 September 1613) he asks his father to send for him, because "both fevers and dissenteries" are ravaging the town and threatening to attack the college, which would be a catastrophe: "If one boarder became sick with it, almost all the boarders would become sick." The following year another scourge appears. The "Grands" have revolted against the king and his mother; the Calvinists of Saumur have reorganized. But the Fathers have reassured their students, and Louis declares in his letter of 2 April, "one thinks that, God willing, this will come to nothing, and that they will decide on peace or on war at the Estates" (the Estates General, which began on 27 October 1614). Then, a month later, he reminds his father that there is still a rumor of impending conflict – and, in confirmation of this, "These last days several companies of soldiers have passed by, but only so that, if there is war, they will be quite ready."

So we are not dealing in this record with a chronicle about the college in the years 1611–1616, but with certain experiences in the life of a simple student, and with the recollection of certain events. These events were also experienced by his fellow student, Charles Huault, and the reactions of the two young men, without coinciding completely, may have had a certain similarity.

There is another point to be made: the importance of the Jesuits in Montmagny's existence. He met them at every turn in his life.

Their main house in Paris was situated on the rue Saint-Antoine, close to his. At the college of La Flèche, directed at this time by someone related to his family, Father Charlet, they took charge of his "classical formation," and that of his brother, Adrien. We have seen that in Orléans he was in touch with them. In Italy, where he spent ten months, he found them in several places, especially in Rome. They also had a house in Malta. When, around 1632, he began to take an interest in New France – and, above all, after 1636, the date of his nomination to Québec – a period of intense collaboration with them began, since they constituted the most dynamic element in the colony. In 1649, a new task fell to him: to oversee the interests of the Order of Malta in the Caribbean islands; there again he found the Jesuits, who in 1646 had replaced the Capuchins as confessors to Commander de Poincy in Saint-Christophe.[48]

Montmagny's ties to the Jesuits seem to us, then, to have been a major event in his existence. The ideals which the Fathers attempted to inculcate in their students certainly appear to have had a certain importance in his life. We shall have the occasion to point this out, especially in the analysis of the *Relations,* whose successive compilers would have nothing but praise for the behaviour and the positions of the old student of La Flèche.[49]

3. The interlude in Orléans (1619–1620)

With college completed, the question arose of university and the choice of a career. The two Huault brothers did not opt for theology, as their mother had suggested in her will.[50] They preferred to follow the family model established three quarters of a century earlier by their grandfather Louis, who went to study law in Orléans.[51] They remained there eleven months, or roughly three semesters.[52] This was not enough to become a barrister; neither Charles nor Adrien ever claimed this title, and the office purchased by the latter, of *contrôleur de l'extraordinaire des guerres*,[53] did not require a diploma in law.

Why thus interrupt studies which in principle would have ensured them a career in the magistracy, the quasi-exclusive profession of their immediate family?[54] Regarding this there is absolutely no indication in the documents that have come down to us. We are reduced to hypotheses. An unexpected event – a duel, for example – which could have forced the two to decamp? Hardly likely. Lack of success in studies? Distaste for the things of the law? That is plausible, but unproven. It is possible that Charles preferred action to study, or – to put it better – the sword to the pen. These are conjectures from which, undoubtedly, we shall never escape.

What is certain is the renown of the University of Orléans. Its originality lay in having only one faculty, law.[55] It was a very ancient specialization – some people even suggest that instruction in it went back to the eleventh century. A famous compilation of laws of the eleventh century is attributed to it. In 1235, the pope authorized the teaching there of Roman law (teaching refused to the University of Paris, which was forced until 1679 to limit itself to canon law). In the sixteenth century, when it was at its apogee, two of the great names of French jurisprudence, Charles Dumoulin (1500–1560) and Guy Coquille (1523–1603) came from it. Foreign students, Germans especially, were numerous there, particularly in the first half of the seventeenth century.[56] The first Knight of Malta to seek adventure in the Americas, Nicolas Durand de Villegagnon (1510–1571),[57] studied there around 1530, and he had as a fellow student (and friend, apparently) Jean Calvin,[58] who in 1556 sent him, at his request, 290 recruits to people the colony that he was trying to establish in the bay of Rio in Brazil.

To match the "coincidences" that we remarked at La Flèche, it is worth noting the presence in Orléans, when Charles Huault was there, of a student who became one of the great savants of the seventeenth century, Pierre de Fermat (1601–1665).[59] Just as we pointed out when comparing Descartes and Corneille with Charles Huault, in this case the educational career presents astonishing similarities: studies with the Jesuits (the college of Toulouse, for Fermat), then the faculty of law. But of the four persons mentioned here, Fermat was the only one to have followed a magistrate's career. He had, among other offices, that of commissioner for the Catholic side in the *chambre mi-partie* of Toulouse, where, after the edict of 1638, the trials implicating the Huguenots took place. But it is above all for his research in mathematics and physics that he is famous; he corresponded with numerous intellectuals, including Mersenne and Descartes.[60]

The interval at Orléans could do no harm to a man who was going to become an administrator: for example, there was the possibility for him to become familiar with the notions of law which would be highly useful to him in a colony still lacking judicial organisms.

But, for the time being, Montmagny abandoned jurisprudence and profited from the revenues which his parents had left him to reflect on his future, and to visit the centre of Christianity.

4.   The journey to Italy (1620–1621)

After spending five and a half months in Paris between March and September 1620,[61] Charles Huault left for Italy. He was absent for a little more than eleven months.[62] If we reckon on two weeks to reach the frontier and the same to return to it, he stayed in Italy for around ten months. He probably had the use of a footman and a horse,[63] and could count on more than 2,000 livres of revenue, which allowed him to bear the costs of the journey without difficulty.[64]

Already, since the sixteenth century, many affluent young Frenchmen left to visit Italy.[65] Louis Huault, Charles's grandfather, went there once his studies were finished, as we have noted. The practice became widespread in the seventeenth century. The *Grande Mademoiselle* remarked in her *Mémoires* that the son of one of her friends had just (in 1657) "finished his studies, and was going to Rome, as the children of Paris ordinarily do upon leaving college."[66]

As an old student of the Jesuits, Montmagny had heard a great deal about Rome, many of his professors having studied at the celebrated college which the Society directed there.[67] In fact, their avowed attachment to the pope made this city into a mythical place, the symbol and incarnation of both classical Antiquity and Christianity. The idea of entering the Order of Malta may also have taken root in his mind during the months that he spent in Paris after leaving Orléans. Knowledge of the Italian language was highly useful for someone who was going to live in Malta, with its numerous ties to Italy; and the best initiation to it would be time spent in Dante's own country. What was more, this was what the Jesuits recommended; at this period they valued courses in modern languages less than a stay in the lands concerned.[68] But we do not know precisely what decided him to leave for this country.

As Charles Huault did not leave an account of his tour – or, if he did write one, it has not come down to us – we have had to consult some of those that do remain from this period: Michel de Montaigne (1580–1581);[69] an anonymous Parisian (1605);[70] Florisel de Claveson (1608–1609);[71] the Sieur de Stochove (1630–1631).[72]

This brief investigation has furnished very useful information on what a lengthy stay in the Italian peninsula could mean for a young Frenchman with education and adequate means.[73] We can now throw some light on the objectives of those men who went off in this way, and on certain aspects of their travels.[74] Essentially, two motivations underlay the Italian trip, one religious and the other cultural; and doubtless in the majority of cases they were both present.

For Catholics, Italy meant first of all Rome, the city which still retained the memory of the persecutions suffered under the Roman Empire and the triumph of Christianity over the pagan gods. All of that was there in concrete form – the innumerable churches and chapels, and the catacombs, of which a new section had been uncovered in 1578. The Counter Reformation had had the consequence, among other things, of accentuating the papal authority that had been temporarily checked by the Protestants. The superbly successful renovation of the basilica of Saint Peter dates from this period, as does the construction of the Jesuit church, the Gesù, the first monument of a style that was destined for a great future, which would later be designated as "baroque." For the great majority of people visiting Italy, Rome was the city where they would stay longest.

But there was another place which most did not wish to miss – and which, for some, was even more impressive than the Eternal City – and this was the sanctuary of Our Lady of Loretto. There they could see the house of the Virgin, which the angels had transported in the thirteenth century.[75] Let us note at once that for the collective imagination of Europeans at the end of the Middle Ages and the start of the modern epoch, there was nothing troublesome about miraculous translations.[76] It is interesting to recall another legend, which Montmagny was soon going to hear if he did not know it already: that of the three Knights of Saint John of Jerusalem, prisoners of the Turks in the thirteenth century, who during their sleep were transported to Eppes, not far from Laon (east of Paris). Today a sanctuary dedicated to Notre-Dame de Liesse[77] still recalls this legend, as does one of the most beautiful churches in Valetta, constructed in 1620 (and therefore brand new when Montmagny arrived).

Furthermore, the devotion to Our Lady of Loretto was planted in Québec under the impetus of a Jesuit who had visited the celebrated pilgrimage place: Father Chaumonot, one of the missionaries whom Montmagny welcomed to the colony in 1639.[78]

Returning to La Flèche, we remark that the Jesuits were already, at the beginning of the century, making themselves the promoters of this devotion. In fact, the book by Father Horatio Torsellini on the history of the sanctuary was already circulating there.[79] Also, in 1604, there appeared another, by Father Louis Richeome, *Le pelerin de Lorette, voeu à la glorieuse Vierge Marie*, re-edited in Lyon in 1607. It is not surprising, given this context, that the most celebrated student of the college, René Descartes, himself made the vow to go to Loretto after the famous night of 11 November 1619 during which he discovered, in a sort of oppressive enthusiasm, the logical principle which was to inspire all his work and make him one of the initiators of the scientific revolution which marked the seventeenth century. Here is how this decision was reported by his first biographer:

> The impression which stayed with him of these agitations led him the next day to make various reflections on the path that he must take. The distress in which he found himself made him turn to God, to pray to Him to let him know His will, to deign to enlighten him, and to lead him in the search for truth. Then he addressed the Virgin Mary, to recommend to her this affair which he judged to be the most important of his life. And to try to interest this blessed Mother of God more deeply, he took the occasion of a journey which he was planning to take to Italy in a few days, to promise a pilgrimage to Our Lady of Loretto.[80]

So Italy attracted plenty of pilgrims. The popes could not remain indifferent in the face of this movement. In 1300 Boniface VIII decided that each year marking the start of a new century would be declared a jubilee, or "holy year." In 1470, Paul II changed this practice to every twenty-five years. Special indulgences were granted, among others, to those who visited the four principal basilicas of Rome.[81] In 1600, a few months before Charles Huault's birth, the city had known a record influx,[82] owing to the fact that Europe was at peace, and the Counter Reformation was experiencing a great vitality, not only in France, but everywhere.

These pilgrims to the high places of Catholicism were also, the great majority of them, tourists; their devotion could be fitted in with their "taste for travelling" (Montaigne's expression), and also their "love of Antiquity and Art,"[83] that we can call their cultural motivation.[84] The Renaissance was born there, reawakening interest in the past and bringing innovation, with much creativity, in all the domains of art. In the fifteenth century the movement had as its capital, so to speak, the city of Florence. Then, at the end of the fifteenth century and all through the sixteenth, it was Rome that took over, thanks, among other things, to the initiatives of the sovereign pontiffs. The population had increased; palaces, churches, and monuments had been built. To make known these treasures, ancient and recent, and to facilitate travel plans, books had been published.[85] Those with an education – which was probably the majority of visitors – could not remain indifferent to the chance to visit the places that they had often heard about – as for example de Claveson, who was thrilled to cross the Rubicon in his turn, or to go into the grotto once frequented by the Sybil,[86] and who sketched into his manuscript all the obelisks that he saw. The artists of the sixteenth century also attracted their attention, Michaelangelo particularly; we have not seen one account in which there is no mention of one or another of his sculptures. Curiously, painting made less impression; it is referred to less often.

And – we should mention this briefly – beside the pilgrims and the tourists of whom we are speaking here, other persons, though in very small numbers, left for Italy. From the second half of the sixteenth century, the custom had developed among artists, especially painters, to go to perfect their formation, generally in Rome, under a master.[87] This, for example, is what Rubens (1577–1640) and Velasquez (1599–1660) did. During his stay in the city of the popes, Montmagny might have met his compatriot Simon Vouet (1590–1649), who lived there from 1612 to 1627.[88] This talented artist so impressed the Roman milieu that he was elected "prince" of the Academy of Saint Luke, a sort of guild of the city's painters.

It is not inappropriate, in closing these remarks, to mention a very great artist who had a profound influence on the period with which we are concerned, that is, the first half of the seventeenth century: Michelangelo Merisi, also called Caravaggio (1573–1610). He was trained in Lombardy before coming to Rome to practise his art, painting. The realism that characterized him,[89] as well as his incisive treatment of light, gave his pictures a remarkable dramatic force – especially the strikingly effective picture, "The Beheading of Saint John" which he painted in Malta in 1607 (Saint John being the patron of the Order of Malta).[90] Caravaggio painted a Virgin of Loretto, which is a masterpiece of grace and realism: the Virgin leans forward in her seat in a familiar attitude; Jesus is anything but a formal child; the peasant couple looking at Mary and her Son is poorly dressed, but altogether rapt with ecstasy before them.[91] This picture represents to perfection the great painter's style, and what we can call the popularity of this celebrated sanctuary.[92]

So the motives for making the Italian tour were numerous for every Catholic who possessed the financial means, and especially anyone who had had the opportunity to pursue classical studies.

The details of Montmagny's tour are unknown to us; at the most we can infer some characteristics, using the contemporary examples that we have mentioned. Did he travel alone or in a group? We do not know. Perhaps his brother Adrien accompanied him. There were two ways to reach Italy: to go to Marseille and travel by sea to Genoa or Livorno, or else – which was more frequent – to go from Lyon to Turin through Savoy. His trip may have included, as well as Rome and Loretto, some other attractive cities, including Venice, Bologna, Milan, Florence, and Naples – the "tourists" of the times seem not to have risked going farther south. Ten months gave him ample time to get to know the principal curiosities of Italy, to make his pilgrimages, to immerse himself in classical Antiquity and – who knows? – to learn the language of the country.

A last thought comes to mind from the readings to which we have been referring. Italy was the occasion, for our future chevalier, of his first contact with the Islamic threat. At this time the peninsula's coastlines, both eastern and western, lived in continual fear of an attack by Muslim corsairs (doubtless as often Berbers, from Algiers or Tunis, as Turks). Was it in Italy that Montmagny first thought of becoming a corsair himself and of participating in the struggle against Islam?

Four of the elements that contributed to the development of the personality of Charles Huault de Montmagny, and prepared him for the role which he was to play in the world, have been briefly sketched out (in the light of the meagre sources at our disposal). There were certainly others, such as, for example, relationships that arose from neighbourhood contacts (in his quarter, his parish) or out of friendship (at college or elsewhere); nothing has survived out of all that. What is important to remember is that the education that he received did not dissuade him – indeed, quite the contrary – from embracing a state of life in which he would be simultaneously a monk and a soldier.

We can close this chapter with a twofold reflection: the importance that religion had exercised from the beginning of his life, and the initiation to things of the spirit.

His mother, a pious enough woman, had sensitized him to a Christianity that was demanding yet balanced, along the lines pointed out by the holy bishop of Geneva. His time spent with the Jesuits had reinforced this tendency by inculcating in him a solid doctrine, offering him models of behaviour, and making him understand the preeminence of Catholicism, for the promotion of which it was glorious to risk one's life. The visit to Italy had permitted him contact with the heroic origins of Christianity (the memory of Saints Peter and Paul and the first martyrs); he had been able to see, either in a ceremony or in an audience,[93] the successor of Peter, the head of a Church that was becoming worldwide under the drive of, among others, the Society of Jesus.

From an intellectual point of view, the major event had been his time spent at the college of La Flèche. Christian humanism, the foundation of Jesuit education, was going to mark his life.[94] The opening to the world – another trait specific to the Society – was given concrete form with the Italian tour. Rome, in Montaigne's words, was "the most open city in the world, where strangeness and national difference is the least considered; since by its nature it is a city made up of strangers; everyone there is as it were in his own home."[95]

One can imagine that such a formation, with its broad ambitions, led to a new perspective, that it did not privilege any profession, but, rather, was marked by openness – witness the careers that we have sketched of four celebrated pupils of the Fathers: the dramatist Pierre Corneille, the philosopher René Descartes, the mystic Jérôme de La Dauversière, the mathematician Pierre de Fermat. One last example can be cited: another fellow student of Montmagny at La Flèche.

Jean-Baptiste Budes de Guébriant (1602–1643) was one of the most brilliant French officers in the Thirty Years War.[96] After college, he, too, made an attempt at legal studies; his birth into a nobility of ancient extraction explains to some extent his behaviour during his stay at the faculty: the practice of equestrian arts, of gambling, and of duelling. Like Descartes, he went to fight in Holland, then he had to flee to Venice (Italy again!) for having taken part in a duel.[97] Richelieu had begun to crack down. He redirected his life, and in 1630 finally entered the army, where his daring and his successes in military operations won him, in 1636, the rank of *maréchal de camp*. He collaborated as an equal with Bernard of Saxe-Weimar, one of the heroes of the moment, then, in 1642, was named *maréchal de France*. He died in the summer of 1643 of a wound received during the taking of a German town. Some weeks before, he had met Condé (1621–1686), then at the summit of his glory[98] – who was, also, an ex-pupil of the Jesuits.

Montmagny's entry into a military order was, in this context, nothing unusual.

ILLUSTRATION 1

Paul Le Jeune, first superior of the Jesuits of Québec, first author of the *Relations*, one of Montmagny's most important collaborators. Engraving, R. Lochon, 1665 (National Archives of Canada, C-21404)

ILLUSTRATION 2

Jacques de Souvré, of the Order of Malta, ambassador of the Order at the court of the king of France. It was he who, in 1651, presided at the ceremony of solemn vows of the chevalier de Montmagny. They worked together for several months in the affair of Saint-Christophe. Bibliothèque nationale, Paris (C7363)

CHAPTER 4

Corsair for Christ

On 1 July 1622[1] Charles Huault left Paris for the island of Malta. He had chosen the definitive direction of his life, even though he did not make his solemn profession in the Order of Saint John of Jerusalem until 1651, twenty-nine years later.[2] Did he truly know what lay ahead of him? He had been able to develop an approximate idea of the "chivalrous life" in talking with members of the Order, of whom there were several among his relations.[3] But he did not suspect that in fourteen years he would journey ten times between the capital of France and that of Malta, that he would end up serving the king of France and the Grand Master of the Order simultaneously, and that he would take ship for the colonies.

The motivation underlying his decision remains hidden, but it is not a surprising one, taken as it was in the atmosphere of a relatively troubled age.[4] The religious wars had not yet ended – it was precisely in the summer of this year, 1622, that Louis XIII was fighting against the Protestants of the Midi, at the very time that several Knights of Malta were battling in the ranks of the French navy against La Rochelle. The Thirty Years War had recently begun. Duelling was in its heyday.[5]

As will be shown later, violence did not intimidate Charles Huault; he lacked neither courage nor audacity. All through his life, he demonstrated a total readiness for all tasks, from the most perilous to the most delicate.

The aim of the present chapter is to consider the period from the beginning of July 1622 to the beginning of January 1636, the moment of his appointment to Québec. But first will come a description of the Order that he was choosing to join, followed by a brief examination of the events which marked this new phase in his life; and finally, a consideration in some detail of his activities after completion of his novitiate: his service in the Mediterranean, on behalf of the Grand Master or on his own account (as when he went on a privateering expedition with a boat which he himself had bought), and then, from 1632 on, his participation in the *Compagnie de la Nouvelle-France*.

1.   The Order of Saint John of Jerusalem, also known, since 1530, as the Order of Malta

There seems to be little value in offering a simple definition of a reality as complex as the Order of Malta. It would seem more useful to give a three-part description of it: a brief look at its past, an outline of its organization, and a summary of its strictly religious requirements.

An outline of the history of this institution can be made under two headings: the eastern Mediterranean until 1522 and Malta from 1530 onward (see Table 14).

It all began around 1060, with the creation in Jerusalem by Italian merchants of a hospital for the treatment of sick pilgrims.[6] In 1100 an enterprising man[7] decided to found a religious community to take charge of patient care (the word "hospitallers" was often used to designate the Knights of Malta). In 1137, military responsibilities were added (in the beginning, essentially, for the protection of the pilgrims); these would remain in effect until the end of the eighteenth century. The hazards associated with the political upheavals in the region forced a retreat to the coast, then to two islands, Cyprus and Rhodes. The Knights were installed on the latter for two centuries.[8] The Ottoman Sultan Soliman II forced them to leave it in 1522.[9]

In 1530 Emperor Charles V granted them the fiefdom of the archipelago of Malta.[10] As at Rhodes, the Knights were made responsible for the government of this territory, which though relatively small in size was densely populated – the population,[11] 100 per cent Catholic, would in 1530 have numbered between 35,000 and 40,000.[12]

Even here the Ottomans pursued the Knights. Their siege of Malta in 1565 is an important date in the annals of Europe. For one thing, the Knights' victory guaranteed the Order a great renown and won it numerous vocations, above all in France. For another, it began the decline of Ottoman naval power in the Mediterranean, a decline that would be confirmed by the battle of Lepanto six years later. Equally, it was at this moment that a systematic defence of the place was undertaken; the fortifications of the capital, Valetta, still impress today's visitor. Palaces and residences, hospitals and churches were also built, some of which are very handsome.

It was in this quite exceptional place that Montmagny was going to learn, and then to devote himself to, not only the religious life but also the art of war, navigation, and privateering.

Let us examine the organization of this unconventional Order.

TABLE 14

The Order of Malta,
Chronological Points of Reference

1050–1070	Foundation by merchants from Amalfi of a hospital in Jerusalem for the care of pilgrims
1099	Capture of Jerusalem by the crusaders
ca. 1100	The director of the hospital, Gerard (d.1120) creates a hospitaller order, under the title of Saint John of Jerusalem
1137	The Order adds military duties to its hospitaller functions
1187	Departure from Jerusalem, retaken by Saladin
1187–1271	The Order occupies Krak, known as Krak of the Chevaliers, in Syria (Krak, an Arab word, signifes stronghold)
1271–1285	It occupies Margat, on the Syrian coast
1285–1291	It occupies Saint John of Acre (today in Israel, close to Lebanon, on the sea)
1291–1308	It occupies the island of Cyprus
1308	It seizes the island of Rhodes
1521–1534	Philippe de Villiers de l'Isle-Adam, Grand Master
1522	Soliman seizes the island of Rhodes
1530 24 March	The island of Malta given in fief to the Order by Emperor Charles V
1557–1568	Jean de Valetta, Grand Master
1565 May–September	The great siege of Malta by the Turks, who are forced to retire
1601	Aloph de Wignacourt, Grand Master
1622 September–March	Luis Mendez de Vasconcelos, Grand Master
1623	Antoine de Paule, Grand Master
1632	An important general chapter
1651	Purchase of the island of Saint-Christophe in the Antilles (resold in 1665)
1798 12 June	Napoleon seizes the island of Malta. Departure of the Order
1835	The "Grand Magisterium" of the Order establishes in Rome

The supreme direction was in the hands of the Grand Master. Like the pope (to whom he was answerable from an ecclesiastical point of view) he was elected for life, and his authority was both religious and territorial.[13] To assist him in his administrative tasks he had councils, some of which were directed by *baillis* (the official representatives of the eight *langues*).

The Order was divided into eight *langues*, or "tongues" (rather like "provinces" in the religious sense of the word);[14] each one having a grand priory responsible for local administration. The French Knights had six grand priories; those of France (the Temple),[15] of Champagne, and of Aquitaine for the French *langue*; those of Saint-Gilles and Toulouse for the *langue* of Provence; and that of Auvergne, for the *langue* of the same name.

The Order included not only chevaliers (knights), but also men-at-arms and chaplains. Those who entered as men-at-arms were commoners or nobles whose "nobility" was of recent origin. Only the chaplains were allowed to be priests, and no proof of nobility was demanded of them.

How was this institution financed, given its numerous obligations, which included maintaining a large hospital at Malta and a sizeable fleet?[16] The ordinary sources of revenue were twofold: the legacies of the knights, and the commanderies. At death, the knights – most of whom came from rich families – had to leave the Order 80 per cent of their goods, while disposing of the rest as they wished. The commandery was an estate which, over the centuries, had been given or left to the Order, which transferred the usufruct to one of its members, who then became a "commander." Every year he had to remit to the Grand Master a portion (between 5 and 30 per cent, generally around 10 per cent) of the revenues which he drew from it. This was the "responsion."

But it was in the area of religion that the Order acquired its specific character, and its unique place in the Church. It was characterized by three elements: a hospitaller vocation; the pursuit, even by warlike means, of the "enemies of the faith";[17] and a spirituality in keeping with these tasks.

The title which the Grand Master adopted in official documents was the following: "Servus pauperum Christi et custos Hospitalis Jerosolimitanis."[18] The rule explained in detail how "our lords the sick," symbolic personifications of "Our Lord Jesus Christ," were to be served. The most important building in Valetta, after the conventual church, was the "sacred infirmary," containing more than 350 beds and a common room a hundred metres long. This hospital was open to all, even to infidels or to Protestants, on whom, however, discreet catechism lessons were lavished.

How were the Knights able to prolong the Holy War? Of the reconquest of Jerusalem, whose name they still bore, there was no longer any serious question. They had two aims: to contain the countries that had been acquired by Islam, and to harass them. They had prevented the Ottomans from establishing themselves in their island in 1565, and, thanks to the impressive fortifications which they built, they succeeded in fending off subsequent attacks. The greater part of their activity was harassment: raids on coastal towns and villages and, above all, attacks on the ships, whether alone or in convoys, that travelled the great sea. The expedition which Montmagny undertook in 1627 furnishes an illustration of this.

By his three vows[19] the Knight of Malta placed himself among the elite of the Christian people; he became one of those souls prepared to consecrate the bulk of their energy to the imitation of Christ. The cross which he wore on his breast symbolized, by its eight points, the beatitudes reserved for the exemplary faithful, and by its four arms, the cardinal virtues.[20] And among these virtues, particular value was placed on strength, because of the arduous and dangerous tasks that could fall to him, the difficulties that awaited him and before which he could never retreat.

There is, however, a qualification to be added to what appears, at first sight, very rigorous: the religious life of the Knights could be adapted to suit different circumstances. It could be practised not only on the galleys or in the houses of the Order, in the inns of the *langues* in Malta or in the Temple in Paris, but also in the world – by the commander on his estates, the sailor aboard ship in the service of the king, the privateer on the vessel that he was commanding. The application of the rule, then, was left to the discretion of the individual. This certainly gave rise to abuses with regard to the three vows or the exercises of piety – though on this last point the recommendations were strict: daily Mass (some, like Commander de Poincy,[21] had their personal chaplain), meditation, and frequent recitation of the Lord's Prayer. Furthermore (and this is easily understandable in the context that we have been describing) it was relatively easy for the knights to obtain dispensation from their vows from Rome.

Three devotions were particular to the Order. They were symbolized by three relics brought from Rhodes: a piece of the true cross, whence the importance of the Mass; the icon of Our Lady of Filermos,[22] whence the cult of the Virgin; and the right hand of John the Baptist, the official patron of the institution.

2. Montmagny enters the Order of Malta

It was within this religious fighting force, a continuation of the work of
the crusaders, that the entire life of Charles Huault would henceforth
be played out; even when working for the king, he would continue to
bear its name and follow its rules. Two years, 1622 and 1623, would
be dedicated almost entirely to the formalities of admission and to the
canonical initiation in this new life.

Three stages will be retraced here: his emancipation from the
guardianship of his older brother, the inquiry undertaken by the grand
priory of France, and the novitiate.

By sentence of the Châtelet of Paris, 15 January 1622,[23] Charles
was declared "emancipated by age, under the authority of Messire
Claude Anjorrant, seigneur of Cloyes, his trustee."[24] By this juridical
decision, he was freed from his brother's tutelage, which is to say that
he could enjoy and dispose of his goods as he wished; but as he was
still a minor (he was not yet twenty-five) he was required, before doing
so, to consult his trustee.[25]

Next, it was required that an exact accounting be made of the
financial management of the trusteeship. This was signed before the
notary by the parties concerned on 11 June.[26] The receipt for the forty-
five months that it had lasted (from 1 September 1618 to 10 June 1622)
amounted to 9,412 livres, 2 sols, 6 deniers – 207 livres per month, for a
total of 2,500 livres per year. Charles made use of this very comfortable
revenue prudently, but without skimping: his expenses for the same
period totalled 8,578 livres. Still due to him from his tutor was the sum
of 830 livres, 10 sols, 10 deniers; this was paid to him forthwith.

There is further detail to this account of expenses: 6,469 livres,
10 sols, 6 deniers in cash were made over to him "on sixty different
occasions, as is shown in the book of expenses of the said Charles
Huault, written and signed by his hand, taking up five entire pages."
Another sum of 1,633 livres, 6 sols, 8 deniers[27] covered his studies in
Orléans, the journey to Italy, and the five and a half months between
the return from Orléans and the departure for Italy (though the place
in which he stayed was not indicated, as we see in the extract in the
annex to the previous chapter). It was clearly specified that this paid
"both for his room and board and for a lackey and a horse."

Just as indirectly, the account gives us a statement of Charles
Huault's fortune. Since the division of the estate in 1619,[28] he owned
half of the seigneurie of Messy,[29] which brought him 937 livres, 15
sols, 6 deniers annually. "The sum of the half-share of two large

MAP 2

The Maltese Archipelego

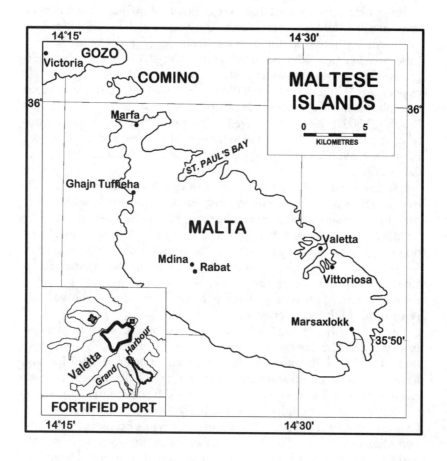

houses situated in Paris on the rue Saint-Antoine called the hôtel de Baillet" – this was the famous hôtel that Louis Huault would sell some months later to Mesme Gallet.[30] The larger of the two was rented to Monsieur de Cénamy for 1,100 livres, 550 of it for Charles; the rent of the other, smaller house was worth 700 livres, which brought him 350. Furthermore there were the revenues from the *greffe des tailles*[31] of four little parishes near Meaux, of which his half-share brought him 126 livres, 10 sols. The total amounted to 1,964 livres, 5 sols, 6 deniers, or close to 2,000 livres of revenue for the current year. And, as we have seen above, his revenue between September 1618 and June 1622 was roughly 2,500 livres per year; we must suppose that the surplus came from the sums which Louis paid to him (and to Adrien and to Charlotte) in compensation for relinquishing the two seigneuries of La Baillie and Goyencourt.

Following the division of the estate in 1619 his estate totalled 73,870 livres.[32] This was certainly not poverty; but if he wished to make a good career – to possess a country seigneurie and a hôtel in the city, and own an office of some importance – it was not enough. A sizeable marriage dowry could certainly have corrected the situation; but it was difficult for a younger son to make a good match. Thus, under the circumstances, Charles's choice suited his family well. However, as we shall soon see, the family would prove its generosity towards him during the difficult years of his Maltese experience.

So, on 7 March 1622, before "the brothers assembled in the priory inn of the Temple in Paris,"[33] Louis Huault came to request the admission of his brother Charles into the Order of Saint John of Jerusalem. In the group there appeared a knight related to the Anjorrant cousins, Dreux Courtin de Rosay – he would be one of the inquisitors for the proofs of Alexandre Huault in 1629[34] – and a person with whom Charles would have to pass the last years of his life, Brother Philippe de Lonvilliers de Poincy. Two brothers, Claude de Revenel-Sablonnières and Charles Brocchier-Arqueville, were named to proceed with the necessary inquiry to verify the antiquity of the candidate's nobility.

This inquiry took place between April 24 and 29. Following the traditional procedure of the Order, it began by hearing four witnesses who were not related to the family, but acquainted with it. They all bore the designation of Messire and the title of knight; one was a marshal of the camps and armies of His Majesty, the others, gentlemen ordinary of the bedchamber.[35] They declared "in all sincerity," following the accepted formula, what they thought of the social status of the Huaults de Montmagny. Essentially, their testimony was as follows: Charles

I, father of the postulant, was indeed "a gentleman in name and in arms" (that is, of ancient extraction and possessing a coat of arms). They had seen him fighting in the siege of Paris in 1591. The Huaults were held by common opinion to be "true gentlemen"; they had never derogated from that rank. As to the mother, Antoinette Du Drac, she was "a gentlewoman in name and in arms, of the ancient house of Dudrac, known as such among the nobility; their escutcheon being: on a gold background a green dragon, with claws, crown, and tongue of the colour red."[36]

Louis then presented the titles which were meant to prove beyond a doubt that the nobility of the paternal and maternal forbears was more than a hundred years old. These documents were acts of fealty and homage, noble successions, noble services, provisions of office – for example, that which Charles I received when he became *maître des requêtes* in 1592 – and calls to feudal service. The oldest of these were counterfeits, or, if they were authentic, they had no connection with the Huaults de Montmagny – but we have already passed judgment on them, and there is no point in returning to this.[37]

The two inquisitors then visited three Parisian churches, Saint-Jean-en-Grève, Saint-Médéric, Saint-Gervais, to examine the epitaphs confirming the burial of the Huault and Du Drac ancestors. The earliest date remained, for the former, that of the decease of Isabeau Le Brest, the second wife of Pierre Huault, which took place on 21 July 1525. For the latter, it went back to Jehan Du Drac, a president of parlement, who died on 4 January 1403; his wife, Jacqueline d'Ay, who died on 8 June 1404, was buried at his side.

This was not all: they had to go to the seigneurie of Montmagny, north of Paris. The two men were unanimous in recognizing the "great antiquity" of the château and of the park – an additional proof of the antiquity of the family's nobility. On the lintel over the door to the manor were engraved the arms of Montmagny. On one "pane of the window which overlooked the courtyard" were painted the arms of the seigneurs and those of the spouses who followed each other in the château: Isabeau Le Brest, Claire de Billon, Antoinette Du Drac.

They then went to the parish church, where behind the main altar there was a window displaying the arms of Pierre Huault and Isabeau Le Brest; "beneath the arms of the said Pierre we remarked a legend in very old lettering, no longer in use: 1526." Lower down there appeared the emblem of the family: "Faitz bien et laisse dire." The keystone of the vault at the entrance to the chapel of Our Lady bore the arms of Montmagny and Billon (Claire de Billon, wife of Louis Huault). Three altars were "furnished and decorated with altar cloths of white damask" on which were emblazoned their arms. The Huaults de Montmagny had not been slow to profit by the means of publicity which the system of the contemporary age offered them.

There remained one last task, the "secret proof." The two commissioners made inquiries among various inhabitants "and other ancient and notable persons of good faith" in the neighbourhood. They received confirmation that all the countryside considered that the Montmagnys were "gentlemen in name and in arms," and that their establishment in the seigneurie was "of great antiquity"; that they had always lived nobly, and, indeed, that Louis and Charles had borne arms in the service of the king in the previous century, the first at the siege of Metz in 1552, the second at that of Paris in 1589. The testimony of the inhabitants agreed with that of the four gentlemen. The inquisitors were satisfied. They made their report, and Charles was authorized to begin his novitiate in Malta.

On 1 July, the religious aspirant left Paris for Malta, carrying with him his proofs of nobility, which he was required to deliver to the competent authorities.[38] The seniority of the knights, by which the granting of commanderies was decided, depended on the day of their arrival on the island. He reached the port of Valetta on 3 August.[39]

According to practice, his novitiate would have begun at once, and lasted for a year. Under the direction of a master of novices, chosen among the Grand Crosses (dignitaries of the Order), and assisted by two experienced knights, the new members studied the history of the institution, its rules and its spirituality; at the same time, they learned to care for the sick, and practised the handling of arms – a combination which appears strange at first sight, but which corresponded well with their vocation and the life that they would later lead.

The years 1622–1623 were rich in spectacular events in Malta. Shortly after Montmagny's arrival came the death of the Grand Master Aloph de Wignacourt who, despite his advanced age of seventy-five years, had gone hunting during the extreme heat of August.[40] Four days later, according to custom, there took place the election of his successor, a Spaniard, Louis Mendez de Vasconcelos, whose reign only lasted six months (17 September 1622 to 6 March 1623), and who was replaced by Antoine de Paule, a Frenchman of the *langue* of Provence, who would lead the Order until 1636. A chance event which took place shortly after his election must have impressed the men beginning their apprenticeship in the Order: "Jean de Fonseca, Portuguese novice, was beheaded in Malta in the great square of the Palace (the palace of the Grand Master), after having been found guilty of theft and murder."[41]

About the novitiate of Charles Huault we have no information; it ought in theory to have ended in August 1623. If he wished, he could now pronounce his vows – in other words, make his profession. He chose to wait. He also had to decide on another requirement of his vocation: to complete his "caravans" – the name given to the expeditions (four as a rule) during which the young knights were introduced, on the Order's ships, to navigation and military life. There as well, he was in no hurry; he decided, rather, to return for a while to France. He obtained permission on 12 October.[42]

In leaving for Paris, Charles had a precise objective in mind: to reach a convenient arrangement with his brothers and sister which would allow him to profit as much as possible from his fortune – which he was going to put into service in the fight against the infidels.

Before addressing the details of his activities in the months and years that were to follow, we should briefly consider the various ways in which he made use of his time, and then make a chronology of his stays, his comings and his goings, from the day he left Paris (1 July 1622) to the day he arrived in Québec (16 June 1636). This is what we shall call the Maltese period of his career.

The table which we have developed is drawn from diverse sources: those of the Order (permissions to go to France, authorizations to go privateering), as well as notarial records in Malta,[43] detailing loans or repayments of money in the presence of Montmagny or a third person, and also powers of attorney arranged before a departure (with the destination sometimes indicated). And there are the French notarial minutes, which indicate his stays in Paris or elsewhere.

Thanks to these documents, Table 15 illustrates the chronology which we have been able to establish. Mentions of exact date are very rare, so we have retained only the months which appear to correspond most exactly with the information received.[44] It was impossible to be more precise.[45]

We note at once that we are dealing with a very active life. In twelve years, he made ten journeys between Paris and Valetta, journeys that must have lasted a month, sometimes more. It took a week from Paris to Marseille; then, having reached the port, he had to seek out a vessel leaving for Malta, or for another port between Provence and the island – Syracuse, for example. The crossing from France to Malta could take ten to twenty-five days, depending on the caprices of the climate and the hazards of the "privateering risk."

TABLE 15

A Knight of Malta's Schedule of Activity:
Charles Huault de Montmagny, July 1622–June 1636

		Months
I.	July 1622: Paris – Malta	1
	- August 1622 to October 1623: Malta (for novitiate)	15
II.	ca. November 1623: Malta – Paris	1
	- December 1623 to March 1624: Paris	4
III.	ca. April 1624: Paris – Malta	1
	- May 1624 to November 1625 (two caravans?)	19
IV.	ca. December 1625: Malta – Paris	1
	- January to March 1626: Paris and Marseille	3
V.	April 1626: Marseille – Malta	1
	- May to September 1626: Malta	4
	- September to December 1626: corso	4
	- January to March 1627: Malta	3
	- April to September 1627: corso	6
	- October to December 1627: Malta	3
VI.	ca. January 1628: Malta – Paris	1
	- ca. February and March 1628: Paris	2
VII.	ca. April 1628: Paris – Malta	1
	- May 1628 to July 1631: Malta (three caravans?)	39
VIII.	August 1631: Malta – Paris	1
	- September 1631 to ca. August 1632: Paris	12
IX.	ca. September 1632: Paris – Malta	1
	- ca. October 1632 to June 1634: Malta	21
X.	ca. July 1634: Malta – Paris	1
	- August 1634 to March 1636: Paris	21
TOTAL		166
XI.	Early April to mid-June 1636: Paris – Québec	

His other periods at sea were long: two privateering expeditions, five "caravans,"[46] and, we suspect, other campaigns. We should therefore reckon on many months aboard ship (the lack of sources does not allow us to be more precise) – which implies that Montmagny was in good health and that he was able to acquire a profound knowledge of seafaring.

According to the information we have collected, he would have spent 114 months out of 166 (July 1622 to May 1636) in Malta and in the Mediterranean, ten in transit between Paris and Valetta, and forty-two in Paris and Marseille.

So the life that he knew during these years was marked by mobility – in contrast with the great majority of his contemporaries, even among the élite. The only possible comparisons can be found in the army, the navy, or even in foreign trade. A sailor, a soldier, a merchant disposing of his goods: a privateer of Malta was all these things. We could add that many missionaries knew a similar mobility, but the Order was not a missionary order, though it was in this direction that Montmagny's activity tended after 1632.

In fact, until August 1632, the time spent in the Mediterranean and in the service of the Order predominated, while afterwards, it was the French capital and the service of the king that took up most of his time. And the contrast goes further: the Mediterranean meant privateering and maritime expeditions, with all that this involved in risks, preparations of every kind, and the busy life of the great port of Valetta. Paris, by comparison, meant calm, comfort, tranquillity – despite all the liveliness of the Marais. But the period from 1632 to 1636 was only an interval; in some respects life in the Canadian colony was going to reflect the years of warfare experienced between Valetta and Alexandria.

3. Privateering activities in the Mediterranean

It was Montmagny's privateering activity that left the most traces in the archives during this period – notarized borrowings or powers of attorney in Malta or in Paris, for instance. He carried off a spectacular action which was set down by a contemporary historian. Since the "corso"[47] was, in the seventeenth century particularly, one of the major occupations of the Order in the Mediterranean, we should start by defining it.

MAP 3

The Eastern Mediterranean and the Order of Malta

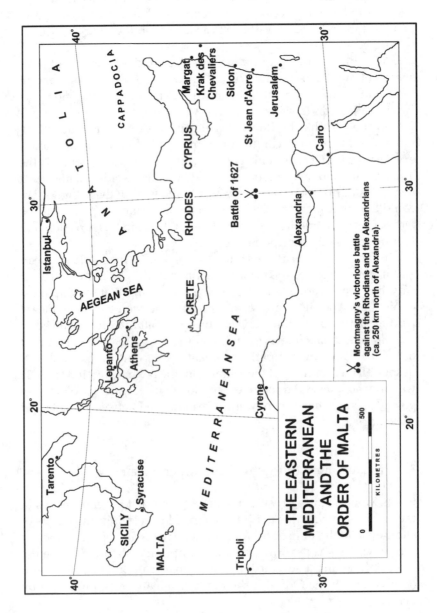

The corso (the term favoured by many historians) was a regular activity exercised after the granting of official letters by the competent authorities. It was permanent and built into the economy of the city or the region which supported it; and it had come to represent the last remnant of the struggle which – from the viewpoint of the year 1623 – had set Christian against Moslem for close to a millenium. Ever since their establishment in Rhodes, the Knights had been known as redoubtable corsairs. In the sixteenth and seventeenth centuries the Berbers (from Tripoli, Tunis, and Algiers) were also very dynamic, but it seems that the Maltese were the most successful.[48] The Knights undertook to diminish, if not to eliminate, the danger that the Moslems – and the Turks in particular – posed to the Christian positions; a menace that was not just a figment of the imagination, as we can see by the simple recitation of some dates: the capture of Constantinople (1453), the conquest of Rhodes (1522), the great siege of Malta (1565), and the conquest of Crete (1669).

We shall recall here only a few elements regarding time frame, place, organization, and impact, which will allow us to understand the special, very interesting, case which the chevalier de Montmagny's Maltese adventure constituted.

Charles V had ceded Malta to the Knights in 1530 upon two conditions; the first one, highly utopian, was that they should return the island to Spain if they succeeded in recovering Rhodes; the second, more realizable, was that they should wage perpetual war on the infidels (and especially their privateers); in this they did not fail. The golden age of the corso began soon after the great siege, and ran roughly from 1580 to 1680. After this date, privateering activity waned little by little, under the combined effect of two interventions, that of the French government, anxious to preserve its interests with the Porte, and that of the Vatican, eager to gain control over the Greek Christian communities, whether or not they were attached to Rome.

The subject can be seen from a different point of view. According to the reasoning of an excellent analyst, Michel Fontenay,[49] the aggressive intervention of the Order of Malta was the West's response to the negative impact which the Ottoman conquest had had on European commerce in the Mediterranean. But in this respect it must still be noted that the long-time masters of this commerce, Venice and Genoa, gradually gave way to the more dynamic countries of the time, Holland, England, and France. It was the latter two, after all, that would oversee the dismemberment of the Ottoman Empire in the nineteenth and twentieth centuries.

There were in theory two possible geographical theatres for the ongoing war against the Moslems of the Mediterranean. The first was the North African coast – commonly called Barbary – from Salé (a Moroccan town on the Atlantic) to Tripoli (in today's Libya). This region was itself well equipped for the corso: it did damage to French commerce to some degree, but above all, it harmed that of the Spaniards. The Maltese were not so active in this region; on the other hand, they attacked the Berbers who dared to approach their island, or Sicily, or Sardinia. The second zone was the Levant, that is to say the Greek coast, the Aegean sea, and the eastern Mediterranean south of the Aegean sea, from Anatolia to Egypt. Within this great basin, three sectors were of prime interest to the corsairs (and the galleys) of Christ: the archipelago, that chain of islands of every size parallel to the Turkish littoral, starting at Rhodes and running north; Palestine, that is to say the eastern shore of the Mediterranean; and the seas north of Egypt. One of the corsairs' dreams was to capture the convoy travelling from Alexandria to Istanbul with the tribute exacted from Cairo, as well as the goods that the Turks had bought there.

A privateering expedition might be financed by a contractor, who furnished the boat and the funds and settled with the captain for a share of the profits and expenses. Or the captain might own his boat and arrange his own financing by borrowing the full amount – as was the case with Montmagny. The crew was mainly Maltese, for whom seafaring was, next to farming, their principal occupation. On oar-driven vessels there were always slaves; on the others, there may or may not have been.

How was this important activity regulated? To begin with, it should be noted that in some ways all the voyages which the galleys and other vessels of the Order undertook in the Levant can be classed as part of the corso. Each year, as a rule, these ships made one expedition, sometimes two; the caravans required of the Knights supplied part of the manpower. These expeditions were decided upon and organized by the sovereign power, and they were directed, from near or from afar, by the Grand Admiral. There remained the private corso, led by knights or by laymen; it is to this that we are referring. As privateering activity increased with the end of the sixteenth century, it became necessary to regulate it. The Grand Master Alof de Wignacourt undertook this task in 1605. He issued a series of laws concerning, among other things, the granting of privateering commissions and the sharing of booty (of which, in the end, he kept 9 per cent for himself). The "tribunale degli Armamenti"[50] was created to see to the application of the rules and the examination of litigious cases.

There is one more question: was the game, relatively complicated and highly dangerous, worth the candle? Do we know if the corso was successful? It had a very heavy impact on Turkish commerce: large cargoes were lost, for instance in 1605 and 1608. What Michel Fontenay calls the "corsair danger" cost the Ottomans dear, to the point that they left a good part of their long-distance commerce, and even their coastal traffic, to ships flying the English, French, or Dutch flag.[51] On certain occasions, the resupply of African produce was dislocated, creating price rises in Istanbul. On the whole it was advantageous to Malta, occupying a considerable labour force not only in the manning of ships but also in what are called "spin-offs,"[52] ship building, for instance, or the arming of boats. It brought in many slaves,[53] mostly for the galleys, but also for domestic service; there was plenty of money to be made in their resale, as well. Malta, like Algiers and Livorno, was an important slave market throughout the *ancien régime*. The corso brought Malta a lot of booty, including food products which could be invaluable to an island for which reprovisioning was a long-term problem.[54]

A detailed examination of the Montmagny case shows concretely what it meant for a knight to undertake such an adventure. It required long preparation, as well as determination and courage. He had to find the funds, engage the crews, arrange for their revictualling, and know how to navigate on a changeable sea. Our man emerged unscathed, though not without difficulty, but he left a part of his fortune behind – was this what most often happened? It is impossible to say, given the current state of research.

So it was that, with his novitiate ended, the young knight returned to Paris in the autumn of 1623. On 19 December, he presented himself to the notary, in the presence of his brother Louis and his sister Charlotte, Dame d'Arsy. The following is the important contract which they were preparing to sign:

> *Noble homme* Charles Huault, received as a Knight of the Order of Saint John of Jerusalem, resident in the island of Malta, but living at present in this city of Paris on the rue des Barres, parish of Saint Gervais, who before making the vows of religion in the same Order, wishing to dispose of the goods belonging to him, of his own free will has recognized and confessed to having given .... [55]

The formula which he retained for "disposing" of his possessions was that of the donation; the recipients were his two brothers, Louis and Adrien (then absent),[56] and his sister. He ceded them all the goods that he possessed, the composition of which we already know: the land at Messy, the Hôtel de Baillet, the office of *greffier des tailles*. In return, they promised him a yearly income of 2,400 livres "for life." The transaction was retroactive to 1 July 1622, the date of his departure for Malta. If Charles were to die – and the corso which he was already planning was full of risks – the income would lapse, the estate remaining with the family.

Other possibilities were envisaged: "in the event of the captivity and enslavement of the person of the said Chevalier" the recipients would be jointly obliged to "redeem him and pay his ransom to the sum of nine thousand livres." What was more, during the months passed at Malta, Montmagny had had the time to study the possibilities of arming, and even buying, a vessel for a corso. His brothers and sister undertook "further, to give him and to pay out in the next eight months the sum of fifteen thousand livres to be used in whatever expense, arming of a vessel or other occasion he will think fit." To be able to count on 15,000 livres gave him a considerable margin of manoeuvre. He would avail himself of this clause in January 1626, twenty-four months later, when he was preparing his first expedition.

After this important operation, he remained a further few weeks in Paris, for on 8 March 1624 he affixed his signature to a notarized document;[57] but undoubtedly he returned soon afterwards to Malta. It is probable that he completed one or two caravans before coming back to France at the beginning of January 1626.

To have an idea of what a caravan involved, let us use the account left by a contemporary of Montmagny.[58] Jean-Baptiste Luppé du Garrané (1586–1660)[59] was presented in 1597, at a very early age, to the provincial chapter of the grand priory of Toulouse.[60] In 1600, he went to Malta for his novitiate, and he pronounced his vows the following year, aged sixteen.

On 24 April 1605 his first caravan began. It lasted fifty-four days.[61] The squadron in which he was serving comprised four galleys. The campaign took place around Greece and the islands of the Aegean sea. The flotilla crossed the strait separating Rhodes from the mainland; there it had numerous encounters, with Christian ships ("which it took time to recognize," says the narrator), then with a Turkish frigate, which escaped. Then "a ship from Linde [sic]" came along, with Turks and a cargo of carpets on board; "we took the Turks and the carpets and let the rest go." These pieces of information are concrete and very interesting – and, for the young sailor, they make exciting adventures. He did not fail to note the bad weather that he experienced and the pitiable state of the galley *Saint-Martin* on which he was sailing; this, he says, was its last voyage.

From mid-June to mid-July there was a respite at Malta; then, on 22 July, the second caravan began, which lasted several months and paid off with the capture of three Turkish brigantines.[62]

The third was anything but boring. Some days after departure, Luppé contracted smallpox near Naples, where he was nursed back to health; he returned to Malta "in a longboat."[63] He was left to rest for several months, then he "wearied of idleness" and begged the Grand Master to allow him to go to the Levant. He spent five months there, from 27 February to 13 July 1608; he was extremely happy to speak of the booty brought back by his galley.

Obviously this life suited him well. As a matter of fact, when he returned to Malta he learned of the death of his older brother and of his father's order that he return home. This he did, to learn that he was being ordered to leave his "profession." His father wanted the patrimony to remain in the family, and knew that Rome dispensed from vows without too much difficulty. But this was not to Jean-Baptiste's taste; he refused, and returned to Malta where, between December 1610 and June 1612, he completed three caravans, one more than was compulsory.

Also – and this is very instructive for the Montmagny case – during the months that he was not on the Order's galleys, Luppé decided to take part in the corso with another knight, who had armed a little boat; he himself invested 700 scudi (approximately 1,750 livres).[64] They took several prizes of minimal value, but the expedition ended in catastrophe: the crew mutinied and sailed the boat to Tunis. Luppé succeeded in escaping. He even helped to finance another arming: the boat was seized by two Turkish galleys. The corso was an extremely hazardous career!

He spent several years in other activities (service in the French navy,[65] the office of receiver for the grand priory of Saint-Gilles in Marseille), then in 1649, at the age of sixty-three, he sought to return to active service. Unfortunately, he had insufficient funds for that. He fell back on a little boat which he bought at Dunkerque for the sum of 10,000 livres (all the money remaining to him, he says); but bad luck stayed with him, and the boat was sunk by the English.

These few details[66] say a lot about what a career as a Knight of Malta could mean if one took his vocation as a scourge of the infidel seriously: sea voyages, troubles, endless dangers, the possibility of ruin,[67] of captivity, of sickness, of death. All this was experienced by

Montmagny (in caravans and in corso), and it remains to recount it for the period that began in December 1625.

On 26 November 1625, Charles obtained permission to return to France.[68] Some weeks later, he was in Paris. On 31 January, he arranged the payment in cash of the 15,000 livres that his brothers and sister had promised him – the same day they were selling *rentes* to obtain liquidity.[69] But this disbursement meant that his pension dropped from 2,400 livres per annum to 1,800. He then went to Marseille, where he was in March.[70] There he found the vessel that he was looking for to undertake his privateering expeditions.[71]

And so he returned to Malta with this vessel and began to prepare for the campaign that he would conduct the following autumn. In notarized contracts dated in August he is designated as "Carolus de Montmagny, capitaneus pittacii nominati San Giovanni."[72] With another notary the formula is slightly different: it is a question of "navigii ipsius Domini de Montmagni, nominati San Giovanni Battista."[73] Thus Noble Charles de Montmagny was the owner of a *patache* named *Saint-Jean-Baptiste,* and also its captain, which implies that he had a good knowledge of the sea, that he had proved himself (apparently in the course of his caravans), and that he was accepted in the maritime circles of Malta.

How much might the vessel have cost him? The contract of purchase has not been found. But an act passed in Malta on 28 December 1626[74] mentions a *patache* (by the name of *Notre-Dame de la Garde de Bonne Espérance,* coming from Ancona) of which a quarter-share was sold to Jacques Paulet, a Frenchman residing in Valetta, for the sum of 720 scudi, signifying a total cost of 2,880 scudi, or around 7,200 livres.[75]

The *patache*[76] carried two masts,[77] averaged 120 feet in length,[78] carried a crew of fifteen to thirty sailors (though it could take up to 120 men for the corso), was equipped with cannon (from eight to sixteen), and was capable of transporting 50 to 100 tons of freight.[79]

Such a vessel must have required quite considerable outlays, for purchase, equipment with cannon, sails, cordage and other tackle, overhauling, sailors' salaries, and victualling. Since the tidy sum that he had brought from Paris did not suffice, Captain Huault had to have recourse to the moneylenders.

From 17 August to 31 August, he raised ten loans, for a total of 3,670 scudi (around 9,165 livres).[80] This was all in cash, except in two cases where there was also merchandise. The amounts ranged from 100 to 800 scudi. The *risico* was 25 or 30 per cent – the risk being the interest predicated on the success of the expedition. Someone who risked 400 scudi at 25 per cent gained back 500 "in the fortnight following the return from the voyage";[81] in case of total loss (shipwreck or seizure by the enemy, for example) the 400 scudi were lost. To this was added the sum of 4,562 livres, 10 sols, which his two brothers arranged to be delivered to him by 8 June,[82] but no time limit was stipulated for reimbursement.

The letters patent from the Grand Master granting him "faculty and licence" to go privateering in the Levant were accorded on 26 August;[83] on 31 August, he authorized four persons (three colleagues from the Knights and a Maltese man) to see to his affairs in his absence.[84] He left shortly afterwards, to return, apparently, around Christmas.

The expedition was profitable, since in the following January (1627) the lenders were reimbursed with interest.[85] Fifteen people had furnished funds: five knights, five Maltese, three Frenchmen resident in Valetta, with the largest amount (800 scudi) coming from Louis and Adrien Huault, his own brothers, who had decided out of friendship for him to support him in this campaign.[86]

However, of the actual progress of his voyage (his planned itinerary, any chance happenings) we have no other information. But we should remember that it took place during a vast concerted effort by the Maltese authorities in this very year to regain the initiative after the setbacks of 1625 (among other things, the loss of two galleys at the hands of the enemy). The new captain general, Francesco Carafa, made an appeal to the warlike spirit of the Knights,[87] and himself directed the official campaigns of the Order's fleet, with two galleys in the first half of the year, and four after September. The effort had happy results.[88]

Encouraged by his own success and that of the Order, Montmagny went back to work. On 8 January 1627 he started all over again, on a new expedition more extensive than the last.[89] The notarial acts came fast and furious until 5 April.[90] There was no shortage of lenders, a sure indication of the success of the first campaign. This time there were forty-four loans, for a total of 13,059 scudi (but probably around 13,660, because two mentions are ambiguous). These were loans of money, except in one case which dealt, oddly, with clothing; and in two others, with slaves, who, it was declared, were for "the service and arming of the boat." The *risico* was 25 per cent, except for one at 20 per cent and three at 30 per cent. Of the forty-four lenders, nineteen were members of the Order (almost all French); the others were laymen: thirteen Maltese, nine Frenchmen and three Italians – a good illustration of the international character of the island.

To these loans must be added the sales which Montmagny himself arranged. Thus he sold eleven tapestries of Flanders (brought from France or purchased elsewhere?) to a lady of Valetta, for the sum of 330 scudi (75 livres each);[91] he also sold four slaves who belonged to him and who appear to have come to him from the prizes taken the previous autumn.[92] Perhaps he owned others; it was commonplace for a corsair to bring back a good number from his campaigns (on 19 August of the same year, one of his colleagues of the *langue* of Auvergne, Blaise d'Arfeuille, charged a Maltese man to go to Sicily on his behalf, to dispose of eleven slaves in his possession).[93] In any case, he had some in his crew, as is attested by the presence of a slavemaster of Italian origin, who furthermore lent him 186 scudi for the voyage.[94] In total, the funds he received came to around 14,000 scudi, which translates into around 35,000 livres tournois.

He left the island between 5 and 13 April.[95] According to a text which we shall soon analyze, he came back around the end of the summer, covered "with honour and with booty." There is no doubt about the honours, but as to the prizes, we are much less sure. Two matters will receive brief mention. We must first try to describe – as best we can, given the scarcity of sources – the exploit which he appears to have achieved in the western Mediterranean. Then we shall examine the financial results of the operation, much more negative than the account by Baudier, to which we are alluding, would have us believe.

Michel Baudier (1589–1645), a soldier turned historian – he was even accorded the officer of "historiographer to the King"[96] – published eight works during his lifetime,[97] including the one that concerns us. He wrote not only about France, but also about Spain, England, Italy, China, Persia, and Turkey. He knew several languages – in all, an author who deserves a certain credibility.

The third edition of his *Inventaire de l'histoire générale des Turcs* appeared in Rouen in 1631. In it he recounted, year by year, the important (or picturesque) events which marked the life of the Turks, especially in their relations with the West. This is the passage that concerned Montmagny (included in the events of 1627):

[In the margin:] A Maltese vessel escapes from the midst of a Turkish fleet.

The Turks' fortune favoured them no better on the sea than on land. We have said before that the Cossacks with their little boats rendered the Sultan's great vessels useless, and brought terror right to the port of Constantinople. Some months afterwards, fifty leagues from Alexandria, a Bassa with three galleys and six sailing ships met a vessel from Malta commanded by the chevalier de Montmagny, a Parisian. It fought him for five hours without being able to take him; the vessel sailed away in full view from the midst of the galleys, and carried back to Malta the honour and the booty that it had taken from the Turks.[98]

A short account, a few lines long, obviously does not replace the shipboard journal of the captain.[99] We do not know Baudier's sources. Was he only repeating stories being told in Paris or in Malta? The scope of his book obviously did not allow him to go into detail. But it does seem that the essentials were there. That the engagement took place 150 miles north of Alexandria is highly likely. That Montmagny resisted an enemy superior in numbers – one against nine – and that he escaped unharmed, is confirmed by another source, as we shall see. In comparing this engagement to the Cossack raids in the Black Sea, the author draws the conclusion of the Turkish fleet's decline. But there is an element that he avoids: the real cost of the operation: the number of deaths, the material damages, and the loss of effects.

A Maltese document dated 6 April 1629[100] (thus some twenty months after the event) confirms the prowess of the "most illustrious captain Charles de Montmagny,"[101] who waged combat singlehandedly ("singulare certamine") "against nine galleys of Rhodians and Alexandrians" ("Alexandrinorum") with an unmatched prudence and strength.[102] So much for the glory! And, it must be added, for the justification of the favour that would follow. On the other hand, he sustained multiple damages ("multa damna"), of the nature of which only one detail is given: the vessel came back in very bad shape ("fort avarié").[103] It was for this reason that his creditors, in the contract that we are citing – and which the notary calls "relaxatio" – absolved him from paying the *risico* and the legal interest on the capital they had advanced. Up to that point, only one creditor had had his money reimbursed.[104]

It is remarkable, all the same, that in his dictionary[105] Moreri took up Baudier's enthusiastic version, but gave it a singular transformation.[106] According to him, the "outstanding victory" took place on 6 August 1627 – a quite believable date. Baudier's pasha becomes the Bey of Rhodes – that is possible, but highly unlikely. Montmagny "was commanding the galleys of the Order"[107]– that is altogether impossible. The Captain General of the galleys at this time was François de Crémaulx, of the *langue* of Auvergne. Obviously, there was no mention of damage.

What comes out of all this is that, in the Levant in the summer of 1627, Montmagny achieved a remarkable feat of arms, standing up by himself to ten enemy vessels. He was able to return to Malta, bringing with him, though doubtless with difficulty, a vessel which had been severely damaged in the encounter. No one speaks of other losses (human lives, merchandise), which may have been high.

Montmagny was not the only corsair to distinguish himself during the year 1627. Other French knights also knew glory: several ships taken, numerous slaves captured. One in particular, René du Bailleul, of the grand priory of Aquitaine, of the *langue* of France, and a native of Maine, captured the attention of historians.[108] Crossing between Turkey and Egypt, he suddenly found himself surrounded by five heavily-armed Turkish caramusels.[109] He had the audacity to attack the flagship, and this so stupefied his aggressors that they abandoned it to him and took flight. This first capture, and that of two vessels (a *patache* and a merchant ship) that he succeeded in seizing, gave him prizes of great value, apparently in the order of 200,000 scudi.[110]

Charles Huault was not as lucky. It is possible more or less to follow the financial sequels of his adventure, traces of which remain in the studies of the notaries of Valetta and Paris. It is a sort of three-sided game, involving the chevalier himself, harassed by the demands of his creditors, who sometimes threatened to take him to court; his brothers, Louis and Adrien, who continued to show him their confidence, and who lodged him in Paris "with his people"[111] for several months; and their common agent, a French merchant residing in Malta, Jean Revest.

About the facts and actions in the weeks following the end of his campaign little is known. There was a slave sold on 15 September;[112] a loan of 342 livres from his brother Adrien,[113] a possible stay in Rome,[114] and a first reimbursement in Malta, made in his absence and dated 8 January 1628.[115] In mid-March he was back in Paris: he gave his two brothers and his sister a receipt for two years of board (1626 and 1627).[116] In the same act he recognized that he owed the two men the sum of 6,402 livres, 8 sols, which they had lent to him at various times in 1626 and 1627. Then the documents are silent until April 1629, the moment when he obtained the famous *relaxatio*.[117] The lenders gave him until the end of November to pay back their capital; he was exonerated of all interest, as we have seen.

But by the following February 1630 nothing had yet been paid.[118] A contract bearing this date contains first of all the statement of a debt amounting in all to 17,777 scudi (about 44,500 livres), and then the promise by Louis and Adrien to turn over the sum of 11,000 livres to Jean Revest, the merchant of Malta, on condition that the latter undertook to liquidate all the debts within eighteen months (thus the final date of 18 August 1631).

It was in March and April 1631 that the reimbursements – all except three – finally took place.[119] The following 15 September, Jean Revest appeared before a Parisian notary in the company of the three Huault brothers.[120] Thus, four years after Charles ended his second expedition to the Levant, he was almost at the end of his troubles.

The 11,000 livres were returned, as promised, to the Valetta merchant. Nine hundred livres were also given to Charles for the costs and other expenses "which are required for Paris and for the journey to Malta which he hopes to take soon." So what was involved was a payment of 12,000 livres, for which the two brothers had to raise some loans.[121] To defray their losses, they reduced the chevalier's annual pension from 1,800 to 1,200 livres, and guaranteed only 6,000 livres (instead of the 9,000 livres initially promised) in the event of a ransom – a sign, by the way, that Charles had not forsworn adventures in the Mediterranean. Louis and Adrien were hoping that their brother would soon obtain a commandery: they reserved a third of its revenues for themselves in advance. It was no doubt with this hope that they cancelled an obligation of 2,400 livres, corresponding to the amount of the money lent at the time of the first expedition which remained to be repaid. They did not fail to mention, in a very interesting detail, that they would reimburse themselves for "the room and board" which they had undertaken "for him and his people," and for the furnishing of horses by Louis, during his recent stays in France.

Louis had to intervene with Jean Revest again in July 1633: there were still 310 scudi (about 775 livres) outstanding, and Charles was being taken to court by one of his colleagues.[122] We do not know how this story ended; but it represents the banal and prosaic end of a great dream – to fight against the infidels, and to try, with God's help, to get rich at the same time.

Note here the important part played by the chevalier's close relatives in his enterprises. They boarded him and his "people," they financed him tirelessly – against a vague promise of reimbursement from a commandery which, incidentally, never materialized. They formed a team, almost;[123] in any case, in many documents it was mentioned that it was "by friendship" and, it seems, with a certain admiration that Louis, Adrien, and even Charlotte were willing to participate financially in the war that the Order was waging in the Mediterranean. One way or another, the Order did not have a bad press in the family; Louis would arrange for his younger son, also named Louis, to be received there as a minor on 7 June 1631;[124] and a grandson of Charlotte, the "chevalier d'Arcy," another younger son, would enter the Order in 1661.[125]

Around September 1632 Charles returned to Malta for his last long stay; leaving there sometime around July 1634 – a period, then, of close to two years.[126] He may have fought against the Turks, but this time it would have been on the Order's vessels, or at the expense of another knight, and thus without any financial participation, as far as we know.

In April and in May 1634,[127] he found procurators for the purpose, on one hand, of attending to his affairs if necessary, and on the other, of representing him, if the need arose – a possible dispensation, doubtless, to be sought in Rome – before the pope and the cardinals of the curia. Then, on 11 June, he obtained permission from the Grand Master to return to France.[128]

But in fact, ever since the beginning of 1632, he had been simultaneously at the service of two Grand Masters, the Grand Master of the Order and the Grand Master of Navigation and Commerce of France: none other than the Cardinal de Richelieu.[129]

4.   The *Compagnie de la Nouvelle-France*

In 1632, and above all since the effort of renovation undertaken by Cardinal de Richelieu, it had become common practice to exchange the navy of the Order for that of His Most Christian Majesty. To make one's caravans, that is to say to fight at sea against the Turks and Berbers, was incontestably the best naval school imaginable. Besides their competence, the Knights of Malta had the reputation of being trustworthy, courageous, and daring. The term " nursery of French sailors" has been used in reference to the Order's navy.[130] In an 1844 book in which "the illustrious seamen of France"[131] were passed in review, more than a third of the individuals whose names the author recorded were hospitallers.

But, on the other hand, it can also be said that France was a nursery for the Knights of Malta. In all Europe it was the country that provided the greatest number of them: between 1529 and 1798, twelve Grand Masters of the Order out of twenty-eight came from the Hexagon; many of the "illustrious seamen" of the Order came from there also.[132]

In this context, we can understand why the French authorities would have had the idea of using the expertise of these specialists of the sea, of appealing to these devoted and courageous men. Thus they are found participating actively in the first campaign which King Louis XIII mounted against the Protestants of La Rochelle who, in 1621, had raised a war fleet to defend themselves.[133] Notable among others were Paul-Albert de Forbin,[134] Jacques de Vincheguerre,[135] and Isaac de Razilly.[136] This last person, whose good name caught the attention of the supreme power, in 1624 found himself entrusted with a delicate and dangerous mission: an embassy to the Moroccan authorities of the port of Safi on the Mediterranean coast.[137]

The year 1624 coincided with the return to power – permanent this time – of Armand Du Plessis de Richelieu. He very swiftly understood the serious handicap represented by the country's weakness in naval equipment. In 1626, he arranged for the king to name him Grand Master of Navigation and Commerce of France.[138] He was determined to modernize this sector which his predecessors had neglected. He turned naturally toward the Order – his uncle, Amador de La Porte, was one of the most visible members of the *langue* of France.[139] The chevalier des Roches[140] was charged with drawing up a report on the Maltese methods of constructing and maintaining galleys: the Levant navy was going to be reorganized on the model of that of the Order.

The cardinal asked for something more fundamental from Razilly: general principles and guidelines for the wholescale renovation that was about to take place. They were presented to him in a memoir, famous to this day, which in actual fact gave direction to the policy of the State and, to a certain point, prepared the work of Colbert.[141] It started with a maxim which has deservedly become celebrated: "the mastery of the sea assures great land power;" and gave, among other examples, the highly appropriate one of Malta, a tiny state that was feared throughout the Mediterranean. It was to shake up the centuries-old inertia of France in this sphere. Some principles were clearly set forth: the State ought to intervene – the king ought to be the premier armorer of the country. All social classes were to be invited to participate, including the clergy: "the charity of the Church has truly grown cold," he commented; her wealth is unproductive, she ought at least to assure the cost of evangelization in the colonies. There had to be an interrelationship between the navy and overseas trade – surely Razilly was thinking, as Colbert would think a generation later, of the example of the Netherlands. To promote foreign trade, there was a need for colonies.

But how to realize this immense programme? The anwer: create two solid navies, one for the Levant and one for the Ocean – Razilly even specified the character and the number of vessels to be armed, their military equipment, and the funds that would be required. Second, establish public companies, monopolies guaranteed and overseen by the State. Third, found colonies in Africa or the Americas – more in the south than in the north, he suggested; forget the Indies, apart from sending a merchant fleet there from time to time.

Razilly's interest in the colonies came from personal experience in the Maranhaô, a region in northeastern Brazil where the seamen of Dieppe had been active since the end of the sixteenth century. In 1612 François de Razilly, his brother, who with the help of his relations had set up a trading company, left to explore the country; Isaac commanded one of the ships. He was highly impressed by the natural richness of the country and the friendliness of the natives. The Razilly brothers returned to seek funding in the mother country; they had great plans. The regent gave their efforts verbal encouragement but no financial backing, at the very time when she had just distributed thousands of livres in pensions to the "greats" of the realm, those restless and greedy men. Whence came the reaction underlying Razilly's memoir: to defeudalize France and modernize its institutions, an idea which appealed to Richelieu.

For our purpose, what is important to note is the part that the Order of Malta played in the colonial activity of France. Its participation as an entity was never more than sporadic – though later we shall study the interesting case of the island of Saint-Christophe. The Knights' involvement was always on a personal basis. The Brazil that Razilly and his brothers sought to penetrate had already, in the sixteenth century, been the object of an equally abortive attempt at establishment by another hospitaller, Nicolas Durand de Villegagnon.[142]

Richelieu's rise to power did not in any way change the attitude of the Order; colonial enterprises were not, in theory at least, consistent with its vocation. But in applying the measures suggested by Commander de Razilly, the minister was going to give a new impulse to the French colonizing effort, and he recruited knights, beginning with Razilly himself. An agreement was reached between the two men in March 1632, for the setting up of Acadia.

It was about the same time that Montmagny made contact with the *Compagnie de la Nouvelle-France,* of which he would become one of the directors.[143] As governor of New France from 1636 to 1648, he again found himself dependent on the Company. Thus he was at its service for sixteen years (from 1632 to 1648), the most productive years of his life. His second career was beginning.

The Company, also called the *Compagnie des Cent-Associés*, had been founded by Richelieu in 1627. It was an initiative on his part to put into application the new principles of his colonial policy. Twelve persons (four of whom had to be merchants) were charged with ensuring the progress of this complex enterprise. It was doubtless through the combined influence of the director general of the Company, Jean de Lauson, and the Jesuits, who had been chosen to take over the religious services in the colony, that Montmagny was designated to participate in the management. In fact, as noted, Lauson was the first cousin of Louis Huault's wife, Isabelle Lottin; and the ties that bound the Jesuits to the Huault family have already been discussed.

Now, the candidates to this post would not have been legion in 1632. The Company had not taken long to go into hopeless ruin. From 1628 on the situation across the Atlantic went from bad to worse. The English occupied the post of Québec from 1629 to 1632. When Montmagny became one of the directors, everything was back to square one.

Somehow the Company survived. Richelieu was occupied elsewhere: the war against the House of Austria monopolized almost all his attention, and it cost him dearly.[144]

Today there is no way of knowing what part Charles Huault played in the management of the Company during those years. Between the beginning of 1632 and the end of 1634, he spent eighteen months in Malta, during which time he could not have been present at the meetings which supposedly took place once a week. But he must have impressed the other directors, because at the end of 1635 they presented him to the minister as the replacement for Champlain. Doubtless, also, the fine performance of Razilly in Acadia prompted them to send another knight to America.

We are now in 1636, at the end of what can be called the pre-North American part of Montmagny's life. We have briefly explored its outlines in two stages: the first extending from his birth to his departure for Malta (1601 to 1622); the second extending from his first journey to Valetta to his taking ship for Québec (1622 to 1636).

In characterizing the first period, two names should be retained: Paris and La Flèche.

Paris meant the family, solidly ensconced in the magistracy – even more on the Du Drac side than on the Huault side. It meant the fine hôtel, well-placed and comfortable though not luxurious, and the country manor, two or three hours' ride from the city centre. The rue Saint-Antoine was a busy quarter, one of the capital's most travelled arteries, which, from 1605, experienced a rebound of activity with the building of the Place Royale. Paris, as has been said, was still "the city of a hundred spires";[145] religion was omnipresent – the Jesuits lived close by the Huaults, for example – and it occupied a place of honour in Antoinette Du Drac's household. It was in this privileged milieu that Charles Huault received his first education, his first socialization.

Then the Jesuits of La Flèche took up the work. There, as well, the environment was hardly disagreeable: a valet, the presence of his brother which must have been reassuring, and the liveliness that can be imagined in a great house teeming with adolescents. It was, as Descartes has so ably pointed out,[146] a training in competitiveness, in individual worth – the competitions and debates were designed for this – in a form of egalitarianism, tempering the differences in birth. In addition, it was an opening to the world, which one could say was both horizontal (the Jesuits were at work in Asia and America) and vertical, in the sense that historical reality was at the heart of Jesuit education: the theatrical pieces put on at the college between 1610 and 1618 were set in the ancient Near East, the Roman Empire, and the Middle Ages. Obviously, the Christianity which all these pieces were intended to celebrate was foremost in the preoccupations of these educators. It was a demanding religion, as a key text, the *Spiritual Exercises* of Ignatius Loyola, clearly shows; but it rested on a balanced view of the human being – body, intelligence, will.

The two brief experiences of his Italian tour and his stay at the University of Orléans did not significantly alter his previous formation, except to make it clear that the legal profession, the appanage of the Huaults and the Du Dracs, was not for Montmagny. To make his career, he chose a completely different direction: religious life in a military order. Two names can represent the period 1622 to 1636: Valetta and Paris.

From 1530, the cornerstone of the Order of Saint John of Jerusalem was Valetta, which, after the great siege, became an impregnable fortress. The Knights who, to all intents and purposes, made this city[147] had highly original rules, when compared to those of other religious orders. Not just anyone could enter: proofs of nobility were required. The predominant virtue was strength – the members had to be ready to fight to the end. Charity (first and foremost towards the poor) and devotion were their other two priorities. They also took the three vows;

but many accommodations were possible. Few religious institutions functioned like this in the Church.

The life of the sea – the very essence of Malta, one might say – imposed many adaptations. A seaport – and this was the principal purpose of Valetta and its environs – meant international interaction; and the Order itself, with its eight *langues,* was essentially international. It meant being constantly busy, with workplaces in perpetual activity, storehouses to be filled, and prisons to hold the galley slaves. And of course there was the sea,[148] capricious in its climate, infested with pirates and privateers. More than two-thirds of the Mediterranean coastline was held by the "enemies of the Christian Faith," and, therefore, of Malta. To travel on it was always an adventure. One word says it all: war, permanent war. Valetta, like Algiers, Tunis, and Alexandria, made the corso its central activity. The chevalier took a full part in this dangerous life.

But this participation allowed escape to another place, the city of his birth. There Montmagny could enjoy a sure repose, since the war affected the capital only indirectly. He also came back into the bosom of the family, which cannot have been so bad, since he always lodged with his brothers during his stays. Above all, his siblings gave proof of their generosity; it was almost like a bank, from which he drew abundantly – we are reminded of the consortium that the Razilly family had formed some years before. Paris was also the seat of the management of the *Compagnie de la Nouvelle-France.* The interest which he developed in the colony would turn his life in a new direction; but one in which other knights had gone before.

Of this period of his life, the most striking aspect can be summed up in one little phrase: "to be a corsair for Christ." For this he practically ruined himself financially, despite help from his moneylenders; but out of this he achieved renown. The habits that he developed would serve him well in the New World: tact, coolness, determination, and audacity in dangerous situations.

CHAPTER 5

From the Mediterranean to the Saint Lawrence

In a spectacular reorientation of his career, Brother Huault de Montmagny was named, perhaps as early as the end of 1635, governor – the first of that title – of New France. The territory entrusted to him, the Saint Lawrence River valley, was dominated by a stretch of water presenting an extreme contrast with the Mediterranean that he had now left forever.

For a good dozen years, he had lived most of his time in contact with a great inland sea, densely populated along its coastline and on its islands, and heavily travelled not only by its own people, but also by northern Europeans, especially the English and the Dutch. Sailing ships and galleys ploughed through it in every direction, for trade or for war, the collision of two great civilizations being, as we have seen, extremely violent. The Saint Lawrence, which Montmagny entered at the end of May 1636, was a kind of maritime corridor emptying into the Atlantic and rising at the very heart of the continent. From the Gulf, the river narrowed until it reached Québec, from which point its width remained more or less unchanged as far as the Great Lakes. It was relatively little frequented; the population along its banks was scattered; Québec had only 200 inhabitants; Trois-Rivières, barely fifty. The native peoples of the Saint Lawrence were nomadic, those of the Great Lakes, semi-sedentary. Their way of life – their culture, among other things – was diametrically different from that of the Mediterranean peoples. Within this immense network, which included the Saint Lawrence's many tributaries, travel was by canoe or small boat, with ocean-going vessels coming up as far as Tadoussac or Québec, save in the winter, since climatic constraints were severe.

Indeed, when this aspect is taken into account, the contrast deepens. The great sea is bracketed between the North African desert and the temperate zone of southern Europe. This results in mostly sunny days and an endemic dryness against which men have had to struggle since the beginning of time.[1] On the other hand, the winter, without being cold (the temperature rarely drops below 10° C) is wet and stormy.

In 1659, Venice forbade long voyages between 15 November and 20 January.[2] Also, going back to the New Testament, it is recalled that in the autumn of 60 A.D., the boat carrying the apostle Paul to Rome was shipwrecked near Malta.[3]

In eastern Canada, the situation is completely different:[4] as far as Québec there is a boreal zone to the north and a temperate cool zone to the south that, from this point, curves slightly upward to include Montréal and most of the Great Lakes region. The result of this is a cold, damp climate. The winter is, properly speaking, the dead season: navigation is blocked by the ice; snow covers the ground to a depth of a metre or more; the cold is persistent. The *Relation* of 1637[5] describes the trip which Montmagny took, at the very beginning of March, across a lake situated "about four leagues from Québec."[6] "As the cold was intense," he and his companions were forced "to pass [the night] between the fire and the snow under ... the mighty vault of heaven." He "had some fishing done there under the ice during Lent." In the summer the temperature is more agreeable, and it rains enough, most of the time, to produce an impressive vegetation.

The antithesis continues with examination of the human milieu. Not the immediate milieu – in both cases Montmagny found brother hospitallers (of whom there will be more presently), Jesuit priests, and compatriots – but, rather, the very different civilizations with which he was confronted. The nations belonging to Islam were, as we have seen, the *raison d'être* of the Order. In seven campaigns (maybe more) he had taken the measure of their wealth and their strength. More than half the Mediterranean seaboard belonged to them. They fought as equals with the Christian nations of Europe. Their culture was refined, with works of art,[7] impressive monuments, and, above all, palaces and mosques. Istanbul was one of the most beautiful cities in the world. Their monotheistic religion was based on the interpretation of an inspired book. But the Koran is not the Bible, and on account of that they were, according to the well-known formula, "enemies of the true faith";[8] and they were in control of the holy places of Christendom. The aboriginal people with whom Montmagny came in contact as soon as he arrived at Tadoussac and Québec were at a stage of technical development closer to the paleolithic than to the post-medieval Mediterranean epoch. They had no experience of urban life or of monarchical power. However, their way of life, their mentality, their culture were well-adapted to the geographical environment which supported them. Their religion had nothing in common with Christian or Muslim monotheism; they were even more "infidel," if it can be put that way, than the Mohammedans.

MAP 4

New France at the Time of Montmagny

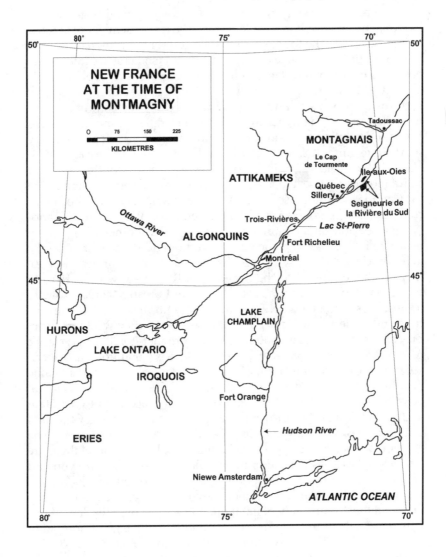

This fact could not leave a Knight of Malta indifferent; he was going to find in it another kind of crusade, adapting his activity to the methods developed by his old schoolmasters, the Jesuits.

A final comparison must be made: the responsibilities which Montmagny had to assume in New France bore no resemblance to those he had carried in the Mediterranean. According to his own testimony he had participated in five caravans,[9] without (so far as we know) any positions of command. He had led two campaigns as captain of his own ship. This demanded courage and also a sense of organization, both for the financing and preparation and for the conduct of and the follow-up to the expedition; but the number of men under his command was limited and the duration of the operations relatively short – a few months. To the Parisian directors of the *Compagnie de la Nouvelle-France* he was only one of a dozen proposed for this task, and he was absent from several meetings. When he received his commission for Canada, an immense territory (even if sparsely inhabited) was confided to his care. He was the representative of the king of France "in Québec and on the Saint Lawrence River and other rivers which flow into it."[10] Once there, he was "governor and lieutenant-general"; in his official acts he chose to use the second term,[11] doubtless because this was better-suited to the thinking of Richelieu, who distrusted provincial "governors" whose authority and prestige could prove to be obstacles to the monarchy's strategy of centralization.[12] The Jesuits constantly referred to "our governor," or, when they wrote in Latin, they said not only "gubernator," but also "moderator,"[13] or – a classic reference – "regius praefectus."[14] His tasks were manifold, as we can see from the text of his commission of 1645 (the only one that has come down to us).[15] First, he had to "command all the men at war who will be in the said country both to guard the said places and to maintain and protect trade, [and to] take care of the said colony of the said country, the conservation and surety of this under our obedience." The exercise of justice was also in his hands: "until such time as there are sovereign judges established in these places ... we authorize you and the lieutenants whom you appoint to exercise sovereign and supreme judgment." A final clause concerned the control which the Company, by means of the "community of habitants," exercised over the "business" which was taking place in the colony, and which the governor had to supervise. Thus the entire administration of the colony fell under his jurisdiction, not only in military but also in all civil affairs, commerce (the Company that he represented) and justice included.

The magnitude of the mission entrusted to him quickly becomes clear. Under each of the elements just mentioned there lay realities much more complex than would appear at first sight; they have already been explored, often authoritatively, by geographers,[16] anthropologists,[17] and historians.[18] There will be frequent references to these authorities. The following chapters will draw upon them in order to understand the work of this man during the twelve years of his life which he passed in North America in the service of both Crown and Church – being a man "of the church," this was part of his vocation.

The next chapter will study his dealings with the native peoples, who made up the majority of his "subjects" (so to speak). The following chapter will analyze the way in which the colony developed under his administration. Chapter 8 will seek to draw up a balance sheet of these twelve years, examining, first, what New France represented in 1648 when he left it, and, second, the quite unexpected repercussions, in the mother country, of his posting in Québec.

The present chapter is a sort of introduction to those that follow. Three questions will be addressed: first, how to explain this Mediterranean–Saint Lawrence convergence; in other words, how to understand the presence in Canada of a religious order whose mother house was situated on the island of Malta; then, what were the basic outlines of the colony which the chevalier inherited at the start of 1636; and, finally, what explains the enthusiasm which seized Father Le Jeune when, in his *Relation* of 1636, he recorded the notable events of this year in New France, at the forefront of which he placed the arrival of Montmagny.

1. The Knights of Malta in the Saint Lawrence River valley

Throughout the *ancien régime*, France drew great benefit from the competence of the Knights,[19] most of all perhaps during the first half of the seventeenth century, when, as has already been noted, many of them served at sea under the banner of the Most Christian King.[20] Such was the case of the Forbin family of Marseille, for example: of the many members of this family who entered the Order,[21] four distinguished themselves in the king's ships between the end of the sixteenth century and the start of the eighteenth.[22]

Some Knights passed into colonial service. This sector, considered briefly in connection with the reverses which the *Compagnie de la Nouvelle-France* experienced at the outset, was brought to an impasse at the outbreak of the Thirty Years War. What was needed were men who were trustworthy, courageous, and used to the sea. The Knights were perfect candidates.

Acadia benefited, though for too short a time, from the genius of the Commander de Razilly.[23] He died in the autumn of 1635, after a sojourn of less than four years.

A few months later, Montmagny arrived in the Saint Lawrence River valley. We know his qualifications: long experience at sea, an unusual degree of endurance and combativeness, and some practice in the management of men (the crew of his ship). To the best of our knowledge, unlike most French knights who were involved in the colonies, he never served in the French navy.

He would not be the only member of his Order in Québec. The man who welcomed him officially into the colony in June 1636, Marc-Antoine de Brasdefer de Châteaufort, may have been one. The lieutenant whom he chose to accompany him across the Atlantic was a confrère, Achille De Lisle. One of the ships in the fleet that transported Montmagny and De Lisle was commanded by the Chevalier de la Roche-Jacquelin.

Concerning these persons, whose stay in New France coincided for a while with that of Montmagny, our knowledge is very slight; there is even some doubt whether the first and the third belonged to the Order.[24] One thing is sure, however: they collaborated closely with him, and if one takes the *Relations* at their word, they possessed the distinctive qualities of Knights of Malta.

The only known Brasdefer genealogy[25] gives, as Marc-Antoine's great-grandfather, a Scottish gentleman by the name of Gemmes de Brasdefer,[26] who had married the heiress of Châteaufort, a little seigneurie situated in southern Normandy, in the *bailliage* of Evreux, "close to Verneuil au Perche."

More certain is the information that comes from the Paris archives. The father was Jean de Brasdefer, *écuyer* – this was his only title. On 16 July 1582[27] he married Anne Gillot, daughter of Claude, *maître des vivres* for the king in Normandy, Brittany, and Poitou.[28] Now, Claude Gillot was not noble; this is important to note, because it constituted an obstacle to entry as Knight into the Order. The young Marc-Antoine lacked the necessary quarterings of nobility, but he could very well have become a man-at-arms; that is a distinct possibility.

Jean de Brasdefer appears to have been a minor country noble; he engaged in technical activities, which was not the custom for a gentleman. A document of 25 June 1611 tells us that he and his son Marc-Antoine, each at the rate of a "half-quarter," and a carpenter of

Paris at the rate of a quarter, shared in the profits that came from the invention "of certain mills which grind without either water or wind," the brainchild of Sieur Christofle de Neufville, *écuyer,* sieur of Beaumont. The two Brasdefers offered "their good offices and good will"; as for the Parisian artisan, he assisted in the production.[29] This is all we know about Marc-Antoine Brasdefer before he came to Canada. At the death of his father in 1616,[30] he would have been in his early thirties.

When the documents (those that historians have been able to consult) speak of him, he was in Canada, and when Champlain died, letters of commission which had been prepared in advance were officially turned over to him by the superior of the Jesuits, as a way of safeguarding the interim.[31] It was perhaps under the influence of the Jesuits that, less than a week after assuming office, he issued an ordinance forbidding blasphemy, drunkenness, and absence from church services. As early as 6 January, he had the occasion to put it into action, condemning a blasphemer to the pillory.[32]

Shortly after the arrival of Montmagny, whom he welcomed officially, Brasdefer was named commander of the post at Trois-Rivières. In his relations with the indigenous people, he knew how to alternate gentleness and firmness. He seems to have co-operated fully in the evangelizing work of the Jesuits.

Concerning the second person, we will now offer the hypothesis which at present seems the most likely. First we shall examine the evidence originating in New France itself, before laying out what has come from the Maltese archives.

Father Le Jeune, at the end of his account of the negotiation which "Monsieur le chevalier de l'Isle" conducted at Trois-Rivières in 1637 in the name of the governor, used these highly flattering words: "In short, I could not have wished for more than this gallant gentleman did for the welfare of this infant Church, and to prove his love for the new Christian who was present among these barbarians."[33] The other mentions he made of him in the *Relations* are all in the same vein.

Brasdefer also figures in certain documents conserved in the archives of the Seminary of Québec. These concern judgments, many of which were rendered "with the advice of Sieur de L'isle, one of the lieutenants" of the governor.[34] One of these acts (dated 20 August 1638) is more explicit: the matter is passed, it is reported, "before us, Achille De Lisle, *écuyer,* sieur de Lisle, Knight of the Order of Saint John of Jerusalem"; in an adjoining page, it is added that the said Knight is "licencié ès lois."[35] In another act, this one dated 20 April 1639, he apposes his signature, which reads as follows: "A. De Lisle." There is a final mention in this series: on 4 May 1642, the governor affirms that he "is acting on the advice of Achille de l'Isle ... our lieutenant in this country, who alone is with us at this time."[36]

So Montmagny had succeeded in having for lieutenant a brother knight who, like him, had undertaken studies in the law, but had completed them and obtained his "licence," as it was then called.

The Maltese archives have revealed elements rather difficult to interpret with certainty. The only person we encountered who could answer to our requirements was the man-at-arms, Brother Achille Le Boucher de Lisle, to whom the Grand Master gave permission on 4 September 1624 to go to France.[37] Supposing that this was indeed the same person, we might ask why, when in Canada, he never used the first part of his patronym (Le Boucher) (though it must be pointed out that this was frequent practice: Charles Huault de Montmagny was almost always referred to as the chevalier de Montmagny).

It would also be reasonable to ask how he passed from the status of man-at-arms to that of knight (by meritorious action, for example? – we think here of the chevalier Paul, of humble origins). It was by this latter title that he was always designated in Canada (where, seemingly, he lived from 1636 to 1642). There remains some doubt on the identification that we are suggesting here.

Another hypothesis has been proposed by some Québec historians.[38] According to them, the Maltese documents might have been referring to Antoine-Louis Bréhant de Lisle – "Antonius de Lisle." As to the antiquity of this man's nobility, there is no problem.[39] He entered the Order in 1631. After his novitiate he took part in a caravan. A papal brief, dated 24 October 1634, rehabilitated him in the wake of an unfortunate episode which should normally have led to his expulsion from the Order.[40] In 1639, he is to be found in the royal navy.[41] As was quite frequently the case among the Knights of Malta, it seems that when his father died he left the community to marry and assure the continuity of the line.[42] It is hardly likely that the "chevalier de Lisle" who came to spend several years in New France during the first part of Montmagny's mandate would have been Antoine-Louis Bréhant de Lisle.

We note, further, that one of the vessels sent by the *Compagnie de la Nouvelle-France*, the *Saint-Jacques*, was commanded in 1635 and in 1636 by the chevalier de la Roche Jacquelin, who may have belonged to the Order.[43] He also seems to have been a friend of the Jesuits,[44] and on his first voyage he took a close interest in the conversion to Catholicism of a young Huguenot who made the crossing in his ship.[45]

For some time, therefore, there had been more than one Knight of Malta (possibly three or even four) in the capital of the colony. That fact is already significant. It must also be pointed out that one of their confrères, and an important one at that, was taking a concrete interest in New France. He did not cross the Atlantic, but his intervention had clear effects upon the missionary strategy of the Jesuits. This was none other than Noël Brulart de Sillery (1577–1640), one of the most remarkable members of this family which had several alliances in common with the Huault and Du Drac families.[46] After a few words on this lineage, we shall outline the career of the chevalier, and retrace the beginnings of his contribution to the missionary work in Canada.

The Brulart family presents a highly interesting case of social ascension.[47] From *conseillers au Parlement* at the beginning of the sixteenth century they rose, at the end of that century, to the post of *président;* and in 1607 Nicolas, Noël's brother, became chancellor of the realm, having been *garde des sceaux* since 1604. Their contribution to the ecclesiastical sector was no less important: many monks and nuns, some canons, two bishops, and several hospitaller vocations.

Noël Brulart served for two years as page to the Grand Master before making his novitiate.[48] He returned to France in 1607, at the same time that his brother was named chancellor; this explains why he was chosen as ambassador to Spain, then to Rome. He had his entrée into the court, where he lived in grand style. He was one of the familiars of the queen mother, who, it appears, awarded him a gratuity of 60,000 écus in 1615.[49] In fact, he never lacked money. On 31 January 1639, still some months before his death, he made over to "his great-nephew and godson, Messire Noël de Bullion, who was preparing to marry Demoiselle Charlotte de Prie, a sumptuous gift: 100,000 livres in cash."[50]

The year 1626 marked a turning point in his life. He felt himself touched by grace, and converted to a more austere life and a greater perfection in the practice of Christian virtues. It is a clear sign of the seriousness of his decision that he took Vincent de Paul as his spiritual director. He retired from the court, gave part of his goods to charity, and decided finally to join the priesthood (on Holy Thursday 1634), something that was very rare among the Knights of Malta.

It was, undoubtedly, the reading of this same year's *Relation* that aroused in him the desire to assist in the foundation of a seminary for young aboriginals.[51] And it was at this very time, as we have seen, that Montmagny came back to Paris for good. They must have met often at the Temple. In March 1637 Noël made a decision. He had just been granted a new commandery, with revenues in the order of 6,500 livres.[52] This was the moment at which he wrote to the governor of Québec, who replied to him by return of mail.[53] The exchange of letters is most telling: we are in the presence of two hospitallers both profoundly marked by the spirituality of the Counter Reformation. "In the thought that God has been pleased to enable me to contribute what I could to the well-being and the advancement of the faith in New France," this was the phrase with which the letter opened. In fact, this pious "thought" coincided with two events that he considered providential, the nomination of Montmagny and his own access to a new source of funds. It must of course be recognized that for a fortune as imposing as his the effort was not overwhelming; but it was, at least, the beginning of his involvement. He then arranged for the Company to grant him territory in Québec, and he sent workers to clear the land and to build. He asked the governor to support his project.

The response is filled with the same resonances: God is visibly at work, "from all eternity the great God has destined you to this" – that is to say, He has destined you to this admirable "total renunciation of the world [his conversion of 1626]." And Montmagny continues:

> But at present, we see in you projects and designs much more sublime, more holy, such as is the establishment of a seminary in New France. This is most truly to follow the intention of God, to Whom be honour and glory forever. How can it all not succeed to your contentment, since it is for the exaltation of His name and that of the most holy Virgin our good mistress.

Such a matching of thought and sentiment between two men whose careers were so different is, at first sight, rather surprising; but it is quite understandable given the spiritual context of the times, as well as the dynamic that characterized the Order of Malta. It was certainly through their contribution to the French navy that the Knights came to be interested in the colonies, and more particularly in New France; but it is not surprising that some of them should have applied their energies to the spiritual conquest of the New World, given that their first calling, the defence of Christianity against Islam, was only the reverse side of a vast project oriented to the extension of the reign of Christ throughout the world.

2.   Where was New France at the start of 1636?

To understand the challenge facing the chevalier de Montmagny, we need to know of what the New France entrusted to him in late 1635 or early 1636 consisted.[54] The candidate would have been informed of this nomination several weeks in advance, as was the case with his two terms in the Antilles in the 1650s.[55]

We must first, as far as possible, outline the territory that was placed under his authority, and then establish what the colony represented in demographic, economic, and social terms.

Montmagny's official title was that which is found in the only commission extant, that of 1645: "Governor and lieutenant-general at Québec and on the Saint Lawrence River and other rivers which flow into it."[56] He was entrusted, then, with this immense expanse which covered the entire network of the Saint Lawrence River and its tributaries, from the Gulf to the Great Lakes. In effect, the concession made to the Company in 1627 had included "All the country of New France called Canada, from the Island of the new land ... to the Great Lake of the Freshwater Sea and beyond ... and throughout the lands and along the rivers which pass through them and fall into the river called Saint Lawrence or the Great River of Canada."[57] The frontiers of this territory were strictly speaking immeasurable, given the means available to the French who were established there; and, in the map which he had published in 1632, Champlain avoided being precise on this subject. The work of exploration was only just beginning. In 1634 Jean Nicollet went as far as the Baie des Puants on the western shore of Lake Michigan,[58] and, very probably, Lake Superior. On the island of Newfoundland, mentioned in the commission cited above, there was no permanent post. A few French were settled in Acadia, but they seem to have been attached to Paris and not to Québec.

An immense territory but, it must be added at once, a very tiny population! At Champlain's death, the number of French could not have exceeded 320.[59] At the post of Trois-Rivières, founded in 1634 at Champlain's urging, there were as yet only agents of the Company and missionaries. At that of Tadoussac, there was still no permanent resident. The heart of the colony was Québec and its immediate environs. It was there that the personnel of the Company (including the king's representative, his lieutenant, the domestics, a few soldiers, and men working in the port) had their offices, their warehouses, and their homes. The Jesuits lived in a house close to the church of Notre-Dame de la Recouvrance. There is no doubt that the greater part of the population was made up of the artisans who had been engaged to construct the first buildings of the town. Guillaume Couillart, son-in-law of Louis Hébert,[60] was even running a farm there. Ten kilometres north-east of Québec a seigneurie was under development; on 15 January 1634, one Robert Giffard[61] had secured from the company a concession of land stretching for a league along the river bank, and a league and a half inland, and the following summer he landed at Québec with forty-three persons (including family members) whom he had recruited at Mortagne-au-Perche, and began to work his domain. At the beginning of 1636 this, along with the domain of the Jesuits situated close by, was the only enterprise of any size established on the banks of the Saint Lawrence.

As for the indigenous population, it was not very numerous in the eastern end of the territory; the Algonquian nations who were scattered about there were nomads without much cohesion. It was the Iroquoians, a semi-sedentary people, who constituted the most coherent, most compact group of nations and tribes. They were established in the eastern part of the Great Lakes. (See Map 4, 119.) They may have numbered around 100,000.[62]

The colony's economy depended, essentially, on the fur trade which remained somewhat problematical. In 1635 the trade was good; the Company paid 284,000 livres to subcontractors for the purchase of the cargo which arrived in France.[63] But in the previous year only a very few canoes had come down from Huronia, because of the threat which the resumption of warlike activities by their traditional enemies, the Iroquois, represented to these allies of the French. Only a few beaver pelts had been sent to the mother country. Yet it was the colony's sole source of revenue, the only reason why people with capital were persuaded to participate. This would be the principal concern of the new administrator; he would have to take important decisions in this regard.

Agriculture, it has been seen, had barely made a start. There had been lands under cultivation since 1625, but various factors – among others the slow pace of clearing – delayed their multiplication. The colony still had to be provisioned from France; even the fishery was slow to develop, though fish were abundant.

What sort of a collection of men was Montmagny going to find in his colony? It is difficult, one can easily see, to talk of a "society," since development was not yet sufficiently advanced; the transition was still taking place between the structures of the old country and those new ones that the colonial phenomenon, once it was truly under way, would put in place. But there are some elements that present a certain originality. They help to explain the action of the new governor.

First of all is the important position already occupied by the clergy. In late 1635 there were in the colony fifteen Jesuit priests, four lay brothers of the same order, and a secular priest – twenty persons out of a population of 320.[64] That represents a significant proportion. In reality this phenomenon is explained, for this period, by the Jesuits' activism. Encouraged by their experience in other parts of the world, especially in Latin America, they were going to make a considerable effort among the native peoples of Canada.[65]

From 1615 to 1629, Recollets[66] had come to work, mostly in Huronia. Notable among them was Brother Gabriel Sagard,[67] who left a dictionary of the Huron language,[68] and who, in 1636, published a *Histoire du Canada* in which he showed that this country was only one of his Company's missionary fields, alongside India, the land of the Tartars, Slavonia, and China; and that its exclusion from the Saint Lawrence in 1632 in favour of the Jesuits was an injustice.[69]

It was in 1625 that the Society of Jesus was set up in New France, and in 1632 it obtained the exclusive right to apostolic work in the colony, only recently recovered from the English. There is no need to expound at length on this Order which, in 1634, would celebrate the hundredth anniversary of its foundation. Simply note two of the qualities that characterized it: dynamism and competence. It attracted powerful personalities;[70] and it is a fact that the men chosen to come to Canada were indeed remarkable – Jean de Brébeuf, Paul Le Jeune, Charles Lalemant, Isaac Jogues ... and the list goes on. For a long time the Canadian mission acted as a powerful magnet for Frenchmen entering the Order.[71] The year 1632 saw the first publication, justly famous, of the *Relations* in which the Jesuits "related" the vicissitudes of their apostolic work in New France, as a means of promoting missionary vocations, of gaining prayers for the missions from those who could not aid them otherwise, and of inciting the wealthier *dévots* to contribute financially to this work which was a continuation of that of the apostles and the first propagators of the Church of Jesus Christ. It has already been seen how the Commander de Sillery responded to their appeal; there will soon be other examples.[72]

Their first task was the conversion of the natives. In the year 1634 they had begun their mission among the Huron. At the same time they applied themselves to finding ways of evangelizing the nomadic peoples.[73] To the French colonists they gave the assurance of religious services; better still, in the autumn of 1635 they opened the doors of their house – or rather, the presbytery which they occupied – to young boys whose parents wished to have them instructed. This was the start of the college of Québec.[74] Montmagny, as one can imagine, was completely ready to collaborate with these religious whom he knew well and with whom he had much in common.

The *Compagnie de la Nouvelle-France* still maintained firm control over the colony; all the personnel derived their authority from it. In the first place was its official representative, who became in fact (if not in title, as was the case with Champlain) the governor; he had his lieutenant – on 25 December 1635, as we have seen, Brasdefer de Châteaufort replaced his patron, following a prearranged mechanism. These two men had at their disposal a few domestics and some soldiers. The fur trade required a more or less specialized personnel: a commissioner general – the man who was in place when Montmagny arrived, François Derré de Gand,[75] had high standing with the Jesuits. Le Jeune was full of his praise; in mentioning his decease he used these very powerful words: "He died as he lived, that is to say as a man who seeks God in truth." There were also agents at Québec, Trois-Rivières and, probably during the summer, at Tadoussac. They took care of the tasks involved in the fur trade: barter of merchandise for pelts and storage. They also had to distribute, or sell, the goods brought in from France to the colonists. They had a few workers to assist them in their work, sailors or dockers for instance.

There was, finally, a need for interpreters to assure communication with the native people. The role of these men was among the most important in the colony; the civil and religious authorities had constant recourse to their services. Some of them have passed into history; one, Etienne Brulé, cut his way to the centre of the continent before being killed by the Huron in 1633.[76] At the time of Montmagny's arrival, the most visible, without a doubt, was Jean Nicollet, a skilful diplomat who had been able to maintain friendship between Huron and the French during the English occupation. In the autumn of 1635 he returned from a long journey into the Great Lakes region.[77]

A new colony had need of artisans – carpenters, roofers, masons, navvies. The Company had persuaded the king to grant them the right, after six years of work in Canada, to return to the mother country with the title of master. As for the other sectors – clothing, shoemaking, and the preparation of food – the little colony required only a few practitioners; but for the first two, the climate presented some challenges that were unknown in the provinces from which the first colonists came.

Entrepreneurs in agriculture were few in number; the constraints posed by land clearance, and also those of the climate (the brevity of the growing season, for example) required a numerous and robust labour force. Two family enterprises – the older one, Hébert-Couillart at Québec,[78] and the other, brand new, team of Robert Giffard[79] – seemed set for prosperity. In 1626 the Jesuits had been granted a property which was also developing well.[80] It is impossible to know the exact extent of land under cultivation but, for the above-mentioned reasons, and given the limited number of immigrants, it could not have been increasing rapidly.

But it is important to note that from these early days the system known as "seigneurial," which was going to characterize the distribution and the exploitation of the land, was already in place: at the start of 1625 for Louis Hébert, at the start of 1634 for Robert Giffard.

Alongside this, an original system was developing by which the country would be peopled, or (better put) settled: that of indentured service. A man concluded a contract with the holder of a fief by which he engaged to work for him for a certain period of time, usually three years (indentured servants were often called "thirty-six monthers") on the understanding that after this period he would be granted a piece of land, most often on the basis of a quit-rent, where he could set up with his family. Thus at the beginning of 1634 Robert Giffard recruited two men, Zacharie Cloutier and Jean Guyon,[81] who in 1637 each obtained a parcel of land, conceded to them in sub-fief.

The little colony which the king confided to the chevalier de Montmagny was still, perhaps, only the beginning of a country, but it already possessed original characteristics which distinguished it clearly from other enterprises undertaken by Europeans farther to the south, the English and the Dutch: the importance of the ecclesiastical element and the beginnings of a seigneurial system. But compared to them it had a serious handicap: the slow rate of settlement, explained by the fact that, for various reasons, France had still done little to develop the immense territory over which it had claimed sovereignty. Did the enthusiasm of Paul Le Jeune over the events of the summer of 1636 presage a change of attitude on the part of the French authorities?

3. Reasons for hope, according to Le Jeune

"I shall begin by referring to the joy with which Our Lord filled our hearts on the arrival of the fleet." It is on this cheerful note that Le

Jeune began his "Relation of the happenings in New France in the Year 1636."[82] Two observations gave him grounds for this attitude: first, that the "great preparations for war" in the mother country – the war declared against Spain in 1635 – had not prevented the sending of ships to Canada; and second, that after the widespread fear within the religious community regarding the replacement for Champlain ("we were anxious as to what zeal his successor would have for this infant Church"), the arrival of Montmagny overjoyed them. His first actions "have made us hope for everything that can be expected from a spirit filled with piety, with firmness, and with discretion." The government of the chevalier began under favourable auspices.

We should like, in the following pages, to make a brief analysis of the *Relation* of this year 1636, basically for two reasons. We believe, first, that the arrival of Montmagny was partly responsible for Le Jeune's euphoric reaction. From this point on, throughout his writing, Le Jeune intended to present his readers with the two elements that, according to him, underlay the joint effort of the missionaries and the monarchy in Canada: the conversion of the native peoples and the establishment of a solid colony. It was precisely for these two objectives that Montmagny would work.

Under these two headings, there were, according to the author, reasons for optimism. First he would show that the persons who had just arrived from France met his expectations; then he would explain that the multiplication in the mother country of expressions of support for the missionary project indicated that his appeals in the preceding *Relations* were being heard. Equally, he would note the appearance among the Amerindians of the first signs, timid still but real, of an interest in the Christian religion. Finally, he would draw a picture of the colony as he saw it at the end of the summer of 1636.

"The arrival of the fleet" aroused his enthusiasm. First there were the "two brave chevaliers" – meaning the Knights of Malta, the governor and his lieutenant. Then there were new fellow Jesuits, come to join the group already in Canada. Two noble families had joined the ships; that was an exciting event.

Montmagny's actions and demeanour upon his arrival impressed Le Jeune.[83] "If first actions are prognostications of those to come" – and citing the case of Louis XIII – "we have reason to bless God in the person of Monsieur de Montmagny, as I shall show in the course of this Relation." He disembarked from the ship in the company of two Jesuits; that was a good sign. Coming ashore, the governor saw a cross – Le Jeune called it "the Tree of our salvation" – and exclaimed: "This is the first cross that I encounter in this country, let us adore the Crucified in His image." He fell to his knees. After the Te Deum, he went to his residence – the "fortress," according to Le Jeune – and received the keys from Chateaufort. No sooner was he installed than he was asked "to be the godfather of a savage who desired baptism." He accepted with joy and "went to the cabins of these poor barbarians, followed by a smart retinue of nobles," that is to say, an entourage in formal dress.[84] This greatly impressed the natives, remarked the author: "So much scarlet, so many elegant persons under their birchbark roofs!" To the newly baptized, the chevalier gave the name of Joseph, "in honour of the holy spouse of the Virgin, patron of New France," and, during the dinner, "this noble godfather said aloud, in the presence of a distinguished company, that he had received that day the greatest honour and the most genuine satisfaction that he could have desired in New France. Are not these things that give us cause for rejoicing?" Three days later, after a palaver, the Jesuits recovered the body of a "young adult savage" whom they had baptized and who had just died after a long illness. A priest came to inform Montmagny that the funeral was about to take place. He at once left the work that he was doing – "the outline of the fortifications which he was tracing and which he is now having built" – "in order to honour us with his presence."[85]

Montmagny also insisted on being present at the departure of the canoe carrying Fathers Chastelain and Garnier to Trois-Rivières and into the Huron missions; he behaved "with matchless courtesy and affection, having three cannons fired as a salute at their departure."[86] To leave for Huronia required some courage, as Montmagny quickly learned from his contact with the missionaries and the other people whom he met.

There is another anecdote to note, which Le Jeune dated 2 July, some three weeks after the governor's arrival.[87] He was receiving the Amerindians officially for the first time, accompanied by the Jesuit and by the captain of the ship, Duplessis-Bochart. The Montagnais of Tadoussac were seeking the support of the French in the war which they wanted to wage against an enemy tribe. One argued for the sincerity of the Franco-Indian friendship, another for their need to find a protection, as one seeks a shelter against bad weather; a third, "a hoary-headed old man, talked in the ancient fashion," that is to say, in the traditional manner of his people, pointing to the gifts that they had just offered and that were supposed to incite the soldiers to fight bravely against the enemies of those who had given them. The French explained that they "had not brought any men for them,"[88] and that furthermore their idea of forming "one People with us" was pointless, since no marriages had yet been celebrated between "Savages" and "Frenchmen." Then came the fourth harangue: if your soldiers help us, they "will have no trouble in obtaining our girls in marriage"; furthermore, "you are continually asking us for our children, and you do not give us yours," in other words, reciprocity does not figure in our relations. This was Montmagny's reaction upon hearing this argument: "I do not know what a Roman senator could have answered that would have been more appropriate to the subject under discussion." Le Jeune intervened: "I replied that in France our Savages were thought to be far more obtuse [massifs][89] than they really are." The French had the last word, and refused everything. From the time of his arrival in the country, Montmagny was thus able to grasp first-hand what it meant for the French to negotiate with the Amerindians from an ambiguous position: on the one hand, a shortage of men, making military assistance illusory; on the other hand, a clear sense of superiority, inhibiting exchanges at the social level.

Montmagny did not intervene directly; he was wise enough, before involving himself, to wait until he was well-initiated into the arcana of New France, the complexities of which he was now beginning to glimpse. Nor did he interfere in the annual trade of Trois-Rivières, leaving Le Jeune and Duplessis-Bochart to take on the task of meeting there with the Huron.

From these images projected by Le Jeune there emerges a first portrait of the governor. He was a man filled with religious spirit; his vocation as a Knight of Malta was not just a façade, it informed his interests, sympathies, and actions. He was energetic – witness his readiness to start work as soon as he arrived – and benevolent, even towards the aboriginals whom he was discovering for the first time; he was discreet. Between him and the Jesuits there was a complicity, most especially in the field which was closest to their hearts, the conversion of the natives to Christianity.

In June and July six religious came to join the team that Le Jeune directed. There were four priests: Nicolas Adam,[90] whom Montmagny may have met at La Flèche between 1615 and 1618; Charles Garnier (who, incidentally, came from the same quarter of Paris as the governor);[91] Pierre Chastellain,[92] and Isaac Jogues.[93] Two lay brothers, Ambroise Caulet[94] and Louis Gobert,[95] returned to Canada to finish their novitiate.[96] Jogues would die in Iroquois country in 1646, Garnier in Huron country in 1649. They were canonized by Pius XI in 1930. As for Chastellain, he was able to return from Huronia in 1650; he spent the rest of his life at the college of Québec; and it is to him that we owe the first treatise on spirituality written by a "Canadian."[97]

Some of the other new arrivals impressed Le Jeune: "Our Savages themselves, who are not great admirers of the Universe, are astonished to see, they say, so many Captains and so many children of Captains. Among the families who are newly arrived, those of Monsieur de Repentigny and Monsieur de La Poterie, gallant Gentlemen, hold the first rank."[98]

There was, in fact, a whole clan coming out of Normandy to settle in New France:[99] Pierre Legardeur de Repentigny, his mother, his wife, his children; his brother, Charles Legardeur de Tilly and his sister Marguerite who arrived with her husband, Jacques Le Neuf de la Poterie; the brother and sister of the latter, along with his mother – we shall return to them later, because they were involved in the fur trade at the end of Montmagny's mandate.[100]

There was, then, cause for optimism in the contingent which crossed the Atlantic in the spring of 1636. But what of the others, that is to say, those who remained in the mother country? There, also, Providence was at work. "I can say, seeing so much fire, so much zeal, so much holy love, in persons so different in age, in sex, in condition, and occupation, that none other than a God can cause these thoughts, can kindle these coals, which are fed only by the aromatic woods of Paradise."[101]

The style was always inflated – publicity demanded it. This consideration – the interest of the home audience – was, in his mind, so important that a chapter was consecrated to it: "Chapter One. Of the sentiments of affection which many persons of merit entertain for New France." "Persons of merit": that was what had to be emphasized, so as to convince others to participate in this generous enterprise.

Very naturally – and fairly – pride of place went to the highest authorities in the kingdom: "the tender and noble desires of our great King for the conversion of these peoples," and "the attentions of Monseigneur the Cardinal," head of the Company. Louis II of Bourbon, Prince of Condé,[102] who was fourteen years in 1635, had written " a word from his own hand" to Father Le Jeune, to tell him of his admiration for the missionary work. Le Jeune considered him as "a new star, which begins to appear among those of the first magnitude." The prince had promised him that when he grew older his affection would be translated into concrete actions. A fine adolescent enthusiasm! The head of the richest fortune in France stayed well clear of doing anything whatsoever for New France and its missions.

It was good policy to praise the members of the *Compagnie de la Nouvelle-France*.[103] The letter which Pierre Lamy, the secretary, had sent him convinced the priest of the purity of their intentions and their disinterestedness.[104] To the thanks which the Jesuit had sent them the previous year, Lamy had the good grace to declare: "but it [this letter of thanks] will be well suited to what we desire to do, whenever God gives us the grace to carry it through." The associates were, all the same, conscious of the limits – not to say the meagreness – of their contribution.

Individuals and religious societies were now taking an interest in New France. An annuity donated by the Marquis de Gamaches[105] was assigned to the college which opened in Québec in 1635.[106] Someone had the idea of "founding a seminary for young Hurons. Oh holy thought!"[107] Richelieu's own niece, Madame de Combalet, touched by the *Relation* of 1635, promised to contribute to the foundation of a hospital.[108] Many religious in various congregations (hospitallers, teachers) showed great eagerness to offer their services for the missionary cause.

So the *Relation* had won over a certain audience in France. Le Jeune saw in that a great "affection for the advancement of the glory of God and for the conversion of the poor Savages."

Other positive elements appeared, this time on the ground in America: the native communities were beginning to evolve. Conversions were more numerous in the last twelve months (115)[109] than in the year that ended in 1635 (22).[110] But more noteworthy than the raw figures was a perceptible change in attitude,[111] in two respects: "The first is that they are not angry[112] with us for baptizing their sick children; indeed, they even summon us to do this. The second is, that the more aged are even beginning to wish to die Christians, asking for baptism when they are sick, in order not to go down into the fires with which they are threatened." Thus the threat of the fires of Hell gave pause for reflection to adults or the parents of children; but for the most part the people being baptized were still the dying.

The native people were coming to appreciate the charity of the missionaries.[113] Thus a captain addressed his guests in the presence of Father Buteux, who was staying among them:

> These people [the Jesuits] have great knowledge; they are charitable, they are kind to us in our necessity .... However they never ask anything in return; but, on the contrary, they feed our sick people, while restoring them to health.[114]

Little by little they were losing "the fear that they had of baptism;[115] they even handed over, for the purpose of forming them in the Christian life, "some of their girls, which seems to me an act of God." Sometimes they were willing to discuss religion, an evident proof for him that a serious questioning was now taking shape on the very essence of the religious phenomenon.

But the forces of resistance were still hard at work. For Le Jeune, this meant above all those customs which he called "pseudo-religious"[116] – the belief in Manitou, for example, a sort of invisible power to which were attributed the things which the human mind could not explain. Only the Devil could suggest such fooleries.[117] But there were men who came forward to profit by this belief – and to exploit their countrymen. These were the medicine men, and on that subject his vocabulary was rich: mountebanks, healers, doctors, interpreters of dreams or (more unkindly) imposters, charlatans, false healers, profiteers.

Other traits in the Amerindian culture bothered the Jesuits: the "excessive" love which, according to them, the natives bore towards their offspring – refusing to let their children go into the seminaries – or, again, their "human respect," that is to say, the force of social pressure. Speaking of the father of a child whom he had baptized on his deathbed, Le Jeune had this comment: he did not have "enough courage to embrace and profess the truths that he approved in his heart."[118] More severe by far were their judgments on the cruelty practised towards prisoners taken from enemy tribes. Montmagny himself, shortly after his arrival, exclaimed at this "barbarism insupportable to our eyes."[119] Like the Jesuits, he shared the prejudices of the French, who considered the horrible punishments inflicted on regicides or sorcerers, and even the fate reserved to galley slaves, to be reasonable, but found certain local warrior practices to be atrocious.

Despite everything, the forces of resistance were beginning to abate – as proved by the number of conversions. To what was this due? To several factors, according to Le Jeune. Most importantly, divine intervention: the solemn vow which the Jesuits had pronounced in honour of the Immaculate Conception, on 8 December 1635,[120] had been heard in heaven. The personnel which the Company had hitherto sent out collaborated fully in the work of the missionaries.[121] In France itself, "an infinity of the purest souls pray to God for the savages."[122]

The fourth heading in Paul Le Jeune's presentation was the state of the colony. Here, again, optimism prevailed; and despite a situation that was actually rather gloomy, he succeeded in finding arguments to justify an almost rapturous enthusiasm: "I see an Aurora emerging from the profound darkness of the night, which, lighting up the surface of the earth with its golden rays, finally changes into that great Ocean of light brought in by the Sun."[123] Central to his reasoning was the contrast between the dark years (1628–1633) and what he had witnessed since 1633: regular arrivals[124] (though far from the quotas that the company had set in 1627!).

However, his description of New France, if we know how to read between the lines, was nuanced and realistic. His exposé can be broken down into four propositions: the country's resources were very abundant, though there was not enough manpower to exploit it; the population was growing; it was living in security; it was enjoying a certain quality of life.

The land was fertile, producing the same crops as the country north of the Loire; but self-sufficiency was not yet assured, though it would be once there were enough labourers. Le Jeune calculated that a man in good health could clear an acre and a half a year. There was as yet no exploitation of the food supplies that hunting and fishing could provide; he made a special point of the migratory birds, "geese, bustards and ducks," which in their season invaded the skies to the very gates of Québec, and of the fish in their prodigious numbers and variety. "But there are not yet enough people here to gather in [these] riches."[125]

Only one thing was running relatively well (though with significant fluctuations), and that was the fur trade. But the company "reserves this trade"; in other words, it was not, in 1636, open to individuals.

Could one live really safely in this territory? the readers asked.[126] The fortifications at the two posts of Québec and Trois-Rivières had just been improved – especially those of the former, the plans of which Montmagny altered shortly after his arrival.[127]

"As to the inhabitants of New France, they have multiplied beyond our hopes," wrote the Jesuit; but he hastened to add that his point of comparison was the year 1632. At that time, when the French returned to Canada, only six or seven persons remained (the family of Louis Hébert). If in August 1636 the count was around 400, that was quite a considerable increase.

The colony enjoyed a certain quality of life: a peaceful climate prevailed "thanks to our ecclesiastical and civil policy." The Jesuits' ministry was experiencing a clear success. Their catechism lessons were bringing together not only the children, but also a number of adults. There was the obligatory mention of the college: "A great number of very respectable persons can assure us that they would never have crossed the Ocean to come to New France, if they had not known that there were persons there capable of directing their consciences, of procuring their salvation, and of instructing their children in virtue and in the knowledge of letters."[128]

Le Jeune hoped that his description of New France would incite many people to cross the ocean, but he was careful to make them understand that these first years would not be easy, and he included a highly realistic chapter which he entitled: "Some advice for those who desire to cross over into New France."[129] In spite of all he remained optimistic, and ended the chapter with this exuberant phrase: this land would "someday be a terrestial Paradise, if Our Lord continues to bestow upon it His blessings, both material and spiritual."

It remains, in closing this series of reflections that has taken us from the heart of the Mediterranean to the banks of the Saint Lawrence – or, to put it better, from a heavily urbanized island to a colony still in its infancy (though "full of promise" according to the Jesuits) – to return to the question of what this year 1636, which changed the course of his life, represented for Montmagny. It divides into four periods of comparable length (between six and twelve weeks).

Between his nomination, at the beginning of January at the latest,[130] and his departure from Paris, which can be placed around 20 March, there was a preparation phase: choosing and collecting what he was to bring by way of personal objects, such as clothes, furniture, books; informing himself about Canada – already some publications were available,[131] and he could consult the Jesuits, including that Brother Caulet who had just started his novitiate after staying two years in Québec; holding discussions with the authorities of the company to find out what they expected of him. Only one act has come down to us from this period: the general and special power of attorney that he concluded before a notary on 18 March, empowering his two brothers, Louis and Adrien, "to undertake in his name" all necessary "pleadings and oppositions," to receive all sums of money destined for him, as well as the emoluments arising from "his office of lieutenant general for the King in New France."[132]

He must have left for Dieppe one or two days later, that is, 19 or 20 March, if embarkation took place on the 30th.[133] The voyage lasted a little more than ten weeks, which was rather long, but does not seem to have involved any disagreeable incidents. A letter from Father Garnier emphasizes the climate of piety which prevailed on the flagship, the *Saint-Joseph*. Two Masses were celebrated every morning "except

12 or 13 times" (too many waves, no doubt), in the stateroom of the commander of the fleet, Charles Du Plessis-Bochart, for whose conduct, like that of Montmagny, the priest had praise; their devotion and their charity impressed him. There were also catechism lessons and readings from the lives of the saints; one might have called it a floating convent, so much so that the sailors made an agreement among themselves, to "punish each other when any oath escaped them."[134]

Once landed, he spent three months in his capital. We know already how he passed his time: in works of fortification, town planning, first contacts with the native peoples, introduction to the people of Québec – the Jesuits, collaborators such as Derré de Gand or the interpreters, and, most certainly, the colonists, his immediate subjects. The *Relation* adds that he took an interest in the Canadian fauna; the moose seem to have impressed him greatly,[135] and he had some of them captured with an eye to domesticating them.

In the autumn he finally decided to visit his colony, before snow and ice impeded the movement of men and materials. He asked Father Le Jeune to accompany him,[136] doubtless because of the latter's knowledge of the territory and of indigenous languages. This suggests that the Jesuit had considerable influence on him. They visited Trois-Rivières, the mouth of the Iroquois River,[137] and the Montréal region with its network of lakes, rivers, rapids, and islands – the account even called one of these (now Île-Jésus) the "île de Montmagny."[138] Next they visited the eastern part of the colony and went as far as Cap Tourmente, where the Company maintained a farm. There, ten days of bad weather delayed their return to the capital, which would have occurred at the end of October or the very beginning of November.

And so Montmagny came back to Québec to take up his winter quarters, so to speak. He would now for the first time experience the dead season, and have the leisure to mull over the management of this extravagant territory which the king had confided to him.

ILLUSTRATION 3

Arms of the Huault de Bernay in 1714, "the only survivors of Huault de Vayres and of Montmagny." The had adopted the device "Me virtus, non praeda trahit," which can be translated as "It is virtue, not the lure of gain, which distinguishes me from other men." Bibliothèque nationale, Paris (DB, 362/1bis, dossier 9421)

ILLUSTRATION 4

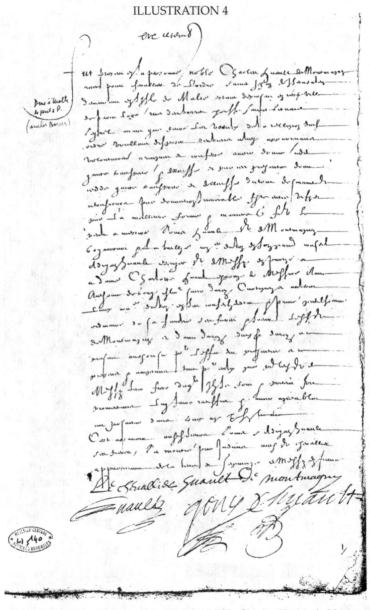

Donation of his goods, 19 December 1623, by "noble Charles Huault de Montmagny, received as Knight of the Order of Saint John of Jerusalem," to his brother and sister, in exchange for an annual pension. AN de France, Paris, Minutier central (notarial acts), Étude LI, liasse 140

CHAPTER 6

Onontio

"Onontio, your name shall be great throughout the earth."[1] It was in these terms that, in his farewell address, the Iroquois ambassador who came to Trois-Rivières in the summer of 1645 saluted the governor of Québec. This nickname had been given to Montmagny by the Hurons, whose language was very close to that of the Iroquois. The allies of the French had picked up the habit of giving them names that were both conceptually significant and accessible to their phonetic patterns. This is how Father Lalemant[2] described the phenomenon:

> The reason for these nicknames is that since the Savages cannot ordinarily pronounce either our names or our surnames, not having in their language the use of several consonants which are found in them, they do what they can to come close to them, and if they cannot succeed, they substitute words used in their country which they can easily pronounce and which have some relation either to our names or to their meaning.

Onontio, literally translated, signified Mons Magnus,[3] or Montmagny. And this name would afterwards serve for all the governors of the French regime. The Amerindians, according to the *Relations*, even attached poetic connotations to this name, "High Mountain." Onontio has "a voice of thunder," one of them commented;[4] for another, "he is a great friend of the Sun," and this gave him supernatural powers.[5]

In a different tone, the Jesuits themselves used every occasion to exalt the most important person in the land; we have already seen several examples of this, and here is another, which pertains to the subject which we will now address: "These words [of a native of Sillery] were highly consoling to Monsieur the Governor, whom I would gladly call the Knight of the Holy Spirit, so much do I see him given to holy and courageous actions, filled with the spirit of God."[6] Here, Le Jeune was evoking the entire domain of relations with the native peoples. In the governor's conduct he perceived attitudes and positions that were close to his own; he approved of them, but in his own style.

We now wish to address this important subject, and to describe, as well as the sources allow us,[7] Montmagny's activities among the nations, both friendly and unfriendly, that were carried out in the territory of New France.[8]

By virtue of his mandate, as defined by the commission of 1645,[9] he was to "take care of the colony," that is, to assure "its conservation and security;" his priority being therefore to see to the protection of his French subjects, surrounded as they were by numerically superior populations. For this purpose he had to preserve alliances already established and defend colonists and allies against the tribes which, since the incursions of Champlain at the beginning of the century, had become hostile.

Another task was assigned him: "to protect trade." He was, in fact, the representative of a commercial company to which the king had given the colony as a seigneurie. According to the statutes approved by Louis XIII and Richelieu in 1627, the fur trade was closely tied to the peopling of the territory and the conversion of the natives. For the Jesuits, this last objective was undoubtedly of first importance, and they never tired of recalling the fact.

Nothing illustrates this better than the meeting which took place at Trois-Rivières on 22 July 1635 (a year before Montmagny's arrival) between the Hurons who had come downriver to trade and the French authorities. Champlain "told them, through an interpreter, that if they wished to preserve and strengthen the friendship that they had with the French, they must receive our faith and worship the God that we worshipped." This adherence would benefit them in every way; notably, it would seal the Franco-Huron alliance: "The French will go in goodly numbers to their country; they will marry their daughters once they are Christians; they will teach all their people to make hatchets, knives and other things which are very necessary to them; and for this purpose they [the Hurons] must next year onwards bring many of their young boys, whom we will lodge comfortably, and feed, instruct and cherish as though they were our younger brothers.[10] And Le Jeune added a revealing detail: "I suggested these thoughts to Monsieur the Governor, which he approved, and even amplified, with a thousand praises and a thousand expressions of affection towards our Society." There could be no clearer evidence of the influence of the Jesuits in the government of the colony. And, as though to provide further proof, Le Jeune mentioned that in his speech the company's commissioner, Charles Duplessis-Bochart, took exactly the same line as did Champlain.[11]

These precedents clearly showed Montmagny the path that he must follow. In the same way the choice of alliances was imposed on him; it was Champlain who had made common cause with the Algonquin[12] and the Huron,[13] by that fact creating what has been called the Laurentian coalition,[14] but automatically alienating the Iroquois confederation, traditional enemy of these nations. During Montmagny's administration this antagonism would assume hitherto unequalled proportions, threaten the very existence of his colony, and result in the dispersal of the most important group among France's allies, the Huron.

To study the vicissitudes of this adventure, we shall proceed chronologically. The first period (1636–1640), which can be qualified as "a highly relative peace," is followed by a second (1641–1645) which was, rather, a time of sporadic hostilities; and by a third period (1646–1648) which began with a fragile peace, only to turn into permanent guerilla warfare.

1.   A highly relative peace (1636–1640)

The new governor's period of adaptation was one of relative calm, allowing him to become familiar with the diverse elements that made up the native checkerboard. There were no serious incidents on the Saint Lawrence or the Ottawa River. There was only one significant battle on the shores of the Great Lakes: a brilliant Huron victory, which would, however, have considerable repercussions, since it moved the Iroquois to adopt European weapons. This modernization of their military equipment by the Amerindians was one of the new developments that would mark the middle decades of the seventeenth century in Canada. Still more serious, perhaps, was the reappearance of a scourge of a biological order, the "contagion"[15] which had first appeared in 1634. The Amerindian mind was quick to identify those responsible: the Europeans, and above all the Jesuits, who, because they used writing, were deemed to be dangerous "magicians." Their lives were often threatened. At the same time there were events of a political and economic order – the growing shortage of furs in Iroquois country, the result of increased demand by the Dutch who were now settled to the south of the territory of New France. And in this territory, at the same time, innovations appeared, namely the installation of services for the native peoples, a "reduction" at Sillery, a hospital, and two schools.

This inquiry will begin with a look, first, at the French allies, and, after that, at the Iroquois phenomenon. This order of priority corresponds to that of Montmagny's preoccupations; it would change in the subsequent periods.

As far as the new governor's relations with the allies are concerned, there are two stages to deal with: first, a consideration of his behaviour in the many meetings he had with them from the end of 1636; then, a study of his attitudes regarding the activities directly related to conversion: sedentarization, hospitalization, and education.

From the beginning of his mandate, it seems, Montmagny chose to collaborate actively with the Jesuits in the promotion of Christianity. On 26 November, when they inaugurated their catechism lessons "for the young savages," he promised "to reward those who should remember well what had been taught them, which he did not fail to do."[16] A few days later, when some Algonquins came to set up camp close to the fort of Québec, he decided to give them a feast to celebrate Franco-Algonquin friendship. In response to the friendly remarks of some of the elders of the group, he expressed astonishment that "living as they did face to face with the French for so long a time, they had not yet accepted their faith." Then "he asked them if what was taught them was bad, pressing them strongly on this point."[17] He was, above all, appealing to their intelligence: if it was bad, they must show it to be so; if it was good, they must act accordingly. In their response they were equal to the occasion: until then, they said, nobody had mastered their tongue sufficiently to give a clear explanation of the Christian truths. They promised to meet with the Jesuits in the following weeks.

The year 1637 gave Montmagny the occasion to become acquainted with three other nations, the Montagnais, the Abenaki, and the Huron. On 24 April, a "captain" [a chief] from Tadoussac[18] who was leaving on an expedition against the Iroquois, passed by Québec to greet the governor who offered him some gifts and sent him to the Jesuits "to hear something about our holy faith."[19] This was becoming a habit with Montmagny – some weeks later he would do the same with an Algonquin captain. He suggested to him that he and his men meet with Father Le Jeune, telling them that "if they did [what he taught them] they would learn the secret of preserving their nation and of diminishing the number of deaths."[20] In fact we note that in the speeches of the natives, the theme of their high rates of mortality compared to those of the French – the epidemics of which more will be said – was becoming insistent.

It was with a far more precise request that a group of Montagnais came knocking at the governor's door on 27 April.[21] Champlain had promised them that he would establish a "bourgade" [fortified village] at Trois-Rivières, where they could "stop," or in other words, settle down. Many were now ready to do this – and there were reasons enough. They realized that in addition to the Iroquois they had another enemy, ignorance. Furthermore, they said – and the formula is striking – "the country is failing them": the French presence had driven the game far into the hinterland. The two interpreters confirmed that Champlain had, in fact, promised to reserve them an enclave as soon as the post at Trois-Rivières was opened, an opening which had taken place in the summer of 1634. But Father Le Jeune intervened in the exchange. He had been a witness to this promise of Champlain's. He reminded them that they had forgotten the essential clause: they had been promised the help that they spoke of on condition "that they would settle down," but also – and it was this that interested the Jesuit above all – "that they would give over their children to be instructed and reared in the Christian faith." Montmagny took up the point; he was ready to "abide by these conditions on their side, provided they would carry out those which concerned them." But, as has been explained already, the aboriginal people were reluctant to abandon their children; and in any case the affair fell through for lack of means to finance the establishment of a "seminary" at Trois-Rivières.

The presence at Québec in July of a group of Abenaki [from Acadia, allies of the Algonquin] allowed Montmagny to discover other facets of the Amerindian reality.[22] The visitors wished to go to Trois-Rivières to meet with their friends; he suspected them of seeking to divert the fur trade to other markets – the English colonists of the Atlantic coast. So he forbade them to go farther. They feigned an eastward departure, but in fact went upriver. Learning this, the governor alerted his subordinate at Trois-Rivières, who searched their baggage. There were no furs, only arquebuses, which he confiscated at once.[23] Two new elements – indeed two dangers – became clear to Montmagny: the diversion of the sole source of revenue for the colony, and the employment by the Amerindians of firearms, which until then had assured the military preponderance of the Europeans.

Around the end of July, the chevalier and Le Jeune left for Trois-Rivières to meet the Hurons who were to arrive there at any time.[24] Even before they got there, they were met with two pieces of bad news. The Hurons had decided to withhold from the priests the boys whom they had previously agreed to confide to them to be formed in the

Christian way of life in a seminary. Montmagny thought that the best policy was to encourage these people to leave their country and to come and settle close to the French habitations; his desire would be fulfilled thirteen years later, but in circumstances very different from those that he imagined. At the same time a canoe arrived at the beach with Father Pierre Pijart aboard, returning from the mission to report two discomfiting facts: the slow pace of Christianization, and the disaster represented by "contagion" in Huronia. Montmagny could witness this second reality with his own eyes: the man who paddled the canoe that brought the Jesuit down was stricken as he disembarked; he was baptized after being rapidly instructed; he gave gifts to the governor, and died a few hours later.

On 6 August there was an Iroquois alert that will be recounted in due time. The skilful handling of operations by Montmagny made them turn back – but only for the time being.

Before returning to his capital, the governor personally conducted Father Pijart to the canoe which took him back to Huronia, and he offered gifts to his crew.[25] Doubtless he wanted the gesture to mark his admiration for the courage of this missionary who was about to risk his life to preach the gospel.

By the end of the summer of 1637 Montmagny had gone through the essential stages of his initiation to "nations" that he doubtless considered more "barbarous"[26] than those against whom he had fought in the Mediterranean. What he had been told, what he had read in the *Relations* that had appeared between 1632 and 1635, took on concrete form. The next three years also brought with them events which are worth examining, because they allow us to complete the picture which we have started to paint.

The Jesuits have provided numerous details about Montmagny's attitudes towards the aboriginal people who lived in his vicinity. Two things stand out: he did not disdain to associate with them – indeed, far from it; and he did not miss any occasion to make an impression on them to educate them.

A Montagnais of Trois-Rivières "who was camping" close to the fort of Québec with his companions in the autumn of 1637 had himself inscribed in the catechumenate. Shortly afterwards he fell dangerously ill. The governor sent him choice meats from his own larder; he assisted at his baptism which took place on 3 December, the feast day of Saint Francis Xavier. His lieutenant, the chevalier de Lisle, was godfather. In the following weeks he went twice to visit him in his cabin. The poor man recovered enough to follow his companions to the hunt in March and April. He made his First Communion on the eve of Corpus Christi. Montmagny insisted that he should carry the dais with him in the following day's procession. "It was a spectacle agreeable to both heaven and earth," commented Le Jeune, "to see this neophyte – covered with a truly Christian modesty under his fine savage's robe – bearing the canopy in the procession, with the foremost person in the land." The salutes of muskets and cannon accompanied this celebration. Montmagny agreed, a little while later, to be godfather to one of his daughters.[27]

Shortly after her arrival in the country in August 1639, Madame de La Peltrie, the benefactress of the Ursulines who had also accompanied them to Québec, came to the church to take communion; "she saw at the Holy Table only Monsieur the Governor, and some Savages who were performing their devotions this day."[28] This gesture of solidarity with the native peoples was customary to him, noted Le Jeune a year later in his *Relation*: "The good examples of the chief men of this colony influence them powerfully; Monsieur our Governor sometimes approaches the holy table with them; he honours them by his presence, coming to visit them at Saint-Joseph [Sillery]. Having learned that these neophytes were to receive communion on the feast of our father and patriarch, Saint Ignatius [31 July], he came to perform his devotions with us in our chapel of Saint-Joseph."[29] Without any testimony coming directly from the man himself, we have to take that of the Jesuit and form a double conclusion: Montmagny was not lacking in devotion, and he hoped that his example would have a beneficial effect on his native subjects.

It is doubtless in the same perspective that we must consider the displays of brilliance with which he punctuated the life of the community – salvoes at the arrival and departure of missionaries, or on great feast days, or to mark some event that he considered important.

When, at the end of July 1639, news arrived of the birth of the dauphin, Montmagny hastened to celebrate this happy event with a fireworks display. Le Jeune's poetic pen was aroused: "Fireworks were sent flying towards Heaven, to fall in showers of gold, to shine like stars; fiery serpents ran everywhere."[30] Then, on 15 August, there was a great procession – the native people from the neighbouring countryside were there. Montmagny led the French. He had given the natives the six sets of clothes which the king had sent for them. He had the cannon fired when the line moved off. A feast followed.[31] In his eyes, as in those of the Jesuits, all this display was meant to inculcate a sense of authority and therefore of fidelity to the monarch, the lieutenant of God, in people who had nothing similar in their mental universe.

Perhaps more important still, and richer in significance, was the ceremony which he organized in the spring of the following year [1640]. Three Amerindian marriages were to be celebrated at Sillery. He ordered that the ceremony should take place in Québec itself, his purpose being to demonstrate the importance which Christians attached to the sacrament of marriage and to illustrate in a symbolic way the harmony which ought to exist between the French and the native peoples. It was a celebration: the brides were dressed by French ladies, Madame de La Peltrie at their head; the bridegrooms were fitted out in the clothes sent by the king the previous year. "Our leading Frenchmen conducted them with honour to the Church." Montmagny "wished himself to make a magnificent feast for all those invited to the nuptials."[32]

Some weeks later – more exactly, 15 August – he arranged for the staging of a "tragi-comedy," to the great astonishment of Le Jeune, who did not believe that "such handsome apparel and such good actors" could have been found in Québec. His secretary, Martial Piraube, directed the whole operation and played the principal role. For the benefit of the natives, still barely capable of understanding the French language, Montmagny had the idea of asking the Jesuits to add something to the spectacle that would make a strong impression on them.

> We had the soul of an unbeliever pursued by two demons, who finally hurled it into a hell that vomited flames; the struggles, the cries, and shrieks of this soul and those of the demons, who spoke in the Algonquin tongue, affected the hearts of some of them so deeply, that a Savage told us, two days afterward, that he had been greatly frightened that night by a horrible dream. "I saw," said he, "a hideous gulf, from which flames and demons came forth. It seemed to me that they tried to destroy me, and this filled me with great terror." In short, these poor folk are coming from day to day to surrender to Jesus Christ.[33]

Thus the Company had given Montmagny the task of maintaining friendship with the allies – those whose proximity threw them into close contact with the colonists, and those whom the economic ties created at the beginning of the century had bound to them. As we have just seen, he knew how to make himself available to meet them; he tried to assist them, as far as the paltry resources at his disposal permitted.

The unity which can be observed in the actions of his first years in New France arose from a position that, in keeping with his own religious vocation, he adopted at the outset: constant support of the work of the Jesuits – in concrete terms, the promotion by all means of the Christianization of the indigenous people. This, understandably, was the aspect that received the most attention in the *Relations* – by Le Jeune certainly (in the *Relation* of 1637),[34] but also by others, such as Charles Lalemant.[35]

And it should be remembered that, in order to realize this objective, various formulas had been proposed. Le Jeune listed them clearly and concisely: "Now, I must say in passing that we have here four great works bound together in a single knot: the settlement of the savages [sedentarization], the hospital, the seminary for little savage boys and the seminary for little savage girls. These last three depend upon the first. Let these barbarians remain nomads, and their sick will die in the woods, and their children will never enter the seminary. Render them sedentary, and you will fill these three institutions, which all have need of powerful assistance."[36] Thus it was the constant preoccupation of the priests during these years: to "reduce" or "settle" the native peoples of the Saint Lawrence valley.[37] The experience of the Paraguay "reductions" was on all lips; they had begun in 1609, and Montmagny must have heard tell of them at La Flèche, as we have pointed out earlier. It was constantly on the minds of the Canadian missionaries. In answer to a letter expressing doubts on the possibility of ever really converting the indigenous people of Canada, Le Jeune said this: "My answer to this is that if he who wrote this letter has read the Relation of what is occurring in Paraguay, he has seen what shall some day happen in New France."[38] In his report to the superior of Québec, Father Le Mercier explained how in conversation he had informed his Huron hearers of the positive results of the work of the Jesuits in Latin America: "The argument that satisfies them best is that which we make from our own broad experience of idolators and infidels, such as those of recent date in Paraguay, who have finally opened their eyes to the truth of the Gospel."[39]

As we have seen, Montmagny's nomination to Québec had inspired one of his hospitaller confrères, Noël Brulart de Sillery, to contribute financially to the missionary effort. The latter's first idea was to found a seminary for young aboriginal girls. In the spring of 1637 he sent workers to Québec to commence construction of a building. But at this time Le Jeune believed that the first priority was to encourage the natives to settle in a village, the permanence of which would restrain their "vagabond wanderings." So he decided, after consulting with the benefactor – who accepted this change – to divert the workers to the preparation of a reduction in the neighbourhood of Québec.

The spot chosen – the bay of Kamiskoua-Ouangachit, seven kilometres from the fort at Québec – was well known to the native people, who traditionally went there in the summer to camp and to fish for eels.[40] In July the work of clearing and construction began. A Montagnais chief, Noël Nagabamat,[41] immediately showed interest in the project. The following spring he was permitted to come with his people to settle at Sillery – the name that was soon given to the village. Another chief, Negaskoumit, did the same.

The foundation of the reduction can be dated to 14 April 1638, the day on which Fathers Le Jeune and De Quen took possession of their residence. Once the Company had given its approval, Montmagny officially conceded the lands, on 19 February 1640.[42] Slowly the village took shape, with little cabins rising around the houses. When Le Jeune wrote his report to the provincial in September 1640, "four little lodgings" had just been built for the natives, at a cost of 400 écus. He did not dare to comment on the meagerness of the effort – all that was permitted by the gifts from the mother country; he simply commented: "Alas! It is only one throw of the dice in France, or a simple meal."[43] All the same, the project was under way.

Montmagny took great interest in the reduction and went there often. The day after the arrival of the religious sisters at the beginning of August 1639, he put his boat at their disposal, so that they could go and visit it.[44] In the spring of 1640 he lent a boat to a group of Montagnais who wanted to settle in.[45]

When the settlement had taken on a certain size, it was necessary to provide a form of local administration. The Montagnais held a council, then the group of those who were Christians had the idea of having the governor name "some Captains to lead them in their small affairs."[46] He preferred to call together the more "important people" – Christians as well as pagans – and, after extolling the benefits of sedentarization and those of Christian matrimonial practices, suggested to them (no doubt taking the example of French towns) that they elect their leaders. The election, by secret ballots, was in actual fact supervised by the Jesuits, and it was decided that those elected should be named for the period of a year. Then the people went "to entreat [the governor] to authorize those whom they had elected." He gladly granted their wish, simply adding a consideration of a theoretical nature that they could grasp: as he had the duty of maintaining the authority of a father of the family in his own house, in the same way "he would make sure, since they required it, that their countrymen obeyed whatever they decided among themselves."

On 9 July 1640, Montmagny presided there at the blessing of the foundation stone of a hospital.[47] The Duchesse d'Aiguillon, who financed the enterprise, had asked that the building be constructed in a place inhabited by indigenous people. Sillery was solely dedicated to that. The hospital sisters entered it the following 1 December. And this brings us to a second preoccupation of the Jesuits: hospital services.

The missionaries were not long in discovering structural deficiencies in Amerindian medical practice, and they soon faced a biological reality of massive dimensions, the "contagion," caused, as noted, by viruses brought from Europe – though, given the current state of knowledge, the immigrants of the day could not know this.

Native medicine comprised two approaches. The first consisted of treatments which the priests called "natural." "They have natural medicines which can be called interior and exterior."[48] The internal medicines were potions derived from certain herbs – the *Relation* called them "simples"; they ground up and boiled branches of cedar or pine, certain roots, and wild sorrel. As for the external medicines, these were superficial incisions. Often the open wounds were filled with ointments prepared with the same ingredients as the aforementioned potions.

The second approach was that of the medicine man. "Among these people there are men who presume to command the rain and the winds; ... others [who claim] to restore health to the sick, with remedies that bear no relation to the sicknesses."[49] Le Jeune treated them as "cheats" and "quacks," when he did not accuse them of being tools of Satan.[50]

Another failing the Jesuits denounced: the native people did not isolate their sick: "The Huron, no matter what plague or contagion they may have, live among their sick with the same indifference and sharing of everything as if they were in perfect health. As a result, in a few days almost all those in the cabin of the deceased found themselves infected; then the sickness spread from house to house, from village to village, and, finally, throughout the country."[51]

It is not difficult to guess the conclusion that the missionaries drew from these several observations: that there was an urgent need to bring hospital services into New France. They were certain that the natives would greatly appreciate this measure; their bodies would be infinitely better treated than before, they thought, but – what seemed most important of all – their souls would derive profit from it; the baptism of the dying would take place without hindrance; and those who recovered would be more receptive to the gospel message.

There is no doubt that Montmagny, who during his novitiate in Malta had been initiated in the medical practices of the day, approved of this idea of the missionaries – his readiness to back the hospital sisters who arrived in the summer of 1639 amply demonstrates this.

What was more, when he arrived in New France a sad reality was already facing him: epidemic disease.[52] A type of influenza ran through the colony from August 1636 to June 1637, from which the Amerindians all suffered considerably and the French very little. Note also that this had been preceded by a wave of measles between June 1634 and the spring of 1635. And even before the devastating effects of these contagious illnesses had been obliterated, a third appeared: smallpox, from the summer of 1639 to the autumn of 1640.

In fact, these epidemics seem to have struck particularly hard at the Huron nation, who were less nomadic than the people of the Saint Lawrence River valley. It has been calculated that between 1634 and 1640 more than half of this population was mown down by the disease.[53] And as it was principally in Huronia that the Jesuits had decided to follow a systematic effort of Christianization – living in the very heart of the villages – many people who did not favour converting to the Christian religion saw them as responsible for these scourges. In Québec there was fear for their lives. Montmagny had had the idea, in the spring of 1640, of sending soldiers "to know how things stood."[54] However, since it was impossible for him to send a good-sized party into Huronia without dangerously reducing his garrison, he resigned himself to another solution. He replaced the soldiers with a delegation made up of the two Huron seminarians who were then studying with the Jesuits, and Guillaume Couture and Father Antoine Daniel. Truly, there was fear of "a general conspiracy throughout the country." The catastrophe did not take place, but a few missionaries had to put up with some affronts. The perpetrators of these acts, turning up in the convoy of 1640, were denounced to Montmagny, who saw fit to punish them as an example.[55] These calamities made the improvement of sick care ever more urgent. The foundation of a hospital close to Québec brought a first solution to this need.

The appeal launched by the first *Relations* had been heard. Richelieu's own niece, the Duchesse d'Aiguillon, had offered to finance the enterprise. The hospital sisters of the Hôtel-Dieu of Dieppe had enthusiastically agreed to furnish the first recruits. The official contract of establishment dates from 16 August 1637.[56] A place at the Québec site was reserved for them by the Company, as well as a piece of land close by, which later became a seigneurie.

The first three religious arrived in Québec on 1 August 1639. As soon as he heard the news, Montmagny had his personal boat decorated and sent to transport them from the ship to the quay in the lower town. He was there to greet them, accompanied by Father Le Jeune. He invited them to lunch at his table, and at suppertime had food from his own pantry served to them in the house, not far from the fort, which the Company had placed at their disposal. The following day, as we have already mentioned, he sent them, still with the use of his boat, to Sillery to meet the people for whose well-being they had crossed the Atlantic.

And they arrived precisely at the moment when an epidemic was breaking out.[57] The sick room in their temporary residence was soon full. The Jesuits' wish was fulfilled: all who died there received baptism before expiring. It was possible to save a few. At the beginning of 1640, Montmagny acceded to the request of the inhabitants of Sillery who wanted the hospital to be built in their reduction – thus meeting the express desire of the Duchesse d'Aiguillon.[58]

And so it was that, with the approval of the governor and through his facilitation of all the formalities, the religious established themselves amidst the native people, some kilometres from the centre of the capital. Monsieur de Puiseaux,[59] a colonist who lived close by the village, lent them his house until the opening of the hospital, which took place in December 1640.

The priests' third preoccupation was education, the two other activities – sedentarization and hospitalization – acting as an underpinning for the teaching of the truths of Christianity. It is well known that, from the end of the sixteenth century, teaching had become a specialty of the Society. Le Jeune had been a professor at the colleges of Rennes and of Bourges; afterwards he had taught rhetoric at Caen, before becoming preacher at Dieppe – and it was from there that he left in 1632 to direct the mission of Canada. Montmagny, who had studied with the Jesuits (we have already noted that for three years [1615 to 1618] he was the fellow student of the same Paul Le Jeune) could not have been better disposed to support all the efforts made in this direction.

Three things must be distinguished here: catechesis (that is to say collective or individual catechism lessons), and two institutions which we shall call "seminaries," one for boys and the other for girls.

The catechism lessons inaugurated at Québec in the autumn of 1636 with, of course, the full collaboration of Montmagny, continued throughout the winter. The governor's enthusiasm never let up. "Monsieur our Governor took so much satisfaction in, and so thoroughly approved of this instruction, that, after making sure that I was provided with little presents to give them, he told me several times that he would be displeased if he found out that I had spared anything which was in his power, to keep up this most pious work."[60]

In his personal dealings with the native people, he never missed an occasion to press them to meet with the priests. Here, for example, is the case of Makheabichtichiou.[61] This Montagnais chief had desired to enter "into the good graces of our governor"; the governor directed him to Le Jeune. The latter's commentary is very revealing both of his own mentality and of Montmagny's manner.

> Now as Monsieur de Montmagny, our governor, is rich in piety, courtesy, and magnanimity, and as he knows how to use these weapons efficiently, he gave this savage a warm welcome, but in such a way as to make him understand that he only granted his special friendship to those who took instruction in our faith. It is thus that we should use our influence and credit for the glory of the sovereign King, and not for our own vanity. This savage now had a flea in his ear. As they honoured the great Captain of the French, he desired to enter even further into his good graces.[62]

At the time of his arrival in New France in 1632, Le Jeune had undertaken an original experiment, to teach the "ABCs" as he called it,[63] to native children. Straight away he had "two scholars," one "little savage ... and one little negro." The following year he welcomed two more. Since the experiment seemed to him to be conclusive, he decided to open what he grandiosely called a "seminary."[64] In fact, in the *Relation* of 1636 he wrote: "See already, by the grace of God, a Huron seminary begun."[65] In his enthusiasm, he announced that a similar seminary would be founded right in Huronia, and that the Montagnais would also have their own (he was probably thinking of Trois-Rivières). He had Montmagny's unconditional support: "Our governor has shown it all possible zeal." In fact, three chapters of the *Relation* of 1637 describe the vicissitudes of the early days.[66] In the summer of 1636 the missionaries to the Hurons had recruited twelve youths whom their parents considered ready to leave. When it came time to board the canoes to leave for Trois-Rivières, only one appeared: "When it came to separating the children from their mothers, the extraordinary tenderness which the savage women have for their children put a halt to everything, and nearly smothered our project at its birth." By exerting various pressures, it was possible to detach two others from a group coming downriver to the colony. A second convoy appeared, from which three more candidates were obtained. With these six youths an experiment began that, it was believed, held promise of a brilliant future.[67]

But the first months were trying. One of the youths took flight. Two others died – it was then a time of epidemic. Father Daniel, who cared for them most attentively, almost lost his own life. Le Jeune's diagnosis is revealing of the medical knowledge of the times: "The true cause of their death lies in the change of air and of exercise, and especially of diet."

Even with reduced numbers, life remained precarious at the seminary; when the ships (and the provisions that they brought) were late in arriving in 1637, there were fears that the experiment would have to be ended. They went to consult Montmagny. Le Jeune wrote: "I admire his courage; he replied that, as we had had so much trouble in getting these young men, he did not think we should have the heart to send them back, since they were behaving so well. 'It is a matter of suffering,' he said, 'and of saving something from your rations and from ours.' He fully appreciates the importance of this Seminary for the glory of Our Lord, and for the commercial interests of these gentlemen (of the Company)."[68]

The following year, 1638, began well. Two of the students asked for baptism. Montmagny wished to be godfather to one of them, whom he named Armand-Jean, "after Monseigneur the Cardinal, judging it appropriate that a Prince of the Church, who favours this infant Church, should gather its first fruits."[69]

But what happened afterwards was very disappointing – Le Jeune's commentary was correspondingly so: "We have always thought that the powers of Hell would unite all their forces against the project of this Seminary, and others like it; and that if it were to succeed, as we have good reason to hope it will, it would only be after having sustained many battles and endured a lot of misfortunes."[70]

The Jesuits found themselves in mid-summer with six students. A first soon fled. Three others proved resistant to discipline – "aiming at nothing but the enjoyment of their pleasures and the gratification of their senses." They secretly equipped a canoe and left for their villages. The remaining two were sent into Huronia by Montmagny, to make sure that the missionaries there were still alive. The governor's godson, according to Le Jeune, did wonders there to promote the French cause and the expansion of Christianity.[71]

So at the end of 1638 there was no longer a Huron seminary. Le Jeune added, however: "Seven little children, both Montagnais and Algonquin, have been given to me ... four or five others have been presented to me to be put in the Seminary, and they have promised to bring me more in the spring."[72] Were the children of these nations, now beginning to settle down, on the way to replacing the Hurons at the seminary? It is not certain. There was question of it again in the following year, 1639,[73] and everything seemed under way; then, in 1640, no mention of it.[74] Had a page been turned? It is a mystery. However, in the Huron case, this is what seems to have happened. In 1639, the author of the *Relation from the Country of the Hurons* speaks thus of the seminary: "It is a work that will some day produce greater results in the service of God in these countries than those whom God inspires to contribute to it believe, although it will not be, perhaps, in the way they thought."[75] Apparently the missionaries were beginning to believe that it was preferable to educate people within their own traditional lifestyle, or that it was more effective to instruct the adults, who would then take responsibility for the children, or prepare them for the priests' lessons.[76]

Early on, too, there was preoccupation with the female children. In 1636 Le Jeune sent two little Montagnais girls to France; they were baptized in Paris on 6 January 1637.[77] He was counting on them, as he said, "to bring some of their wandering compatriots to a halt"; which is to say that he hoped a seminary for girls would be opened soon. As well, at his instigation a Québec couple had, for some time already, been boarding some girls in their house.[78]

His appeals to France did not go without response. The Ursulines in particular sent him enthusiastic letters: "[T]hey write to me with such fire, and in such great numbers, and from so many different places, that if we gave in to their wishes, a city of nuns would be formed, and there would be ten teachers to each pupil."[79]

The practical realization of the project resulted from a crossing of paths. A lady of Normandy had made a vow to consecrate her life and her fortune to the native peoples of New France. A Jesuit[80] put her in touch with an Ursuline of Tours who felt called by God to go to Canada to put her teaching skills and her religious fervour at the service of young aboriginal women. They left the port of Dieppe at the beginning of May 1639: Madame de La Peltrie and Marie de l'Incarnation,[81] who brought with her two Ursuline sisters. From Montmagny and the rest of the colony they received the same warm welcome as the hospital sisters. A private house, situated in the lower town close to the port, was placed at their disposal. Hardly were they settled in when they were entrusted with "six savage girls," and even "some French girls [who] began going to them for instruction."[82] Without delay they set about learning the Algonquian dialects. There do not seem to have been any Huron students at the outset.

The beginnings were very difficult, mainly for two reasons. First, the lack of space: three nuns, between ten and fifteen native girls, and at least two little French girls had to be lodged in two small rooms. Secondly, the omnipresent "contagion"; between September and February 1640 four little aboriginals were carried off by the disease. Despite these handicaps the work prospered; the results, according to Le Jeune who dedicated a whole chapter to "the Seminary of the Ursuline Mothers,"[83] were up to expectations: the religious rejoiced "in the good qualities of their children" – docility, piety, modesty, good manners, and "civility."[84] This success met the hopes of the governor, for whom everything that could contribute to the promotion of the aboriginals was to be praised and encouraged.[85] It was one of the most significant achievements of the first years of his term.

All the same, the burning question of Montmagny's administration remained the Iroquois phenomenon. This nation was related linguistically and culturally to the Huron and other peoples (Petun, Neutral, Erie) who were also settled in the Great Lakes region. Today the term "Iroquois" is used to denote all these nations. We should note that in the sixteenth century certain groups of these Iroquois had been living on the banks of the Saint Lawrence, notably on the sites of Québec and Montréal; but before Champlain's arrival in 1603 they had left this region for reasons that are unknown. The Iroquois nation was composed of five tribes which formed a kind of confederation: from east to west these were the Mohawk (or Agnier) tribe, the Onneyout (or Oneida), the Onondaga, the Goyogouin (or Cayuga), and the Tsonnontouan (or Seneca). In 1636 their territory stretched roughly from the Hudson River to the Niagara.

To understand where the problem of Franco-Iroquois relations stood at the time of Montmagny's arrival, we must recall – very briefly – the action and initiatives of his predecessor.[86]

On his first voyage into the Saint Lawrence River valley in 1603, Champlain came into contact with the Montagnais and Algonquin tribes who lived there or who came there to trade, hunt, and fish. They were in a state of war – centuries-old perhaps – with the Iroquois; and that very summer, the Algonquin succeeded in winning an important victory over the Mohawk. But they were well aware that the

Iroquois nation was on the way to revitalization after a long period of misfortune. The support of the French could prove necessary for their very survival. Thus in a solemn meeting, Champlain heard the great chief Anadabijou[87] glorify the friendship that he saw being established between the two nations; one of the natives who had been taken back to France on a previous voyage had met with King Henri IV, who had promised that he would send colonists, and that he would protect the allied nations against their enemies.

It was five years before Champlain could begin, very modestly, to fulfil this program of action that he seems furthermore to have adopted as his personal affair. He was at that time the lieutenant of the Sieur de Gua des Monts, holder of the fur trade monopoly.[88] The following year (1609) he mounted a campaign against the Iroquois. The Algonquin and the Huron (also enemies of the Iroquois) formed the bulk of the force, and he had with him a few French soldiers. The use of the musket sowed panic among the enemies. This was the beginning of a new Hundred Years' War, almost (1609–1701). In 1610 the Iroquois did not wait to be attacked; they settled in at the mouth of the Richelieu River (known also as "the Iroquois River"), from where they could control the upper Saint Lawrence. Champlain succeeded in beating them a second time. This was his last victory over them. In 1615, the attack that he directed against an Iroquois village ended in fiasco because he did not know how to use the allied fighters effectively. He had reached the limit of his possibilities, since the French government lent only a distracted ear to his appeals for military assistance.

Instead he thought now of making peace with the Iroquois, and in fact from 1624 to1627 there was something like a general pacification in the region. But henceforth other factors intervened. It was no longer the old tribal antagonism that underlay the quarrels, but rather the search for profit. After 1609 the Dutch were settled on the island of Manhattan and along the Hudson River, with Fort Orange only sixty kilometres from the nearest villages of the Mohawk. They would try to monopolize the trade in furs that had already begun at this fort, which meant preventing the Hurons and other allies of France from coming there; they even wanted to divert the traffic that moved along the Saint Lawrence valley to this post. Obviously this meant, sooner or later, a return to hostilities.

Champlain returned to Québec in 1633, after the English occupation had ended. He sent two boats to meet the Huron, who were coming downriver for the trade; above Trois-Rivières three of his men were killed and two wounded, ambushed by a party of Iroquois.[89] He saw at once how the situation had developed. He promised his allies to work out-and-out for the destruction of the Iroquois. For this purpose he asked Richelieu for 120 soldiers. As well, he was aware that a new factor had now to be considered. The shortage of furs in the Saint Lawrence basin meant that they had to come from the hinterland; there was no peaceful way for the Iroquois to procure them. The Huron wished to remain the middlemen. The Algonquin also wanted that; in fact one of their most respected chiefs, whom the French called La Grenouille,[90] tried in January 1635 to come to an understanding once and for all with the Mohawk[91] – even though his attempt was not supported unanimously by his tribe. He went to one of the Mohawk villages, where he was very badly received; neither he nor any of his companions survived the assault which followed their arrival.[92] It seems that this surprising reaction suited the Dutch who could have been damaged by this potential alliance. These were some of the facts that dominated relations with the Iroquois when Montmagny arrived in New France.

The year 1636 was relatively calm. In the autumn the governor toured his colony from Île-Jésus to Cap Tourmente, without incident. If he had conceived the idea of doing it in the winter, he would undoubtedly have run into a strong Iroquois party – 150 of them came to within two days' travel of Trois-Rivières but, in keeping with their customary tactic of surprise, they did not dare to attack a fort where guards were posted day and night.[93]

The only indication that he had of the Iroquois presence at Québec was the torture which the Montagnais inflicted on a prisoner in the town, not far from his fort: whipping, cuts with stones and knives, deep bites; "it is said that they [the Amerindian allies] exercised another cruelty on him, which would make this paper blush," added the disgusted Le Jeune. Montmagny, as we have already said, had the reaction of all newcomers to this country: he ordered the Montagnais to be told "that he was displeased with these cruelties, and that they should go somewhere else so as not to offend our Frenchmen's sight with barbarisms which in our eyes are intolerable."[94]

For the discussions with the allies that took place that summer, in which the central subject was the Iroquois question, Montmagny had the good sense to leave the initiative to men more experienced than he: François Derré de Gand,[95] the commissioner of the Company, and Duplessis-Bochart.

The year 1637 began rather badly for the allies. A raid by the Montagnais and Abenakis against the Mohawk turned into a disaster;

they returned to Trois-Rivières "overcome with mourning and sadness,"[96] having lost a considerable number of their force.

In mid-summer Montmagny was in Trois-Rivières when warning came that Iroquois were close by.[97] They were encamped at Lake Saint-Pierre a few kilometres west of the post, ready to challenge all the Huron canoes coming down to trade. The governor made careful preparation to sustain the siege that he thought was imminent. The warriors who were there, and whose instinctive reaction in those moments of excitement was to resort to noisy and exciting rituals, he placed under close surveillance. Some Iroquois, in a show of bravado, appeared on the river. He then sent some men, including Nicollet, to reconnoitre around the fort. They reported that the Iroquois were there in force: as many as 500 warriors, armed to the teeth. He at once sent a messenger to Québec to alert his lieutenant, the chevalier de Lisle. The latter played his part well: less than five days later two fully-equipped long-boats arrived, four others and a canoe followed a few hours later. He had succeeded in pressing a number of vessels that were in port, as well as a few colonists, into service.

With this help Montmagny felt ready to confront the enemy. He had Le Jeune (who seems to have become his universal counsellor) accompany him, and under cover of night he moved in the direction of the mouth of the Richelieu River. He crossed Lake Saint-Pierre and arrived at the islands at its extreme west end, then went onto the river, only to find that the enemy had fled. Once aware of the arrival of reinforcements and the determination of the governor, the Iroquois preferred not to take on an adversary who was resolute, methodical, and armed with muskets and cannon. It would have been useless, and even dangerous, for the French to pursue them in boats heavier than theirs.

The operation had been conducted with calm and determination – the chevalier had experienced other actions of the sort in the Mediterranean – and it had impressed the Mohawk. Montmagny had also succeeded in controlling the native allies and in avoiding the defeat that Champlain had experienced in 1615. He was beginning to show what he was capable of: to be able to hold fast with limited forces.

It was war, but it was not yet war, if we can put it like that; and this situation was going to continue for the next three years. In fact, the Mohawk did not return to the Saint Lawrence in 1638. But the respite did not last, as we shall soon see. The battle was carried on elsewhere. The Huron, assisted by the Algonquin, won a spectacular victory over them, thus avenging the loss in 1637 of one of their captains, Tarantouan. They took more than eighty prisoners.[98] The dark side to this brilliant action was that it persuaded the Iroquois to acquire firearms.[99] More to the west, some young Huron warriors left at the beginning of 1639 on an expedition against the Tsonnontouan[100] (or Seneca, the westernmost tribe of the Iroquois nation), breaking a truce that had lasted since 1634. The guerrilla war was beginning with a vengeance.

And in fact, in the summer of 1639, the Mohawk tried to take revenge by coming to fight on the Saint Lawrence. They put up a fort at the entrance to Lake Saint-Pierre, not far from Trois-Rivières. This time they hoped, by surprise raids, to trap the Algonquin who, it seems, were more and more nervous over the enemy menace, and for this reason were coming to find refuge with the French.[101] Montmagny arrived quickly and succeeded in chasing them off again, but he had no chance of defeating them, apparently because of the state of excitement among the Algonquin who accompanied him – this time he did not succeed in controlling them. This is how Le Jeune described the event: "Monsieur our Governor went up to Trois-Rivières with a ship and some longboats, well armed, and removed these obstacles. For, although contrary winds and the haste of the Savages robbed him of the opportunity that he was seeking to defeat their enemies, nevertheless, seeing the good will which a man of such merit had for them, they [the Algonquin] met and held several discussions among themselves, in which they decided to embrace the Christian faith and to spend time near our residence at Trois-Rivières, giving us a fine opportunity to instruct them."[102]

The enemy were highly mobile. Despite his efforts, Montmagny could not catch up with them, or seriously weaken them. The Huron community found itself in an uncomfortable situation. As Jérôme Lalemant put it, speaking of the year between spring 1639 and the end of May 1640: "As to the war, their (the Huron) losses were greater than their gains."[103] Some Algonquin who had gone into Iroquois country were overcome by their enemies during a magic ceremony.[104] From the end of 1640, the Iroquois were on a war footing, and prepared to keep a close eye on the Saint Lawrence.[105]

Thus Montmagny's first years were marked by a relative calm on the Saint Lawrence. The Iroquois had to some degree been contained. The allies' raid in the summer of 1638 was hard on them, but it did not destroy them; to the contrary, it seems to have sharpened their fighting instincts, as would appear in brutal fashion in the period that opened with the winter of 1640–1641.

2.   Open but sporadic hostilities (1641–1645)

The period that opened with the beginning of the year 1641 would be marked by a series of raids which, this time, did not spare the French. The situation became so bad that, in a letter of 2 September 1644, a Jesuit priest would write these very strong words: "Fishing and hunting are forbidden to the French, it is difficult even to pick a salad in the garden safely, and to go to fetch wood it is necessary to put everybody on guard and ready for battle ... We have to fear them [the Iroquois] all the time. If this persecution goes on, we shall have to leave the country."[106] The Iroquois menace dominated the colony's whole life during these years; and so it is with this aspect that we must start our study.

The winter of 1640–1641 had hardly begun when a hundred Iroquois left their territory.[107] Once arrived at the Saint Lawrence River, they separated into two groups. The first, which went up the Ottawa River above Montréal, captured some Algonquin. The second took cover at the very gates of Trois-Rivières. They succeeded in seizing two interpreters who had gone out on a hunting trip, François Marguerie and Thomas Godefroy. These men had the presence of mind not to attempt a desperate defence. Their assailants took them to their village and treated them very well – because they were going to be used for a projected negotiation. The Mohawk wished to propose peace with the French.

At the end of April, 500 warriors left their villages, taking with them their two prisoners.[108] Once at the mouth of the Richelieu the expeditionary force split: one party set up an ambush to attack all the convoys passing by, and the other appeared, on 5 June, at Trois-Rivières. A canoe with a white flag advanced rapidly towards the post; Marguerie was quickly recognized and received warmly. He went at once to meet François de Champflour, the post commander. The message he had to transmit was very clear: the Iroquois were there in force, 350 warriors armed with, among other things, thirty-six arquebuses. They wanted to make peace with the French, but to continue the war against their allies. They demanded that they be given thirty arquebuses. They kept Godefroy as hostage. Champflour answered that a proposal of this importance could only be discussed by the governor of the colony. The Mohawk agreed to wait, and they began to put up fortifications on the right bank, opposite Trois-Rivières.

Montmagny arrived on the tenth, only five days after Champflour had sent the messenger. He came in an armed long-boat; other boats followed with reinforcements, arms, and ammunition. Immediately he entered into negotiations. He travelled in an armed canoe to a position not far from the bank, and from there he sent Nicollet and Father Ragueneau who, two days before, had represented Champflour in a meeting with the Mohawk, who were beginning to get impatient.

The two emissaries received gifts as a witness of the friendship of four of the five tribes. The two French prisoners were officially freed. In a symbolic evocation, an orator declared: "Here is the house that we shall have at Trois-Rivières, when we come to trade with you; we shall smoke there without fear, since we shall have Onontio for our brother."[109] In conclusion, Montmagny was asked to force the Algonquin and the Huron to bury the hatchet – but at the same time, to the great embarrassment of the French, four Algonquin canoes were ransacked a few kilometres away.

Two days later, Montmagny gathered all his forces on the beach. The Iroquois made it clear that they desired his presence on their bank, together with that of Nicollet and Ragueneau. Sensing a trap, Montmagny refused. Finally three Mohawk captains came forward. The governor offered them rich presents, to symbolize the invitation that he was making to them to come and trade with the French. But he offered no arquebuses. The captains responded: set up a trading post among us; give us arquebuses; we are ready to break with the Dutch. Montmagny let them know that a universal peace would be welcome, but that it had to be accompanied by the immediate release of an Algonquin prisoner. He was told that he would have this answer in the morning. Montmagny retorted that he wanted this answer at once – the reply was that it would come the following day.

The response did indeed come the following morning. The message was shouted out to the French: "No arquebuses, no peace." Montmagny ordered his men to destroy the little fort built on the bank – it was practically empty, a second one having been built behind it, out of reach of the cannon. He decided not to set out at once; the risk was too great. But shortly after ordering the attack, he realized that, under cover of the night, the enemy had carefully prepared for flight. The canoes were ready a mile upstream, and they left before the French, with their slower boats, were able to catch up with them. Once again, the enemy escaped him.

How could he have done otherwise, with limited forces, and above all with enemies who knew the terrain, were equipped with light boats, and accustomed to rapid attacks? How could he foresee their action plans? Not feeling very sure of himself, the governor had consulted his principal companions; they were as uncertain as he. He even asked for advice from the Jesuits, who were reluctant to become involved in a purely military question. What is important to note is that he recognized the gravity of the situation. The enemy warriors who were on the warpath were as numerous as the whole neo-French population, and they were highly cunning – they had pretended good will by returning the prisoners. And they knew perfectly well that the French were powerless before them, that, given the current state of their forces, they could not mount an expedition to destroy them. So Montmagny took the decision to ask for help from the mother country; towards this end he would send Le Jeune to try to make Richelieu conscious of the military weaknesses of New France.[110]

The year ended without confrontation, but not without danger, because the check that they had experienced in front of Trois-Rivières fired up the Mohawk. At the end of autumn a war party set out to surprise any colonists who risked leaving the post, retreating only after the death of two chiefs, which appeared to them as a bad omen.[111] Another expedition took some prisoners along the Ottawa River, and there the warriors boasted of having killed several French soldiers at Trois-Rivières[112] – their motive being to impress France's allies. Thus there was, on their part, a clear determination to spy on and harass the colony – and they had the means to put it into action.[113]

It was in this tense atmosphere that there arrived at Québec a group of immigrants whose mission was to settle in the very centre of the hornets' nest, on the island of Montréal. Montmagny received them cordially, but tried to show them how untimely and imprudent their decision was, given their small numbers and the mediocrity of his own means. He respected their determination, but explained to them the danger of their situation.[114]

The very year that Montréal was established (1642) turned out to be rife with violent attacks. The Iroquois initiatives would, in different ways, affect the Algonquin, the Huron, and the French.

The winter was not yet over when the Algonquin of the Outaouais were vigorously attacked and, thereafter, plagued incessantly. A group of Algonquin and Montagnais warriors left for Iroquois country in the spring to try to avenge these provocations. On the way they met an enemy detachment, whom they attacked with fury; they succeeded in defeating them, and returned to Sillery.[115]

The Hurons, less fortunate, experienced a series of disasters. A first defeat occurred on 8 June; the details of this encounter remain obscure.[116] But on the subject of the following defeat, that of 5 August, the *Relations* are inexhaustible – and for good cause, as we shall see.[117]

A shipment of furs had arrived in mid-July at Trois-Rivières. The crews were impatient to go home. Montmagny, who was there waiting for a favourable time to go and build a fort at the mouth of the Richelieu River, advised them to wait; he was ready to convoy them with his boats through the danger zone that extended to the des Prairies River, when he was headed that way. They disregarded this prudent advice, and set off on 1 August. Some of the best captains of the nation were there, as well as a seminarian on whom great hopes were placed, and three Jesuits, Father Isaac Jogues, Brother René Goupil (a practised surgeon), and a *donné*, Guillaume Couture.[118] The very day after their departure they were attacked by two enemy contingents who had hidden themselves in the brush on a point on the left bank. The ambush succeeded perfectly. Those who survived were taken to Iroquois country. Some of them were tortured: Brother Goupil was hacked to death, and Father Jogues was forced to serve as a domestic in a hut. He would later be liberated by the Dutch. Simultaneously, above Montréal, eleven canoes coming downriver with their stocks of furs were seized by the Iroquois, and several members of the crews were killed.[119]

The construction of a fort on the Richelieu appeared every day more urgent. Le Jeune's journey did not have all the desired success: the cardinal gave a miserly 30,000 livres[120] with which to enlist a few soldiers, erect a fort, and put the Jesuits' house at Sainte-Marie in Huronia into a state of defence. What was needed was not that, wrote the Jesuit to the General of the Society, but a good, strong detachment – at least 200 soldiers, well equipped – to settle the Iroquois question once and for all, to weaken this nation beyond recovery, and to prevent it from doing harm to commerce and the work of evangelization.

On 13 August, Montmagny put his soldiers and labourers to work at the mouth of the Richelieu.[121] A week later they had almost finished building their fort and were just completing the palisade, when, the following night, in their usual unexpected way, 300 Iroquois warriors appeared. Their attack was well organized: they were divided into three groups and they moved with discipline and speed. The French managed, more or less, to resist this first assault. Montmagny, who was at that moment in his brigantine, returned to the fort as fast as he could and took over the direction of operations. He succeeded in dislodging the adversaries, who retired to a little fort which they had constructed a league upriver, before returning to their villages. According to Vimont, it was the governor's coolness and good judgment that saved the situation: "Had [he] not been present, all the workmen would have been cut to pieces."[122] The attack was so vigorous that pursuit of the enemy was impossible. But at least they were temporarily halted and, as the *Relation* again pointed out, Montmagny drew a lesson from this fight: "Our soldiers learned that they had to be constantly on their guard against an enemy who pounces like a bird on his prey, who fights like a thief (*larron*), and who attacks like a brave man."[123]

Morale reached rock-bottom in New France. The first sentence of the *Relation* that Jérôme Lalemant sent his provincial from Huronia at the end of September 1643 read as follows: "The scourge of war, which has hitherto carried off a great number of these peoples, has continued so strongly this last year, that it could be said that this country is but one scene of massacre."[124]

In this same year 1643, the Iroquois basically used a tactic in which they were already experienced: making war by little groups, which guaranteed great mobility and made tracking difficult.[125] To the French, it seemed that they were here, there, and everywhere; for they multiplied their strikes. We can only take note of a few.

On 9 May two Algonquin canoes, loaded with furs, were pillaged twelve miles west of Trois-Rivières,[126] close to the fort that Montmagny had built the previous year precisely to prevent this piracy. In June, the Iroquois circled Montréal. First they intercepted the Huron convoy that arrived in the colony on 9 June; "They saw sixty Hurons coming downriver in thirteen canoes, without arquebuses and without arms, but loaded down with furs, on their way to Montréal and from there to Trois-Rivières for their trade. They were carrying the letters from our Fathers with the Hurons, and a copy of their *Relation*. The forty Iroquois came out of the woods, fell upon them, frightened them with their arquebuses, and put them to flight, taking twenty-three of them prisoner together with their canoes and furs."[127]

After completing this strike they were seen, an hour later, on the outskirts of the post, where they tracked down five colonists who were putting up a house frame. They surprised them, killed and scalped three of them, and took away two prisoners. Everyone felt the effects of this, including Montmagny: "Monsieur the Governor, however, who was anxious for the Father's [Jogues's] release, and peace if it were reasonable, equipped four longboats, and went, prepared for war or for peace, to Trois-Rivières, and thence to Fort Richelieu, to see if the Iroquois would appear on the river or before the habitations."[128] During the whole month of July he attempted, without success, to catch up with one group or the other, whenever he had news of them. He frequently left his boat to follow their trail, but without success – they were always beyond his reach! He was obliged, regretfully, to refuse the offer that the allies made to lend him up to 300 warriors.[129] Without European enforcements, he was not sure he could use these troops suitably.

Three other alerts are mentioned by the *Relation* between the end of July and the end of August; they took place between Montréal and Lake Saint-Pierre. But this time there were victims on both sides.[130] For example, the Huron, returning to their country, after having been on their guard during the first leg of the trip up the Ottawa, believed that the danger was past. Alas! Halfway through a portage that they were undertaking in good spirits, the enemy pounced on them, killed or captured some of them, seized their merchandise, and immediately took off.

Vimont, who was due to send his annual *Relation* to Paris, finished his letter of introduction thus:

> At the time of writing, I learn that they are captured for the third time on the way upriver. This has forced us to send Father Le Jeune, who has long experience in the affairs of these regions, to your Reverence, to explain them more clearly to those who care for this poor land. This has been the advice and wish of Monsieur de Montmagny our governor, and all the inhabitants, who have earnestly begged me to do it.[131]

And so the governor's emissary undertook his second voyage to Paris. Would he succeed in persuading the administration of the kingdom to give him more substantial assistance than that of 1641?

The year 1644 began with fireworks; the Iroquois carried out raid upon raid until mid-spring. Then there was a let-up, so to speak. It seems that there was some weariness on their part.[132] And all the time the idea of some sort of negotiation was timidly gaining ground. Montmagny himself thought of it more and more, given the reluctance of Anne of Austria to send him adequate means.

The *Relation* of 1643–1644 reports that at the end of the winter "in less than a month, ten bands of Iroquois warriors left their country to come and make war against the French, the Algonquin and the Huron."[133] All the strategic points between Trois-Rivières and Chaudière Falls on the Ottawa were under their close surveillance.

On 30 March, at Montréal, trained watchdogs gave warning of a suspicious presence.[134] The commander, Maisonneuve, sallied out with thirty of his men and gave battle. Some of them fell, and the munitions began to run short, so he ordered a retreat toward the fort. Without snowshoes the French had difficulty walking through the snow. As soon as they reached a road with some footing, general panic set in and there was a rush toward the post. Maisonneuve remained alone before the enemy – the honour of killing him was left to a chief. He, however, managed to fell the chief, and while the warriors were attending to him, was able to reach the fort.

The Mohawk could not let the elimination of one of their captains go without reprisals. Two strikes followed. Father Bressani,[135] who was leaving to begin his missionary life among the Hurons, was captured and brutalized.[136] On the des Prairies River, some Algonquin were taken by surprise; not one succeeded in escaping; they were led back to the villages and burnt alive.

The pressure did not let up until the end of the summer. A group of Algonquin and Huron succeeded, in late July, in capturing three Iroquois, who in the early morning were shadowing the French of Fort Richelieu as they went to collect fishing nets spread out not far from the palisade.[137] They arrived triumphant at Trois-Rivières. The prisoner who belonged to the Algonquins was already undergoing torture when Champflour intervened. He "sent them word to stop, that Monsieur the Chevalier de Montmagny, the Governor of the country, had to be informed of the capture of the prisoners and that the matter was important."[138]

Upon arriving, Montmagny first addressed the Algonquin, who were dancing with impatience to send their prisoner to the stake that they had already prepared; he ordered them to be spoken to "with a good accent," that is to say in severe tones. The prisoner's life was saved, but he could no longer walk, since his feet had already been burned with red-hot stones. With the Huron, it was an altogether different story. "They handed him thirty-two or thirty-three straws, saying that an equal number of presents would argue more effectively for the deliverance of the prisoners [the two who belonged to them]." The governor complied with their rites. He prepared a great feast for all who were there, with numerous gifts, "consisting of axes, blankets, kettles, iron arrowheads, and suchlike." The Algonquin said that it was not the presents that interested them, but the prospect of the peace that would render their life more agreeable. The Hurons, meanwhile, had changed their position; they insisted now on another sentiment, pride. The presents have come too quickly, they said; we are men of war and not merchants; our chiefs will be displeased with us; they will punish us, without a doubt. It is up to them to decide if these prisoners should be used for parleys of peace. Montmagny yielded to this reasoning, believing that "if the Hurons undertook to negotiate peace, they would do it more effectively than the French, as they have a better knowledge than we of savage usages." So he left them the initiative, though taking a risk: that one individual, full of rage and revenge, would let loose "a hatchet blow at these prisoners." As their return to Huronia represented great dangers, he had them accompanied by twenty-two soldiers; three Jesuits, one of them Brébeuf, were also included in the party.

Montmagny had succeeded in securing some help from the regent – 100,000 livres[139] that allowed the dispatch of sixty soldiers – not enough to launch a large-scale offensive, but sufficient, more or less, for the defence of the few posts that the colony boasted.

The skirmishes continued through the autumn and winter. Lalemant told of some of them in the *Relation* which he sent off in 1645. He added, with a touch of humour, that "the folks in the forests of Richelieu and of Montréal have been walled up and enclosed more tightly than any monks or nuns in the smallest monasteries of France." And, a little further: "The French had, as a cloister [at the fort of Richelieu] a palisade of stakes, not very large; but finally the Iroquois ambassadors who came at the beginning of July [in the summer of 1645] broke down the cloister of these poor recluses, who, since they did not have the gift of prayer, did not take too much pleasure in such a tiny monastery."[140] In fact, the year 1645 would see the arrangement of a truce.

The peace process began after an Algonquin victory at the end of April. The incident took place at Lake Champlain. Using Iroquois tactics, seven Algonquin warriors succeeded in overcoming two enemy canoes manned by fourteen men. Eleven were killed, one succeeded in escaping, two were taken prisoner. These were treated gently – a novelty, in which we can see the influence of the governor and the Jesuits. The same self-control was shown upon their arrival at Sillery on 17 May.

The next morning Montmagny appeared. At once a council was called and the chief of the victorious band turned the two prisoners over to the governor, who declared to the Algonquins: "that he honoured their valour and their courage, that he had always loved them, especially those who had become his brothers and his family through Baptism, that for the rest he did not wish that the thanks which he gave for their gift to him should remain a naked word, that he wished to dress it with robes and arm it with powder and lead, using language that matched their way of speaking; and upon that, he gave them fine presents."[141] The two Iroquois, whom Montmagny released at once, were wild with joy; one of them danced and threw an hatchet in the fire, to signify his desire to see peace flourish. Lalemant commented: "If there are barbarous actions in these peoples, there are also thoughts worthy of the spirit of the Greeks and the Romans."

Shortly afterwards, Montmagny turned them over to the governor of Trois-Rivières. The latter was to send the warrior taken the previous summer, whose feet had been cared for and healed, back to Iroquois country, with the following message: the two prisoners captured on Lake Champlain would be returned to their families as soon as talks were seriously undertaken with a view to "a universal peace among all the Nations."[142]

In truth, despite all the risks that an Iroquois peace represented, the governor had no alternative. His military forces were extremely limited; the "Laurentian coalition" was seriously threatened in its very existence, not only by the losses suffered at the hands of enemies, but perhaps still more by sickness and famine. The colony was in danger of suffocation: the fur trade had diminished significantly, and the movements and even the daily tasks of the colonists were seriously hindered.

So on 21 May the Iroquois left Trois-Rivières – there was no wish to let the affair drag on. For fear of some provocation on the part of the allies, he was made to leave alone in his canoe – a fact with which the Mohawk negotiator who came later would with some justice reproach Montmagny.[143] He carried letters for Guillaume Couture. This donné, who was made prisoner at the same time as Jogues and Goupil, had been adopted by the victors and, in proof of an extraordinary adaptibility on both sides, had risen to the rank of chief. The tribal council sent him to Trois-Rivières in the company of two of its principal captains, one of whom was Kiotsaton, a very able speaker.[144] On 5 July they were at the post, where Montmagny himself arrived a week later. It was grand theatre.White drapes formed an impressive roof over the group, which was itself set out in symbolic fashion: the Iroquois were placed at the feet of Montmagny and his men, in whose first rank sat the Jesuit superior; facing them were the Montagnais and the Algonquin; the rectangle was closed by the Huron on one side and the French colonists on the other.

Out of courtesy, the first word was given to the enemy. In the shape of seventeen porcelain necklets, the Mohawk presented the same number of grievances or wishes, the thrust of which was obviously the need to restore peace and friendship; a certain reticence, however, was shown to the proposal of reconciliation with the Huron. The following day, Montmagny gave a banquet for everyone. Then it was his turn to offer "fourteen gifts all of which had their meanings and carried their words"; and the *Relation* continued: "Thus the peace with them was concluded, on condition that they should not commit any hostile act against the Huron, or the other nations who were our allies, until such time as the chiefs of the Nations who were not present had met with them."

It must be recognized that this peace had its limits; no important allied chief was present and of the five Iroquois tribes, only the Mohawk were there. But circumstances did not allow Montmagny anything else.

For the return, the governor had the delegates accompanied by "two young French boys, both to help them carry their canoes and their presents and to demonstrate the confidence that he had in these peoples." Once he had embarked, Kiotsaton, always true to his reputation as an orator, called out to the governor: "Onontio, your name shall be great throughout the earth; I did not think that I would carry away my head which I had risked, I did not think that it would pass back through your gates, and I am leaving them loaded with honour, gifts and benevolence."

This highly inflated speech would not have impressed the governor overly much – there remained too many risks: reactions among the Iroquois, for example, or responses of allied chiefs. But in the final analysis, the ceasefire was respected throughout the summer, and parleys commenced again at the beginning of September. The delegates of the various allied tribes concerned began to arrive, including the principal Huron captains who came with an impressive convoy of furs; they "had orders from all their country to treat fully for peace and to follow the thinking of Onontio."[145] On 18 September the four Mohawk ambassadors arrived. They were received with great pomp.

The ceremony took place with the same rites as the July meeting. This time Guillaume Couture was the orator for the Iroquois party; he laid eighteen bands of mother-of-pearl before the governor. Some of the gifts were simple expressions of politeness; others were intended to celebrate the Iroquois peace (which, however, covered up a lacuna: of the five tribes, only the Mohawk had ratified the accord); almost half of the gifts were concerned with future negotiations with the allies, who were invited to go and make known their intentions to the same Mohawk in the coming months. Then a captain announced that the allied prisoners would be freed, but that the young Huron girl who had been captured at the same time as Jogues in 1642 would remain as a hostage.[146] Finally he declared to Montmagny that the gifts which he had sent to the other tribes had been passed on. In fact, the governor intended to include them in the peace, but the success of his initiative remained most uncertain; the Oneida, for example, had found that their share of gifts was not generous enough, doubtless a pretext for not allowing their hands to be tied.

The following session was reserved to Montmagny and his allies. It was their turn to offer something. The Huron freed their last Iroquois prisoner and, with the Algonquin, promised to send ambassadors as soon as possible, a promise which Montmagny formally undertook to see respected. In an emphatic style, worthy of the orator of July, the chief of the Iroquois delegation cried out: "Onontio, you have banished all the mists, the air is still, the sky appears unclouded, the sun shines, I see no more trouble; peace has made everything calm, my heart is at rest, I leave contented."[147] A great banquet for more than 400 guests put an end to this important series of meetings.

In the religous circles of New France there was optimism. Marie de l'Incarnation wrote shortly afterwards: "We are on the eve of seeing the kingdom of God extend over all the infidel peoples of our America."[148] More realistic, however, was the reaction of the Jesuits:"If these barbarians ... do not trouble this peace concluded for the French and well advanced for the Savages, there will be an opportunity to go and suffer for Jesus Christ among a great number of peoples."[149]

Basically, what they meant to say was that peace remained precarious; Montmagny himself was well aware of this. Someone could compromise everything on an impulse or during a drinking session. The Iroquois had not all adhered to the treaty; the majority of the tribes (four out of five) had abstained.[150] Further negotiations were up to the allies, and it was not certain that they would succeed. And to add to the complication, there was a secret clause which Montmagny had had to accept solemnly in the treaty concluded with Kiotsaton in July.[151] The latter demanded a private interview with the governor, Guillaume Couture serving as interpreter. The chief demanded, in the name of his tribe, that the French abandon the Algonquin, though peace could be made immediately with the Huron. What was their intention in making this proposition? To come to an agreement with the Huron over the fur trade? To settle with the Algonquin, then go after the Huron, and then the French? Nobody has ever known.[152] After consultation with the Jesuits, who, like him, found the situation highly difficult, the governor proposed a compromise: the Christian Algonquin were "natural Frenchmen" and they had to be included in the peace; as for the others, it was up to them, if they could, to negotiate their own understanding with their enemies. Kiotsaton accepted this. All this shows, among other things, first, that the Mohawk were masters of the situation, second, that Montmagny's room for manoeuvre was very limited: he did not have the means to protect the Algonquin, with whom the French had been tied in friendship since the beginning of the century. Also, this clause may be seen as a lesser evil, impossible to avoid, given the political situation in which he was struggling; but he may also have seen it as a delaying tactic, since he was still hoping to receive reinforcements from France that would allow him, in his turn, to assert himself. What is clear is that his back was against the wall, because in any case this famous clause was very difficult to respect: how would a Christian Algonquin be distinguished from a pagan Algonquin in the ordinary course of events?

Obviously we are in the presence of "a crippled peace" – an expression often used to qualify a mediocre accord between European belligerents. Subsequent events will show the justice of this description in the case of New France for the period that concerns us.

All these events – those which we have just examined for the years 1641–1645 – were not without repercussions on French-allied relations. Let us remember some of the more significant facts in following the same schema as before: sedentarization, hospitalization, and education. Some examples will suffice.

The idea of "settling" or "reducing" the native people was beginning to make headway in North America, and also in France, where interest was expressed in a practical manner – in the case of the "Montrealists." However, the Iroquois war hindered the normal development of the process.

In the colony, it was on the village of Saint-Joseph, otherwise known as Sillery, that efforts were concentrated.[153] First to establish there were Montagnais and Algonquin. For the former, it became more or less their centre,[154] as they regrouped around the Jesuit house. The latter settled close to the other pole of the village, the Hôtel-Dieu. In 1642, forty families lived there, in other words at least 300 people. They resided in birchbark cabins; four little French-style houses sheltered the chiefs.

Quite clearly the *Relation* was insisting – for the purpose of encouraging the benefactors – on the efficacy of the experiment. The native people were gradually being Christianized: "During the time that the savages have been at Sillery [that is to say, outside the hunting seasons], they have frequented the sacraments with as much assiduity and fervour as do our French people in Québec." They were adapting themselves to Western good manners: "the Savages show little gratitude in their natural state, especially towards the Europeans. Christianity trains them, little by little, in this virtue"; thus they went "of their own accord" to bring two presents to Montmagny, the first for having risked his life in fighting against the Iroquois, their enemies, and the second "for having wiped away our tears for the capture of Father Jogues and our men by the Iroquois."[155]

The autumn of 1642 also saw the resumption of an experiment already attempted, the "seminary of the Hurons."[156] No longer were children received, but "older persons, more capable of instruction." This time the initiative came from a young man who, some years before, had stayed at Notre-Dame des Anges. In danger of drowning in Lake Ontario, he "made a vow to God that, if he escaped, he would lead a more disciplined and perfect life." So he presented himself with a companion at the door of the priests at Sillery. They received them joyfully but, because of their limited means, refused at first to accept some other candidates who also wished to attempt the experiment. But "the charity of the Governor and of the hospital Mothers gave the means to add three more to the first two, and to baptize those who were not in our house," wrote Father Vimont, who was only too happy with their conduct.

Thus the reduction of Sillery experienced a certain diffusion – the proof of this can be seen in the time which the Attikamek stayed there in the autumn and winter of 1642. This nation lived above the Saint-Maurice River, some 200 kilometres north of Trois-Rivières. A captain from Sillery invited them "with presents"[157] to come and try, if only for some weeks, the experience of the sedentary life. After their customary stop at Trois-Rivières for the fur trade, they came downriver to the outskirts of Québec and set up camp beside the Montagnais (to whom the Attikamek were related linguistically). The group comprised sixty people. The village bore the expense of furnishing them with the provisions that they lacked.

The captain of the group, accompanied by "five or six of the most notable," went at once to meet Montmagny. They had been told of "the great care which the governor takes of those who wish to believe in God"; they promised him that they would be baptized and that they would spread the new belief among their compatriots. He assured them of his protection and encouraged them "to heed the Fathers and learn well what they needed for their salvation." He even made them a gift of "a good provision of wood and of biscuit."

Half of them converted before their departure for the hunt, which apparently took place around the end of February. Montmagny wished to be godfather to the first two to be baptized, a boy of twenty-five and a girl of fifteen. For the ceremony he chose the hospital chapel, "consecrated to the precious blood of Jesus." After the ceremony "he gave a feast, remarkable for the country, to forty of the foremost savages."

It was the beginning of the Christianization of this nation. The subsequent *Relation* devotes a whole chapter to them: "Of the good conduct of the Attikamek."[158] "During the two years since they left Sillery," wrote Vimont, "they have preserved their Faith and the fervor of their piety." The missionary's only regret was to be unable, for lack of means, to visit them in their country.

It remains, however, to mention a less attractive aspect, which the *Relation* does not omit: the impact of the Iroquois war on the settlement. It was not actually attacked directly, but the danger would become so serious that all its life would be severely disrupted.[159]

In June 1641, the rumour spread that the enemy, already installed on both sides of the river around Trois-Rivières, was going to come down to Québec and start by attacking the surrounding, less defensible localities. In reality nothing happened, but the following summer (1642), faced with the persistence of Iroquois aggression, Montmagny encouraged the Jesuits to persuade the nuns to leave the reduction and return to Québec. Shortly afterwards came the capture of Jogues and his companions. This defeat had the effect of noticeably increasing the population of Sillery. The regular inhabitants and the new arrivals pleaded with the nuns to stay – and this was, in any case, their intention.

The end of 1642, and also the year 1643, was quieter for the region. It was in 1644 that the situation took a turn for the worse. At the beginning of May, alarming news came to Montmagny. Father Bressani, captured by the Mohawk, had managed to send a distressing message: the Iroquois intended to invade Sillery and carry off the nuns. A sort of confirmation of this plan came from the fact that some French and aboriginals had been killed at Cap Rouge, about twenty miles from the capital. The governor immediately called a meeting at Fort Saint-Louis (his residence), to which the Jesuits and the principal inhabitants came. It was decided to send the nuns back to town. Filled with a powerful sense of duty, they refused. As was his way, Montmagny did not insist; he sent them six soldiers to assure their protection twenty-four hours a day. At the end of the month, the enemy raids resumed with a vengeance in the environs of Québec. The allies began to move out. This time Montmagny came in person to plead with the nuns to come into town – he could not, for lack of soldiers, strip any more from the defences of Québec. They gave in. He provided them with a little house close to the fort, where the Ursulines had lodged upon their arrival. The construction of the Hôtel-Dieu was resumed in the capital; they were able to enter it in the summer of 1646.

The success (relative though it was) of Sillery made people think that the experiment could be transposed elsewhere. The site of Trois-Rivières was an obvious suggestion: a great number of natives passed by there for the fur trade and, as was their habit, stayed for a longer or a shorter time. In 1643, Vimont could still write: "It would be a great blessing if these people could once become fixed and settled in some suitable residence, as the others have done at Sillery."[160]

The reduction could not progress rapidly because of two factors: the constant coming and going of the natives, accentuated still further by the Iroquois menace, and the fact that most of them were Algonquin, who appeared to the Jesuits even more ill-disposed than the other nations to the reception of the gospel. Some individuals who were extremely hostile to the missionaries, such as that "apostate" called Chibanagouch of whom the *Relation* of 1643 spoke at length,[161] sowed distrust among the population. They were also found to be slow to conform to French habits, or to the simple demands of the military situation; thus Montmagny had considerable difficulty, in 1642, in preventing the murder of a Sokokiois prisoner[162] whom he wished to use in his dealings with the Iroquois.

Despite these handicaps, the nucleus of a Christian population had succeded in forming and in 1641 Vimont counted eighty neophytes.[163] In the autumn of 1643 four Hurons left their country, "to come and winter here, and to be instructed at leisure, hoping to profit greatly from the good examples both of our French people and of the Christian Savages, of whose virtue and good behaviour they had heard tell by their countrymen who had wintered here in previous years and had been greatly impressed thereby."[164] It was the reconstitution, this time at Trois-Rivières, of the new-style seminary of the Hurons that had opened at Sillery – that is to say, the grouping together of adults desiring to perfect their practice of the Christian religion. Two other compatriots who had been prisoners of the Iroquois joined the first four. They chose Brébeuf for their spiritual director – and that speaks for their high demand for perfection: "There they found Father Brébeuf, whom they were seeking; and he received them into our house, and took charge of their instruction and their food, being greatly assisted by gifts from Monsieur the Governor, who spares nothing on such occasions."

The writer of the *Relation* had nothing but praise for their generous spirit – these examples reassured the Jesuits as to the efficacity of their methods, and could not fail to gladden the hearts of pious readers in France. But a sad fate awaited these seminarists in the spring of 1644. On 26 April, they left Trois-Rivières for their country, "promising to speak highly in favour of the Faith, and to make their relatives and compatriots participants in the same good fortune which they had received from us." Father Bressani and a domestic accompanied them. Three days later, they were taken prisoner by the Iroquois in an ambush in a bay in Lake Saint-Pierre. One more trial for New France.

It was, again, the idea of "reduction" that was at the origin of an important achievement of the 1640s in New France, the foundation of Montréal. Here again we must see the direct influence of the *Relations*. The initiator of this enterprise, who lived in La Flèche (we have already mentioned his name, since this man, La Dauversière, had been at college in this town at the same time as Montmagny) had chosen a Jesuit as spiritual director. The body that he set up ended by being called "The Society of Notre-Dame of Montréal for the conversion of the Savages of New France." What is important here – we shall return to this foundation a little later – is the aim which the associates proposed. It is found clearly defined in a little work, *Les véritables motifs*, published in 1643. They were to

> bring together [at Montréal] a people made up of Frenchmen and of Savages who will be converted in order to render them sedentary, form them in the mechanical arts and farming, unite them under the one same discipline, in the exercises of a Christian life, each according to his strength, complexion and industry, and to make the praises of Jesus Christ resound in a desert where Jesus Christ has never yet been named; [that has been] until recently a lair of the demons, and [is] now, by His grace, His dwelling and the delightful resting place of His angels.[165]

Thus it was fundamentally the same approach as that of the Jesuits, as Vimont showed clearly in the *Relation* of 1642. "Their intention is to have houses built in which to lodge them; to clear the land in order to feed them; to establish Seminaries to instruct them, and a Hôtel-Dieu to assist their sick."[166]

These fine plans, the execution of which began in 1642, did not materialize as predicted. The Iroquois war prevented the realization of the initial project.

The programmes of sedentarization normally included hospital care. It has been seen that the Augustinian nuns, who had laboured at Sillery itself for several years, were forced to return to the town of Québec, where they continued to take care of the natives. Chapter 6 of the *Relation* of 1641[167] enumerated the five sectors in which they worked: 1) "They gather in all the poor abandoned savages" – the indigenous people's practices did not always permit them to take along people who could not keep up with them in their travels, such as the sick and the elderly, who were left to shift for themselves as best they could in order to survive. 2) "All sick persons, both French and savage, are welcome in this House" – this was the specific function of the hospital sisters. 3) "As soon as a savage feels ill, he goes to the Hospital to be purged and bled; some of them ask for medicine, which they take in their own cabins" – a sort of dispensary, in fact. 4) "This house is ... a refuge for the needy poor" – a service of social assistance. 5) "The young savage girls ... meet at the House of the hospital sisters, to be instructed there." It should be added that their chapel was often used for catechism,[168] and that certain native women learned to be nurses: "They move the sick, assist them, treat them and are better at preparing their *sagamités*, or their kind of food, than we are."

We can understand the interest shown to them by the colonial authorities, and in particular by Montmagny, who himself belonged to an Order dedicated to the care of the sick.

He was also eager, as was fitting, to support the efforts made by the Ursulines in the field of education. If the seminary for young aboriginal men was a failure, the same was not true of the seminary for girls.

There certainly were difficulties, as for example the disagreement between Marie de l'Incarnation and Madame de La Peltrie.[169] The latter would have preferred a school installed within an Amerindian neighbourhood, like the Hôtel-Dieu at Sillery; the nun, who could apparently count on the support of Montmagny and the Jesuits, preferred a house separated from the natives' cabins. When the Montréal contingent appeared at the end of the summer of 1641, the lady warmed to the project and decided to abandon the Ursulines and attach herself, instead, to the new foundation.[170] Despite the difficulties that this caused her, Marie continued with her work. She was even able, on 21 September 1642, to enter the building which would serve both as a monastery and a seminary. It was situated in the upper town, less than 100 metres from the fort.

Vimont summed up the nuns' achievements thus: "They have always had a fairly good number of savage girls, both transient and permanent boarders, as well as the little French girls and the many savages, men and women, who often come to visit them and to receive some help and instruction."[171] So their work went on at two levels, that of the classroom and that of the parlour.

First, it was necessary to make the students punctual (which was not natural to them),[172] to teach them to read and write (it was above all writing that fascinated them), and to introduce them to Christian doctrine and practices. Furthermore, these young women were expected to serve as mediators in the transmission of the message to their neighbours; and there is evidence that this was indeed the case.[173]

As for the parlour, it was not only a place for friendly meetings: "The parlour of these good women often serves as a classroom, the savages from outside coming there expressly to see them, and to ask to be instructed or to repeat the prayers."[174] The Attikamek, during the several months that they spent at Sillery, seem to have made thorough use of this convenient way of being instructed – and, often, of enjoying a generous meal: "Usually after instruction it is necessary to assuage the hunger of these poor people." For the nuns this was a strong contrast with the cloistered life that they had known in France. Basically, they learned very quickly to place themselves at the service of the natives and to adapt to their way of life.

Montmagny assisted them as much as his means allowed. Above all, he knew how to support their work. One day he summoned an Algonquin who was threatening the life of a Montagnais girl, instructed and baptized under the Ursulines, who refused to become his son's wife. "He told him through his interpreter that he should take care not to attempt anything against the Christians, that he could not attack them without offending his own person."[175] And remember "the little Thérèse," one of the Mothers' most promising students, who fell prisoner to the Iroquois at the same time as Jogues.[176] During negotiations he tried by every means to have her returned to the colony.

3.   From fragile peace to permanent guerilla warfare (1646–1648)

Montmagny's last three years in Canada were difficult. The peace was short-lived. The climate of insecurity, so briefly dispelled, was rekindled in the colony. The systematic devastation of Huronia began in 1647, to be completed in 1649, a year after the chevalier returned to the mother country. Again, the chronological plan works best, since each year had its own characteristics.

The year 1646 was the year of Jogues, so much did this courageous missionary occupy centre stage, even after his death on 18 October.[177] Mid-June was also the tenth anniversary of Montmagny's arrival in the country; and his zeal for the work had not slackened. Jérôme Lalemant recalled it in these terms in the *Relation* of 1646: "Monsieur the Chevalier de Montmagny, our Governor, has also been one of the principal instruments which Divine Providence has used to bring matters to the point and the light in which they are; the labour of ten years has not shaken his constancy, nor diminished his concern for everything related to the advancement of Religion and of the public good."[178]

Four stages, which we shall cover briefly, divide this year that should have been the first of a long and durable understanding: new peace parlays; the sudden about-face of the Mohawk; the tragic adventure of Isaac Jogues; the resumption of guerilla warfare in the colony.

The month of February had not ended when a group of Mohawk appeared at Montréal with the object of confirming the re-established peace which, so far, was still in effect.[179] Arriving at Trois-Rivières, they had Montmagny informed of their presence in the colony, but, since the river was not yet navigable, they put off their meeting with him until later and went on a hunt with the Algonquin – which meant that they were applying the agreed programme of joint activities to the letter. The year was starting well.

On 7 May Montmagny was able to receive the Iroquois delegates.[180] The ritual exchange of gifts began again. Of especial note was the gift which the Mohawk presented to the Jesuits for the disappearance of Father Anne de Noue, frozen to death several kilometres from Fort Richelieu at the beginning of February. The governor's gifts were designed to congratulate the erstwhile enemies for having kept their word: an end to the raids, and the inclusion of the Huron and Algonquin in the peace. Under pressure from the Ursulines, there was again question of Thérèse, the Huron girl: a gift invited them to bring her back to Québec. The Algonquin, speaking through one of their grand chiefs, remained suspicious. The Mohawk ambassador, Kiotsaton, who had already come in 1645, reproached the Huron for not having communicated with the other Iroquois tribes; as for the Algonquin, he let them understand that their visit was eagerly awaited in his country.

Montmagny, for his part, decided to send two ambassadors "to bring them his word and to express his joy and contentment over the peace so happily concluded." He chose Jogues, whose missionary fervour had not been eroded in the slightest by the indignities he had suffered there, and one of his advisers, Jean Bourdon. Montmagny was not unaware that the Jesuit wished to profit by the Iroquois' apparent good will to found a Christian mission among them some day.

The two men's mission went off very well (seemingly, at least) – so well that the priest decided to return to the Mohawk in the autumn and settle among them. He had the imprudence, however, to leave them with a little chest full of objects, which he was to take back upon his return – objects that were harmless, but that ended up appearing mysterious to them, and even dangerous.

At the end of June, the two diplomats returned to Fort Richelieu. Jogues spent his whole summer preparing for his apostolic sojourn in Iroquois country. But even before he left the colony for their country the Mohawk had diametrically changed their strategy. Here is how the *Relation* [181] presented this change: "This people [the Mohawk] had [on a date not given] sent presents to the Iroquois of the upper countries ... in order strongly to continue their alliances, and to conjure [conspire][182] for the ruin of the French and their allied tribes." It was a complete reversal: all Montmagny's policy was thrown into question, all his patient efforts of two years ruined. Father Jérôme Lalemant attributed this "perfidy" firstly to "their warrior humour," secondly to "the glory and the military profits which they gain from war," thirdly to their "superstition," and fourthly – and for him probably the determining element – to "the hatred which the Huron captives have given them for the doctrine of Jesus Christ." We have already mentioned how certain Huron had accused the Jesuits of being the cause of various epidemics (at least three in ten years) which had ravaged their country. Obviously they were not speaking of microbes; they reasoned in terms of magic spells and dealings with the Devil – and under the circumstances the chest that Jogues had left in an Amerindian village took on the appearance of a baleful object.[183]

Unaware of the Mohawk change of attitude, the missionary left Trois-Rivières on 24 September,[184] accompanied by a *donné*, Jean de La Lande. His mission was above all a spiritual one: to begin the conversion of this nation. The governor enjoined him equally to see to the preservation of the understanding so dearly won. But the Huron who went with him had a sense of what was coming; all but one of them deserted after several kilometres on the road.

Upon their arrival, the two Frenchmen were stripped, beaten "with heavy blows of fists and sticks." They were spared the agony of fire, being told: "Have courage, we will strike you with the hatchet and set your heads on the palings ... so that when we capture your brothers they may still see you."[185] The following day it was done. This was the equivalent of a declaration of war.

In November, Iroquois warriors were lying in wait on the island of Montréal. Some Huron returning from the hunt were taken prisoner there, as were two Frenchmen who were a little "distant from the settlement."[186] The guerilla war had well and truly begun.

After a calm of some months, the situation returned to what it had been in 1642 and 1643. Montmagny was no more capable than before of initiatives on the ground; he could only guarantee the defence of the territory. Negotiations which had still been possible in 1646 were unthinkable in 1647. The climate of insecurity that had been felt before paralyzed the colony once more.

In Huronia, it was not yet outright war, but there were some events which presaged no good.[187] The Huron tribe of Arendaenronnons, whose territory was closest to the Iroquois, decided to move out and disperse among the villages farther to the north and west. At about the same time, a neighbouring settlement of Huron belonging to the nation known as the Neutrals was practically wiped out by the Seneca. The latter were equally successful in a raid on the inhabitants of the village of Saint-Ignace (in Huron country), who were "encamped for the purpose of hunting, at a distance of two days' journey into the woods, in the direction of the enemy's country." They fell upon one of the cabins which stood a little apart from the others, killed seven people and made twenty-four prisoners. They took off at once, and could not be pursued. Thus the initiative was with the Iroquois, to the point where the Huron decided not to come to Trois-Rivières that summer. And that meant no European tools for them, no provisioning for the Jesuits and their personnel, and no furs for the *Communauté des Habitants* (the organization set up in 1645, of which there will be mention later), for whom this trade was practically the *raison d'être*.

Life was just as difficult along the banks of the Ottawa and the Saint Lawrence. In the month of May, the post at Trois-Rivières became the object of close surveillance by the Mohawk.[188] First, two Algonquin going out to the hunt were taken. Their aggressors extracted from them a number of details concerning "the condition of the French at Trois-Rivières," and "the places where the Algonquin had recently gone for their great hunt," information that would be put to use immediately. The morning after this capture, while the French were attending the Ash Wednesday ceremonies, two houses "somewhat removed from the fort" were ransacked from top to bottom: "clothing, blankets, powder, lead, and arquebuses, and other like things" disappeared in less than an hour. The pillagers then went off in search of other Amerindians, to the north and to the south of the river. In so doing they met Piescaret,[189] the most famous of Algonquin warriors, and, by a subtle feint, succeeded in outwitting his vigilance: "He began to sing his song of peace, telling to them of his joy at their coming"; he had not yet finished his song when a warrior "thrust a sword into his belly and pierced him from one side to the other."

Montmagny's action in 1647, the last full year that he spent in New France, was extremely limited; as we have explained, the meagreness of means at his disposal did not allow him to do more than assure the defence of his European nationals. In the spring he gave the people of Sillery some soldiers whose purpose was to patrol the Saint Lawrence and chase away as many enemies as they could.[190] They found nothing on the way out, and spent two days feasting in Montréal. But the return journey was painful. Three Hurons were taken prisoner, one of whom was at once burned and devoured. The rest of the party was saved by the intervention of Montmagny, who happened at that moment to be at Fort Richelieu. But he was no luckier than before in the pursuit of the Iroquois, since they took advantage of a torrential rain to flee. At the start of autumn another enterprise of the same kind was organized. Two natives were killed and six French wounded. They managed all the same to bring back an Iroquois prisoner; he was delivered to Montmagny, who judged this time that the man ought to be punished. He "gave him a few days later to a Savage captain, with orders not to torment him for as long as is their custom, nor reduce him to a filthy nakedness, nor to make a quarry of him as dogs do." Before dying, the man embraced the Christian faith. From various indications the Jesuits believed that it was he who had killed Father Jogues.[191]

The year of Montmagny's return to France (1648), the Iroquois played a cautious game. They were more and more convinced that it was not possible to defeat the French outright – the latter knew too well how to defend themselves. All their effort would be concentrated on the elimination of the Huron. No doubt they calculated that once the fur trade's networks had been dismantled, the French would leave. So as not to have enemies along the Saint Lawrence during the execution of this plan, they had to pretend to want to negotiate, and this succeeded up to a certain point.

At the beginning of the year there was a real attempt among the Huron to make up with the Iroquois. The central nations of the Iroquois (the Oneida, the Onondaga, and the Cayuga) lent an attentive ear to these appeals for peace, but the Mohawk and the Seneca remained intractable.[192] They even killed six of the Huron ambassadors who came to the Onondaga.[193] One of the members of this nation who was on his way to Huronia was so disgusted by this treachery that he killed himself.[194]

At the end of the winter Montmagny decided to send a canoe, manned by a soldier and two aboriginals, into Huron territory. He ordered them to be escorted as far as Montréal.[195] Their mission was to urge the Huron to come down for the fur trade. For their part the latter were beginning to feel the lack "of axes and other French goods."[196] A large contingent – 250 men, 60 canoes[197] – set out, but with infinite precautions. Not without difficulty, they succeeded in reaching the post at Trois-Rivières. Shortly after their arrival, Montmagny came himself to meet them. Exchanges of presents took place; it was necessary, according to their custom, to renew alliances with gifts and speeches. The governor expressed his pleasure at the reprobation which they had shown for the murder of a Frenchman committed by one of their own, and, employing their symbolic language, "showed them by this present that in his mind the dead man had come to life again."[198] Always true to himself, "he made another gift, to urge them strongly to keep the promise they had given to listen readily to the preachers of the Gospel." The group left Trois-Rivières again on 6 August.[199] The governor lent them eight soldiers to help in the building of defences around the villages. This was his farewell to the Huron allies. Some days later his replacement, Louis d'Ailleboust, arrived at Québec.

But no one in the colony was yet aware of the disaster that had struck Huronia. At daybreak on 6 July the village of Saint-Joseph (Téanostaiaé), though well-fortified and situated at the southeast extremity of Huron territory, was attacked by the Iroquois.[200] In several hours they succeeded in taking it and setting fire to it. About 700 people out of its 2000 perished on this day, or were led into captivity. Father Daniel, who had helped many of them to escape and who had administered the sacrament of baptism to some, was finally riddled with arrows and musket balls; his body was thrown into the flames of his blazing church. In the other towns of Huronia where the fugitives from Saint-Joseph fled, there was disarray and discouragement; no one dared to work in the fields, and this led to a famine in the region.[201]

On the Saint Lawrence, the Mohawk followed an altogether different tactic, as we have already indicated: a pretence of peaceful intentions. On 18 May two of their canoes appeared at Montréal.[202] They brought peace proposals, which however did not include either the

Algonquin or the Montagnais; what they wanted was to take back one of their warriors who had remained in New France in 1647, the one that Montmagny had given to the Algonquin to be punished. The "peace mission" came up short. It was the same thing in June at Trois-Rivières; from a little fort erected on the south shore 400 warriors, accompanying some ambassadors, made their appearance. It was only a bluff. In mid-July another detachment comprising a hundred warriors stopped at the same post, demanding to be sold provisions – another ruse, since more than eighty sacks of corn were found in their fort.[203] A Huron prisoner who had escaped from their hands unmasked their pretence: "The Iroquois, he declared, were planning to invite the French to a conference during which they would kill them all."[204] These Iroquois were finally defeated by the Huron who arrived for the fur trade.[205]

Montmagny's mandate was ending on a depressing note.

Despite these incidents – for 1649 the word would be catastrophe – life went on. With altogether insufficient means, Montmagny still managed to keep his colony running. The institutions set up at the start of his administration continued to prosper; we allude here only to the bodies devoted to promoting the Christian life among the aboriginal people: the reduction at Sillery, the Hôtel-Dieu of Québec, and the Ursuline seminary. A few minor events are to be noted during the last months of Montmagny's term at Québec.

"The aspect of the country, which appeared to me wholly frightful in the war, when I saw it for the first time, having changed and become very beautiful in the quiet of peace"; truly "digitus Dei est hic"; the finger of God is here. These highly optimistic remarks of Jérôme Lalemant set the tone for the letter which served as introduction to the *Relation* of 1646.[206] Note that he did not know, at the date of writing, of the martyrdom of Jogues. What impressed him above all was the expansion that the experiment of sedentarization was undergoing. "After a night of so many centuries, the light has appeared over these countries. The Faith is in its dawn ..."; the 300 converts that they had counted during the last twelve months were the most striking proof of this. That was the important point, but recognizing that other factors had powerfully contributed to this success, he named five of them.[207] The first was "the good condition into which the gentlemen of the Company of New France have put the country and the colony" – an amiable waft of incense towards an institution that was in fact moribund and ineffectual. The other factors can be taken at face value: the help of the "Messieurs of Montréal"; the devotion of the two female communities of Québec; the good example of the inhabitants; the courage of the governor: "Monsieur the Chevalier de Montmagny, our Governor, has also been one of the principal instruments which Divine Providence has used for bringing affairs to the point and to the light in which they now are."

But the tone adopted at the beginning of the *Relation* of 1647 contrasts sharply with that of 1646: "The state of life at present is the reign of instability, of trouble, of obscurity";[208] to this observation dictated by his human wisdom there is a corresponding Christian reaction, hardly less pessimistic: "all times and places are filled with the judgments of God, incomprehensible to our minds; and ... the paths and the ways [taken by] His Divine Majesty to arrive at a goal, are very different from those which men would have chosen."

The major event was evidently what he called "the treachery of these barbarians" the Iroquois; it was responsible for the death of Jogues and his companion, as well as the attacks against the French and their allies. This disaster had its spiritual counterweight: "Over six hundred savages have been baptized, what can we desire further?"

In fact, the reduction at Sillery knew a certain success. The church of Saint-Michel, which had been inaugurated at the end of 1646, "has not, in truth, the magnificence of those great miracles of Europe," but it thrilled the native people, whose edifying examples filled numerous pages of the *Relation* of 1647.[209] The Iroquois incursions unnerved them to some extent, but, as we have seen, did not slow down the rhythm of conversions.

Jérôme Lalemant seems to have been fascinated by the behaviour of a tribe from the north of the Mauricie, the Attikamek.[210] As we have already mentioned, they had once passed a winter at Sillery, and this had been the beginning of their conversion to Christianity, for which certain admirable natural qualities prepared them: "It seems as if innocence, banished from the majority of the Empires and Kingdoms of the World, has withdrawn into the great forests where these people dwell. Their nature has something of the goodness of the Terrestial Paradise before sin had entered it. Their practices manifest none of the luxury, the ambition, the avarice, or the pleasures that corrupt our cities." In spite of their nomadic lifestyle and the absence of missionaries among them, they remained faithful to the practices into which they had been initiated. They came to Trois-Rivières in the summer of 1648. They took only three hours to set up their cabins and prepare a feast. "When this was done, each one came to give an account of his conscience"; and the priest commented: "I do not know if in Monasteries of the strictest discipline there are many people more sincere and more candid than those good folk, who have dealings only with God, and with the animals of their great forests."[211] The Iroquois attacks had not snuffed out the hopes of implanting and developing Christianity in Canadian soil.

The *Relation* of 1646, like those that preceded it, praised the courage, the zeal, and the charity of the hospital sisters.[212] But in fact the work was evolving, and they now seem to have been receiving as many French people as aboriginals.[213] Yet it was still the latter for whom they cared the most, allowing them to set up their huts close by the hospital, furnishing them with food in case of need, and teaching them Christian prayers.

In the autumn (5 November) of this year 1646, the foundress and first superior of the institution, Marie Guénet died. Only thirty-six years old, she had lived as a religious for twenty, including the seven passed in the service of the Amerindians,[214] whom she loved as much as if they had been her own children. The mortifications which she had not given up in spite of the hardship imposed by adaptation to a new climate and precarious conditions of life (of which a religious had died in 1641)[215] were justified, according to Lalemant, by her "strong constitution." After the funeral, there was a "funeral feast for the Savages."[216] One of these "pronounced an oration and in his own manner gave the eulogy" of the deceased.

The loss of this admirable nun was compensated two years later by the arrival of a remarkable woman – the equal, one may say, of Marie de l'Incarnation: active and devoted like her, and also a mystic in her prayer life. It was at the moment when Montmagny was relinquishing the reins of power (19 August 1648) that Catherine de Saint-Augustin arrived; she was only sixteen, having been born in 1632.[217]

As for the "seminary" of the Ursulines, it continued to be "a great blessing to both the French girls and the Savages."[218] More than eighty girls were "aided and instructed" between the summer of 1646 and that of 1647. And it was a charity that went a long way. The native "seminarians" in fact received quite a different treatment from the French students; they were lodged and fed without charge, all the more because it was as a favour that the Amerinidians were asked to confide their daughters to the religious. As well, they had to be dressed in the French style. When they left, their parents were offered gifts; sometimes there was even a dowry given to someone who was going to marry upon leaving school. Occasionally adults were confided to the religious, as for instance a Huron who was fed by them throughout the winter of 1646–1647.[219] A woman, who had "escaped from the country of the

Iroquois," came to complain to the Jesuits "that a Demon tormented her"; they handed her over to the Ursulines who delivered her from her anguish. "After a few days the poor creature came to tell us that she was quite free, and that God had cured her in the house of the virgins."[220]

The activity of the superior, Marie de l'Incarnation, was always boundless; no task discouraged her in the service of young people and of adults. The business experience that she had had at the start of her widowhood made her eminently suitable to oversee the work of the employees whom she engaged. She even took it upon herself to straighten out subtle questions of religious administration,[221] while living, in the midst of this hubbub, an intense spiritual life. The mortifications that she imposed on herself for her "offences" to God are evidence of a great delicacy of conscience. Her mystical experiences make her one of the most brilliant representatives of the great spiritual force of the seventeenth century.

For twelve years Montmagny had to direct a colony the territory of which was peopled principally by Amerindians – a sharp contrast with his first career in the Mediterranean. In conclusion to this long chapter, it seems fitting to present some brief reflections on his status as representative of the king of France, on the attitude that he adopted toward the native people, and on the essential features of his military activity.

The governor was the first person in importance of the country, and, according to the testimony of the *Relations*, the native people were well aware of this, even as they knew that he held his title from the king, the "great captain" of the French. Montmagny lost no occasion to develop this sense of authority in them – by which we mean the monarchical authority; the feasts which he organized for the birth of the dauphin and for Anne of Austria's assumption of the duties of regent were directed toward this end. He acquitted himself most worthily in his role as representative of the most powerful king in Europe. He lived up to the name – Onontio, "Great Mountain" – which had been given to him; he was imposing, even as he remained accessible to all. But there remains an ambiguity: the power of the king which the missionaries and the governor presented as being so impressive was slow to manifest itself concretely on Canadian soil. When he promised to aid his allies and defeat their enemies, Montmagny could not feel perfectly at ease, so puny was the assistance provided to him.

In no way did this affect his fundamental attitude toward them. He was a religious; this implied that he would do everything to promote the conversion of the Amerindians. And even toward the enemies, the Iroquois, he showed all the benevolence that he could – he did not oppose Jogues's somewhat ambitious plans to go and live among them.[222] He knew, when duty demanded it, how to use strength, to fight them with all his energy, to make the best possible use of the poor means at his disposal. He even came to make contact with the Dutch authorities, allies of the Mohawk.[223] To his native friends he multiplied his exhortations to become pupils of the Jesuits; he was ready to mix with them, above all, it seems, in cultural activities. He knew, as well, how to attune himself to them, offering gifts and feasts and thus closely following their traditional customs.

His military initiatives were dictated by the security of his European nationals and, at the same time, by the demands of the alliances concluded with the various nations. He paid for this with his own person, moving around to meet an enemy that was highly mobile and better armed than his allies, often himself directing the operations. He twice asked the mother country, whose interest was elsewhere, to give him military aid. It was exasperatingly slight, but he did not become discouraged. When he deemed it opportune, even necessary (it being the only option possible) to negotiate with the Iroquois, he used all his benevolence and his skill. He was only too willing to assist the allies – had they not been promised in 1603 that they would be helped to vanquish their enemies? To escort the convoys coming down from Huronia, or heading back, substantial forces would have been needed; he could only offer tiny contingents. To prevent the disintegration of the Huron nation, he would have had to send some dozens of soldiers; he could not do so without dangerously reducing his garrison. What a grievous situation for the representative of a powerful state!

At once the question arises: Could he have done more? Did he lack initiative? The response, it seems to us, has been given throughout this chapter. With the means at his disposal, we believe that he could not have done more. He twice sent Father Le Jeune to warn the French authorities of the dangers that threatened their colony – without success. France was at war, and there was an almost total lack of interest in Canada. The royal power had a convenient alibi: the *Compagnie de la Nouvelle-France*, which was useless, and, from 1645 onwards, the *Communauté des Habitants*, also powerless.

Should this indifference be seen as a conjunctural phenomenon? One would think so, in view of the fact that Richelieu, heavily preoccupied with the war in central Europe, turned a deaf ear to Champlain in 1633 when he asked him for "a hundred and twenty men lightly armed."[224] Much more significant (and to our mind indicative of a fact of a structural order), was Colbert's response in 1666 to Intendant Jean Talon, who had been trying to make him understand that the riches of Canada were immense and that people must quickly be sent there: "The King cannot agree with all the argument that you make regarding the means to form Canada into a great and powerful State ... It would not be prudent to depopulate his kingdom, as one would have to do, to populate Canada."[225]

ILLUSTRATION 5

IROQUOIS. HURONS ALGONQUINS, ET DIVERS
PEUPLES EN CANADA, ET EN LA LOÜSIANE

Etching, 1676. (National Archives of Canada, C-070615)

ILLUSTRATION 6

Château Frontenac, Québec: Cornerstone bearing the Cross of Malta, deposited in 1647 by the chevalier de Montmagny

CHAPTER 7

"Wise and Prudent Conduct"
in the Internal Management of the Colony

On 6 June 1645 a "governor's commission" was delivered to Montmagny.[1] The royal authority gave as its principal reason: "You have acquired so great a reputation by your wise and prudent conduct." It was the third renewal of his mandate. In 1639 the Jesuits had expressed satisfaction at "the continuation of his government."[2] In 1642, the king, satisfied with his "services," had reappointed him and granted him a pension of 3,000 livres.[3] What is more, this reputation of his had not been slow to take shape, since when, after a study in depth, Father Du Tertre wrote his history of the Antilles, he made this remark: "The Company[4] believed that Poincy [another Knight of Malta, sent to Saint-Christophe in 1638] would govern the islands with the same prudence as the chevalier de Montmagny governed Canada."[5] The term "prudence" used here by the author undoubtedly signified that, compared to the rash and sometimes inopportune initiatives of Poincy, the "conduct" of Montmagny had been marked by a greater submission to the authorities – the king, the Company – and a greater respect for persons. The Jesuits of New France never missed an occasion to eulogize the governor, sometimes grandiloquently; we have just seen this on the subject of his relations with the native peoples. Likewise, Father Vimont's remarks concerning his management of the colony's internal affairs came very close to panegyric: "For the rest, it would be difficult to explain the cares and the trouble that Monsieur de Montmagny, our governor, has taken and still takes, every day, to smooth out the colony's difficulties. Anyone else would have lost courage a hundred times."[6] These remarks appear at the beginning of the *Relation* of 1643. And in that of the previous year he had used different words to say the same thing: "The entire colony has passed the winter in good health. Monsieur the chevalier de Montmagny, our governor, always as amiable as he is beloved, maintains everything in peace, repose and good order. Everyone is happy to honour and respect him."[7]

So it is the other part of the mandate confided to Montmagny that we wish to examine in this chapter – namely the administration of New France.

At this level, which could be entitled the internal life of the colony, the governor was charged with two imperatives: to ensure respect for the king and the Company, to assure a certain quality of life for the inhabitants.

To learn how he performed these two tasks, we shall proceed in two stages. First, we shall examine his actions in the various domains that were under his authority. Second, we shall try to discern the part he played in the most important events of this period in New France.

1.   Managing a colony: some points of reference

Montmagny, we must remember, was the representative of a commercial company. The French government, still hesitant to launch into colonial adventures, had been willing to head a body that, in principle, was to assume all the costs of colonization. The funds placed in this Company by the associates could profit, or at the very least be maintained, only by trade – essentially, the fur trade, which by this fact became the primary responsibility of the person whom they designated to the king to be the governor of Canada. The study which we shall make at the end of this chapter of the innovation represented by the *Communauté des Habitants* (created in 1645), of which the chevalier was one of the promoters, will provide the occasion to consider the development of this activity between 1636 and 1648.

His second task was that of assuring the security of the inhabitants. The aspect we should consider here is what Vimont has called "peace," that is, internal peace: the administration of justice and the equitable distribution of lands.

His third task was the "conservation of the country" – otherwise put, making sure that the inhabitants could enjoy a normal supply of consumer goods, including those of a cultural nature.

The laws of the kingdom were applicable to New France, and the legal code which prevailed there was drawn not only from the Custom of Paris, but also from those of both Orléans and the Vexin. The judicial framework was extremely simple, given the tiny size of the colony in those days; the governor remained the ultimate authority to whom to appeal. All the same, jurisprudence was a discipline with which Montmagny had a certain familiarity, seeing that his family had included numerous magistrates, and that he himself had for several months attended the faculty of law of Orléans. As well, in Québec he found a colonist (and what is more, a member of the Company) who held a licence "ès loiz," Noël Juchereau des Chatelets, who became one of his principal advisers.

The prevailing impression that comes out of the testimony that the Jesuits have left us of his performance is summed up in the three words of Vimont cited above: "peace, repose, and good order." This was a restatement of the judgment brought by Le Jeune some years earlier:[8] "It remains to speak of our ecclesiastical and civil policy. I have already said that there is no work here for legal quibblers. Any differences that I have seen arise so far have appeared only to disappear quickly. Each man is his own advocate, and the first person he meets is his judge in the last resort without appeal. If something deserves to be carried to Monsieur the governor, he dispatches it in a couple of words or has it dealt with by those who have knowledge of the affair."[9]

For the Jesuits, then, "good order" was explained by several factors, chief of which was the personality of the governor himself – the constant application to his duties and the prudence that characterized him. In 1646, Jérôme Lalemant recalled, with justice, that all his concern was for the advancement of "the public good" and religion.[10] But we must keep in mind the fact that the population was still very small – and this lessened the occasions for quarrels and lawsuits. In 1646, at a time when local interests were at loggerheads with the *Communauté des Habitants*, we see "murmurs" building up, and certain colonists frustrated by the advantages that the new arrangement would give the more fortunate. Montmagny swiftly intervened to put an end to this incipient rejection of the established order; but soon afterwards he encouraged the efforts that were made to improve the formula – and this would culminate in the amendments of 1647 and 1648.

From this a little light is thrown on his method: to assure the principle of authority while accommodating to concrete realities and seeking to understand people. Of the cases that he had to judge, only a few examples have survived. In two disputes which set some tenants against their seigneur in the summer of 1646, he pronounced in favour of the latter – we shall return to this case.[11] At about the same time, some native men in Sillery had killed a Frenchman's cow "which had been in their corn."[12] Montmagny made them appear before him, and exacted a fine of 75 livres, or six beaver pelts; but he declared to them "that once they made a complaint, justice would be rendered to them for the damage that the cows had done in their corn." And on 28 April of the following year, he published an ordinance on this subject: "All the inhabitants, and others of any quality and condition whatsoever [are obliged] to enclose, or have enclosed, pigs and other animals belonging to them; or to have some person to guard them, in order to avoid the damage which the said animals could do to grains and newly-sown fields; on pain of arbitrary fine."[13] We can see at once the concept he had of public order: property should be respected, but it was not up to the individuals themselves to enforce its maintenance in case of conflict. Still more significant was the judgment which he rendered on 19 July 1647, against a certain Lafontaine, who broke the law forbidding the sale of alcohol to the natives.[14] He sentenced him to a fine of 30 livres; however, since the guilty man confessed his fault, he ended up charging him only 10 livres – a way of making the judgment more humane and, in the final analysis, more effective.

He had to be severe with some misdeeds, and he did not hesitate to condemn the guilty to the "chevalet."[15] For instance, two Frenchmen who were drunk while attending Midnight Mass on the evening of 24 December 1645, to the great scandal of the native people, were punished this way. Five men who were drunk at Easter, in 1648, were similarly chastised.[16] It certainly seems that Montmagny took the role of guardian of order, which the king had confided to him, seriously. He did not compromise principles – the indigenous people were obliged, like other subjects of the king, to respect their neighbours' property – but he showed flexibility and understanding in the application of the law. He knew how to be "expeditious," as has been mentioned above.[17]

A task just as urgent – and what is more, essential, we should say, to the maintenance of internal peace – was the settlement of the country and the division of the land among those subjects who were going to develop it. Four aspects will hold our attention: 1) what may be called the occupation of the territory, or concretely put, the distribution of seigneuries – the system common to all the provinces of France, that was transferred to Canada; 2) the exploitation of the lands thus shared, that is to say the redistribution by the seigneurs within their fiefs to tenants, or even vassals (the sub-fiefs); 3) urban management – already the cluster of dwellings that formed the capital, Québec, was the object of the Company's preoccupations; 4) Montmagny's own contribution to this work of colonization; he had a seigneurie granted to himself, which he rapidly put to exploitation.

At the end of the summer following his arrival, the governor was quick to tour the heart of his colony – the Saint Lawrence, from Cap de Tourmente to the Saint-Louis rapids at Montréal and its environs.

The land grants had begun before his arrival, but, except around Québec, there was as yet no tangible result. The first settler of Québec, Louis Hébert, had two fiefs granted to him by the viceroy of New France, one in 1623,[18] very close to Québec, the other, in February 1626, some kilometres to the north; and alongside this second fief, some days later, the Jesuits received a grant of land, which they christened Notre-Dame des Anges.[19] The first grant made by the *Cent-Associés* in the region, on 15 January 1634, was the *côte* of Beauport, northeast of Québec, to Robert Giffard, who wasted no time in coming to settle there with his colonists.[20] Beyond this narrow perimeter, nothing had yet been done (despite the two grants made in 1633 and 1634 in the Trois-Rivières region).[21]

For 1635 there are two grants to note: La Citière, given to the oldest son of Jean de Lauson, the Company's intendant – an immense territory south of Montréal, containing, in theory, five million acres,[22] that was returned some years later to the royal domain; and the fief of Cap Rouge (west of Cap aux Diamants), granted to Noël and Jean Jucherau.[23]

In Montmagny's first years, distributions were more numerous: five in 1636, six in 1637, two in 1638, two in 1639, three in 1640. A total of eighteen in five years; and from 1640 onwards, the geographical area which they covered extended – going from east to west – from the tip of the île d'Orléans to the western end of the island of Montréal.

Note some details about these grants. The île d'Orléans and the *côte* of Beaupré (situated on the mainland just north of this island) were conceded to a consortium formed by eight members of the *Compagnie des Cent-Associés*. The Lausons were still present; a great seigneurie on the south bank opposite Québec, which was to bear their name, belonged to Jean de Lauson, and it should be noted that he also owned an eighth part of the land that had been granted to the aforementioned consortium. Thus from 1636 this family held a significant part of the lands distributed in New France. In 1636 and 1637, the surveyor Jean Bourdon was endowed with two seigneuries,[24] possibly through the influence of Montmagny, who greatly appreciated his services.

The other beneficiaries of the period were mainly religious bodies. The Ursulines would receive three fiefs,[25] the hospital sisters, by way of the Duchesse d'Aiguillon, the property of the Grondines.[26] In 1640 the two founders of Montréal, the baron de Fancamp and the Sieur de La Dauversière, acquired the island of Montréal and the seigneurie of Saint-Sulpice.[27] Two fiefs were also made over to the Jesuits in 1638 and 1639: the île aux Ruaux,[28] just beyond the île d'Orléans, and Batiscan, close to Trois-Rivières.[29]

There followed a dead period of five years; no concessions were made between 17 December 1640 and 5 May 1646. Two factors explain this pause: first, the shortage of manpower (almost no rural workers were coming to Canada, and thus, in accordance with regulations, the unexploited lands risked lapsing out of the hands of their holders); and second, the Iroquois menace, which discouraged even the most enterprising. François de Chavigny de Berchereau, one of Montmagny's men, had to give up the exploitation of his seigneurie west of Québec, land which would later be called Deschambault after his son-in-law.[30]

Montmagny's last three years (1646–1648) marked a resumption in the granting of lands. The Iroquois peace of 1645 gave hope for a period of tranquillity. Furthermore, the setting up of the *Communauté des Habitants* (also in 1645) seems to have had an invigorating effect, since it was its promoters who during those years were largely the recipients of fiefs – beginning with the governor himself, who by three deeds dated 5 May 1646, received the seigneurie of the Rivière du Sud. We shall return to this soon. Three of the twelve directors obtained lands: Robert Giffard, the fiefs of Saint-Ignace and Saint-Gabriel, enlargements to his seigneurie of Beauport;[31] Pierre Legardeur de Repentigny, the fief of Becancour south of Trois-Rivières and, close to Montréal, on the north shore, the contiguous fiefs of l'Assomption and Lachenaie; and Jacques Le Neuf de la Poterie, the fief of Portneuf.[32] On 18 September 1647, Montmagny granted Jean Juchereau, Sieur de Maure, the general agent of the Community's store during 1646 and 1647, the seigneurie which, in fact, bore the name of De Maure.[33] Two interpreters, Jacques Hertel and Nicolas Marsolet, also became seigneurs in April 1647, of two small properties in the region of Trois-Rivières.[34]

Finally, on 1 April 1647, François de Lauson began to divide up his immense fief of La Citière, south of Montréal, and he granted the seigneurie of La Prairie de la Madelaine to the Jesuits "who, he said, still [expose themselves] every day to danger in order to draw the savage peoples of the said country to the knowledge of the true God."[35] The official occupation only took place on 3 May 1649,[36] after Montmagny's departure.

These, then, were the thirty-three grants that were made under his administration; the impetus was given, and it would continue for many decades. In 1648, the seigneuries were spread out – though not yet contiguous – between the Cap de Tourmente and the west of the island of Montréal. Québec was no longer the only centre of development; Trois-Rivières, and even more, Montréal, were also beginning to play a role.

To be sure, the final aim of this important work of sharing out territory among the seigneurs was not to offer them an increase in prestige, but rather to promote the development of the colony. This was one of Montmagny's great preoccupations.

In the Company's deed of 20 March 1638 that granted the île aux Ruaux to the Jesuits, this remark is found: "we have been informed by Monsieur de Montmagny, governor of Québec, of the nature and quality of the île aux Ruaux, situated in the Saint Lawrence River below the île d'Orléans, and what the aforesaid island has to offer to those who are ready to put it into cultivation."[37] Montmagny had visited the region in the autumn of 1636, and he knew that the Jesuits, who had domestic servants, were capable of assuring the exploitation of this little island. It was with the same view that he insisted to the same Jesuits that, in their seigneurie of Notre-Dame des Anges, they distribute lands to tenants in return for payment of dues. The Father Provincial of Paris agreed to this, but faced with the hesitations of the general, it took until the year 1647 to conform to the governor's wishes.[38]

Montmagny did not spare himself in making certain that the rules concerning property were respected, or that the surveying was exact. He can be found, on 22 June 1646, on the banks of the Saint Charles River with Father Lalemant, working on the verification of the boundaries of the lands granted to the Ursulines; the question was complex, and he postponed "the whole matter until the return of M. Bourdon who had gone to the Iroquois."[39] The following month he came to the aid of his counsellor, Noël Juchereau, in rendering judgment in a dispute which pitted Robert Giffard against two of his vassals who were refusing to render homage for their holdings.[40] The governor obliged them to meet their obligation. The same sentence was passed a few days later, on 20 August 1646, when they again defied the law by refusing to make the official declaration and to pay the dues for the two lands that they held from Giffard.

It remains to examine what, concretely, the distribution of tenant holdings in the Saint Lawrence valley represented during Montmagny's administration. Marcel Trudel has counted, year by year, the acreage thus conceded by the seigneurs.[41] For 1637, 1,418 acres – an impressive figure, since only 240 had been allotted in the preceding ten years. For 1638 and 1639, 1,054 acres. Then comes the great trough of 1640–1643 – in four years, an acre and a half. The activity began again in 1644 with 351 acres, to reach a peak in 1647 with 2,563 acres; then, in 1648, 1,772 acres. These are not overly impressive numbers; in 1654, under Jean de Lauson, the distribution reached 12,792 acres. But the conditions were different: the civil war that had followed the Thirty Years' War was over; the colonist arrivals were more numerous (in 1653 the *recrue* totalled 232 persons).[42] For the Montmagny period, the factors which accounted for the fluctuations in the grants of fiefs were equally at play: the numerical weakness of new arrivals and the warlike activities of the Mohawk. In 1643 Jacques Hertel had established colonists in an sub-fief of his, downriver from Trois-Rivières; he had to abandon the clearance work and return to the post with his tenants.[43]

The seigneurs had another means of getting value for money: the exploitation of their "domain," that is to say, the part of the seigneurie which they reserved for themselves. They cultivated it themselves, or turned it over to a farmer. For the period that concerns us here, the evidence is too slight to allow any significant conclusion.[44] Suffice it to say that Robert Giffard held onto a domain of 450 acres, on which, in 1634, he built a manor, including a chapel; and that the Jesuits exploited two *métairies* in their seigneurie of Notre-Dame des Anges.[45]

On 15 August 1648, just before leaving his post, Montmagny, in the name of the Company, made over to the "inhabitants of Trois-Rivières" "a shared field to serve as pasturage for their animals." This institution had existed in France since the Middle Ages, but one spoke, rather, of "commons": tracts of land, mostly pasture, which were reserved for the use of the "community of inhabitants" of a parish. Inspired by these precedents, the residents of Trois-Rivières had then asked for the grant of a parcel of land, which they would clear in common, to protect their cattle against the incursions of the Iroquois.[46] They were doubtless aware that the seigneurs of Beaupré included in their deeds of grant this little phrase: "the fields along the said river, [held in] common."

In keeping with his limited means – a reflection of the poor health of the Company that employed him – Montmagny did his best to supervise the distribution of the lands in his territory. At the time of his departure in 1648 the French grip on the Saint Lawrence valley was beginning, in spite of everything, to have a certain strength.

In the *Relation* which he drew up at the end of the summer of 1636, Le Jeune was no doubt repeating for the Father Provincial conversations that he had had with Montmagny, when he wrote: "The courage of these gentlemen [of the Company] incites them to go forward. They are thinking of various dwellings or habitations all the way to the great falls [Sault Saint-Louis, close to Montréal] which will perhaps some day all be towns."[47] In fact, the directors of the Company must have had long discussions in their meetings at the beginning of the year about the management of territory; this can be proved by the letter which Jean de Lauson, then intendant of the organization, wrote on 19 March 1636 to the two brothers Noël and Jean Juchereau, in which he informed them: "that the Company had resolved to keep a *banlieue* around this city of Québec and around each residence of the said Company, in which no-one may have a fief; so that all this area will be held by the said Company; and that the boundaries of the said Sieur de Maure [Jean Juchereau de Maure] may only begin at the end of the said *banlieue*."[48] The Company was beginning to preoccupy itself with town planning. Montmagny was quick to comply with its wishes. He immediately notified the Juchereau brothers of the decision which concerned them: "Monsieur de Montmagny, newly acceded to the government of the country, has found that the said grant would end too close to the city."[49] Then he personally went to work. As we have said, he was not there three days before he traced "the delineations of the fortifications,"[50] on which he made work begin without delay. But here is something more interesting: "The alignments of a city have been drawn up, so that all that is built now will be in good order."[51] Apparently the Company left it to Montmagny to define what was the "good order" in question. To help him in this work he had an engineer, Jean Bourdon, with whom he soon developed close bonds. It was necessary to envisage an overall plan for the space reserved for the city. The layout which was adopted for the upper town, the seat of government, the main outlines of which endured throughout the seventeenth century, was characterized by the close connection between the imperatives of defence and those of urbanism; from the point of departure constituted by the "fort," the fortified residence of the governor and his garrison, and the adjoining *place d'armes*, the streets were planned so as to fan out – what is called a "plan rayonnant."[52] On the outer curve of the fan there were to be fortified walls (which would not be erected until later in the seventeenth century).

"Military town planning," one may call this arrangement.[53] Montmagny had lived several years in a city of similar conception: Valetta, as well as being a secular city and the centre of a religious order, was an ingenious fortress.[54] In a way he found himself in his element in Québec.

One last task faced him: to redistribute the lands while taking account of previous decisions. Champlain had visualized building the city along the Saint Charles River, north of Cap aux Diamants; its centre, now, was going to become the high ground which commenced precisely at this cape and for this reason would be called the upper town. Around this site, also, a *banlieue* was planned, where the properties would be distributed *en roture*.[55]

The Juchereaus, as has been seen, had to move westward. Guillaume Couillard, Louis Hébert's son-in-law and heir, ceded the properties he owned within the perimeter designated for the city, in return for land in the *banlieue*. The operation lasted until 1645, when, on 6 June of that year, Guillaume Bense sold the Company the two pieces of land that he still held there.[56]

The beneficiaries of the operation were the religious bodies; but the dimensions of their grants were made uniform, each allotment containing about six acres; they were compensated with lots in the *banlieue*. In 1645, the administration of Notre-Dame parish received from Guillaume Couillard a site on which, starting in autumn 1646, the church would be built. There was only one grant to a private person: on 9 September 1640 Montmagny gave Louis Hébert's widow a piece of land to serve as a courtyard and garden for the house which she occupied.[57]

Thus the upper town was still only thinly populated when Montmagny left Canada in 1648. Apart from the religious houses, it comprised the fort, the construction of which was now well under way, and some dwellings.

In the *banlieue* that gave towards the west (in the direction of Cap Rouge) some properties were distributed: for example, to Jean Coté, on 27 August 1636;[58] to the Juchereau brothers; to the two interpreters Le Tardif and Nicollet; to Pierre Puiseaux, who spent close to 100,000 livres of the money he had acquired in the Antilles to build a little château;[59] to François Derré de Gand, a land of 130 acres, given afterwards to the Jesuits for the reduction of Sillery;[60] and to Adrien Duchesne, surgeon.

On the side of the Saint Charles River, the distributions were still more numerous. We note only that of 25 February 1637 to the two brothers Jacques and Robert Caumont,[61] who were later joined by Pierre Gadbois; ten years afterwards, on 7 April 1647, they sold the lot to the Hôtel-Dieu for the sum of 1,500 livres.[62]

There remained, at the foot of the escarpment, an enclave which was soon given the name of Lower Town; it had its own configuration (more or less rectangular) and its own purpose as a port and a commercial centre. The Company had had its store there since its foundation; a bakery, a brewery, and chalk- and brick-ovens were attached to it. The Jesuits acquired a warehouse there. Toward the end of his mandate, Montmagny granted a space to the *Société de Notre-Dame de Montréal*, and Jacques Le Neuf de La Poterie, "perhaps the greatest businessman of the period,"[63] obtained permission to establish there.

The title of "city" is certainly applied to Québec's cluster of houses, but it does not correspond to the definition which Richelet gives: "A place full of houses and encircled by terraces and ditches or walls and ditches."[64] Here, in 1648, in the upper town, were the fort under construction, the three religious houses, the church, a few dwellings and, for the rest, fields and gardens. In this regard two contemporary witnesses are very enlightening.[65] In 1644 Marie de l'Incarnation described for her son what she saw with her eyes:

> In response to what you want to know regarding the country, I will tell you, my dear son, that there are houses of stone, of wood, and of birchbark. Ours is all of stone, it is 92 feet long and 28 feet wide; it is the largest and most beautiful in Canada ... The fort is of stone, as are the houses belonging to it. Those of the Reverend Fathers [the Jesuits], of Madame our foundress, of the Hospital Mothers and of the sedentary savages, are of stone. Those of the inhabitants are half-timbered and gravelled; two or three also being of solid stone. Some of the savages have their portable houses of birchbark, which they erect very neatly with poles.

And here, in 1650, is what Father Ragueneau had to say: "Québec is called a city; it would be truer to say that apart from the fort, our house and the two convents of nuns, it has almost nothing which even has the appearance of a humble village, let alone a city. There are some thirty houses of French people, scattered here and there without any order." Thus, for the Jesuit, it was not even a humble village. The plan conceived by Montmagny and Bourdon was not yet visible; there were not enough houses to speak of real streets. The political situation, both in Canada and in France, had played against them. Development would only come later in the seventeenth century.

Montmagny decided, when he found the circumstances favourable, to participate personally in the colonizing effort. The first mention that we have found of this dates from 25 October 1645; it is drawn from the *Journal des Jésuites:* "On the 25th Monsieur the Governor left for the Isle aux Oies where he was having the ground worked and had seven labourers."[66] We can suppose that he had charged one of the "habitants" who went to France in the autumn of 1644 to negotiate the creation of the "Communauté," to obtain a verbal agreement from the Company. The official concession was signed 5 May 1646.[67]

It seemed to him a propitious moment: the king had appointed him for another term; the Iroquois had promised to remain peaceable. So he set a team to clearing the land and constructing buildings. He was able, at the beginning of November, to send a priest (abbé Gilles Nicollet, who had accompanied him to the site in October) to assure religious services for the workers over the winter.[68]

As was proper, the name of Montmagny was given to the town which now occupies the site of the original seigneurie, of which this first description is drawn from the deed of grant:

> [the] lands and places declared hereafter, to wit: the river called du Sud at the place where it discharges into the Saint Lawrence with a league of land along the Saint Lawrence going upriver towards Québec and a half-league along the same river in the direction of the Gulf, the whole running four leagues deep in the lands flanking the said river on one part and the other, and this included in the total extent, and furthermore two islands situated in the Saint Lawrence river close to the said place downstream on the said river, the one called the Île aux Oies and the other called the Île aux Grues, with the shallows between the two, the whole containing about four leagues along the same river, the aforesaid grants to be enjoyed by the said Sieur de Montmagny in full property, justice and seigneurie.[69]

This seigneurie was situated on the south shore of the river (or close by, in the case of the islands) at a distance of about fifty kilometres from Québec.

Montmagny could not immediately exploit all the acreage that had been granted to him; he decided to begin with the île aux Oies, where natural fields already gave hay in abundance.[70] He swiftly introduced cattle-raising – in 1647 there were already a dozen head[71] – and a fishing industry – on 24 July 1647, the Jesuits received a cask of salmon coming from the Île aux Oies.[72] He did the same for hunting, which he enjoyed as well: as we have already mentioned, game, and particularly wild fowl, was in great abundance at certain times of the year.

Once the labours of clearance and construction were assured, he was ready, in 1646, to settle a farmer on the island: Jacques Boissel, who remained there until 1649.[73] By this date Montmagny was in Paris, and we do not know who replaced the first farmer. At any rate, on 6 May 1650, he presented, as he was required to do by custom, "avowal and enumeration" "for the fief and seigneurie granted to him" but he promised, "in case of profession to the Order of Saint John of Jerusalem to place the said holdings out of his hands so that they would not fall into mortmain."[74] There was danger that the land would become the property of an institution, considered as "perpetual,"[75] and by this fact the then seigneur would be deprived of the rights due at the moment of transmission by succession and alienation (by sale or otherwise). And indeed, on 17 May 1651, Brother Charles Huault de Montmagny did make his solemn profession in the Temple in Paris. We shall return to this subject later.

So he was thinking of putting his affairs in order and, when a serious buyer turned up, he sold. This transaction took place in Paris on 10 January 1654.[76] His brother Adrien Huault, to whom he had left a power of attorney before departing for Saint-Christophe, ceded the seigneurie to "Louis Théandre Chartier, Esq., Sieur de Lotbinière and Demoiselle Elisabeth D'Hamour his wife, and Jean Moyen, Esq., Sieur des Granges and Demoiselle Elisabeth Lebrest his wife," in return for the sum of 300 livres cash and, for the rest, a *rente* on a principal of 2,700 livres.

Montmagny had doubtless desired above all to give an example and to incite the seigneurs to develop the resources of the Saint Lawrence valley. It required a certain dose of courage to cultivate an isolated spot such as the Île aux Oies, some distance from the capital, and difficult to defend; the truth of this is shown by the fact that in 1655 Jean Moyen, one of the two men who, the year before, had bought the seigneurie, was killed with his wife and doubtless with his employees, by the Iroquois, who at the same time destroyed the buildings and other effects.[77]

Seeing to "the protection and security of the country" also implied overseeing its provisioning, a service provided by the Company, and then by the *Communauté des Habitants*. It was to the store in Lower Town that the inhabitants of Québec went to buy arms and ammunition, tools, clothes, and other consumer goods of the day. The functionary assigned to the supervision of this service had the title of "victualling agent,"[78] so much was it the case that his principal concern was for the distribution of foodstuffs. The provisions arrived from overseas during the summer in the Company's ships. Interesting to note in this regard is "the memoir of what was sent to the Hôtel-Dieu" in March 1640.[79] Just to mention the foods: there are listed, first the ordinary foodstuffs:[80] flour, barley, oatmeal, biscuit, peas, rice, lard, oil, butter, cheese, honey, wine, brandy; and then the foods serving above all to nourish the sick: "dried fruits," described separately as "raisins," "prunes," and hops (houblon).[81]

We can well imagine that dependence on the mother country could present difficulties, as for example the anxiety felt when ships were late arriving. At the beginning of July 1639, since no one had had any news of the ships that were supposed to be coming from France, François Derré de Gand, who was at that time the victualling agent, asked Montmagny to publish an ordinance to prevent the shortages that always remained a possibility – through seizure of the ships by enemies or pirates, or just simple shipwreck. Three commissioners were then designated "to inspect the lands under cultivation in the environs of Québec as well as the victuals which the inhabitants of Québec and surrounding places have in their stores and in their houses, to be sure that the report that they have made to us adequately describes the need for and shortage of food in the country,"and, after the inspection, to issue "very express prohibitions and interdictions on the part of the king ...against their removing, subtracting or using in any manner whatsoever any of the said victuals, except what is necessary to them daily for the nourishment and maintenance of their family."[82] The rigorous terms which the governor used show how serious the situation appeared to him; in this regard his stay in Malta should be recalled, a rocky island that depended on the outside for its food supplies, and where similar measures were not unusual.

In fact – and his interest in turning lands to agriculture has proved it[83] – Montmagny was aiming at self-sufficiency (in essential products, of course) for the colony; it would almost be guaranteed in 1653, at least where cereals, the staple in the diet of westerners in the seventeenth century, were concerned.[84]

There is also the impression that, from the time of his arrival, Montmagny was fascinated by the wildlife of the country. Le Jeune reported in his *Relation* of 1636, the drawing-up of which was completed at the end of August, "that Monsieur our Governor arranged to domesticate" some moose;[85] elsewhere he specified that "two males and a female" were involved. The success of the operation is not certain: "if they become tame, it will be easy to feed them, since they eat only wood,"[86] but undoubtedly the experiment was not crowned with success, since there was no further mention of them.

Le Jeune again recounted that in the autumn of 1636, on the way back from the journey that he made with the governor, the latter could not resist chasing a moose which crossed his path:

On October 4, we left Trois-Rivières. Hardly had we gone four or five leagues when we saw a moose walking along the edge of the woods.

We were sailing along gently in the middle of the great river, in the beauty of a golden day. Monsieur the governor, having seen this great animal, at once ordered the sails lowered and everybody silenced, while two or three of our Frenchmen went stealthily in a little canoe, to bring this huge beast down into the water, or to shoot her dead with the arquebus, if she took to the woods. Hearing the noise, she leapt into the water. At once Monsieur ordered a longboat equipped, which was rowed over to her. The poor beast did not know which way to flee; she saw arquebuses on land and, on the water, a longboat bearing down on her. Finally she was killed and brought on deck. If all the voyages undertaken in New France passed as pleasantly as this one, there would be too much pleasure and perhaps the body would profit more than the spirit.[87]

A highly interesting scene, in which we do not know what to admire most, the narrative ability of the Jesuit or Montmagny's mastery of the chase – there was hunting in Malta, too. Without a doubt the chevalier also loved to have game on his table. He was in a position, at the New Year, to send the Jesuits partridges out of his larder, or wild geese coming from his seigneurie. He also took an interest in the aquatic resources of the region, as witness his fishing excursion to Lake Saint Charles in March 1637, and the stocks of salmon which he harvested in the vicinity of the île aux Oies.

He seems, then, to have been convinced that the food-producing potential of Canada was immense. What remained was to find people to exploit it. In this respect, the political circumstances were totally unfavourable to him. But we must remember that "man does not live by bread alone." Even in a colony where numbers were still very limited, there were celebrations – if only thanks to the elaborate liturgy of the Church. All this was in the domain of what is also called cultural consumer goods. There again, it is tempting to see the chevalier at work. What part did he play in this? Does he appear to have been involved? Did he innovate?

At first glance it may seem surprising that the information on this subject is more plentiful than that, for example, on diet. But a moderately attentive reflection will allow some insights. The sources at our disposal for this period were for the most part religious – the Jesuits and the female communities. Feast days and Church ceremonies were of particular interest to them; and the governor himself belonged to an Order in which ceremony was still imprinted with medieval symbolism.[88] It has frequently been pointed out that Christianity had profoundly marked the life of Montmagny, by the very vocation that made him a successor to the crusaders. But he was just as much filled with the culture of the age: he had studied under the Jesuits; he had passed time at the university; he had lived several months in Italy – an Italian influence which his stay in Malta could only accentuate.[89]

Furthermore, these events, which came out of daily life and belonged to the spiritual domain, were more easily retained by our chroniclers than the material reality that was essentially commonplace and, in their eyes, valueless except as a substratum for the spiritual.

The most numerous solemn occasions of New France in this period came, it can be surmised, from the domain of the sacred. First of all there were the moveable feasts of the liturgical year. The only two about which we have some detail were connected to the Eucharist, the sacrament which the Counter Reformation had chosen to rehabilitate. On Holy Thursday in the spring of 1640 the practice was begun at the Hôtel-Dieu of "washing the feet of the poor ... as is the custom in well-regulated hospitals." Montmagny "wanted to be at this holy ceremony." He "was the first to begin to wash the feet of the men," he was followed by his lieutenant the chevalier de Lisle and "some of our foremost Frenchmen."[90] The two chevaliers were familiar with this rite, which had become traditional in their Order, and which re-enacted Christ's gesture of humility at the Last Supper.[91] For the feast of Corpus Christi,[92] the monstrance was carried triumphantly through the public square; the choice of bearers of the canopy[93] was left to the governor.[94] It will be recalled that he had insisted in 1638 on having at his side a native man who had just made his First Communion. "Monsieur our Governor spoke to us of giving him one of the supports of the canopy under which the Blessed Sacrament was carried, taking one himself with truly generous humility."[95]

Some of the fixed feast days received a particular lustre under Montmagny. The first one for which he was responsible after his arrival was the feast of the Immaculate Conception, the patronal feast of the church of Québec, which the Jesuits served. "At the beginning of Vespers a flag was planted on a bastion of the fort, to the sound of cannon; and at daybreak the artillery reawakened our joy." The inhabitants responded with "a salvo of muskets or arquebuses and many approached the Holy Table in her Honour [the Blessed Virgin]."[96]

More impressive still was the spectacle which Montmagny reserved for the people of Québec the following 19 March,[97] the feast of Saint Joseph, the patron whom the Recollets had chosen for New France.[98] "Monsieur the Governor arranged for bonfires with as many fireworks as I have seen even in France." The illumination which came at the end was in fact quite ingenious, and even astonishing, for the tiny outpost that was Québec in 1637. It took place in three stages. First there was a stake, bearing "the name of Saint Joseph in lights"[99] above which twenty "little snakes,"[100] little twisting jets of fire, were sent skyward. Behind the stake, "Fourteen large rockets (fusées)[101] were lit," which were shot up one after the other; they fell "in showers of gold or of fire." A third "wonder" was a miniature castle built on a levelled surface at the end of a beam; it was "flanked by four towers filled with burning candles," and surrounded by "four big trompes[102] from which thirteen dozen little snakes were seen to leap, rising up six by six at regular intervals, and four dozen rockets which were fired twelve at a time." Montmagny had looked for help to his engineer, Jean Bourdon, and to Sieur de Beaulieu.[103]

It was not possible to use such riches every year. On 18 March 1646, the fireworks were very simple, and the feast day itself, 19 March, so loaded with devotions that "Monsieur the Governor became unwell with them." In 1647 "there were no fireworks" on the eve of the feast. Jerôme Lalemant said, however, that he himself was the cause of this change; he had explained "that a Benediction in honour of the Blessed Sacrament was better" – a rigorist reasoning which was certainly not to Montmagny's taste, but to which he conformed out of respect for his old educators.[104]

The feast of Saint John the Baptist, June 24, was celebrated in Canada as in France, Christianity having transformed the ancient rites tied to the cosmic phenomenon of the solstice and to the return of the summer season. For Montmagny it had a particular significance, because the precursor was the name-saint of the Order to which he belonged.[105] The Journal des Jésuites described the procedures followed in the years 1647 and 1648. In both cases, Montmagny invited the priests to the opening of the ceremony: on the evening of 23 June he lit the traditional bonfire, and allowed the guns, cannon, and muskets to sound; the priests sang a hymn and recited a prayer.[106]

The Jesuit feast days did not pass unnoticed. On 31 July 1646, Montmagny wanted to give a cannon salute to commemorate that of Saint Ignatius, founder of the Society, canonized in 1622, the very year that he entered the Order of Malta. But Father Lalemant dissuaded him for a very practical reason: the fleet from France that they were expecting daily had not yet arrived, and the sound of the cannon might make the colonists believe that the ships were finally in port.[107] On 3 December Saint Francis Xavier was honoured;[108] in 1645, Montmagny had the "Diane" – a drum roll at daybreak – sounded;[109] in 1646, he had a three-gun salute given at the fort, and he sent the priests "two bottles of Spanish wine and a suckling pig."[110]

We must also remember that the number of days of rest – Sundays (fifty-two) and feasts of obligation (forty-five until 1642, and thirty-one thereafter) – was considerable: between seventy-five and ninety (there would have been fewer when Sunday and feast day coincided). Added to these were the special celebrations – for example, the "jubilee," which lasted for two weeks in Canada in 1645, or the political/religious solemnities which were connected to the vow of Louis XIII and to the birth of the dauphin.

These jubilees or holy years had existed in the Church since 1300, and fell on regular dates.[111] The faithful in a state of grace could, on performance of certain practices, obtain a plenary indulgence – a new occasion for multiplying acts of devotion and revitalizing the Christian faith. The pope could also proclaim an extra Holy Year, which is what Innocent X did for 1645 (he had been elected in 1644). In New France it ran from 17 to 31 December.[112] Montmagny co-operated fully: three cannon salutes at the moment of the *Veni Creator*, the traditional opening hymn; and above all, alms to the needy: two pistoles given on the spot, and a promise to furnish a significant sum: "he ordered M. Deschatelets (the general agent of the *Communauté de Habitants*) to give whatever we ask of him for the poor, to the amount of 200 livres."[113] The native inhabitants of Sillery also wanted to have their part in the jubilee; on 26 December they came in procession to Québec, visited the three chapels – the parish, the Ursuline convent, the Hôtel-Dieu – and, "despite the great cold," went home fasting. "On their return to Sillery they were given a banquet on behalf of Monsieur the Governor."[114] On 15 August 1638, there were two reasons for great rejoicing: "The savages of these four cabins [which had been infected with sickness] all came into our house on the day of the glorious Assumption of the Virgin, in order to take part in the procession which we made to recognize this great princess as superior and protector of both Frances, according to the holy affections of our good King, and as well to bless God because in His goodness He has been pleased to give [us] a child of miracle and benediction."[115] The priest's first allusion concerned what has been called the vow of Louis XIII, the solemn act by which he "vowed," or consecrated, his person and his kingdom to God under the patronage of the Virgin – a promise which, faced with the danger which the Spanish invasion of 1636 represented for his country, and devout man that he was, he had made to God.[116] A commemorative procession recalled this event each year, on 15 August. The second allusion was to the pregnancy of Queen Anne after twenty years of marriage, which many saw as a blessing from heaven.

"Monsieur our Governor," continued the Jesuit, "did not forget anything of all possible magnificence necessary to honour this procession." The natives and the French filed two by two, and at various places they passed before "hedges of soldiers" who saluted them with musket volleys. "The cannon ashore and those afloat, firing in good order, caused I know not what rejoicing, accompanied by a holy devotion that all offered to God for the accomplishment of our great King's designs and for the salvation of these peoples." What a fine example of the spiritual enthusiasm of the author of the *Relation*: "holy devotion," offered by "all" to God!

In July of the following year, it was the birth of the dauphin that was celebrated; a whole chapter of the *Relation* of 1639 was devoted to it: "Chapter One. Of the joy which New France received with the birth of Monseigneur the Dauphin and of a council which the savages held."[117] Montmagny immediately ordered the staging of an already prepared event, which we may suspect contained fireworks and cannon salutes. He judiciously shared out the gifts which the king had sent to the aboriginals: six formal suits of clothing, very showy, which impressed them greatly. The procession of 15 August was accompanied by the usual deafening gunfire, and followed by a banquet presented to the native people. Thanks to the latter, the celebration ended on a realistic note: they held a great council in which they tried to make the Jesuits and Montmagny understand that their fine promises to help them settle down would not be taken seriously as long as they could not bring in people to teach them European techniques (in construction and agriculture among other things).

In the seventeenth century there still survived in Europe traces of an ancient custom, the "May." Furetière defines the May as "a tree or a great green branch, which by honour is planted before the door of a person whom one wishes to honour on the first of May."[118] In 1637, Montmagny took the initiative of introducing this practice into New France, though giving it a religious orientation. "On the first day of May [Le Jeune tells us], Monsieur the Governor ordered a great tree with a triple canopy to be raised in front of the church, at the base of which were three great circles, one upon the other, decorated with festoons, bearing these three beautiful names inscribed as on an escutcheon: Jesus, Maria, Joseph. It was the first May Day with which New France has honoured the Church. It was saluted by a troop of arquebusiers who surrounded it."[119] But parallel to this first act, another took place at the fort. "The soldiers planted another tree in front of the fort, bearing a crown under which were fastened the arms of the King, of Monsieur the Cardinal, and of Monsieur our Governor." This second version more closely resembles what we find in the dictionary cited above; but it was, perhaps, the expression of a sense of respect owed to the authorities – the governor, representative of the minister (head of the *Compagnie de la Nouvelle-France*), and of the sovereign. If the idea for this decision came from the soldiers themselves, as the author seems to suggest, it must be concluded that they held their superior in a certain esteem.

We have noted in passing the way in which these events punctuated daily life. It was necessary to engage the senses: first and foremost, to seek out visual effects (the fireworks, some of them quite ingenious as we have seen, were altogether appropriate) as well as more plastic images, such as those superimposed crowns or the miniature castle prepared for Saint Joseph's feast, and movements like the processions to which the medley of costumes added colour. There were sound effects, too, some of them ear-splitting, basically produced by firearms; others, more melodious and poetic, were obtained by hymns and religious chants[120] or by a musical instrument.[121] All this display, we should note again, was meant to touch the imagination, to put across ideas, and to incite to do good.

Another dimension comes across: the sense of community, expressed in liturgies, processions, gatherings to watch a spectacle, visits, and exchanges of presents on certain occasions.

There is one more element to point out, and not the least: the omnipresence of Christian symbolism; even the May tree, an essentially profane act without religious connotation, took on new meaning under Montmagny's inspiration. We can see how much the formation that he had received from the Jesuits had shaped him. One more example of this will suffice, one that was more complex: the inauguration of the practice of theatre in the Saint Lawrence valley.

This art, as we have already shown, was an integral part of life in the Society's colleges.[122] During his stay at La Flèche, Montmagny had many occasions to learn its secrets – and perhaps to participate in it. In 1614,[123] for example, on the occasion of the passage of the young Louis XIII, Fathers Petau and Caussin wrote and produced a piece which they entitled "Pompa Regia";[124] there was also a performance of a tragedy, "Godefroy de Bouillon,"[125] and "Clorinde,"[126] a play which was staged in one of the avenues of the park.

In the preceding chapter we have mentioned the first piece played (in 1640) in the Saint Lawrence valley – a tragi-comedy of which we do not know the title or even the theme developed in it; what Le Jeune retained of it was the pedagogical value for the Amerindians of a scene where Satan took part.[127] More significant from many points of view was the presentation on 31 December 1646 of the greatest success of the day on the Parisian scene, Le Cid by Pierre Corneille.[128] First of all, it should be remembered that the author had been a student of the Jesuits in Rouen (he was slightly younger than Montmagny, having begun his studies in 1615). And the piece was, and still is, one of the masterpieces of universal literature, not only for the language (many verses remain justly famous) but also for its dramatic qualities. It is one of the great works of baroque art, through the skilful presentation of the spirit of chivalry – which the "chevaliers" (or Knights) of Malta claimed to perpetuate. But what is still more remarkable is that so elaborate a piece could have been staged in Québec in 1646. Jérôme Lalemant, whose tendency towards a certain form of rigorism has already been noted, was reticent about Montmagny's undertaking, as is evident from the brevity of the mention which he made of this obviously important event. But it should be noted that, throughout the century, the attitude of the clergy in New France was, on the whole, very severe with regard to the theatre, or at any rate that which did not explicitly aim to promote Christian values. "Our Fathers attended out of consideration for Monsieur the Governor who was fond of it, and for the Savages as well," wrote Lalemant; he asked Montmagny to excuse him from attending; but in the end his judgment was not unfavorable: "Everything went well and there was nothing which could cause scandal."

It is not without interest to mention that Jean de Lauson, who arrived in the colony in the summer of 1651, did not wish to fall behind the chevalier. On the following 4 December he had another piece by Corneille staged, Héraclius, which he had no doubt seen in Paris when it first appeared in 1647; then, four months later, on 16 April 1652, he returned to Le Cid. Does the dry mention of the two events by Father Ragueneau in the Journal[129] mark his disapproval?

Thus Montmagny gave strong support to the clergy in all celebrations, mostly of Christian inspiration – and relatively numerous, as we have seen – which punctuated the life of the colony. He took part personally in all the solemnities, in the same spirit as his one-time masters of La Flèche; but he was able all the same to keep a certain distance from them – as the staging of Le Cid demonstrated.

2. Concerning some outstanding events

During the years 1636–1648 the internal history of the colony witnessed three events of great importance: the arrival of the nuns (1639); the foundation of Montréal (1642); and the setting up of the *Communauté des Habitants* (1645). Actually, colonial life was so marked by the aboriginal phenomenon during this period that in studying this we have already discussed the first two events; it only remains to add some further details to underline the part played by Montmagny. The third will merit more attention, because it could be said that it was to some degree his work, or, at least, that it could not have succeeded without his agreement and his participation.

We have already pictured the joy which ran through the little colony on 1 August 1639, the day of the arrival of the hospital sisters and the Ursulines. Here is how the author of the Annales of the Hôtel-Dieu described their welcome: "Monsieur the Governor received us with all possible demonstrations of benevolence. He told us how much he had wanted us, the pleasure that he had in seeing us and the care that he wanted to give us, to prove by his actions the sincerity of his esteem and affection for us. He ordered several cannon fired in our honour."[130] Montmagny understood perfectly what the presence of two communities of women meant to a young colony. To begin with, from the religious point of view, the consecration of their life to Christ and the practice of the greatest of Christian virtues – charity – had to be an inspiration to the colonists and the native peoples. From the social point of view, essential services like education and health were going to be assured, and there would be, for women wishing to enter religion, the possibility of finding houses to receive them.[131] Finally, from the economic point of view, these stable institutions, receiving financial support from the mother country, were to play a part with respect to property (urban building, rural land development) and employment (workers and servants, for instance).

When Montmagny left in 1648, they were well established, with impressive houses in the little town, and seigneuries not far from Québec; their work, among the native peoples as well as the colonists, had become part and parcel of the life of New France.

The governor had contributed in various ways to this success. Here is the testimony of the hospital sisters: "Monsieur the Chevalier de Montmagny returned to France. We cannot say enough about how he looked for ways to please us and with what exactitude he used the frequent opportunities presented to him to render us service. He advised us in all things and himself looked after our needs. He helped us greatly in those beginnings and in the moves which we were obliged to make before fixing on our permanent establishment. He was a very brave man, very accommodating, full of compassion for the poor, zealous for religion, and altogether capable of inspiring the love of Christianity by the example of his piety."[132] The portrait which the author traced is highly flattering. It blends with that of the Jesuits; what results is a picture that doubtless bears some resemblance to the real person, in benevolence, readiness to help, the art of accommodation, and gallantry.

It is this last virtue which Marie de l'Incarnation emphasized in a letter to the superior of Tours in September 1642. According to her, his fighting ability and his courage had saved the colony: "If Monsieur our Governor had not been on the spot [Fort Richelieu] all would have been lost, since there remained only thirty or forty men who perhaps were not the most careful."[133] His zeal for religion consoled her greatly; in the same letter she recounted the edifying behaviour of three of her pupils, "who this winter went on the hunt with their parents to help them with the housekeeping and to prepare their furs." She had received letters from them, and she concluded "that everybody [to whom she had spoken of it] admired their spirit," but she added this: "above all, Monsieur our Governor spoke to me of it with a very particular consolation, seeing in these Savage girls, raised in the woods and the snows, sentiments of devotion and a politeness of spirit which often are not found in the well-brought up girls of France." She, too, judged Montmagny's charity to be exemplary; he assisted native people threatened by famine; he "gave them great charities during that time. He was the most charitable man that one could see; all these poor folk had thought to die of hunger."[134]

Based on mutual esteem and constant collaboration, the relations which were formed between the nuns of Québec and Montmagny were excellent; he played his part in the success of their work.

Montmagny participated again, though this time indirectly, in the second great event of these years, the foundation of Ville-Marie. The establishment in his territory of a little village for the purpose of advancing the faith among the Amerindians could not leave him indifferent. What was involved, in effect, was a reduction modelled on the experience of Sillery, comprising the same educational and hospital services. The initiator of this enterprise, Jérôme Le Royer de La Dauversière, is not unknown to us.[135] From his adolescence onwards he had lived in the Jesuits' orbit. It was in 1639, it seems, that his spiritual director, Father François Chauveau, gave him the green light to realize a dream which he had nurtured for some years, the establishment of a Christian colony on the island of Montréal in Canada.

Thanks to the numerous relationships that he had in Paris, some of them by way of the *Compagnie du Saint-Sacrement* of which he was a member, he succeeded in interesting several persons in his project, and in collecting funds. In the spring of 1640, he was able to send material to Québec. On 7 August of the same year, with his principal associate,[136] he obtained from Jean de Lauson the donation of the seigneurie of the island of Montréal, a donation confirmed by the Company on the following 17 December.[137]

At the beginning of 1641, all was ready for the realization of his plans. It was Father Charles Lalemant, the procurator in Paris for the Canadian missions, who suggested to Le Royer de la Dauversière that he engage a demobilized military man, Paul Chomedey de Maisonneuve, to assume command of the mission.[138] Regarding this man, no significant information survives concerning his actions and deeds before 1640, but the Jesuit had recognized qualities in him which made him the ideal candidate to supervise the beginnings of the enterprise: courage and determination, a sense of organization, skill in the handling of men, and solid Christian convictions.

The hazards of navigation delayed Maisonneuve's arrival in Québec by several weeks; thus, when he disembarked in September, it was too late to think of getting to Montréal. Two problems confronted him. The first was to organize the forced stopover. With the help of a woman of some diplomatic ability, Jeanne Mance, he succeeded in finding the needed assistance, and was welcomed with all his entourage (forty persons) near Sillery, at the home of Monsieur de Puiseaux.[139] The second was to confront the opposition which swiftly built up against his project. The "Montréalists"[140] arrived at a bad moment: the island where they planned to establish themselves was a long way from the capital, and thus difficult to help in case of danger – a danger which was no illusion, since the whole upper Saint Lawrence basin west of Trois-Rivières had been living for some months under the terror of Iroquois incursions. Montmagny had just sent Le Jeune to Paris to ask for reinforcements to fight effectively against these enemies. The Jesuits, who certainly approved the principle of a new reduction, were sceptical of its success under the circumstances. "I have difficulty believing," wrote Vimont in 1642, "that there will ever be enough Savages at Notre-Dame de Montréal to master the Iroquois."[141] Montmagny decided to call "an assembly" of "the foremost persons of the country";[142] this was the question that he proposed to their consideration: "Would it not be more suitable to settle the island of Orléans than the island of Montréal?" Maisonneuve, who was present, took the floor to express his surprise "that a matter which concerned him had been brought up for deliberation, before he had spoken of it." Clearly he wished to say that, being the first concerned, he ought first to have presented his project to the group before it was opened to discussion. If this was indeed what happened, the governor's tactic was not a good one. He had probably wanted to show the new arrival that public opinion was against his enterprise. Maisonneuve unequivocally let the assembly know "that he had come to lay the foundations for a town on the island of Montréal, and that, no matter if this plan turned out to be even more dangerous, he would carry it out or die in the attempt."[143] Faced with such determination, Montmagny, in his usual manner, did not insist. He even left a short time later for Montréal.[144] Assisted by his surveyor, and following the instructions given him in the contract of December 1640, he laid out the territory which was to go to the "Messieurs de Montréal."[145] It was he who, on 17 May of the following year, presided over the official takeover of the seigneurie by Maisonneuve, and the foundation of the town.[146]

All the same, two incidents took place during the winter that, without the cool-headedness of the two men, might have soured their relations. Maisonneuve's people had decided to celebrate his birthday on 13 February. Jean Gory, a surgeon by profession and a jack-of-all-trades, used arquebuses and cannon for the celebration, without consulting Montmagny, who alone had the power to authorize salvoes. The latter immediately had the prankster imprisoned. Maisonneuve did not protest, and the governor, not wishing to increase the tension, swiftly released the "culprit." However, upon Gory's return, his patron committed the blunder of glorifying his conduct: "You were put into chains for love of me, you have suffered the punishment and I have received the affront, I love you the more for it and for that I raise your wages by 10 écus."[147] Montmagny, understandably, did not take this slander, which threatened to undermine his authority, lightly; on principle he had an inquiry made, but he did not pursue an affair which might poison his relations with a man whose service record, as well as the good opinion the Jesuits held of him, was known to him.

From then on the relations between the two men seem to have been altogether correct. In their defence, it must certainly be recognized that Maisonneuve's status was not completely clear. It was only at the beginning of July 1643 that Montmagny came to Montréal to deliver a letter from the king (dated the 21 previous February), giving permission to complete the fort and install all the pieces of artillery necessary to its defence. At the same time, the king recommended that Montmagny assist Maisonneuve insofar as he could.[148]

Things were becoming clearer. On 13 February 1644, the king granted the society of Montréal permission, among other things, to designate a "governor," to erect a *corps de communauté*, and to travel freely on the river. The following 26 March, a commission according this title of governor was signed in favour of Maisonneuve.[149] So Montréal enjoyed a certain measure of autonomy – and in fact, it seems that Montmagny would not be seen again in Montréal between 1643 and the end of his mandate. Québec was where the control of the fur trade and the power of sovereign judgment remained. These elements were going to be transformed substantially by the political and economic restructuring which began in 1645 and which remains to be studied.

Before closing these reflections, it is interesting to remark that on the future of Montréal both Montmagny and Maisonneuve were right, but on different levels. The initial project could not be realized; the Iroquois menace continued until 1701, preventing the allies from coming to settle alongside the French. On the other hand the post, better situated for the fur trade than Trois-Rivières, developed rapidly. Furthermore – and this is symbolic of the change that was taking place – the name of Ville-Marie was progressively abandoned for that of Montréal.

The governor's first responsibility, according to the commission of 1645, was "to preserve commerce," that is to say, to protect and facilitate the Company's operations. But it should be remembered that the commission was dated 6 June, and that shortly before, a new distribution of powers had been established in the colony. The role of the governor was going to be transformed, and for that reason, Montmagny was enjoined to "enforce the execution of the decrees and rulings of the Council" on this subject.

From 1633 to 1642, the Company had delegated a part of its responsibilities to subcontracting companies, which had not been as successful as hoped.[150] In 1643 and 1644 it assumed the task itself, and then after the beginning of the year 1645 an original formula was developed: while still under the authority of the parent Company, the *"Communauté des habitants du Canada"* – a sort of new subcontracting company – was formed, this time comprising only residents of the colony. There should be no surprise at this initiative; Montmagny had adopted the habit of consulting the principal inhabitants when there was a question of making important decisions.

In fact, in 1644 there was a small group of enterprising men – one could doubtless call them the 'notables' of the colony – among those who had decided to settle permanently in Canada. Their names are well-known: Giffard, Legardeur, Juchereau, Le Neuf, Bourdon, Godefroy, Chavigny. These men recognized the immense resources of the country; they wanted to develop them, and – why not? – enrich themselves at the same time.[151]

Two things preoccupied them. First, the fur trade remained risky. In a good year, such as 1635, the sale of pelts brought in 284,500 livres tournois;[152] but in 1642, 1643, and 1644 the sums were, respectively, 131,000, 85,000, and 48,000 livres.[153] This considerable drop was due in large part to the Iroquois war. Then in 1644 peace talks were begun, making it possible to predict a period of tranquillity; furthermore, the king had sent help in 1642, and the regent did so again, in 1644; leading to the hope that the metropolitan government was now going to intervene in a serious and rational fashion.

A second cause for anxiety was the Company's indebtedness. At the beginning of 1642, this debt amounted to 411,000 livres. The king had forced the associates to put in a supplementary contribution to meet the deficit, and, at the same time, to facilitate the necessary borrowing. But their ranks were beginning to thin out: from 104 shares counted in 1642, there remained only sixty-four in 1644.[154] Rightly or wrongly, the Canadians believed that they could, by way of the anticipated profits of a renewed fur trade, meet this deficit. Did they hope that the king would, if necessary, continue to exact sums from the associates of the parent Company? It is likely, since some of the notables were aware of what was going on in the mother country; Jean-Paul Godefroy's father was an active member of the Company.[155]

Of the discussions and conversations which preceded this step by the home authorities, no trace remains; but they must have taken place with Montmagny's permission, on the one hand because some of the promoters were close to him, as will be seen; and on the other, because the Jesuits played an important part in the affair. Already Paul Le Jeune's journey in 1643, taken at Montmagny's request, had met with the approval of "all the inhabitants who [had] earnestly requested it of us," according to Vimont,[156] and furthermore the solution of 1645 would be adopted as a result of their energetic intervention.[157] The affair was concluded, says Lalemant, "agente regina et nobis impellentibus";[158] the Queen has added the weight of her authority to the affair and we (the Jesuits) gave it all possible encouragement.

Can we identify the authors of the project? Two names stand out, it seems: Pierre Legardeur de Repentigny and Noël Juchereau des Chatelets.[159] The former had arrived in Canada at the same time as Montmagny, whose lieutenant he became upon the departure of the chevalier de Lisle. The second, who has already been mentioned, had a jurist's formation; he was one of the governor's most listened-to counsellors. Also, they were both about the same age as he. It was Legardeur who would be sent to Paris to negotiate, in the company of the businessman Jean-Paul Godefroy (born in Paris in 1602, and so some months after Montmagny and in the same town as he).

One principle was going to guide their action: the colonial management of the fur trade was "the only way of keeping them (the merchants) there, and calling in new ones."[160] In other words, the dynamic elements already in the colony must be retained, and others must be attracted.

Some points of the decree of 14 January 1645 should be recalled.[161] The Company retained the seigneurial ownership of New France;[162] therefore it still chose the governor. Montmagny remained its official representative in the Community. In principle he ruled the colony, but in everything that concerned commerce, he had to take account of the opinion of the *habitants*, since what the Company ceded to the Community was "all rights and powers in the fur trade."[163] So it was the Community, and it alone, that received and bought furs, just as it was the Community that was responsible for the distribution of commodities coming from France. That implied, among other things, the complete outfitting of a fleet. Equally, the expenses of the colony fell to it: the salaries of agents, employees, and soldiers, the furnishing of munitions, the construction and upkeep of fortifications. There again, the governor's authority was eroded, since part of the defence of the territory now reverted to the *habitants*. As well, it was agreed that twenty colonists a year should be brought over – a far cry from the 266 that Richelieu had foreseen for each of the years from 1628 to 1643! Another important factor was that Montréal was integrated in a more rational fashion into the colony, meaning co-operation in the commercial enterprise, and subordination to Québec for administration and defence.[164]

How was the Community structured? A first level – call it the base – comprised the *habitants*, that is to say the colonists who had settled in New France and opted to stay there. The frequency of their meetings was not spelled out. The second level comprised twelve directors to whom fell the management of the enterprise. It is no surprise that this little group included the entrepreneurs mentioned above, who, on account of their family and marriage arrangements, ended up by forming a sort of clan.[165] It was also from among them that the premier officers of the Community, such as the admiral of the fleet and the general agent, were chosen.

The position of the governor was slightly changed. If he still answered to the Company that had named him, he was now remunerated by the Community; and if he had the last word in matters of commerce and defence, he had in practice to come to terms with it in these two domains.[166] It goes without saying that it is normal for a new body – and one without an equivalent in the mother country – to start out with fumbles, hesitations, and sometimes blunders. This is what was going to happen.

In 1645 and 1646 the situation was favourable; the Iroquois did not intercept anything and the sums drawn from the sales of furs reached an average, for each of the two years, of a little more than 300,000 livres.[167] One might well have believed that the new arrangement would bring peace and prosperity. This was not exactly the case; there were frictions, then recriminations.

Some points should be recalled here. Despite the significant amount of profit drawn from the fur trade – evaluated at 196,000 livres for the Community in the autumn of 1645[168] – the costs were so considerable that a deficit was registered; it was the same in 1646, which meant that no dividend could be distributed to the *habitants*.[169]

A minor squabble put the general agent of the Company at loggerheads with the general agent of the Community, over the surplus of furs brought back by soldiers returning from Huronia.[170] The dispute was settled peacefully and the sum was turned over to the building of a church and a presbytery in Québec (construction of which would begin in the autumn of 1646). This should have put an end to the complaints of those who were nostalgic for the previous regime; but apparently, such was not the case.

At the instigation of the Community's governing council, which now supervised commerce, Montmagny issued a series of ordinances intended to guarantee it strict control over the furs and the articles of trade. On 8 August 1645 it was forbidden for anyone to go aboard ships anchoring at Québec without having first obtained permission from "those who are assigned to the store for the business of the trade."[171] This was to avoid direct trading between the sailors and the colonists, a trade which could include furs and European goods, brandy in particular. The ban was renewed in 1646 and 1647.

More disrupting – and more controversial – was the interdiction on 6 September of any trade whatsoever between the colonists and the Amerindians – even to make themselves coats: in this case, furs would be available "at the store at a reasonable price."[172] As if this was not enough – this considerable upset to established practices – it was necessary in the autumn to "publish the ban" anew,[173] first at Trois-Rivières and then at Québec.[174] Two new ordinances addressing the people of Trois-Rivières were published by Montmagny in the summer of 1646.[175] For years the colonists had been buying pelts from the natives and selling them to the Company at a small profit.[176]

Did the Community have the right to make laws on this point? Montmagny thought so, since he published the ordinances in this spirit. The Jesuits' position was different. In the autumn of 1645 they consulted Juchereau des Chatelets to know if they could continue to trade directly with the native people; their close contacts with them had made this a regular practice. He answered them "that this could go on for us as usual, but that we should do it quietly."[177] This resembled a sort of permission: if it was done without publicity, it would be winked at. It was under the form of a case of conscience that the question was laid to rest some months later. Lalemant, Vimont, and Le Jeune held a council to decide if they should or should not "tolerate ... the beaver trade at Sillery." Since Sillery was a permanent residence or a temporary stopover for the Amerindians, the latter might often have furs in their possession; could one buy from them or had one to send them to trade directly at the Community store? A double response was found: "1) If the store was reasonable, one was obliged in conscience not to divert them elsewhere" (meaning, no doubt, "a reasonable price,"whether for furs or for merchandise). "2) If it was not reasonable, one could in good conscience cover it up, the *habitants* having the right by nature, and from the King, to trade."[178] What did "right by nature" mean? Was the monopoly against nature? This was problematic because when the store was reasonable, the principle did not apply, and because in other respects Montmagny's ordinances and rulings were undermined from the start. Did this "right of the *habitants*" come from the king? But he himself had delivered everything that concerned commerce into the Company's hands, and it was the Company (and later the Community) that had the power to legislate on this.

All this implies that the ruling issued by the directors angered many people. Montmagny supported them with all his authority, believing no doubt that their mandate went this far, and he forced the application of the rules. In June 1647 the Ursulines' almoner saw the confiscation of 260 pounds of furs that he had acquired;[179] the ruling contained the phrase: "If any are found during visits, they will be confiscated."[180] The good abbé had boasted of his possession, and had made it clear "that he would only give it to the store at a good price."

As one might expect, muttering began, and with the help of jealousy, rumours circulated regarding the private life of the men in power. Here is how the *Journal des Jésuites* took note of this incident:

> At the end of this month [January 1646], the lesser *habitants* seemed ready to mutiny against those who had charges and offices. M. Marsolet and above all his wife, and M. Maheu were held to be the authors of this; it was all calmed down by Monsieur the Governor; these lesser *habitants* were in the wrong, having no reasonable foundation for their complaint; they said that M. des Chastelets the general agent was making too much profit, etc. A young man from the Governor's staff named M. Robineau took the malcontents' part; thence came plenty of troubles and angry words and grumblings; lampoons were made. Once Monsieur the Governor punished the guilty ones, everything quieted down.[181]

Speaking in the name of the "lesser habitants," then, was Nicolas Marsolet, interpreter, trader, and owner of a seigneurie.[182] But the principal agitators, it seems, were his wife, Marie Le Barbier, and one René Maheut, whose only known identification is that of "bourgeois of Paris."[183] They received support from René Robinau, who was only twenty years old and who perhaps was, as junior officer, a member of the garrison which Montmagny maintained at the château Saint-Louis.[184] Their "mutiny" was manifested verbally and in writing; the "lampoons" in question here were satires, which were circulated among the population. The Jesuits disapproved of this campaign, because the accusations that were launched seemed frivolous to them. Montmagny put an end to the squabble, ordering punishment for the culprits (doubtless those mentioned by Lalemant): fines, probably, or perhaps prison for the soldier.

Nonetheless, a malaise persisted, and there were matters left in abeyance. Fortifications were the reponsibility of the Community, but Fort Richelieu was falling into ruin.[185] In his usual way, Montmagny first made certain that the principle of authority was safe and that peace was reestablished in his capital. Following this, he himself inquired into the situation,[186] then he allowed a delegation to be organized that would go to the mother country in an attempt to find an improvement to the formula of 1645.

Thus, in the autumn of 1646, Robert Giffard, one of the twelve directors, Guillaume Tronquet, the governor's secretary, and Chomedey de Maisonneuve, who represented both the interests of the *Société de Montréal* and those of the *habitants* who did not take part in the direction of the Community, left for France. They carried with them "several memoranda" which had been "drawn up for a good ruling."[187]

In February 1647 the queen mother named four commissioners whose mission was to make a close examination of "the affairs of New France": Elie Laisné de la Marguerie, Antoine de Barillon de Morangis, Jean-Antoine de Mesmes, and Guillaume de Lamoignon.[188] The first three (and perhaps even the fourth) were members of the *Société de Montréal,* and thus already well informed regarding the colony's affairs. De Barillon and de Mesmes were closely related by marriage with the Huault and Du Drac families. Laisné and de Mesmes belonged to the Company of the Blessed Sacrament. The little working group seems to have been granted a certain permanence, since the council that they formed was required to prepare an annual report on the affairs of the Community.

In the month that followed their nomination, their recommendations were adopted by the King's Council.[189] The *Communauté des Habitants* was fundamentally transformed;[190] the twelve directors were replaced by a small council composed of three members, the governor of the colony, the governor of Montréal, and the superior of the Jesuits – proof, if proof is still needed, of the importance of the fur trade in the life of New France. This council named the officers of the Community; it was obliged, when the admiral of the fleet was in Québec, to admit him to its meetings (though only with a consultative voice), along with three syndics elected by the inhabitants of the colony's three centres, Québec, Trois-Rivières, and Montréal. The role of this body was to supervise the activities of the Community – among other things, to examine its accounts if necessary, and to regulate the fur trade. This was opened up again: all could trade with the Amerindians, so long as they then brought the pelts to the Community's store.

Even before the arrival of the official documents, the essentials of the new arrangement were known to the population. The habitants of Québec at once (on 29 June) pressed Montmagny to have a syndic elected.[191] He referred them to the "general assembly" of *habitants* which was to be convoked at an opportune time, that is to say, after the arrival of the royal ruling. Despite this they proceeded on 21 July to elect a "procureur syndic," and it was one of Montmagny's men, Jean Bourdon, who was chosen. Shortly afterwards, he presented a "request from the *habitants*" to the governor, in which they confided to him "all matters while awaiting the new dispositions sent by Paris;" however, even before these arrived, they wished "to cashier all the officers and directors of the Community"[192] – an abuse of power, certainly, but one which shows clearly the grudge which many people showed against the "directors" named in 1645.

The king's letters finally arrived in Québec, and at once the decisions that they contained were applied. The Jesuits consulted among themselves as to whether they should enter the council or not; the response was in the affirmative.[193] Louis d'Ailleboust, Maisonneuve's lieutenant, was named admiral of the fleet, proof that the integration of Montréal into the colony had been confirmed. However, it was almost the same personnel that were to be found in the various posts (appointed or otherwise) of the Community, proof that the uncomplimentary allegations levelled against them had been set aside.

The new ruling did not create unanimity in the colony. The climate created by this recourse to the population gave rise to all sorts of initiatives. The *habitants* of Trois-Rivières – still a tiny little settlement – demanded the title of governor for their commandant and a seat on the colony's council; what is more, in a novel suggestion, they wanted the trade in furs to be practiced collectively within the limits of their territory. The syndics sought for something more substantial than a mere consultative voice within the council. The expenses of the Community were found to be too high. The abandonment of Fort Richelieu was deplored. And, as a crowning trouble, "the Hurons did not come downriver this last summer,"[194] and the revenues from the trade were minimal.

These complaints were sent on to the "commissioners for the affairs of New France,"who proposed a second reorganization of the Community to the king.[195] This was being acted on just as Montmagny was resigning his position – there will be more on it in the following chapter. The new arrangement lasted until 1663, at which time the king took over the effective direction of the colony's affairs.

It is difficult indeed to draw up a balance sheet of the "internal management"of the Canadian colony by Montmagny. He conformed to the rules that the authorities who had engaged him – the Company and the sovereign – had set for him; he intervened with them, with a certain degree of success, to improve the situation, but without being able to solve the fundamental problem: the shortage of colonists. He used the means at his disposal to assure security and an agreeable life for those under his jurisdiction.

This "balance sheet" was positive, if the testimonies handed down are to be believed. Their unanimity is quite striking. It is fitting, then, to close these remarks by recalling them briefly.

That the king should have praised "the wise and prudent conduct" of the chevalier in renaming him for a fourth mandate in 1645 is normal enough, since he had to justify his decision; but that Father Du Tertre should do it some years later, after a serious study of the question, is more significant.

The same reasoning can be used with regard to the Jesuits and the nuns, who constantly reiterated the virtues of the governor: nothing unusual there, since he was himself a member of a religious Order, and he worthily fulfilled his obligations to his Order and to religion in general. More revealing, however, is the satisfaction which the *habitants* showed in offering him, in 1647 – after eleven years of working among them – a gift both remarkable and heavy with symbolism: the first horse brought from France to the colony.[196]

The first historian of Montréal might have been expected to pass a severe judgement on the man who had "quarreled" with Maisonneuve. But this is how Dollier de Casson recounts the journey which took place in the month of May 1642, from Québec to the island of Montréal: "Monsieur the chevalier de Montmagny, truly a man of good heart who had no other interests than those of his King and of the country which he had the honour to command, knowing that everything had been arranged, wished to participate in this first establishment by honouring it with his presence. This is why he boarded a boat and himself led all this fleet to Montréal, where we dropped anchor on the eighteenth of May in the present year [1642]."[197] Thus the Sulpician made a point of Montmagny's disinterestedness, the way in which he did not spare himself in leading what, in grand terms, was called a "fleet," which took the group of new colonists going to found Ville-Marie – accompanied by soldiers, since the Iroquois menace was taken seriously, as we have seen. Readiness, then, and the enthusiasm to work which is summed up in the words of praise, "truly a man of good heart"; and, underlying this, a great adaptability to circumstances.

When, in the middle of the eighteenth century, the Jesuit Father de Charlevoix wrote his *Histoire et description de la Nouvelle-France*, he had these words about the chevalier, which repeat in colourful language what we have just said: "His conduct was always so exemplary, and he showed on every occasion so much wisdom, piety, religion and disinterest; he spared himself so little when it was a question of acting to repress the insolence of the Iroquois, and he knew so well how to maintain his dignity in the most delicate situations, that he made both Frenchmen and Savages respect him, and the Court, for a long time, even held him up to the governors of the new colonies, as a model whom they could not study too well."[198]

ILLUSTRATION 7

A frigate (in Italian, *fregata*) and a galley (*galera*). Seventeenth-century engraving. Archives of Malta

ILLUSTRATION 8

A *patache* (in Italian, *patachio*) and a galleon. Seventeenth-century engraving. Archives of Malta

CHAPTER 8

Reality and Fiction

The *Journal* of the Jesuits for 1648 reported that "on the 20th day [of August], feast of Saint Bernard, M. d'Ailleboust dropped anchor before Québec, and was received as Governor."[1] Montmagny's commission, already renewed three times, was not renewed in 1648. The previous year, at the suggestion of the *Société de Notre-Dame de Montréal*, the Company offered the post to Maisonneuve, who had been in France since the summer of 1645;[2] he declined the honour, but immediately thought of the man who had been commandant in Montréal during his absence, Louis d'Ailleboust. This is why, on his return in the summer of 1647, he informed d'Ailleboust of the Company's choice, and arranged that he obtain the command of the fleet of the *Communauté des Habitants*, which was then leaving for the mother country.[3] Perhaps Montmagny was aware that a replacement had been named and that barring unforeseen circumstances – death, shipwreck, or some other accident befalling his successor – he would be retiring in the summer of 1648.

According to the Jesuits, the transition took place smoothly: "It is beautiful to see two persons of virtue and merit competing in deference, especially when one of them suppresses the interests which might move him to act otherwise, if he did not fortify his courage with a thought higher and more noble than those commonly held."[4] Thus the praise for Montmagny continued, even as it began for his successor. There is, in his case, an allusion to the bitterness which he must have had to overcome upon learning of his replacement – though there is no evidence to support this assertion.[5]

Further on in the text there is mention of "generous magnanimity" in the welcome that Montmagny reserved for his successor, and of the reaction of the latter, who "answered in like manner to his predecessor, not being able to find enough honour to acknowledge the merit and the virtue of this gallant chevalier." The priests wished, no doubt, to convince their readers that the king would only name worthy and deserving persons to the government of Canada.

But it is worth noting what the two men had in common: a courage beyond question and a total devotion to the interests of the Church. Like Montmagny, d'Ailleboust had developed close ties with the Jesuits: in Paris his spiritual director, a Jesuit, had put him in touch with Father Charles Lalemant, who interested him in the Montréal project; and it was in this dangerous post that he had served since 1643. Their status differed, however, the one being a member of a religious order, and the other being married, and trained as a military engineer.[6]

Montmagny's last month on Canadian soil (20 September to 23 October) passed without incident. He may have been present at the new council, as the royal decree of 5 March 1648 allowed,[7] and he must have had several meetings with d'Ailleboust. Doubtless he visited his seigneurie for the last time and – always ready to serve – he agreed to command the flagship of the fleet that took him back to Europe.[8]

In the first section of this chapter we should like to summarize what the New France that Montmagny left to his successor represented – which can be seen, also, as the balance sheet of a long and challenging administration. This was reality!

Fiction will take us rocketing from Paris to the Québec forest, then to the residence of Montmagny. It was around 1648 that Savinien de Cyrano composed his *Voyage dans la Lune*. From 1650, the manuscript was circulating in the literary circles of the capital.[9] In a first attempt to reach "the star with the silver face," the adventurer makes a false move and falls to earth, only to find himself in another France, beyond the Atlantic. The soldiers of the governor of Québec who discover him lead him to the latter: "He asked me my country, my name and my quality; and after I had satisfied him by telling of the agreeable success of my voyage, whether he believed it or only pretended to believe, he had the goodness to give me a room in his apartment. Great was my good fortune to find a man capable of high opinions, who was not astonished when I told him that the earth must have turned during my elevation, since having begun two leagues from Paris, I fell by an almost perpendicular line into Canada." The details of this unforeseen flight are of great interest to us. Montmagny had become a familiar figure to the readers of the *Relations*, among whom were to be found some members of the erudite circles of the French capital. We need take a closer look at the description which Cyrano made of the governor, and explain its various aspects. This will be the aim of the second part of this chapter.

1.   New France in 1648

Rather than tracing a detailed picture of the colony that Montmagny left in October 1648, this section will highlight the traits which characterized it, and which allow us to see how far it had developed by the end of his mandate.

A first set of reflections will focus on the political and commercial problems that had been intimately intertwined since 1645. Then we shall consider demography and society. The sparseness of the population was undoubtedly the major problem of New France in 1648; but all the same there was to be found in this little society a certain dynamism and some original behaviours, phenomena to which, it appears, Montmagny's attitude was favourable. The religious dimension cannot be shrugged off – the colony's vitality was attributable, in good part, to the action of church bodies, or those which, like the *Société de Notre-Dame de Montréal*, were directly inspired by Christian ideals. Finally, it will be fitting to bring up the Amerindian question, so intimately bound to the spiritual phenomenon just mentioned.

The year 1648 is important as regards the administration of Canada. The efforts of reorganization which had been made since 1644 ended in a compromise by which the subjects had a not inconsiderable part in the exercise of government – an immediate reflection of the political situation in France, where civil war was looming, and absolutism was in abeyance for a few years.

The edict of 5 March 1648 fell into three sections: the council was enlarged; defence was reconsidered; and commerce was transformed.[10]

From that time on the council of the *Communauté des Habitants* comprised seven persons: the king's lieutenant governor (who was also governor of Québec); the governors of Trois-Rivières and of Montréal; the superior of the Jesuits; the past governor, if he was still there; and two representatives of the *habitants,* chosen by the council and by the syndics of the cities – these would become three if the past governor had left the colony. What Montmagny had practised informally now took shape, with the *habitants* participating with full right and on a regular basis in the management of the colony, in all matters that concerned commerce and defence.

In this latter domain there was a promising innovation: for the first time, there would be an attempt to adapt to native tactics. A "flying detachment" of forty soldiers would be formed. Armed with light equipment and trained to surprise attack, it would be capable of moving swiftly to the places where its presence was necessary. A budget was set aside for this. To counter this, the governors' garrisons were reduced: twelve soldiers for the governor of Québec, six for each of the other two.

There was also innovation in the commercial sector. It was no longer forbidden for merchants to set up shop in New France, except where furs and goods for the fur trade, the monopoly reserved to the Community, were concerned. It was foreseen that the convoys of furs from Huronia would from now on be escorted; and the men – specified as volunteers – would be authorized "to do some trading in pelts." All lawsuits involving the Community were forwarded to the king's council – a preventive measure, no doubt, given the long delays and the costs imposed on plaintiffs by such a recourse.

The new arrangements were applied immediately, but it must be remarked that this time the three councillors who ought to have been chosen by the council and the syndics were named by the regent, who designated three past directors of the Community.[11] The syndics of Québec and Trois-Rivières were elected at the end of August and the beginning of September.

So this new system gave the *habitants* an enhanced representation within the council, encouraging them to participate more directly in the colony's affairs, and thus to pay closer attention to the interests of the community. Along with this, the possibility of opening stores served – theoretically, at least – to spur the development of commercial enterprises.

On the other side of the coin, a certain erosion in the governor's powers is apparent. Montmagny, as has been seen, had a certain habit of teamwork; he would have adapted well. His replacement, d'Ailleboust, seems to have conformed well enough to this situation. For Lauson, d'Ailleboust's successor (1651–1656), it would create problems.[12]

It would be interesting to know Montmagny's thinking about these changes, as well as the content of the reports he sent to France for their elaboration. It seems – as noted in the preceding remarks – that his contribution was positive. His habit of consultation undoubtedly allowed him to be attentive to the suggestions which came from his subjects, to discuss them with them, to write about them to the king. In the absence of documents, hypotheses will have to serve.

By every account, Montmagny's term ended on an optimistic note. The principal demands of the *habitants* had found an echo among the authorities at home. The fur trade had been good; in fact, the *Journal des Jésuites* noted, for end of the month of August: "This year the trade from Tadoussac amounted to forty thousand livres of profit; and in all, about 250,000 livres; in weight at least 224,000 pounds, and more than 500 moose."[13] An enterprising habitant had begun the fishery of seals at Tadoussac: "This month [June 1648], Master Abraham Martin, with two of his sons-in-law, went out for the first time to fish for seals; he took some on the eve of the feast of Saint John, at Isle Rouge close to Tadoussac, from which he made great barrels of oil."[14] Did the initiative have a follow-up? There is no way of knowing, given the existing state of the colony, but it had to be pleasing to Montmagny, who was aware of the resources of the Saint Lawrence valley. An interesting note: in 1653, Louis d'Ailleboust (who had quit the governorship of the colony in 1651) joined with Jean-Paul Godefroy and Jean Bourdon to establish a fishing station at Percé;[15] the captain of the vessel had orders to "transport the products of the journey to Saint-Christophe, in the Antilles." And it was precisely in this year that Montmagny arrived on that island, where he was going to finish his days in service to his Order.

Did the reordering of the fur trade and the emerging diversification in the commercial enterprises coincide with a real breakthrough for New France? For that to happen, the mother country itself would have had to change course where its colonial action was concerned. Did its present circumstances allow for the possibility? Could it have started a growth in population, the only way to guarantee the security and prosperity of Canada? In fact, in 1648 the situation in general in the Laurentian colony was dark in this respect.

We will remember that Le Jeune (to enhance his publicity in favour of the colony, apparently) had endowed the beginnings of Montmagny's government with euphoria – "who will now make difficulties over crossing our seas, when such tender children, such delicate young ladies" risk it? He clearly wanted to suggest that the arrival of entire families – in very small numbers, actually – was going to create a significant movement of emigration into Canada. This was not the case. The demographic balance sheet for these twelve years was not very glowing. Despite its limited dimensions – and perhaps because of them – the society which was formed in New France did not lack cohesion or dynamism. Some observations should be made on each of these two points.

At the time of Montmagny's arrival, the colony boasted two centres; a third would be added in 1642. To start with that one: how many inhabitants might there have been in Montréal in 1648? Between eighty and ninety, apparently.[16] There was not an aboriginal among them – though settlement of the native peoples had been the precise objective which had dominated the foundation of the post. The Iroquois attacks had kept them away. They were responsible for some deaths at the same time as they prevented territorial expansion. The first land grant close to the fort took place only in January 1648,[17] and it was in this same year that a windmill was built.[18] Despite a rather uncomfortable situation, in 1645, thanks to a tentative return of peace, construction was started on a hospital outside the palisade.[19]

After fourteen years of existence, the second village, Trois-Rivières, counted perhaps a hundred inhabitants, and many grants had been made to individuals – but to the north of the site, and not on the river bank, because of the Iroquois threat. The natural growth of the population had begun: there were thirty-three births between 1634 and 1648.[20] Unlike Montréal, a number of aboriginals lived close by: "More than 30 native families started to farm" in the spring of 1646, according to the *Journal des Jésuites*.[21]

The most densely populated area still remained the Québec region with, apparently, more than 600 habitants.[22] It was the seat of the governor and of the colony's religious communities. The seigneuries on the outskirts were relatively active; the distribution of tenant holdings continued. Here is what Jérôme Lalemant reported: "On the 14th [of January 1648] Father de Quen returned from his mission from Beauport to Cap Tourmente & Isle d'Orléans; there he found more than 200 souls & more than 140 communicants."[23] Doubtless the sixty or so "non-communicants" were children. Some building sites, employing a number of labourers, had just been opened, such as the parish church and the college. The château Saint-Louis, that is to say the governor's residence, was also under construction – as was proved in the nineteenth century, when a shaped stone was found on the site, with a Maltese cross cut into its side, as well as a date, "1647."[24] This was undoubtedly the stone used for the official inauguration of the works by the chevalier de Montmagny.[25] The development of the south shore had also begun, and it was precisely in 1648 that religious services were commenced for the tenants of the seigneurie of Lauson.[26]

A calculation of the total population of New France in 1648 requires a little math. The number of immigrants who settled between 1632 and 1648 was about 760;[27] add to this (for the same years) the births, 215;[28] subtract the deaths, around 125[29] to arrive at 850 *habitants*. But as the lists of the time were rarely complete, it would be better to say that the population stood between 850 and 1000.

Thus the population, which had been estimated at around 350 at the death of Champlain in December 1635, had more than doubled (had perhaps even tripled) during Montmagny's administration. But these rough numbers do not mean much; they should be seen in a larger context. This was far from the number envisaged by Richelieu, according to whose expectations 4,000 immigrants were to have crossed the Atlantic for Canada between 1627 and 1643. And New France cut a poor figure when compared to the English colonies.

The fine plans of 1627 had been frustrated. The drawbacks of the early days discouraged the men of state, while the war in Europe absorbed more and more of their energy and their attention. They lost interest in the colonial sector. Snap decisions took the place of a global policy; to the express demands of Montmagny, they responded in 1642, 1644, 1645, 1647, and 1648 with hasty ordinances which did not deal with the fundamental problem – the shortage of colonists.

The consequences of this state of affairs has already been sketched in part. The native people were less than impressed by the French performance. The Iroquois came close, on several occasions, to eliminating the colony. The allies continued to wait for the workers who were to teach them European techniques and the soldiers who were to deliver them from their enemies. Montmagny did not have the wherewithal to fulfil the promises of his predecessor, nor those that he himself had made at the outset of his term. The immense resources of the Saint Lawrence valley – in hunting, fishing, lumber and agriculture – remained almost unexploited. The fur trade was constantly threatened – in 1649, it was disastrous, because of the disappearance of the Huron. At the same time, the French habitat was dispersed – three settlements at two or three days' distance, sometimes more, from each other – and hemmed in; except at Québec, nothing had yet been done in the surrounding areas, so much did the Iroquois danger prevent the people from spreading out. And this was true even in the capital: we have already noted the anxiety that Montmagny felt for the hospital sisters established at Sillery; lacking men to protect them, he was forced in the summer of 1644 to make them return to Québec.

Difficult work for a lieutenant-general of the king, left as he was by his patron to manage as best he could. Good fortune for the sovereign to have found a man both obliging and highly conscientious, and who, what is more, belonged to an Order whose motto was to hold fast to the end.

To describe this embryonic society formed by the French colonists of the Saint Lawrence valley in 1648, two aspects must be considered: the social order, and the community services.

Two groups held the high ground in the colony, though in different ways, and in pursuit of different objectives: the clergy on the one hand, and the "notables" on the other.

In *ancien régime* France, the clergy was the first order of the State;[30] its influence there was still very great – if only by reason of the successive presence at the helm of government, for the period under consideration, of two cardinals, Richelieu and Mazarin. Its importance in New France was no less; it rested essentially on two factors: numbers, and competence.

We have calculated that, after Montmagny's departure in the autumn of 1648, there were between forty-one and fifty-one members of the clergy: twenty to thirty Jesuits (priests and lay brothers); two secular priests; eight hospital sisters at the Hôtel-Dieu,[31] and eleven Ursulines (including two lay sisters).[32] That adds up to a proportion hovering between 5 and 6 per cent of the total population – which is considerable.

The word 'competence' which we use to qualify this clergy in fact covers many realities which cannot be dealt with here. The two congregations of women specialized in the domains to which they were dedicated, hospital care and teaching. The Society of Jesus saw to the ministry among the French, and made very considerable efforts for the conversion of the native peoples. The Fathers had opened a college – education had in fact become one of their specialties. The publicity that their annual *Relation* generated for New France continued to have some echoes in the mother country.

This competence, it should be added, was most often fortified by a generosity worthy of the spirit of the Counter Reformation, still very much alive in this mid-seventeenth century. One need only mention three names which symbolize perfectly that total consecration to spiritual realities which, within the Church, was the ideal of the times: the Ursuline Marie de l'Incarnation; the hospital sister Catherine de Saint-Augustin (who arrived in Québec just as Montmagny was leaving); and the Jesuit Jean de Brébeuf, who was to suffer martyrdom some months after Montmagny's return to France.

At another level (though, like the clergy, part of the elite of colonial society), we find the notables, that group of dynamic men who had come to settle in the colony from 1634 on[33] – the exception being Guillaume Couillard, who had arrived in Québec in 1621 and married the daughter of the first colonist, Louis Hébert.[34] They owed their notability to various factors: nobility; the possession of a seigneurie; a particular ability (like those who became the governor's councillors, the surveyor Jean

Bourdon, for example, or Noël Juchereau, who had a diploma in law), or, simply, personal qualities which compelled recognition; this was perhaps the case of Charles Sevestre, elected syndic of Québec in 1648.[35] The *Communauté des Habitants* gave all these men the possibility of playing a role in the direction of the colony's affairs. Some of them were sent as delegates to France, others figured among the twelve directors named in 1645, or occupied various administrative posts.

Again, note the family and marriage ties that accentuated the cohesion of the group.[36] The Legardeurs and the Le Neufs were already a clan when they arrived in the country in 1636, and they continued to grow: On 3 October 1646, Marie-Madeleine Le Gardeur married Jean-Paul Godefroy; a relative of the latter married Marie Le Neuf, sister of Michel, the syndic of Trois-Rivières, in 1648.[37]

Thus, despite its limited numbers, Québec society already had a structure. We really only possess details on the elite, but the beginnings of an organization in the artisan world are visible. Father Lalemant, reporting on the Corpus Christi procession of 11 June 1648, shows us, in line behind the "savages" grouped around Le Jeune, the representatives of the corps de métiers: "there followed twelve torches of twelve trades (turner, joiner, shoemaker, cooper, locksmith, armorer, carpenter, mason, swordsmith, baker, coachmaker, and nailsmith), and then four lay chanters with candles."[38]

There is one last remark to be made about this incipient collectivity: it enjoyed a set of services – today called "social services" – completely out of proportion to its actual numbers, but justified both by the expectation of a significant demographic expansion, and by the demands of the work among the native peoples. We refer precisely here to two domains: education and hospital care.

From 1635 on, the Jesuits were preoccupied with opening a school for the boys of Québec. In 1647 the construction of a college was begun, to be completed three years later. There were seven or eight scholars in 1647,[39] and a dozen, possibly, in the autumn of 1648. The courses were given in a house belonging to the *Compagnie de la Nouvelle-France*. By the time of the inauguration of the new building in 1651, there were sixteen pupils. The talent of adaptation which characterized the Jesuits is again evident here. There was no question of an elaborate syllabus for Québec in the years 1647–1648; the "college" offered, first, training in reading and writing; then grammar, especially Latin grammar; and finally, an introduction to mathematics.

Parallel with the priests, the Ursulines, from 1639 on, took over the education of girls.[40] They Canadianized themselves; in 1646 they installed a novitiate; the following year they adopted a constitution for their Québec monastery that rendered them independent of the Tours and Paris houses. They possessed the largest building then in existence in New France (92 feet by 28 and three floors), which in 1648 housed nine choir nuns and two lay sisters. They also had in their service, on the lands that had been conceded to them, ten indentured servants. Among their students they welcomed native girls (this had been their original purpose in coming to Canada: to establish a "seminary" of young aboriginals). They also had boarders, as well as day students. The syllabus was simple: catechism, reading, writing, and sewing. To the nuns' regret, few of their native students "francizized"; few married Frenchmen.[41] The marriage of Pierre Boucher to a Huron girl on 17 January 1649 was one of the first; the sisters made over a dowry of 500 livres to the fiancée.

Another service was well and truly underway in the colony: health care. Since 1644 the hospital sisters had been working in a hospital within the city of Québec, and in 1646 their residence had been enlarged.[42] In 1648 eight nuns lived there, and it was in this same year that the first Canadian postulant, Marie-Françoise Giffard, came to join the group. The *rente* which had been assigned to them by Richelieu's niece, the Duchesse d'Aiguillon, and the exploitation of their grants on Canadian soil, enabled them to offer corporal and spiritual services to a population, aboriginal and French, that was threatened by epidemics, Iroquois incursions, and accidents of every kind.

In Montréal, there was as yet no religious institution to provide hospital care;[43] however, Jeanne Mance was looking into this. She could count on funds which came to her from a Parisian benefactress, Madame de Bullion, widow of the *surintendant des finances*, Claude de Bullion.[44] The construction of a building outside the wall was begun in 1645, but did not advance rapidly because of the Iroquois danger.

Thus, apart from the case of Jeanne Mance, the two sectors of education and health were in the hands of three religious congregations. And in the mind of the times, these two domains were an integral part of something larger: the deepening of Christian life. There again, there is much to say about the New France of 1648.

One trait – the importance of religion – so notable in the Canada of 1636, had not weakened; to the contrary, it had to all appearances grown stronger with the years. When Montmagny's term ended in 1648, whom did they find to replace him? Louis d'Ailleboust. To a Knight of Malta there succeeded one of the most active members of the *Société de Notre-Dame de Montréal.* Here is a comment by Jérôme Lallemant: "the other [d'Ailleboust], whose virtue is already known in this new world, gives us, I will say, not just a hope but an assurance that the fruits already well advanced will ripen, and that the Kingdom of God will continue to spread and to grow strong in these countries."[45] It was no small advantage for the clergy to be able to count on the exemplary life and the virtually unconditional support of the foremost person in the land.

The position of the Jesuits themselves was reinforced. Almost alone, they provided the ministry to the colony, leaving, whenever possible, the guidance of the two convents of nuns to the few secular priests who found themselves in Québec. Their number had increased, above all by reason of their foundations in Huronia – among others, that of the reduction of Sainte-Marie.[46]

The nuns had arrived in 1639, and their works had prospered. In 1648, as has already been mentioned, the hospital sisters welcomed into their ranks the daughter of the seigneur of Beauport, Robert Giffard.[47]

The *Société de Notre-Dame de Montréal* was still hanging on, despite the repeated attacks of the Iroquois, but the generous project – the settling of the natives with a view to converting them – which had brought it to settle in the island in 1642, was not yet capable of realization. However, it remained on the agenda. It is not without interest to note, furthermore, that this society was made up largely of lay persons, in Canada as in France; thus apostolic preoccupations were not the monopoly of clerics and persons consecrated to God. All this was in the best spirit of the Counter Reformation, still alive in this mid-seventeenth century, with two of its greatest protagonists, Jean-Jacques Olier (closely connected to the Montréal project) and Vincent de Paul, still very active.

The life of the Canadian colonists was particularly marked by religion; some interesting points can be taken from the *Journal des Jésuites* of 1648, which is voluble on the subject.

It was the activities of worship that first attracted the attention of Father Lalemant. In Holy Week, for example, whose long and numerous devotions he described, almost five full days were taken up by ceremonies and prayers, from the Tenebrae of Wednesday afternoon,[48] until the Benediction of the Blessed Sacrament at three-thirty on Easter Sunday. On Friday, church services lasted from seven in the morning until eleven, with, first, a sermon lasting two and a half hours,[49] then a "service" essentially comprising the chanted recitation of the Passion and the adoration of the cross. For the more devout, there were more Tenebrae later in the day.

At Christmas 1648, "for the first time," Midnight Mass lasted from matins until ten o'clock, "and the whole church was crammed from the start."[50] There was music and singing. The elevation of the Host and the communion were accompanied with "music with a viol"; a Low Mass followed the High Mass. Note that this piety owed nothing to the fact that the governor was a member of a religious order; Louis d'Ailleboust, replacing Montmagny (who had left in October) was no more opposed than his predecessor to the Jesuits' initiatives in this domain.

These feasts were sometimes accompanied by a procession through the streets, for example, on Rogation Days, Corpus Christi, and the Assumption. That of 25 April 1648 (the feast of Saint Mark) had to be cancelled because of the pitiable state of the roads due to a late freeze-up.[51] The superior suffered scruples over this: "I repent [having called it off]: the Church, it seems, and custom ask for greater inconveniences than this before omitting this procession." On 19 July he again noted, "I have announced the procession and the forty hours to the two religious houses, to employ all the week in sanctity."[52] A striking phrase, which well illustrates the ideal animating the clergy of the times.

Every Sunday between October and May, the children, and any adults who wanted it, were offered religious instruction in the form of the catechism.[53] In 1648 the feast of the Purification (2 February) fell on a Sunday. After Mass they proceeded with the blessing of the water and the distribution of candles, "not keeping any precedence, except that of M. the Governor," but there was no preaching, since "that would have been too long; but the afternoon catechism was conducted on the subject of the feast."[54]

The surveillance that the clergy exercised at the time over the conduct of individuals went a very long way. In the spring of 1648 the superior of the Jesuits, the premier ecclesiastical authority of the colony, asked himself the following question: did he have the power to pronounce excommunication on the spot for those who neglected their Easter duty? He decided not to act on this immediately, but to consult the French canon lawyers on this subject.[55]

Another problem arose a few months later: an offence which the priest designated only by the words: "crimine pessimo" – meaning, no doubt, bestiality, which Pierre Richelet defines as "a crime committed with female animals, for which [the perpetrator] is burnt."[56] The priests of Montréal, where it took place, opposed the prescribed punishment, "sed occulte" – that is, without saying so in public, so as not to seem to be ignoring the law. The culprit was taken to Québec: "He was sent here and put into prison. To save him at least from the galleys, he was offered the position of executor of justice [hangman]; he accepted it, but his previous trial was reinstated, and then his sentence was commuted."[57]

This was one of the last judgments that Montmagny had to pronounce in Canada. It should be noted once more that he did it in perfect agreement with the Jesuits, who clearly felt a concern for tolerance, and a will to adapt a ruling of extreme rigour to the specific situation of a colony in its beginnings.

The question of the native peoples was grafted directly onto the religious question. Since 1627 the *Compagnie de la Nouvelle-France* had, among its tasks – along with the development of commerce and the maintenance of peace – the conversion of the Amerindians. Remember their ambiguous status in the colony. Were they subjects of the governor? The Christians, certainly, were considered 'natural' Frenchmen. The others were attached to France in some fashion, since France claimed that the territory belonged to it; but in official meetings they were negotiated with as with a foreign people. Was this an attitude dictated by the weakness of the French? That seems credible. For the Jesuits, the dialectic was different. Commenting on the decision of the new governor, d'Ailleboust, in the autumn of 1648, to take steps against the sale of alcohol or the presence of unconverted or "apostates" at Sillery, Father Lalemant wrote: "It is good to bring them little by little under the orders of those whom God has chosen to command"; and, some lines later, speaking of the "liberty" so dear to the native people, he added: "it must be regulated and submitted to the laws emanating from the eternal law."[58] Put otherwise, for their own good the natives ought to be subjected gradually to French laws.

To assure the conversion of the Amerindians – or should we say their assimilation, in view of what we read in the *Relations? –* the Jesuits concentrated on two territories, the Saint Lawrence valley, and Huronia.

Right at the start of his *Relation* of 1648, the superior of Québec opened on an optimistic note: "In these two Relations your Reverence will see a good number of Savages baptized; you will learn that the Faith is spreading its roots far into the hearts of the believers."[59] But if one pays attention to the reflections scattered through the rest of his report, it becomes clear that this optimism was not without nuance, as, for example, the judgment that he passes on the Iroquois: "It is not to be hoped that the Iroquois will continue to keep their faith, if they are not held to it by some interest of fear or of hope, because they have no religion, and their reasoning is such that if an individual has killed a Frenchman for his pleasure, he need not fear some punishment."[60] Continuing his reasoning, he concluded: "The Iroquois ruin everything ... this scourge is heavy indeed. May God be blessed at all times ..., he is allowing his Church to be afflicted."[61] Banal resignation? Blind submission? Indeed not! In fact, he ended his reflection with these very revealing words: "But He [God] would be well pleased if those who have the power to help her would raise the standard for her glory. Let us change the subject." Too polite, or too diplomatic, to go beyond a simple allusion, he was pointing out the inaction of the mother country.

What was the situation in terms of the apostolate? The two reductions in the centre of the colony were only progressing slowly: there were, perhaps, 200 natives at Sillery, not all of them Christians – thirteen were baptized in 1648.[62] They do not seem even to have made a start in farming; the lands reserved for them were being cleared by French colonists. At Trois-Rivières, there are no complete numbers, but there were twenty baptisms in 1648, a number which grew to forty-two in 1649 and sixty-three in 1650.[63] As had been done at Sillery, a sort of local government was set up there. Thirty families cultivated the soil in 1646. What was the situation in 1648? The record leaves no indication. There is good reason to say that, there as well, the tendency was towards a disaffection for agricultural labour.

The migratory tribes were not neglected by the Jesuits: every year, from spring to autumn, one of the priests set up camp at Tadoussac, an important gathering place, especially for the Montagnais. From there they began to spread out. In 1647, Father de Quen[64] went up the Saguenay to Lake Saint-Jean. From September 1647 to April 1648 Father Druillettes wintered with a group of Montagnais who had come to Matane on the south shore and had gone to hunt in the mountains of the hinterland. At the time of Montmagny's departure this missionary was, without a doubt, the man whose renown was greatest throughout eastern Canada. He had an indomitable energy, a great facility for languages, plenty of tact, an iron constitution – he regained his eyesight in incredible circumstances and, as a result of this, passed among the native peoples for some sort of great Christian sorcerer. He would become the idol of the Abenakis, a nation of the Atlantic coast, where he went for the first time in the winter of 1646–1647.[65]

Moving out again, this time to the north, to the Attikamek of the upper Saint-Maurice: this tribe, as noted earlier, would only be visited, like others in the region, in 1651 and 1652, by Father Buteux.[66] But they came regularly to Trois-Rivières. The chronicler of 1648 was astonished by the vitality of their faith: the absence of a priest had not discouraged them; in the depths of the forests they continued their practices of devotion. The priest was again altogether amazed at it: "Since Baptism made them disciples of the Holy Spirit, this Teacher has been pleased with them, He instructs them far from the clamour of the law courts and the Louvres, he makes them more knowledgeable without books, than all the Aristotles with their great volumes."[67] Since on the whole the Amerindian reality offered little cause for rejoicing, Father Lalemant felt obliged to make the most of a case which he considered exemplary.

However, the central work of the Society of Jesus in New France – which coincided almost exactly with Montmagny's term[68] – remained Huronia. There again, the *Relation* of 1648 is precious for the completion of this portrait of the colony at the moment of his departure.[69]

To start with, this was the year that the French colony saw the last great convoy from the Huron nation reaching Trois-Rivières: "It was good to see about sixty canoes coming gently down the great river, and all the Huron solemnly sitting, beating out a rhythm with their voices and their paddles to the chants and airs of their enemies [some Iroquois prisoners] but it was a doleful thing to look upon these victims, who will, perhaps, be food for the flames and for the stomachs of these barbarians."[70] The Huron had succeeded in overcoming an Iroquois detachment which was blocking their route. They were not all Christians, only half at most, and so had kept their "barbaric" customs – an allusion, here, to the treatment of prisoners. Of 250 men "led by five brave captains," there were "Christians and Catechumens to the number of more than 120."[71] They were able to talk with Montmagny, and there was an exchange of gifts, in what would be the last official meeting of this Nation with a representative of France.

To speak of Huronia in 1648, one must first of all mention the fort of Sainte-Marie. In 1639, the new superior of the mission, Jérôme Lalemant, decided to set up a central post from which to direct and supervise that great operation, the Christianization of the region. Close to the great lake,[72] at the point where a river flowed into it, the missionaries began the establishment of a post comprising houses, church, hospital, and storehouses, with part of the cleared area reserved for Huron Christians. Fields were planted and domestic animals were brought in. In the letter that Ragueneau wrote to the General in March 1644, he informed him that not only had they become self-sufficient, but they now had reserves of most of the essential foodstuffs.[73] Three priests were living there then (fifteen others were dispersed among the territory's missions), and there were also four coadjutor brothers, twenty-three *donnés*, seven domestics, and eight soldiers.

Eleven missions depended on Sainte-Marie, eight for the Hurons and three for the Algonquin tribes living east of Huronia, that is to say in the direction of the Ottawa River. Seventeen hundred baptisms had been performed in 1648 – and to that should be added, according to the chronicle, those which had been performed by Father Antoine Daniel before his death, the number of which could not be known.[74]

Two events marked this year. First, the one which we have just referred to and which we recounted in a previous chapter.[75] And some weeks before (28 April) there had been a tragedy, this time within the Nation itself. One of the Jesuits' domestics had been murdered on the order of six captains who were not yet converted, and who had commanded two of their men to kill the first Frenchman they met. Faced with the worsening of the situation, these chiefs had a reaction which, in the circumstances, could to a certain point be explained: they attributed their ordeals to the presence of the missionaries and their religous message. Here is how the *Relation* presented the event: "We are very certain that these Captains, who are not the least considerable in the country, have always declared themselves enemies of the Faith, and in the aftermath of this affair they have let loose their rage and their spite against us and against our Christians; and whatever pretext they may have alleged regarding this murder, our Christian Captains have informed us that they have a grudge against Jesus Christ in the persons of those who recognize Him and adore Him."[76]

In a general assembly called to study the situation, these captains declared that the priests and indeed all the Christians should be chased out; however, since these had become numerous and strong enough to present a different point of view, they succeeded in making the assembly recognize the need for a collective restitution. The Jesuits yielded to their way of conceiving justice: "given the mind of the Savages, their justice is without doubt very effective in preventing wrongdoing, although in France it would appear an injustice: since it is the public which makes satisfaction for the faults of individuals, whether the criminal is recognized, or whether he remains concealed. In a word, it is the crime that is punished."[77]

There followed exchanges of speeches and of presents. Note in particular the remarks of the captain who presented the nation's excuses: "My brother ... here are all the Nations assembled. ... we are now only a handful of people; it is you alone who sustain this country, and bear it in your hands. A thunderbolt from Heaven has fallen upon our land, and has torn it open; if you cease to sustain us, we shall fall into this abyss. Have pity on us. Rather than to parley, we come to bewail our loss, as much as yours. This land is no longer anything but a dried-up skeleton, without flesh, without veins, without nerves, without arteries; like bones which no longer hold to each other except by a thin thread."[78] Basically, in the very depths of their being, the Huron were feeling a sense of extreme disarray. The Iroquois menace weighed upon them like the sword of Damocles; they had a sort of presentiment of what was going to happen in 1649 and 1650. The words recorded by Ragueneau give an idea of the atmosphere – quasi-apocalyptic – which was crushing them on the eve of the looming catastrophe.

For Montmagny, 1648 was the end of a long and trying administration, as we said at the start of this chapter.

Long: it lasted twelve years, when it was initially to be a term of only three years – the epoch of the founder, Samuel de Champlain, had come to an end.[79] D'Ailleboust would only remain as governor of Québec from 1648 to 1651. His immediate successor, Jean de Lauson, did not finish his second term.

Trying: it is now evident what is meant by this. The enthusiasm proclaimed by Le Jeune in the *Relation* of 1636 was no longer in the air. The colony was underpopulated – what could 900 Europeans do in an immense uncleared territory, peopled with Amerindians, the most dynamic of whom were hostile to them? Their very protection was uncertain; twice Montmagny asked the mother country for minimal support, only to receive a niggardly response. The fur trade, officially the only source of financing for New France, was at the mercy of the native people. To assist the Huron, the principal suppliers of furs, Montmagny was only able in 1647 to send a pathetic protection force: a squadron of eight soldiers. The following year, these allies of France were already experiencing premonitions of their dispersion.

This was the Canadian reality at the decade's end. In France, where this state of things was barely suspected, it inspired fanciful stories.

2.   Between the chevalier de Montmagny and the prophet Elijah: Cyrano

Around 1650 there circulated among the intellectuals of the French capital the manuscript of a tale both ingenious and – in many respects – provoking: *L'Autre Monde*, that came from the pen of a certain Savinien de Cyrano. The work was not published until after his death in 1657, and even then in an expurgated version and under a new title: *L'histoire comique des estats et empires de la Lune*.[80] It is above all the first version of the book that is of interest here.

Convinced that the moon is another world, inhabited like this one, Cyrano decides to journey to it. Retiring to a place apart in the outskirts of Paris, he girds his waist with a string of bottles filled with rose-coloured liquid, and, the sun's rays warming this "subtil" liquid,[81] he is lifted into the air. At the end of several hours, realizing that he is going to miss his target, he breaks some of his bottles, and with gravity no longer impeded, redescends to earth. But instead of returning to Paris, he lands in the vicinity of Québec (though he does not know it right away). Some naked savages surround him, then run away, after seeing his accoutrement close up. He is soon spotted by some soldiers on parade, and he asks them where, exactly, he is. "You are in France, they answered me; but what devil has put you in this state? And how is it that we do not know you at all? Have the ships arrived? Are you going to inform Monsieur the Governor of it? And why have you divided your brandy into so many bottles?"[82] He gives them a direct answer: that the "Devil" [in whom Cyrano surely did not believe] could not have put him in this state; that he does not know that "the Seine carries ships," that he has no report to deliver to M. de Montbazon, the governor of Paris,[83] and that his flasks do not contain brandy. "Ho ho," they say, "you are a sly fellow"; and they decide to lead him without delay to the governor. "On the way, I learned from them that I was in France and I was not in Europe, because I was in New France. I was presented to Monsieur de Montmagny, who is its Viceroy. He asked me my country, my name and my rank, and after I had satisfied him with an account of the agreeable success of my voyage, whether he believed it or pretended to believe, he had the goodness to have a room in his apartment given to me."

The author of this tale, one of the most innovative people of the seventeenth century, was an unusual person.[84] After two painful adventures in the army, he recycled himself, so to speak, by frequenting the erudite circles and the literary salons of the capital. Thus he participated in the ferment of ideas which marked the beginning of the scientific revolution, which has made the seventeenth century one of the key periods in the history of humanity. The habit of disputation – the phenomenon that goes under the name "erudite libertinage" – which characterized the milieu in which he came to move, corresponded perfectly to his restless spirit. He would adopt as his method a systematic criticism of the ideas inherited from the past, whether religious or profane.

In 1645 he decided to devote his life to writing, and it is from this year, probably, that his work *Le pédant joué* dates, in which the caricature of Jean Grangier, the rector of the college where he had studied, was recognizable.[85] He wrote some mazarinades, before taking the cardinal's part. The provocative tone of one of his pieces led to his being accused of atheism.[86] He died in a run-of-the-mill accident, on 21 July 1655.[87]

To return to the traveller: after several hours spent in Québec, he takes advantage of the fires of Saint John to attempt another flight to the earth's satellite – and this time he succeeds. He is received by the prophet Elijah, since it is there that the "earthly paradise" was moved after the sin of Adam and Eve.[88]

His stay on the moon gives rise to fantastic adventures, all marked by a scathing caricature of traditional thought. These are some of the themes he broaches: the creation of the world by God, the resurrection of the body, the immortality of the soul, miracles – the doctor who is assigned to him is altogether put out to hear him use "these fairy-tale terms of miracles"; this is unworthy of a philosopher. "As the wise man sees nothing in the world which he does not conceive or which he does not deem to be conceived, he ought to abominate all this talk of miracles, of prodigies, of events against Nature, which was invented by the stupid to explain the weaknesses in their understanding."[89]

State and society do not escape the novelist's scalpel; two examples will suffice: the undue interference of the lunar clergy in the life of citizens; and the stupidity of war in the European style, compared to the customs which are current above.

But the interlude in Québec does not give rise to such virulence. Cyrano finds in his host, Montmagny, "a man capable of high opinions," who does not object when he tells him "that the earth must have turned during my elevation";[90] their discussions, which furthermore the governor seems to enjoy, bear exclusively on problems of astronomy and physics. Nothing on society. On religion, only a brief allusion as to the location of hell – there needs to be a little room for the facetious. In fact, a Jesuit has told Montmagny that the world turns on itself, but not for the reasons put forward by Copernicus; the Bible, he said, teaches us that since hell is at the centre of the earth the damned who attempt to "flee the heat of the flames" throw themselves "against the vault," and thus trigger a rotating movement, "as a dog turns a wheel when he runs around an enclosure inside."[91]

The long discussion that the two men have on the very day of their meeting deals essentially with the nature and the respective role of the sun and the earth; with geocentrism; with the nature of the universe.

The author places in Montmagny's mouth a series of propositions which would tend not to call into question the traditional teaching on the solar cycle.[92] The sun, a perfect star,[93] which lifted you up, may very well also have set you back on the earth – this is a first response arising from what was once called natural philosophy. Then come arguments from common sense: it is the sun that we see moving; the earth is firm beneath our feet, it cannot be moving as fast as you claim. This is the occasion for Cyrano to present his theory: the sun heats everything – it does the same in microcosms such as fruits, for example, which contain nuts charged with energy which will assure reproduction *ad infinitum*. What is more, the movement of the sun is absurd in itself – one might as well say that the coasts turn around the ship, which is itself stable; and that it is the fireplace that turns around the swallow which is being roasted on a spit. Another objection to this movement: the sun's mass, hundreds of times heavier than the earth. Furthermore there is nothing to prove that the vault of heaven is round – which it would have to be to circle around the earth. The rotation of the earth is easy to explain: the sun's rays which touch it give it movement, "as we make a globe turn by hitting it with our hand."

Montmagny then presents another objection to heliocentrism: how does it happen, "if the system of Ptolemy [theorist of geocentrism] was so improbable, that it has been so generally received?" Very simple, responds the visitor, "most men" allow themselves to be deceived either by a sensory illusion [the sun rising and setting], or by a deformation of a psychological order: it is "the insupportable pride of humans which persuades them that Nature was made just for them, as if it is likely that the sun, a great body [434] times vaster than the earth, was set alight merely to ripen their apples and fill out their cabbages." And according to Cyrano, the stars are themselves suns around which gravitate worlds that we cannot suspect; and, behind the stars that we see, there exist "worlds which we do not see from here because of their small size and because their borrowed light cannot reach us."

Montmagny interrupts. "But, he says to me, if, as you assure me, the fixed stars are so many suns, one could conclude from that that the world is infinite ... and that it goes on eternally in this way."[94] Exactly, retorts the other. If God has been able to make the soul immortal, "he has been able to make the world infinite"; what is more, "God would be finished Himself, supposing the world was not infinite." The governor has trouble following him. "My faith!" he answers me, "Say what you will, I would not be able to understand this infinity at all." Cyrano's reaction is up to the argument: "Is it easier to understand a nothingness beyond?" Basically, what is nothingness? It is much more difficult to conceive than the "infinities" that we know: earth, fire, water, air, the stars, the heavens. "For the infinite is nothing but a boundless interweaving of all this." Better still, the universe continues to create itself, it transforms itself ceaselessly: The Parisian continues, "If I ever have the honour of seeing you in France, I shall make you observe, by means of an excellent spyglass in my possession, that certain obscurities which from here appear as blots are in fact worlds under construction."[95]

These claims were largely imaginary on the part of Cyrano, but the discoveries of the astrophysicists have confirmed certain points. More nonsensical, however, was the theory according to which America had only existed for some decades; it was part of the transformation of the universe of which he had just spoken. It was the reason why "our predecessors who have spanned the Ocean a thousand times" did not discover it.[96]

The conversations continue the next day, "and the days following"; then other cares take Montmagny away: "the pressure of the Province's affairs interrupted our philosophy, and I returned more enthusiastically than ever to the design of flying to the moon."[97]

An opportunity is presented a few days later. The governor is in deep discussion with his collaborators and the native allies, seeking a solution to the Iroquois problem. The soldiers of the garrison are busy with preparations for the Saint John's fire. So Cyrano hastens to assemble a new machine: a central box for the pilot, great wings moved by springs. Then he puts it all to the test; throwing himself with this contraption from the height of a nearby hill. Not having taken his measurements well, he somersaults "roughly into the valley." In no way discouraged, he returns to his room to treat his wounds with beef marrow and to revive himself "with a bottle of cordial essence" – brandy, no doubt. But when he returns to look for his engine, he can no longer find it. The soldiers, in search of wood for the fire they are preparing, have taken it to the firepit – someone has even suggested surrounding it with rockets, so that "when the spring moves the great wings, no-one will believe that this machine is not a Fire Dragon."[98]

Cyrano finishes by repairing it on the pyre, "just as they are setting the fire." He has time to slip into it without warning, to be lifted up immediately "into the clouds." The rockets placed all around it ignite one by one, and send him far into space. When the last one has burnt out, the machine falls to earth and shatters. The word spreads through France that "he has been burnt in Canada in this great fireworks display which he had invented."[99] A false rumour, since he has been able to continue his "elevation" by "a happening which you would take for a miracle."[100] The marrow with which he smeared himself has saved his life, and brought him to a happy landing. "The moon during this quarter, since it is accustomed to suck the marrow of animals [a dig at a popular belief] drank up that with which I was covered." And it was thus that he discovered the earthly paradise.

Quite against his will, Montmagny had become a character in a novel. So far as we know he had no ties to the libertines.[101] In his family circle, which we have been able to observe, one would rather have found *dévots*.

The portrait Cyrano traced of him was flattering. The governor of Québec is a cultivated man; he has read Gassendi, he knows of Ptolemy,[102] and Tyco Brahe.[103] He is interested in scientific questions, especially astronomy.

He is also someone who is attentive to others: he listens; he intervenes without being abrupt. He has an open mind: he converses with Cyrano as with the Jesuits. He loves discussion, he even seeks it out; he does not, in contrast with the lunar priests, resort easily to condemnation. He is welcoming, lending a room in his residence to a visitor, who feels very much at ease there. He is capable of humour. As Cyrano is going to bed on the night of his arrival, he seeks him out to start a discussion: "I would not have come, he said, to interrupt your rest, if I had not thought that a person who was able to make nine hundred leagues in half a day could have done so without tiring."[104] Montmagny is close to the Jesuits. Upon the Parisian's arrival in Québec he goes to consult with them; apparently the conversation turns on the theories of the great astronomers and on sorcery. But he knows how to keep his distance from them; after having met with them, he says to Cyrano: "But don't you know ... the friendly argument that I have just had on your behalf with our Jesuit fathers? They have it absolutely that you are a magician, and the greatest grace that you can obtain from them, is to be considered nothing but an imposter." Here is something very interesting. The Canadian Jesuits, it has been observed, were in the process of evolving in their judgment regarding medicine men. After the vituperation which, upon their arrival in the colony, they hurled against the action of Satan which they saw concealed behind the "sorcerers," they were coming to see them more and more as imposters and tricksters. This shows that Cyrano had scanned the *Relations*. It is then highly probable that these writings constituted one of the bases for his imaginary story, and it can be asked if it is not to render homage of a sort to their authors that he included this incursion into New France in his voyage.

The *Relations*, at least those of the 1630s and 1640s, were evidently a publishing success.[105] They had not escaped the attention of the intellectual circles. La Mothe Le Vayer, a friend of Cyrano, was an assiduous reader of them,[106] as was the royal engineer, Pierre Petit, himself also a man of letters and an erudite.[107]

Several details recorded by Cyrano seem to have been drawn directly from the annual publication of the Jesuits: the celebrations of Saint John, with their fireworks and rockets; the native people who swiftly disappear into the forest, leaving behind them an old man who cannot run; the parade of garrison soldiers; the council where the discussion is about the measures to take to protect the allies from their enemies the Iroquois; the sparsity of the population, which makes anonymity impossible.

Several features in the image of Montmagny were faithful to what the *Relation* described: the warm welcome for new arrivals or visitors;[108] the attentive benevolence to all; the devotion; the constant contact with the Jesuits.

Thus ends the second phase in the career of the chevalier. This one and the first were approximately the same length, a little over twelve years. It might be instructive to outline a few elements of comparison between the two.

The geographic contrast has already been evoked. Montmagny knew how to adapt to it; he lived through a dozen harsh winters, just as he had faced up to the hot climate of southern Europe. He became accustomed to the Saint Lawrence River, just as he had been able to master the capricious waters of the Mediterranean.

When he was on the island of Malta, his contacts were above all those which his Order provided for him. But the preparation of missions put him in contact with a whole series of technicians, as did the privateering voyages or the caravans, where he worked side by side (if he did not command them) with a variety of crews. In Québec (even if, at the beginning, he could count on the presence of the chevalier de Lisle, his lieutenant), his Order was replaced by the Jesuits with whom he worked in perfect symbiosis. With his subjects, there is no evidence of serious misunderstanding – the controversy with the pioneers of Montréal only lasted a short time.

But in fact, his principal occupation differed fundamentally from the one case to the other. In Valetta it had been war against the Turks, either on his own boat (which was the cause of his financial ruin) or on the galleys of the Order: a hard life involving constant movement, ventures of all kinds, wild expenditures of energy. In Canada the management of a colony fell upon his shoulders: the attentive examination of the questions put to him, discussions with his collaborators, but also with the *habitants* and with the natives, administration of justice; and to this was added a military role, to which he had to adapt, since the Amerindians were profoundly different from the Mediterranean peoples that he had fought before.

But it was precisely in that confrontation that he had, in 1627, put up a spectacular resistance to an enemy far superior in numbers. This exploit won him renown in Malta, and he was taken up by a contemporary historian who was interested in Turkey. In the colony of Québec, nothing of the sort occurred. Political circumstances in France made his administration extremely difficult; he coped as best he could. He resisted the Iroquois with very limited forces – it may be said that he had learned that habit in the Mediterranean – but there was nothing spectacular involved. He held out, however, despite all obstacles, and the Jesuits did not fail to bear witness to this in the *Relations* – and that attracted the attention of a storyteller.

CHAPTER 9

On the Service of the Order of Malta
in the Antilles

Upon his return to the mother country at the end of November 1648, Montmagny would find a France very different from the one he had left twelve years earlier, in 1636, the year that the Spanish occupied the town of Corbie less than a hundred kilometres from Paris. Two points will help to explain the change which his career was to experience: the new political climate, and colonial realities in transformation.

The situation of the kingdom, both internally and abroad, had evolved a great deal. There had been a changeover at the uppermost levels. Mazarin and the regent, Anne of Austria (both of them born outside France), had personalities very different from those of Richelieu and Louis XIII, and their style of government bore little resemblance to that of their predecessors. The difficult task of winning the war had not left them with much leisure to give serious consideration to the country's problems. Certainly, from 1643 (year of the victory at Rocroi) to 1648 (that at Lens) the army had succeeded in regaining the initiative – and this culminated in the Peace of Westphalia in 1648. But the effort had cost dear in human lives (it has already been mentioned that it was thus that one of Montmagny's fellow students at La Flèche, Jean-Baptiste de Budes de Guébriant, had seen his brilliant military career end, in November 1643). And it was necessary to find the wherewithal; the expedients to which Mazarin, "the Sicilian," had been forced to resort to finance the operations had not been to everyone's taste. The Marais to which Montmagny returned had been violently shaken by the first manifestations of the Fronde – imprisonment of magistrates, skirmishes, barricades. The court had only returned from its six weeks' exile a few days before, and he would see it depart, at the beginning of January, for several months more.

The sector which, throughout all these years, was most neglected was without a doubt that of the colonies. It is clear what that meant for the Saint Lawrence valley. The historian Charles de la Roncière, speaking of "disarray," of the "collapse of our colonial empire," is thinking primarily of the events in the Antilles.[1] But it is evident that the system put in place by Richelieu – of private companies under government surveillance – was at an impasse. A highly spectacular event illustrates the helplessness of these bodies and the incompetence of their political overseers. When, on 25 November 1645, the new lieutenant general of the islands (whose nomination, suggested by the regent whose protegé he was, was accepted by the Company) presented himself at Saint-Christophe in the lesser Antilles, Commander Philippe de Lonvilliers de Poincy, a colleague of Montmagny who had already served two three-year terms in this post, refused to recognize his replacement. The latter had to take refuge in Guadeloupe and, after several months of ineffectual palavers and failed coups, was forced *manu militari* to return to France. Mazarin, who was totally occupied with peace negotiations, and the regent, who was incapable of asserting herself, had to let it be. The *Compagnie des Îles d'Amérique*, discredited, decided shortly afterwards to sell the islands to individuals, who became their seigneurs. Charles Houel[2] and his brother-in-law Jean Boisseret, seigneur of Herblay, took over Guadeloupe on 4 September 1649, and Jacques Dyel du Parquet,[3] Martinique, on 22 September 1650. On 24 May 1651 the island of Saint-Christophe was sold to the Order of Malta, and some days later (31 May 1651) Poincy received a royal commission as governor of the American islands.

These events would have powerful repercussions on Montmagny's career. Less than a year after his return from Québec, he found himself entrusted by the Grand Master with a most ungrateful task: to represent him personally in the Antilles, which meant, concretely, to conduct the preliminary inquiry before the purchase of the island, as well as to attempt to bring Poincy entirely in line with the interests of the Order. After 1652 he became his lieutenant. This, briefly, was how Montmagny's last years (1649–1657) were spent.

The situations to be studied are scarcely ordinary – indeed, they deal with individual behaviours that are far from commonplace – and they also throw some light on a rather dark period of French colonization, as well as on an episode in the history of the Order of Malta.

It is appropriate here to refer briefly to the beginnings of Saint-Christophe, the starting point in the development of the French Antilles, and then to make a close study of the Poincy phenomenon. On more than one point, his career is comparable to that of Montmagny. A first stage takes us to 1649; after that date a second stage begins, in which the Order was directly involved, through Montmagny among others. The main features of this involvement, which finally ended in 1665 with the cession of the island to the *Compagnie des Indes Occidentales,* will be examined.

1.   France in Saint-Christophe

The French adventure in Saint-Christophe (and in the Antilles) really began in 1625, with the chance meeting of two Norman privateers, "Urbain de Roissey, écuyer, Sieur de Chardonville," and "Pierre Belain, écuyer, Sieur d'Esnambuc."[4] The former, an enterprising and audacious captain, had in the preceding year seized an entire cargo of sugar from an English pirate sailing in the Channel. While in the Caribbean in the summer of 1625, he was pursued by a Spanish fleet cruising south of Jamaica. He escaped, and as luck would have it he took refuge in Saint-Christophe, where he entered immediately into contact with the second, Belain d'Esnambuc, who had recently arrived there. This man, who had been roaming the Atlantic, and especially the coasts of Brazil, since 1603, was as active as Roissey; furthermore, he possessed real organizational talents. Upon arriving in Saint-Christophe, he had met a handful of Frenchmen, who had just begun growing tobacco there. He welcomed his compatriot with enthusiasm, seeing in him a sign that God approved of the project which he was beginning to entertain: the official installation of France in the Antilles, and first of all in Saint-Christophe.

So Roissey arrived at the right moment: it was necessary to raise some capital – which was easier for two than for one; and, also, to find support in high places – and Sieur de Chardonville knew Commander de Razilly personally. They left for the mother country as soon as a cargo of tobacco was ready, in July 1626.

The island which they were beginning to exploit is part of the Lesser Antilles, situated between Guadeloupe and Puerto Rico. Its climate is agreeable, and its ground, though very uneven, is green and fertile.[5]

Its name was given to it by Christopher Columbus, who had landed there during his first voyage in 1492. At that time it was inhabited by the Caribs, who had recently settled there.[6] The Spaniards claimed sovereignty over the territory, but they did not occupy it. When, in 1618, some individual Frenchmen took up occupation, the Caribs did not obstruct them.

The difficulties began when other Europeans decided to move into the island, also with a view to exploiting it. In 1623, some English colonists landed. They were much taken by the climate, and their leader, Thomas Warner, returned to England to seek reinforcements. He came back in 1625 with a hundred colonists. Belain, who did not have the means to oppose him, decided to divide the territory – despite its modest size[7] – in two. What was more, this division was conducted in a rather strange way: one part, two non-contiguous parcels on the northwest and the southeast, going to France, and on the other, the mountainous centre and the two other coasts, going to England. During the seventeenth century another nation was regularly active in the region, though without political pretensions: the Dutch.[8] In return for tobacco (and later, sugar) they exchanged clothing, foodstuffs, and various goods. In this way they saved the badly provisioned and hungry young colony several times.

So here were our two privateers, transformed into colonizers. They arrived in Le Havre at the end of the summer of 1626, unloaded their cargo of tobacco, received the support of an important outfitter, succeeded in interesting Razilly in their project, and obtained an interview with Richelieu. Everything went along swimmingly, and on 31 October of the same year a contract was passed before a notary, establishing the *Compagnie de Saint-Christophe*.[9] The capital of 45,000 livres came from thirteen lenders, including the cardinal, who for his part in it turned over 10,000 livres – evidence of the interest that he felt in the project. The two captains became the agents for the society that was responsible for populating the colony (though no quota was imposed), for developing its agriculture, and for managing its commerce for twenty years.

The capital, it should be said, was not very considerable. The capacity of the three ships that they were able to purchase did not allow for the transportation of more than 240 men, and in rather precarious conditions at that. A comparison, enlightening in many ways, comes from the simultaneous effort that the English were making: Warner had also taken to the idea of a company, and he found enough funding in England to acquire five ships, on which 400 colonists found a place in relative comfort.[10]

It was in fact d'Esnambuc who took charge of the colony. The first three years were very hard. As we have seen, the Company had a limited budget, so the earliest undertakings were necessarily modest. France's enemies profited from this. The tenacity and courage of the captain general (as he was entitled) saved the situation.

MAP 5

The Lesser Antilles (1650–1652)

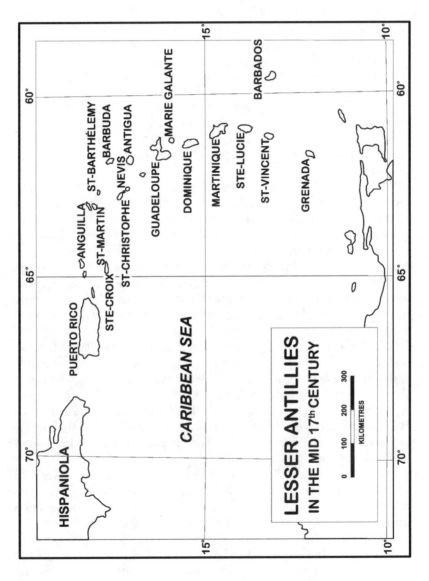

The maiden voyage at the beginning of 1627 took two and a half months. The colonists who disembarked were in poor shape: several had become sick, either during the crossing, or upon arrival on the island. The following year the Company sent 120 men and paid over 9,000 livres. But the English were beginning to encroach upon the land of the French colonists, in spite of a treaty concluded in May 1627.[11] D'Esnambuc had no other recourse than to leave for France to plead for the government's intervention. The Company could not guarantee the defence of the colony.[12]

Richelieu reacted energetically; it is possible that now that he was free of the problem of La Rochelle, he desired to take revenge for the discomfiture which the *Cent-Associés* had suffered in the Saint Lawrence. Ten ships arrived at Saint-Christophe on 27 July 1629. The English had to concede.

This was not the end. An imposing Spanish fleet was soon dotting the horizon. The French had the time, thanks to the ships that newly arrived from France, to take flight to the neighbouring islands, to return some weeks later after the departure of the Spaniards, who were not staying. Since the food situation was catastrophic, d'Esnambuc (and the colony) were only able to survive thanks to the Zealanders – enough tobacco remained to be exchanged for basic rations. This was the beginning of a regular collaboration with them, which the Company directors hastened to denounce, attempting in this way to cover up their own ineptitude.

That was the fundamental problem. The associates failed entirely to understand what the planting and peopling of a colony on the other side of the Atlantic involved. To give a specific example: at the beginning of the 1630s there were only 360 French on the island of Saint-Christophe, where the English had already installed 6,000 of their compatriots.[13] D'Esnambuc did wonders to keep these within their boundaries. In the face of all these difficulties, it was judged prudent to modify the system that had been put in place in 1626.

On 12 February 1635 the *Compagnie des Îles d'Amérique* had its official birth.[14] It was given permission to establish on any islands which were not yet occupied by a Christian prince. Its obligations can be summed up as follows: to people the colony (4,000 colonists in twenty years); to put it into a defensible state; to assure religious services; and to keep a close eye on the economic activity. The governor would be named by the king and he would be forbidden to take part in trade. Since no amount was mentioned in the contract, it must be concluded that the capital of the retiring company – in any case, what remained of it – came to the new company, and that future benefits were being counted on to finance the enterprise. This attests to the modesty of the new group's ambitions.

In spite of everything, new perspectives were opened up, and this unleashed a movement of immigration (by the end of 1636 the French part of Saint-Christophe counted close to 3,000 inhabitants). It also inspired certain initiatives: a lieutenant of Belain's, Liénart de l'Olive, settled in Guadeloupe in 1635,[15] and his own nephew, Jacques Dyel du Parquet, in Martinique in the following year.[16]

D'Esnambuc did not long survive the birth of the Company. He had done good work, but he was worn out and, in 1636, he requested his recall. It was refused. He died at the beginning of the following year. His replacement was difficult: what was needed was a firm, authoritarian man, who also possessed tact and good judgment. The French were dispersed , even into the interior of Saint-Christophe; the English there had shown themselves to be redoubtable neighbours; the Caribs were not all dead. Belain's lieutenant, a man named Du Halde, was designated; but he soon felt himself overwhelmed, and resigned.[17] In January 1638, the Company presented the cardinal with a new candidate: Commander Philippe de Lonvilliers de Poincy.

A new phase – as full of ups and downs as the last – was opening for the islands.

2.   The Poincy phenomenon

The man who would soon be travelling across the Atlantic to start (at fifty-five) a new career – one which would end with his death twenty-two years later – is an enigmatic figure. After an extremely exciting life, he settled down in a faraway island and never moved from it, even refusing to obey an order from the king to return to France. Close to Basseterre, his capital, he built himself a magnificent château, where he entertained sumptuously. His household comprised 300 persons;[18] even the dignitaries of the Order did not have so rich a lifestyle. For twenty years he had served the king impeccably; now, installed in his little realm, he became an autocrat, resisting the *lettres de cachet**
that his sovereign ordered to be delivered to him, throwing the man who was sent to replace him off the island. He proved to be a good organizer, and highly effective – but he did not know how to manage his money, or neglected to do it. From the time of his accession to power

he accumulated debts; even after his death his estate was pursued by interminable lawsuits.

Historians have not been kind to him. In 1667, Father Du Tertre wrote of Poincy: "A man of spirit, a great politican, generous on certain occasions, affecting to appear magnificent in his entertainment and in his buildings, beneficent towards his friends and his domestics, to whom he gave fortunes, the object of fear and severe to excess towards those who were not in his interests."[19] What, for the Dominican, ruined everything was the fact that he was suspicious, litigious, and hard, if not hateful, to his enemies. His only preoccupation was his "interest" – that is to say, the augmentation of his fortune. Nevertheless, when Du Tertre had to summarize the first part of Poincy's career (the part preceding the adventure in the Antilles) he offered this complimentary judgment: "In a word, he was a skilled warrior, a great politician, a man full of riches and friends, and one of the good minds of Europe."[20]

At the beginning of the twentieth century, a serious article devoted to him includes the following reflexion: "Literate by education, pious by profession, cruel by avarice and by ambition, clever enough to have conquered and kept wealth, cultivated enough to know how to enjoy it, too self-absorbed to have given thought to the public good and to have had broad views, Poincy appears to us as endowed with quite remarkable talents."[21] To this historian, too, Poincy seemed a strange person.

After a few words on his social origin, we shall examine the first part of his life, which can be summed up in two phrases: service to the Grand Master, service to the king; and then move on to the beginning of the colonial years, from his nomination in 1638 to the Order's purchase in 1651 of the island of Saint-Christophe.

Philippe de Lonvilliers de Poincy came from an ancient family of the north of France.[22] His great-great-grandfather, Guillaume Blondel, écuyer, was the seigneur of Lonvilliers, an estate situated in Picardie, not far from Montreuil-sur-Mer. His great-grandfather, Gilles de Lonvilliers (the surname Blondel had disappeared), was seigneur of Arnoncourt, close to Langres. His grandfather, who possessed two seigneuries in the neighbourhood of Compiègne, and lived at Fresnois-les-Beauvaisis, bought Poincy-lez-Meaux, which appeared in the surname of his descendants.[23] In this gradual progress toward the centre we can easily distinguish the attraction of the capital.

Jean de Lonvilliers, Philippe's father, had the good fortune to ally himself to a lineage of ancient and distinguished nobility, when on 18 November 1566 he married Sophie de Choiseul. It is interesting to note that between 1527 and 1640, sixteen members of the Choiseul family entered the Order of Malta, which may partially explain the vocation of the young Poincy.[24]

On 16 September 1604 the dossier of his proofs of nobility was presented to the examiners of the Grand Priory of France.[25] Some weeks later he commenced his novitiate. His vows were pronounced on 17 January 1606.[26] He most likely completed his two caravans this year. Like Montmagny, he made several journeys *ad patriam;* on 17 June 1608 he is found there, attending the marriage of his brother Christophe.[27] In 1609, he was in the Gulf of Alexandria, under the orders of a famous captain by the name of Fressinet, who was for a while the terror of the Turks: "Three chevaliers [in an assault on a fortress] entered by a gate, the third was Poincy, who has fought bravely for his Order in many voyages and encounters and has since been made a commander. But a stone striking him on the shoulder threw him against the grille, for the Turks threw masses of stones through the embrasures upon their enemies. Poincy picked himself up and with some others to the number of ten who had entered [the gate] drove the Turks away from these embrasures, and the troops who were outside entered the place, pillaged and sacked it."[28] His courage had given the besiegers the victory.

But having developed a taste for armed combat, he decided to fight for his own benefit. He bought a brigantine, the *Saint-Anne,* arranged for its armament, and, on 2 August 1610, obtained permission to go privateering in the Levant.[29] We have not been able to follow him in this activity.[30] All the same, there is a striking resemblance between his career and Montmagny's.

From autumn 1615 on, he divided his life between the service of the king and that of the Grand Master. In May 1622, we find him commanding two ships in Brittany. He obtained a first commandery in 1619,[31] and a second in 1624.[32] He attended the assemblies and chapters of the Grand Priory of France.[33] For some time he was procurator for the Grand Master in the camps and armies of France,[34] and in January 1634 he was his intermediary with Richelieu.[35]

It was at about this time, apparently, that the colonies attracted his attention. On 28 December 1632, he enrolled as a member of the *Compagnie de la Nouvelle-France,* paying (so it seems) 3,000 livres.[36] This year is notable for two events: Montmagny's entry into the governing board of this body, and the departure of Razilly for Acadia. Could there have been some sort of a connection between these events?

It was, however, naval service that absorbed Poincy most frequently between 1620 and 1638. He took part in the first campaign against La

Rochelle, in 1621–1622. When hostilities broke out again in 1626, he was assigned to the province of Brittany as squadron chief;[37] he became commander of the navy in Brest (the first, it is noted, to bear this title in France).[38] His diligence and ability brought him to Richelieu's attention.[39] In April 1635 he was in service again, this time against the Spanish. In the spring of 1637, he had the rank of squadron chief and played a determining role in the French victory at the islands of Lérins. Was success going to his head? He complained to Richelieu[40] that the office of rear admiral which had been conferred on him, though only temporarily, had been unjustly taken away, following a misunderstanding with Henri d'Escoubleau, Archbishop of Bordeaux,[41] who was at that time president of the council of the navy.

Poincy was offered two opportunities to extricate himself without embarrassment from the impasse into which his quarrel with the archbishop had put him. The Grand Master recalled him to Malta, doubtless to give him an important post in his fleet.[42] The *Compagnie des Îles d'Amérique* proposed that he go to Saint-Christophe, as governor and lieutenant general. He chose the second solution.

Father Du Tertre, reaching the year 1638 in his *Histoire des Antilles*, warns the reader that this date was going to bring in an era of turbulence: "Here we are in 1638, under a new government or rather under new governments, which for twelve years are going to provide us with more revolutions, more revolts, more intrigues, more persecutions of the Church, more innocents oppressed, more criminals absolved, and more tragic stories, than a great empire would suffer during an entire century."[43] At the centre of this effervescence were Saint-Christophe and its governor, who in the long run was going to reveal himself as very different from his brother in religion who, two years earlier, had come to replace Champlain in Québec.[44]

He made a remarkable entry into his capital, Basseterre, with a following of many gentlemen dressed in livery;[45] he was out to impress not only his own subjects, but also the English neighbours. And in fact, one of the first measures of his government was to provide for the defence of the French part of the island. The male population was enrolled in a militia, with twelve companies of 200 men each, and plans were drawn up to provide solid fortification of the strategic points.

He obviously had organizing talents; he was enterprising and effective – and cultivated, as the contents of his library demonstrate;[46] he did not lack intelligence – witness the report which he sent to the Company at the end of 1639.[47] He suggested that, since coexistence with the English was proving difficult, it sell the island of Saint-Christophe, concentrate its efforts on Guadeloupe and Martinique, and then annex Dominica, thus making these three islands into a "great Kingdom." Richelieu turned down this proposition.

The ministerial veto did not discourage him. He made a realistic decision. The island of Saint-Christophe would become his business, his enterprise. Unable to count on a miserly and ineffectual Company, he assumed the cost of his own initiatives. In doing this, he went hopelessly into debt – an uncomfortable situation made even worse by the lawsuits which his quarrelsome habits brought down on him. He occupied himself in beautifying the villages, in joining them to each other by good roads, in improving the port installations. He arranged the building of chapels and a hospital. Four stores were constructed in the name of the Company, but he reserved the fifth, larger and better furnished than the others, for himself – and this provoked complaints. On a height overlooking the capital, he had a château built for himself, surrounded by gardens and terraces.

But there was another side to his administration which was less positive, and which contributed to his bad reputation: his implacability. Here are three examples.

First there was the La Grange affair.[48] The sieur de La Grange, who had preceded Poincy as lieutenant, had not accomplished his duty to his satisfaction, so he turned on him. La Grange's wife put about rumours concerning the governor. Poincy became unmanageable, threatened to have them beheaded, seized their goods, and expelled them along with their friends.

While this was going on, a group of slaves revolted. Those who were not killed in the pursuit that was mounted against them had to suffer the punishment of being quartered alive.[49]

Shortly after the renewal of Poincy's mandate in 1641, his enemies – he had antagonized many of his countrymen – caused a false commission to be circulated, which limited his powers. The presumed author of this document was imprisoned, whereupon his wife made the guards drunk, and the two fled into refuge with the English. But Poincy gathered all the soldiers and summoned the English to give up his two subjects, who were condemned to death. Before his decapitation, the husband was forced to make honourable amends, walking through the streets in his shirt with a candle in his hand.[50]

This excessive severity upset the Company's directors, and resulted in a termination of his commission. A new affair was in the making – without a doubt one of the most spectacular in French colonial history.

A Burgundian gentleman was found to replace Poincy, Noël Patrocle de Thoisy.[51] It was a political nomination, but there is no reason to believe that the new candidate would have been less suitable than Poincy. Noël Patrocle's father was a familiar of the regent, Anne of Austria;[52] and it was undoubtedly she who suggested his name. The royal commission was issued to him on 20 February 1645.[53]

The Company, which distrusted Poincy, had some days before (16 February) obtained a *lettre de cachet* from the king, ordering him to return to France "where [he declared] I desire to give you employment in future functions in my service."[54] It was communicated to him on 13 March. Perhaps it was at that moment that he chose rebellion. Some time before, he had written to the Company to tell it that it owed him a reimboursement of the enormous sums that he had spent in developing the island and, among other things, setting up the culture of sugar cane.[55] In August, the company asked its administrator Leumont to enter into negotiations with Poincy over the details of his retirement; but Poincy had just expelled him from Saint-Christophe.

In a second *lettre de cachet* dated 18 August 1645, the king demanded that he leave the Antilles under pain of disobedience. His nephew was approached to put pressure on him.[56]

In the hopes that he could come to an understanding with Poincy, Thoisy left Le Havre on 2 September.[57] When the new governor presented himself at Saint-Christophe, he was not even able to disembark – his escort was not strong enough to overcome the militia who refused him access to the port. He was forced to take refuge in Guadeloupe. Once there, he and Houel (governor of Guadeloupe since 1643)[58] prepared a plan to compel the intractable governor by force of arms. Du Parquet arrived from Martinique with another idea: to carry off Poincy's two nephews as blackmail. This was accepted. No good came of it for him, because though the nephews fell into his soldiers' hands, Parquet himself only escaped the militia of Saint-Christophe for the moment, by taking refuge with the Capuchins (who were later expelled from the island), then with the English governor, who delivered him up promptly.

Thoisy was finally betrayed by his Martinique hosts, who turned him over to Poincy. At the end of January 1647, Poincy forced him to board a ship leaving for Saint-Malo.

Meanwhile, the Council of State, no more capable than the Company of ensuring respect for its orders at such a distance from Europe, allowed Poincy a year to arrange his affairs, after which Thoisy would replace him.[59] This did not work out. The ousted lieutenant general had

MAP 6

Saint-Christophe (today Saint Kitts) in 1650

no wish to begin the comedy again. He plunged into judicial pursuits against the commander, which were to last for years.

The Company was in open disarray. In May 1647 it had the idea of beginning a criminal process against Poincy.[60] Then it thought about getting rid of the islands. There was even some question of selling Saint-Christophe to Christophe de Lonvilliers, who had remained on Poincy's property, and who would have served as a figurehead for his brother.[61]

As for Poincy, after having rid himself of his enemies the "Patrocles,"[62] he continued to manage his property, his island, and even his family. In May 1649,[63] he married his nephew, Robert de Lonvilliers, to the daughter of Antoine Girault, *écuyer*, first captain of the milita and the richest and most influential man on the island.[64] The wedding ceremony, which took place in his chapel, was presided over by the superior of the Jesuits (who had replaced the Capuchins on Saint-Christophe).

But his position vis-à-vis the king and the Company remained uncomfortable. So he gave thought to the Order to which he belonged.

3. Montmagny on the Service of the Order of Malta in the Antilles

A letter which Poincy wrote from Saint-Christophe on 20 May 1649 to Brother Jacques de Souvré, ambassador of the Order to the King of France,[65] contains the following lines: "Monsieur, I have no doubt that the greater part of our Order believes that I have forgotten the benefits that I have received from it. I beg you to believe that since I have had the honour of belonging to it, I have not gone a single day of my life without intending to recognize it, as I am obliged."[66] Fine sentiments indeed, but one might well think, more prosaically, that Poincy was seeking a solution which would allow him to remain at his post and escape his creditors. The purchase of the island that he had envisaged[67] did not seem capable of realization. By way of his religious community, he might perhaps achieve his ends. But for our purposes what is important is the concrete proposition that he made, to have two chevaliers from the Grand Priory of France come to his capital. Their role – which he mentioned at the outset – would be, at the moment of his death, to take possession of his estate in the name of the Order; then, more generally, to represent the Order's interests. It would even be necessary that they obtain "letters patent from the King sealed with the great seal" to protect him against the false accusations which (he said) continued to assail him, "to the prejudice of our aforesaid Order." He would pay all their expenses and give them each 1,000 livres per annum. He added a brief resumé of his property: two houses,[68] "very beautiful and elegant, together with good sugar mills, furnished with their slaves and all sorts of livestock."

It was very skilful pleading – how could one doubt the good sentiments of a man who opened wide the gates of his palace to the representatives of the Grand Master, and who showed himself so concerned with his interests?

Meanwhile a rumour ran through Paris that the commander was dead. Souvré wrote about this to the authorities in Malta on 5 and 23 September.[69] The Grand Master began to receive requests from the chevaliers who were eyeing the two commanderies which would have become vacant.[70]

It was at this moment that Montmagny's role in the Antilles began. "On the news of the death of Monsieur the Commander de Poincy [he wrote to the Grand Master on 26 November 1649], it was proposed that I go and take command in the Island of Saint-Christophe, and by the same means arrange for the assumption by the Order of the said Commander's effects after his death."[71] The Company, having been alerted, had made him this proposition. He had accepted "with great joy," and had immediately started his inquiry. He was told, for instance, that Poincy's revenue amounted to around 100,000 écus, "to wit, two hundred thousand livres and more in sugar and tobacco, and more than fifty thousand livres attached to the government." He was even told of Poincy's ridiculous claim: "There are few places in France where two hundred thousand livres of revenue are on display through a window." And according to Montmagny, this fine fortune was threatened from two directions: first of all, the nephews, who, already in the Antilles, would claim their share of the inheritance; secondly, the Company, which had "heavy claims against the said Sieur Commander."

But the affair seems to have turned up short, since the news was false. Montmagny was thinking of something else; he hoped to leave Paris for Malta before too long. But in fact, he would never see the Mediterranean again. At the end of January 1650, the Grand Master and his council accepted Poincy's offer – he had succeeded in convincing them of his "good intentions."[72] For the task of going to his side and keeping an eye on the Order's financial interests, two chevaliers appeared to them to stand out, Montmagny and La Haye.[73] On the following 7 March, the Grand Master wrote to the former, informing him that the Council had chosen him unanimously, and that he was to find a companion, La Haye having backed out.[74]

Borrowing a style reminiscent of Poincy, they urged him to go "to save our hopes from the claws of the harpies!" – or, in more concrete language, to "look after the interests of the treasury." He would have the title of procurator general of the Order in the Antilles. The news was sent to Poincy, Souvré, and Delbene (the receiver of the Grand Priory of France) the following 22 March.[75] On the same day, the Grand Master sent Montmagny his instructions. They were drawn from the recommendations of a select committee and were to remain secret.[76]

One consideration dominated all the directives which were meant to guide the procurator general's actions, and it was of an economic order. He must make certain of the commander's "dépouille"[77] "which is very considerable." The Order's finances were in deplorable condition (*"oppressa da debiti et necessitosa"*). The war in Europe had occasioned many expenses; it had kept many of the knights occupied in their own countries. The Turks were menacing again; so it had been necessary to borrow, among other things, to prepare for a siege which threatened in 1645.[78] Because of the war in Candia, privateering had slowed down and was bringing in much less.[79]

Montmagny would have to act quickly. Poincy's good dispositions would perhaps not last for long, and furthermore, his advanced age inspired some anxiety. Montmagny was to use discretion – the Company, for instance, was not to know of the dispatch to Saint-Christophe of an emissary of the Grand Master. The central purpose of his misson was to persuade the commander, "with all possible skill and industry," to use "liberality" towards his Order. After being informed of "his faculties" (that is to say the extent of his wealth), he should suggest immediate gifts (less uncertain than a succession), which for the time being would remain a part of his estate. Various strategies were envisaged, as, for example, a foundation, an annual sum furnished for a specific purpose; or another suggestion, the purchase of muskets, which would bear his name and his arms; a gift of cash or, if he preferred, of supplies like sugar and tobacco; to leave the Order the total revenue from his commanderies, or to turn over annual *rentes* to it.

Montmagny was reminded that he had had much contact with the Jesuits throughout his life, and that they were now Poincy's confessors. He should – though with plenty of prudence – encourage them to remind their penitent of his duties toward the Order.

"A delicate task," the Grand Master admitted, and one requiring "very wise discretion." An impossible task, it might be added. Despite his fine words to his superior, Poincy had absolutely no intention of giving anything at all to his Order. Even had he wished it, he could not, loaded down as he was with debts. Montmagny was supposed to find out what he actually possessed; there was little hope that he could do this, since the commander had only one idea in his head – to stay in place – and he was counting on the Order to help him do it. The chain of events demonstrates this clearly.

Montmagny followed his superior's instruction with all dispatch. He hurried through his preparations for departure, and continued his inquiries. Poincy's niece, Madame des Vergers, was in Paris at this time.[80] He learned from her that the Commander dreamed of establishing a commandery in Saint-Christophe.[81] Razilly had made a similar suggestion in 1634 for Acadia; it had been refused by the Grand Master.[82] According to Montmagny, Poincy's suggestion was not pertinent unless the king accepted that the governor would always be a Knight of Malta. There was no longer any question of that. The niece also brought him up to date on her uncle's bitter recriminations against the Company; he was unforgiving toward these gentlemen "who had wished to take the government from him" – this was made very clear! The procurator general suggested to the Grand Master that if he wished to obtain favours from Poincy, he should let him hope to stay in place for at least three years. He took it upon himself to make the directors of the Company, with whom he had good relations, understand that for the greatest good of the Order it was necessary to be generous toward the commander. Indeed, the Grand Master noted some months later that the Company had changed its attitude, and he attributed this modification to Montmagny's action.[83]

In his letter of 6 May, Montmagny directed the attention of the council to a completely new suggestion, which came from Souvré and from Mazarin: the sale of the island by the Company to the Order of Malta.[84] His first reaction – he did not yet know Poincy – was that the latter would refuse; and he doubted, equally, that the Company would accept. More than anything else, he was thinking of an accommodation.

It was during the following summer that he made the voyage to the Antilles. In a letter to Delbene, the Grand Master congratulated himself on Montmagny's promptness in accomplishing his duty, and he hoped that "his skill will lead Poincy's mind to some good design."[85] In mid-September Montmagny was in Guadeloupe, and shortly afterwards, in Saint-Christophe.[86]

This first sojourn in the Antilles was going to last about three months. The only event which Montmagny was to witness was the recapture of the island of Sainte-Croix by the commander's troops.[87] The report that he made to the Grand Master has not been found, but in the letter which the latter wrote to him on 28 February 1651, the essential has been retained.[88]

The diagnosis is favourable: the island is fertile and, if well administered, could be very profitable. Lascaris speaks of the "hopes" to which his report has given rise. In his letter to Souvré, he is all enthusiasm, and speaks of the "fortunate isles."[89] Now the question arises of the necessary dealings with the Company and with the king. So Poincy has latched onto the idea of having the Order buy the island. The "right of domain and seigneurie" which the Company enjoyed would pass to the Order. The king would accord the territories in fief, exactly as Charles V in 1530 had confided the island of Malta to the Knights. To honour the commander who is at the centre of this deal, the Grand Master suggests that he has more prestigious things to offer: the title of *bailli* and the dignity of the Grand Cross. Note, as well, that he remarks with a certain disappointment on the modesty of the gift (no details given) which Poincy has made to Montmagny, and which he considers well below what he deserves.

And it is a fact that the latter was wasting no time; the negotiations were proceeding apace. At the beginning of May[90] (the Grand Master's letter must have reached him by mid-March) the associates, having been convened, accepted the principle of the sale of the island, and delegated two of their people to prepare and sign the contract in their name. This was done the following 24 May.[91]

For a payment of 120,000 livres,[92] the Company surrendered all the rights which had been conceded to it by the king (who retained "sovereignty" over the territory); it also abandoned its assets – the only things mentioned being "its habitations, its negroes and negresses"; furthermore it allowed to lapse "even that which it can claim and demand against the said Commander de Poincy."

This contract, though only four pages long, was nevertheless of great importance: it signified an entirely new direction for the Order. Several of its members had previously plunged into colonial adventures, such as Villegagnon, or Razilly, or Montmagny. But they had all acted as individuals. It was the Order itself that was engaged by the contract of 1651. For the Knights it was something unheard of. Since time immemorial their vocation had been for the Mediterranean. At the outset, they had assured hospital services and the defence of the

Holy Places. They had become, even more clearly after their installation in Malta, the Christian West's principal rampart against the maritime attacks of the Turks. Were they going to be transformed into colonizers? The chances were slim.

The great beneficiary of all this upheaval was the Commander de Poincy. He got what he was looking for. A week after the signing of the contract, César de Vendôme, who since the death of Brézé had become "Grand Master, Chief and Superintendant of Navigation and of Commerce for France and the conquered lands," sent him a royal commission as governor of the islands of America, no time limit being specified.[93] Helped by the Fronde, the king was able to forget his "rebellion." However, in the instructions that accompanied the commission, an article forbade him to trade with strangers, "as has been practised in the past with unheard-of irregularity ... against the intention of His Majesty and in contempt of France." A warning accompanied this injunction: "if this is not respected by the Sieur de Poincy, the present [privileges] shall be considered null and void." Did these threats cause undue alarm to the commander, who was soon to become the *bailli* de Poincy?

The settlement of the Saint-Christophe affair, as well as the provisional settlement of relations between Poincy and Thoisy,[94] gave Montmagny some respite. Few details have come down to us regarding his comings and goings during this period. All the same, there are two points of interest: his relations with his family remained excellent, and he completed his entry into the Order of Malta by making his religious profession.

The ties with his nearest relations remained close after his return from Canada. He chose, as before, to stay with his lifelong companion, his brother Adrien, who had remained faithful to the Marais, where he lived in the cul-de-sac of the Blancs Manteaux. Even the grant of a lodging by the Grand Priory, after his profession, did not make Montmagny change his residence.[95] In 1651 and 1652, he signed two marriage contracts: those of his nephew, Adrien Huault II,[96] *conseiller au Grand Conseil* (an office inherited from his father, Louis), and of his cousin, Claude Anjorrant,[97] *conseiller au parlement* – whose family had given two knights to the Order of Malta.

Most of the time Montmagny was designated in the documents as "received as Knight in the Order of Saint John of Jerusalem." He had not yet pronounced his vows. In 1650 he notified the Grand Master of his desire to complete his entry into the Order.[98] As he could not go to Malta, a papal brief was required authorizing him to make his profession outside the mother house. Once all the permissions were accorded[99] – a simple formality in his case – the ceremony could take place. It was performed on 17 July 1651, in the church of Sainte-Marie in the Temple enclosure, presided over by the Grand Master's ambassador, Jacques de Souvré, with whom Montmagny had been working for several months.[100]

In the great majority of cases this commitment was made immediately after the year of novitiate. Thus the chevalier de Poincy had received the habit – synonymous with making his vows – on 17 January 1606, from the hands of Brother Galéan de Bellebrune, in a chapel dedicated to Saint Paul in the conventual church of Valetta.[101] For unknown reasons,[102] Montmagny had decided to delay his, which was entirely laudable according to the Rule, but which prevented him from acceding to a commandery or to the dignities of the Order.

Following the ritual, the ceremony took place in the course of a Mass. He was clothed in the habit and given the sword: "Receive the holy sword [the celebrant said to him] to use it for your defence and that of the Holy Cross of God, and to the confusion of the enemies of Christ's cross and of the Christian faith; and, as far as human frailty permits, do not harm anyone unjustly with it."[103] The eight-pointed cross displayed on the robe and the knight's sword symbolized the religious commitment of the members of the Order. Then, after confessing and receiving communion, he promised to observe the rules of the Order, and pronounced the three traditional vows of poverty, chastity, and obedience.

Numerous knights attended, and "many other persons of outstanding condition" – doubtless, in addition to his relatives, some representatives of the Companies such as Jean de Lauson, who had just been named to Québec, and some high functionaries.

Indeed, the event did not pass unnoticed in Paris. It was reported in the *Gazette de France*. This journal, founded in 1635 by Théophraste Renaudot at Richelieu's instigation, was the earliest of French periodicals. It was chiefly interested in matters concerning the court and the men of government. Here is how this "profession" was described: "Today the chevalier de Montmagny, in consideration of the services rendered by him to the Order of Saint John of Jerusalem, having been dispensed by special privilege of the Pope and of the Grand Master of the Order from going to Malta to make his vows, made them at the Temple, and received the habit and the sword by the hands of Commander de Souvray, Ambassador of the aforesaid Order to this Court, who made the ceremony so extraordinary, that there is no memory of ever having seen one so solemn in France."[104]

So there was emphasis on the solemnity of the ceremony – the rites, imbued with the spirit of the Middle Ages, which we have briefly enumerated – and on the services rendered to the Order which justified the privilege of pronouncing the vows at the Temple.

From this time on he participated with great regularity at the assemblies and annual chapters of the Grand Priory of France.[105] On the following 2 November, a pension of 1,000 livres was assigned to him,[106] as well as a house within the Temple enclosure.[107]

He did not remain long without employment.[108] We have the impression that in the autumn of 1651 he was presented for the post of official representative of the Order in Saint-Christophe. In any case, he continued to receive news of the island. Indeed, at the very beginning of January 1652 he was writing to the Grand Master to inform him that a terrible hurricane had just ravaged it, causing enormous losses; and, above all, to tell him of his astonishment at some of Poincy's decisions.[109] On his departure from Basseterre, Montmagny had left him with a man named de Thou, a companion (a layman) whom he had succeeded in finding to accompany him to the islands in 1650, and who was supposed in his absence to continue watching over the Order's interests.[110] To get rid of him, the commander used the pretext of a mission to the marshal de La Meilleraye which he sent him to fulfil. This decision of Poincy's angered the Grand Master, as did the negotiation which he undertook (or pretended to undertake) with the marshal, without consultation with the Order, though it specifically concerned the ownership of the island.[111]

This news prompted the Grand Master to proceed rapidly with Montmagny's nomination. On the following 12 February, he wrote to inform him of two recent decisions of his council: the official acceptance of the "domain" of the islands (Saint-Christophe and the little islands that depended on it) and the choice of himself to make this "establishment."[112] As companion he suggested another chevalier, De La Borde – who, like the man nominated in 1650, declined.[113]

The instructions were only sent to Montmagny the following 23 July.[114] It was hoped that the Court would move quickly in giving its official consent to the transfer of the island, but the civil war was delaying everything. Montmagny was asked to speed up his preparations for departure – apparently they were beginning to doubt the commander's good faith.

In the name of the Grand Master, he was to take possession of the territory (after receiving the official grant that the king would be making). There was to be a ceremony, in which he would confer the titles of dignity that had been granted to Poincy. He was to ensure respect of the clauses of the agreement concluded with the Company (especially concerning the sums due to it). His mission was of the utmost importance: to assure by all appropriate means the "possession" of the island. Upon arrival of the royal letters, Poincy became "perpetual governor for life," while he himself had to serve him as lieutenant. He had to adjudicate the differences between the governor and his subjects. If, upon the death of Poincy, he inherited the government, he was ordered to leave justice to the judges – a direct allusion to Poincy's doings.

Poincy's role was also defined: to keep his "lieutenant" informed of everything: the government of the island, economic questions, his future legacy; to send an exhaustive description of his goods; to acquit the sums which he was constrained by judicial decision to pay to Thoisy; to give as many gifts as possible to the Order of Malta. To be sure of being well understood by Poincy, the Grand Master wrote to him as well, on the same day: Montmagny is becoming your lieutenant "to ease you in the fatigues of government, You will instruct him in all that you deem necessary for a good government."[115]

But, as with the previous voyage, there were also secret directives.[116] To ensure peace with the English, which, according to the Grand Master, was the best way to preserve Poincy's possessions for the Order. To prevent seditious activities – the governor's family was at work, especially Sieur Girault, who had "held dubious conversations in France." If Poincy wished to benefit his relatives and friends financially – by giving "irrevocable fiefs," for example – the Order was to be notified at once. Montmagny was to confront the commander directly, if he showed himself too generous towards them. Finally, he was to give the Order a good image, "to prevent interest groups from forming against it."

The Grand Master sent Montmagny a magnificent gift for his "governor": twelve dozen gold, and twice as many silver and rings, and a casket of small objects of devotion.

Montmagny had suggested that the Order give presents of some value to Girault and his son; the council decided that before making this gesture, their good will toward the Order would have to be confirmed.

At the beginning of January, Montmagny gave power of attorney to a fellow knight, and then to his brother Adrien, to administer his goods in his absence.[117] On 16 January, he drew up his testament,[118] which was placed in a little coffer of red and gold leather and deposited with

M. François Curson, on the rue Vivienne.[119] He left Paris on about 18 January and was in Nantes, from where he wrote to his brother, on 11 February.[120] He then made his fifth and final crossing of the Atlantic.

The work that awaited him was not very agreeable. The years 1653–1657 were gratifying to no one except Poincy.

Montmagny was relegated to a farm outside the capital.[121] In actual fact, he did not have a chance to accomplish any of the tasks that the Grand Master had confided to him. However, instead of taking umbrage like Thoisy, he preferred courtesy and patience – thus he wrote three times to his brother asking him to entertain Poincy's nephew who was making the trip to Paris.[122] The gentle method was no more successful than the use of violence. There was nothing to do but wait for Poincy's death.

The Grand Master, himself also at the end of his career – he was going to die on 14 August 1657 – showed more and more impatience. The king had accepted in theory – and, in 1653, officially – the cession of Saint-Christophe.[123] But there were delays: the admiralties of France had still to be consulted to determine the opinion of the merchants on this transaction; and the registration by the parlement of Paris had to be awaited. A dispatch to Souvré, dated 30 November 1656, recalled it bitterly: "If this unhappy news [the rumour of Poincy's death] were verified, there would be strong doubt as to whether his good will would be fruitful, since the chevalier de Montmagny has nothing in hand with which to give the Order possession of the principality; without which one has little hope in the works of the said venerable *Bailli*, and it is this consideration which prevents us from sending other colleagues to the said chevalier, from whom we have had no news now for ten months."[124] The same complaint came from the pen of the Grand Master on 12 June 1657, by which time he was no longer hiding his disappointment over Poincy's acrimonious attitude: "On the subject of the dissatisfactions claimed by the venerable *Bailli* de Poincy, we have never tried, in all that we have done, to defraud him of his revenue, but only to lend our name to defend him against his persecutors, and it will never be our intention to give him the slightest shadow of a reason for the cooling and alteration of his good will."[125]

As for Poincy, he continued to rule the roost, basking in the congratulations (self-serving) of his Order, and the praises (resigned) of the king.[126] He took advantage of his relations and allies to whom he conceded positions of command and fine properties. They were his delegates in France to ensure his interests.[127] They served him as intermediaries with the population.[128] He was viewed well by strangers.

The Dutch proposed in 1654 to make the trade which was practised with them official, a suggestion that embarrassed the Grand Master.[129] The agreement with the English was renewed, shortly after an impressive demonstration of force on their part in April 1655: seventy ships and 10,000 soldiers.[130]

There was, all the same, one small disappointment: the reconquest of Tortola[131] by the Spanish.[132] Poincy charged a Knight of Malta, Timoléon Hotman de Fontenay,[133] with retaking it, but this was not possible. The island of Sainte-Croix was also attacked, but here the French succeeded in holding on.

But – supreme consolation – he had the ear of the Jesuits. On his return to the islands in 1657 Father Jean Halley wrote: "We have put Saint-Christophe into such a state that, having two parishes, the principal one where we are is second in nothing to the best regulated in Paris or Dijon, and lives in a general example of piety and virtue."[134] Father Pelleprat's witness was more nuanced, though remaining favourable. The years 1652–1653 were difficult for the population, with contagious diseases, food shortages, mortalities, and begging – and the people responded well to the appeal which the priests made to their charitable duty. The latter catechized, among others, the indentured servants, whose condition was often deplorable. Pelleprat recalled that two of his fellow priests, who had died while burying the dead, were "extremely respected by Monsieur the *Bailli* de Poincy."[135]

The presence of the Jesuits in the island must have comforted Montmagny, who had always had good relations with them. It must be supposed that they helped him to bear the exclusion – and the inaction, which certainly weighed on him – that marked his last years; and that they were with him in his last moments.

He died on 4 July 1657.[136] Here is the notice that Father du Tertre gave about him:

> The Order took possession of Saint-Christophe, confirmed M. de Poincy in his charge, and sent Monsieur the chevalier de Montmagny to Saint-Christophe to succeed him. The arrival of this chevalier, who had commanded in New France with so much glory, did not please him; M. De Montmagny noted this, so he retired with M. Menager to Cayonne, which is so to speak the commandery farm, and lived there as a private person, waiting for the death of M. De Poincy. But he died before him in 1657; the people who had had high hopes for his leadership regretted him greatly. During this retirement he devoted himself to the exercise of all the virtues. He was buried in the parish

of Basse-Terre and M. De Poincy saw that he was given all the honours due to his birth and to his merits.

It is quite clear, as we have already mentioned, that Montmagny's presence did not please Poincy. The mandate which the chevalier received from the Grand Master limited his authority and obliged him to present his accounts; all of this displeased him. No doubt the retreat of his "lieutenant" to a "farm" pleased him greatly. Was the retreat chosen or forced? No one will ever know. Today Cayonne is a little village situated some kilometres from Basseterre, on the other side of the island. In the seventeenth century this had to mean complete isolation, since the social and political life was concentrated in the capital, the principal port of the colony.

The "farm" in question was one of the properties acquired by Poincy.[137] It bore no resemblance to a "commandery." The Sieur Claude Mesnager mentioned above was a Frenchman employed by Poincy; he asked – by all appearances at Montmagny's instigation – to be received into the Order as a man-at-arms, and this was granted him in 1659.[138] He was later in the service of the chevalier de Sales, Montmagny's replacement, who sent him to France in 1666.[139] The Order granted him a commandery in 1694.[140]

Montmagny lived as a private individual, we are told; but no detail remains concerning his activities. Did he cultivate the soil, or fish, or perhaps perform works of charity among the poor and the sick? According to Du Tertre, he lived an exemplary life, which is certainly likely, considering what we know of his time in New France. But what does that mean in concrete terms? A mystery.

His attitude and behaviour contrasted strongly with the way of life (and of governing) of Poincy, without a doubt – and this did not pass unnoticed by the population, who "had high hopes" for him, according to the Dominican. The Jesuits could also have contributed to this reputation, since it is probable that those who went to Saint-Christophe had read the *Relations*.

From our research in the notarial archives of Paris we have learned something about his last transactions and the liquidation of the few goods that he possessed.

His principal agent in the mother country remained his brother Adrien. It was he who, on 10 January 1654, sold the seigneurie conceded in 1646 by the *Compagnie de la Nouvelle-France*.[141] On 9 September 1655 Adrien rented the house in the Temple enclosure whose usufruct the Order had ceded to Montmagny.[142] In September 1656 he also recovered a part of the money remaining due to the chevalier from a loan made in the spring of 1649 to a treasurer of France, Monsieur Hilaire Leclerc, for the amount of 8,000 livres.[143]

"By devotion," Montmagny, on 10 May 1654, asked his correspondent to arrange for the saying of "a Mass to the Virgin every Saturday."[144] On 17 January 1657, perhaps feeling that his health was deteriorating, he ordered that two Masses a week be said "for his intentions," one to the Virgin, the other to the Holy Spirit – and this was "begun on Monday 9 April 1657, the day that the said Sieur de La Baillie received the letter."[145]

An inventory of his estate was made in Paris on 22 December 1657.[146] The notary had brought together representatives of the Grand Priory of France and Adrien Huault, who was acting in his own name and that of his nephews and his niece. They were taken for the purpose to the residence of M. François Curzon, with whom were deposited some pieces of furniture belonging to the chevalier, his "papers," and his testament.

There was nothing of great value among the stored objects: a wood cabinet (40 livres) and a "folding table of pear wood." But besides this there was something more revealing: "twenty-five volumes of books of mathematics" (estimated at 10 livres) – evidence, perhaps, of an intellectual preoccupation acquired during his time at La Flèche. Lastly, there were eighteen pictures (none worth more than 4 livres), some of which may have come from Malta: "Stormy sea with several vessels"; "Landscape with house beside the sea"; "Galley being shipwrecked at sea."

The "papers" which were enumerated concerned transactions relating to privateering in the Mediterranean in the 1620s; settlements of accounts between the two brothers Charles and Adrien; diverse contracts arising from the partition of the goods of their older brother Louis, deceased in 1646; and a bull from the Grand Master permitting the chevalier to make his will while paying his debts.[147]

The text of his will has not survived, but the essential of it can be deduced from the account which was made in March 1658 between Adrien Huault and the chevalier de Broc Saint-Martin.[148] The surplus arising from the difference between his assets and his debts was to go to the Order.

To his credit there remained a part of the pension which his brothers and his sisters had promised him in 1624;[149] the remains of the loan which he had made to Hilaire Leclerc in 1649; the arrears from his stipend as governor of Québec, which should in principle have been remitted to Adrien on his behalf by the *Compagnie de la Nouvelle-France;* the rent of the house in the Temple enclosure, the usufruct of which had been assigned to him by the Order, and a sum owing to him by Madame Ribier, his niece. The total came to 20,752 livres, 7 sols, 6 deniers.

The chevalier had debts: a significant remainder of the sums borrowed from his family for the arming of his ship during the 1620s; the Masses requested in 1654 and 1657; shipments to Saint-Christophe of clothes and various articles such as shoes and spices (we learn here that one of these shipments was part of a cargo seized by the English, and that one of the ports at which the freight was embarked was Middleburg in Zealand); the postage for many letters; 60 livres spent by Adrien for "entertaining splendidly" Poincy's nephew in Paris; and lastly, the notaries' fees. All this came to 19,405 livres, 17 sols, 6 deniers. There remained for the Order 1,351 livres, 12 sols. Nothing spectacular, but at least the balance was not negative.

This account, commonplace enough in its details and its figures, nevertheless recalls the stages of the exciting life of a French chevalier of the first half of the seventeenth century: his privateering in the Mediterranean, his administration of a far-off colony, and his service to the Order in the Antilles. In the accomplishment of these tasks, he was able at one and the same time to preserve the spiritual values that supported him and to remain closely connected to the concrete, often brutal, realities that surrounded him. This mix of idealism and realism was truly characteristic of the spirituality of the French Counter Reformation. By a rather remarkable coincidence, the man who replaced him in the Antilles was the chevalier de Sales, the nephew of the spiritual father of this movement.

4. **Epilogue to Montmagny's death: The end of the adventure of the Order of Malta in the Antilles**

The Order's Antilles adventure did not long survive Montmagny's death. The final vicissitudes of this involvement coincided – both for Malta and for Paris – with dramatic changes in the personnel at the top. In the first case, five Grand Masters succeeded each other in seven years.[150] In the second, we see the disappearance of Mazarin, the elimination of Fouquet, the "coming to power" of Louis XIV, and then of Colbert.

First, Montmagny had to be replaced. To emphasize still more firmly the Order's presence beside Poincy, the Grand Master made sure this time that two chevaliers would leave for Saint-Christophe; he chose Jean de Limoges Saint-Just and Charles de Sales.[151] Of the former our information is almost nil;[152] but of the latter, who was also the effective successor to Poincy, we have more, because as has been noted, he belonged to the family of the illustrious bishop of Geneva. Admitted to the novitiate in 1643 at the age of eighteen, he rapidly made himself a name for his courage in the struggle against the Turks,[153] distinguishing himself in an action against them on the island of Crete.[154] His style of life (and then of governing, after 1660) contrasted perfectly with that of Poincy. It is with that of Montmagny, it seems, that it could better be compared. He gained the love of the inhabitants. One example of his goodness will suffice: he stripped himself of almost all his goods to come to the aid of the victims of one of those hurricanes which devastated the region from time to time.[155]

Poincy received his two brother knights with benevolence, it seems.[156] Undoubtedly his declining health obliged him to restrain his bravado. He was nonetheless active. Thus he suggested to the Grand Master that he send him some Maltese people to populate his island, a request which was rejected.[157] His last achievement was the establishment of a "treaty of union and defensive league drawn up at Saint-Christophe between French and English, and of peace with the Caribs."[158] It was signed in January 1660, in the commander's mansion, by himself, by Charles Houel, seigneur of Guadeloupe, and by the English governors of the Antilles.[159] Poincy died a few weeks later, on 11 April.[160]

Some months after the *bailli*'s death, the Order faced the question of getting rid of an island of which the profitability was not evident, at least in the immediate future. In 1660 (probably at the suggestion of the new governor, Charles de Sales),[161] Fouquet, the *surintendant des finances*, and Souvré discussed this, and an amount was even suggested: 400,000 livres.[162] The first mention in the Grand Master's correspondence dates from February 1662,[163] and in the month of August in the same year, the chevalier de Berrieux, receiver for the Grand Priory of France, hoped that the thing would soon be done.[164]

The months that followed (from the beginning of 1663 to the beginning of 1665) were marked by two reactions: intense discussions within the council of the Grand Master, and stronger and stronger pressures from the king[165] and Colbert. The latter, who was very interested in the colonies, wished to return the monopoly of French establishments outside France to the companies which he controlled.

The Grand Master finally agreed to send an ambassador extraordinary to Paris, in the person of Etienne-Marie Lomellini, grand prior of England. He charged him with the mission of offering the islands to the king and obtaining a satisfactory price.[166] The business went along smoothly and the contract was signed on 10 August 1665.[167] The Order surrendered to the *Compagnie des Indes occidentales* all its rights to the islands and all the goods contained "both in the contract of sale by the *Compagnie des Îles d'Amérique* [1651] and others and in the personal possessions (*pecule*)[168] and the succession (*dépouille*)[169] of the late Monsieur le Bailly de Poincy." However it retained the latter's active debts – for example, obligations including those which had been transferred to him as a result of an understanding concluded with the heirs of La Grange (his lieutenant, who had preceded him onto the island by several months in 1638).

The sale price had been fixed at 500,000 livres. However, 78,111 livres, 9 sols, 10 deniers had to be subtracted at once; this was the sum that remained to be paid (capital and interest) to the original Company, the one which, fourteen years before, had sold the island to the Knights. The Order lacked money, as previously noted, and this was a new proof of it. In the following fifteen months, the sum of 421,688 livres, 110 sols, 2 deniers was to be paid to it in three installments. After the ratification of the contract by the Order,[170] Colbert promised, in December, that the payments would begin in January 1666.[171]

Things swiftly became complicated, in totally unexpected ways. Before long a man called Desmartins, a Parisian banker, appeared in the offices of the Company;[172] he demanded reimbursement of the sums that he had lent to Poincy from 16 September 1638, when the two men and an outfitter by the name of Rigault had founded a society for the exploitation of Saint-Christophe.[173] The Grand Master cried foul. This claim, he said, was "feigned and imagined."[174] He had no idea to what point his *bailli's* succession was encumbered.

A second event came to add to the confusion: the conflict that developed that year between the English and the French on Saint-Christophe. The chevalier de Sales lost his life in this, despite a heroic defence which saved the island for France – temporarily. The Grand Master feared that this incident would serve as pretext for an additional delay in the payment.

In fact there was a delay, but it was due to something much more banal (it would seem): the familial concerns of Colbert. The minister, whose complexes regarding his commoner origins are well known[175] – his grandfather, a bourgeois of Reims! – wished at all costs to have this humble lineage forgotten: with his three daughters married to dukes, and his second son in the clergy (to became archbishop of Rouen), he needed to place the third, he thought of the Order of Saint John of Jerusalem, in which the access to title of Knight was, as everyone knew, reserved for nobles capable of proving their eight quarters. The payment of the sum owing to the Order was a condition for the reception of Antoine-Albert Colbert into its ranks. The papal brief dispensing the boy from his minority status did not arrive in Paris until 17 October 1667. However, this was not yet enough to untie the purse strings.[176] It was necessary, in addition, that a commandery be accorded him. Souvré thought of le Piéton, in the Hainault.[177] A problem arose: it had gone into the hands of another chevalier. The ambassador had recourse to a legal quibble: the incumbent had neglected payment of his "responsions," the percentage of revenues that each chevalier had to send to the common treasury; this could be used as a pretext to take le Piéton from him. Colbert even had the idea of arranging for a pension to be paid to him, so stubbornly did he hold to "his commandery". When the deal was accepted in Malta, the money began to flow. One hundred thousand livres were turned over at the beginning of October 1668; in July of the following year, 104,545 livres arrived; in December 1671, another 100,000, and the rest on 15 February 1672.[178]

Thus, very prosaically, ended the Order of Malta's involvement in an adventure far removed from its original vocation, into which the ambition of one of its members had dragged it, and for which Brother Charles Huault de Montmagny had sacrificed the last years of his life. The invitation made to him to add colonization to his hospitaller and military duties had only led, finally, to an episode without a future.

This chapter has revealed new facets of the personality of Charles Huault de Montmagny; and it has given us a fairly close-up knowledge of two other members of his Order, with whom we can usefully sketch a few points of comparison.

Montmagny passed these years (the last of his life) doing three things: administrative duties – essentially, inquiries in France and in Saint-Christophe, or the search for solutions to the problems submitted to him by the Order, the Company, and the French government; long transatlantic voyages (three of them), exacting and challenging in many respects, for the preparation, realization, and sequels; and an exile of four years (from mid-1653 to mid-1657) in a little corner of land lost in the middle of the Caribbean sea, waiting – in vain – for the moment when he could play a role in this part of the world, in the name of the Grand Master and the king. For the first two he was well prepared; for the third, he had to adapt – and this required great patience and a certain self-sacrifice. After having occupied centre stage in Canada, he was forced to accept a sort of seclusion which, it seems, was hardly congenial to his temperament. He had all the time in the world to meditate on the various aspects of the spirituality of his Order, to which, only a little time before, on 17 July 1651, he had definitively adhered, in the "solemn" and "extraordinary" ceremony described by the *Gazette de France.*

But in fact, during the years studied here, three personalities have come to our attention: not only Montmagny, but also Poincy and de Sales. In some ways they resembled each other, but for the rest, it was like night and day.

First, there are some remarkable similarities: their outstanding actions in the Mediterranean against the Turks, where they had filled to perfection their role as swashbucklers against the "infidels." All three of them experienced a long American career, in the realization of which they ended their days: twenty-one years for the first, twenty-two (without interruption) for the second, eight for the third. So they collaborated in a work of colonization which was completely foreign to the true vocation of their institute, but which was accepted by it as a way of extricating the commander de Poincy from his difficulties (with a vague hope of eventual benefits). But the latter – and in this he showed astonishing differences from the two others – ended by transforming himself into a sort of potentate in the colony confided to him. His extreme egocentrism, excessive severity, and even rebelliousness against the king, were behaviours totally inconceivable for Montmagny and de Sales, who shared a vision of relationships with the authorities and the rest of the population that was imbued, so far as we can tell, with benevolence, charity, and respect for the conventions.

"Faitz bien et laisse dire"

When the investigators of the Order of Malta visited the parish church of Montmagny in the springtime of 1622, they found, "in the main window behind the grand altar," beneath the arms of Pierre Huault, the chevalier's great-grandfather, "two scrolls of silver on which is written in gold, in ancient lettering, 'Faitz bien et laisse dire'" – do what is right and let others say what they will.[1] This was the motto he had chosen. There is no way of knowing if Charles Huault adopted it or if he had meditated long on its significance, but it had no doubt been commented on by parents anxious to give his life a direction marked by dignity and virtue. Regardless, what must be remembered is that it applied very well to him, and that it could have served as a theme for his biography. The ideal that it represented – "vertu,"[2] sense of duty – was surely his own. He has not told us this himself; he has "laissé dire" (let others say) – if we can be permitted this play on words – by the Jesuits and other chroniclers.

His family coat of arms is equally symbolic.[3] It has been adopted by two localities, both of which – the one in France and the other in Québec – bear the name of Montmagny. It even appears in the mural painting which adorns the façade of the latter.[4] It reads as follows: "D'or à la fasce d'azur, chargée de trois molettes d'éperon d'or, accompagnée de trois coquerelles de gueule, deux en chef et une en pointe."[5] The spurs evoked the chivalry to which Pierre Huault was already aspiring, and which was realized by some of his descendants, among them his great-grandson Charles and Charles's cousin Alexandre Huault de Vayres, spiritual heirs to the crusaders by way of the Order of Malta. The "coquerelles," or stylized hazelnuts, recalled the country life which the family pursued in its seigneurie north of Paris. His mother's family arms had a similar resonance: "D'or au dragon ailé de sinople, armé, lampassé et couronné de gueule d'or", the dragon representing strength of character, indomitability, service that is all fire and flame for a cause.[6] These symbols could not have left Charles Huault indifferent.

These allegorical images add a certain colour to the picture which is developed from the long description we have given of the deeds and behaviour of the chevalier de Montmagny, a picture which, moreover, is relatively close to the one traced by the Québecois historian, J. Edmond Roy, at the beginning of the century. He was a man of sincerity – the Grand Master called him "une âme droite" – and unselfishness; he took his religious vocation seriously. Prudence was another of his qualities (the *Relations* mention this several times), as was patience, whether in the lengthy preparations for his privateering expedition, or in the long drawn-out activities for the Order in the affair of Saint-Christophe. Nothing discouraged him. Faced with the delays of the authorities in the mother country in sending aid to New France, he did not balk. In dangerous situations he gave proof of courage – perhaps the most characteristic quality of the Knights of Saint John of Jerusalem. A final trait of his personality was cordiality, which we observe, for example, in his relations with the Indians, welcoming them to his home, visiting them in Sillery, and mingling with them without difficulty.

And the little of him that has been preserved – a few letters[7] – does not contradict this portrait that the witnesses of his life have left us.

At the very foundation of his thinking is a great respect for Christian values. To think of founding a seminary for the Amerindians – as did Noël Brulart – was, for him, "to follow the intention of God," and "to labour for the exaltation of his name." To Father de Goussaincourt, who wrote to him in Québec, he recommended that he complete his work on the "martyrs" of the Order of Malta, since it concerned persons who had "sacrificed their life in the service of God." He informed the Grand Master in 1649 that three Jesuits had been killed in Canada "in hatred of the faith"; these were "true martyrs." He suggested that he himself would bring the "relation" of these events to Valetta, as soon as it was published.

His concern for the Order did not diminish during all those years spent far from Malta and from the Temple in Paris. When, in 1650, he wrote anew to his superior, he twice reminded him of it. He had only one ambition: to serve to the best of his capacity. In his letter of 29 April 1650, he told the Grand Master that his missive gave him the opportunity "to render obedience to His Eminence and to the Council, and service to the Order: this is the fulfilment of my desires." It was an idea which he took up again in the conclusion, in slightly different terms: "I shall employ all the industry and the little talent which it has pleased God to give me to satisfy His desire that I render as much service as I can to the Order."

Two traits stand out equally in these writings. The first is humility: he says to Goussaincourt that he "has not deserved" the honour of the fine letter that he has sent him; twice he avows to the Grand Master that he "has not merited" the "favours" with which he has loaded him. The second is kindness, or perhaps better still, benevolence, which seems natural in him – when he speaks of someone, or discusses something, it is, from the very beginning, in positive terms that he does it.

Thus all that remains is the presentation in more general terms, and in a broader perspective, of the characteristics of a life of which the principal events are now known to us.

One word sums up Montmagny's three careers: "service." He was in the service of the Grand Master of Malta, then of the king in New France, and lastly of both in the Caribbean. In all three cases he was "in the service" of Christian ideals. At the start of the modern era these still included armed struggle against the "infidels" (such as Lepanto in 1571 and Crete in the mid-seventeenth century), but since the middle of the sixteenth century they were expressed more and more in the missionary effort, particularly in Asia and in America. It was for the benefit of the monarch of his native land that he used his maritime and military expertise, but even there the conversion of the pagans remained an avowed objective, and a very real one, above all because of the presence of the Jesuits in Canada. The formation that he had received at the college of La Flèche prepared him for this devotion to a cause, which, in his case, was wholehearted and unremitting.

An orientation like this, which from the very start required him to be ready for everything, had definite repercussions on his life. He held command posts – on his ship in the mid-1620s, and later in an immense colonial territory. But he also had to accept subordinate roles (during his caravans, for example), and even to remain provisionally in the shadows and wait patiently for the moment to go into action (as during his life as a recluse in Cayonne in the Caribbean).

Passing to the geography which went with his choice of life, there again we find very interesting facts; his fields of action were immense and dispersed. He touched upon four continents: two, Europe and America, where he made deep incursions; two, Asia and Africa, which he only brushed against in the course of his journeys in the Mediterranean. He became familiar with vast stretches of water – the Mediterranean, the Atlantic ocean, the Saint Lawrence, and the Caribbean sea. And remember, in talking of the sea, the importance of islands in his life: the island of Malta, the île aux Oies in his seigneurie close to Québec, and the island of Saint-Christophe where he ended his days.

All this, as we can see at once, forced him into long voyages. A table of his use of time between 1622 and 1636 illustrates this clearly. From 1636 on, five crossings of the Atlantic, continual excursions on the Saint Lawrence, many of which reminded him, due to the danger of Iroquois raids, of the violent combats sustained against the Turks. In these experiences he was completely different from the majority of the members of his family, who, so far as is known, were occupied with tasks related to their judicial offices, which only rarely entailed travel, and minor travel at that. The sole exception that we know of was his grandfather, Louis Huault I, who visited Italy after his studies. To find some similarity, we have to turn to his cousins, the Huaults de Vayre, several of whom were in the military, and especially Alexandre, who also entered the Order of Malta, and later passed, like many chevaliers of the time, into the service of the king of France, and was killed at the siege of Dôle in 1636.

At a deeper level of analysis, Montmagny's activity in fact fits into two great developments of the age, which gave him all his direction: the transformation of the Church occasioned by the great movement of the Counter Reformation, and the modernization of the French state, begun at the end of the Middle Ages, accompanied, in the seventeenth century, by an opening up to the outside world – the beginnings, tentative until 1661, of overseas colonization.

Thanks to his family he was raised in this reinvigorated Catholicism, with a devout mother, an aunt who had died in the odour of sanctity, and brothers who had a great veneration for François de Sales, one of the principal promoters of this renewal. His environment pushed him in a definite direction.

The Jesuit influence gave this initial attitude the orientation which marked all his life. As it turned out, the Fathers were present wherever he went. But it was at college that he had been initiated into Christian humanism, a term we use to qualify the model which they offered their students: an unconditional but clear-headed acceptance of Christian principles, along with a respect for the human values which had reached their high point in the so-called "classic" civilization of the Greeks and the Romans; the search by all acceptable means for competence in everything – with, at the same time, an attention to corporal, psychological, or social limitations; and the continual pursuit of a just equilibrium.

The preceding pages have furnished numerous examples of Montmagny's zeal for religion; he has been seen constantly searching for the most balanced solutions to the problems which he had to resolve.

To the second great phenomenon – the passage of France into modernity – the chevalier's family had already made its contribution; its abandonment of the Loire for the capital was part of two complementary phenomena of this evolution: the centralization of the kingdom, and the creation of an administrative bureaucracy. In taking part against the League, the Huaults accepted the absolutism represented by Henri IV's rise to power. After all, this was the king who sent Charles Huault into Poitou to foil the false nobles who were challenging his authority.

As for the chevalier himself, it was to another stage in the same modernization – the colonial effort – that he devoted the latter part of his life. We have explained at several points how this work turned out to be less than gratifying for him. France had succeeded, thanks above all to Henri IV, in climbing out of the stagnation into which a long civil war had cast her, and because of which she had fallen behind other European countries in planting groups of her citizens in the not-yet-settled lands of the globe. Then came the Thirty Years' War, and the resumption of the civil war. It was in the midst of this stagnation that Richelieu attempted to develop a maritime and colonial policy of some breadth. Misfortune came of it: some English merchants, the Kirke brothers, aborted everything in the valley of the Saint Lawrence, where the greatest effort had been made. Champlain launched the experiment again in 1633, but with limited means. In 1636, when Montmagny left for Québec, France was on a war footing with the House of Austria. The government was miserly in its contribution of manpower, resources, and equipment, and most particularly by using as intermediary a commercial company which it headed, but which was ruined from the start. To govern in these conditions was not very easy.

New France is indebted to Montmagny for having persevered in these difficult conditions; he played his part, less spectacular no doubt than that of Champlain – in the survival of the colony – and, all told, he made a contribution to the expansion of France overseas.

Notes

Introduction

1. L. Moreri, *Le Grand Dictionnaire historique ou le Mélange de l'histoire sacrée et profane*, 10 vols (Paris, 1756). The first edition, in one volume, dates from 1674, and was published in Lyon; that of 1725, in six volumes, comes from Paris. The work was also published in Amsterdam (1694, 1698, 1702, and 1740), and in Basel (1731 and 1733). In fact, it went through nineteen editions in French and one in Spanish (Paris, 1753).

2. It is found in the Cabinet des Titres of the BnF (Bibliothèque nationale de France, Paris): DB (Dossiers bleus) 362, and Cabinet d'Hozier 193. See, in the various notes to Chapter 1, critical remarks concerning this documentation.

3. J.-E. Roy, "M. de Montmagny," *Nouvelle-France* 5 (1906), "Son administration," 1: 105–21, 161–73, "Son caractère," 2: 417–28, 520–30.

4. J.P.B. Julien, known as the Chevalier de Courcelles, *Dictionnaire universel de la noblesse de France* (Paris, 1820–1822).

5. The *Dictionary of Canadian Biography* (hereafter *DCB*) devotes rather a short article to Montmagny (three and a half columns compared to twenty-five columns for Champlain). In it is a resumé of material contained in J.-E. Roy's work and in G. Lanctot's *Histoire du Canada*. Without a search in the archives mentioned later in this Introduction, it was not possible for the author to correct the current errors regarding the dates of his birth and death, for example, or his occupation upon his return to Paris in 1648.

6. J. Rouillard, ed., *Guide d'histoire du Québec du régime français à nos jours: Bibliographie commentée* (Montréal: Éd. du Méridien, 1991), 39.

7. H. Méchoulan, ed., *L'État baroque, 1610–1652* (Paris: Vrin, 1985).

Chapter 1

1. Moreri, *Le Grand dictionnaire*. See Introduction n. 1.

2. J.X. Carré de Busserolle, *Dictionnaire géographique, historique et biographique d'Indre-et-Loire*, 3 vols (Tours, 1878), the word "Huaudière" (la): farm, commune of Azay-le-Rideau.

3. F.A. Aubert de la Chesnaye-Desbois, *Dictionnaire de la noblesse*, 3rd ed., 19 vols (Paris, 1863–1876), Villiers de l'Isle-Adam entry.

4. See this chapter, n. 14.

5. La Chesnaye-Desbois, *Dictionnaire*, Huault entry; de Courcelles, *Dictionnaire universel*. A recent work, though in general very seriously written, has taken it up. See A. Lapeyre and R. Scheurer, *Les notaires et secrétaires du roi sous les règnes de Louis XI, Charles VIII et Louis XII (1461–1515)* (Paris: BN, 1978), 2: plate 56.

6. See J.C. Dubé, *Les intendants de la Nouvelle-France* (Montréal: Fides 1984), 14 ff.

7. AOM, Arch 2926, document reproduced in BN, Carrés d'Hozier, fols. 136–7.

8. 1464–1534, elected in 1521.

9. See Carré de Busserolle, *Dictionnaire géographique*.

10. Lapeyre and Scheurer, *Les notaires et secrétaires du roi*, vol. 1, entry 63, Philippe de Billon.

11. Unfortunately, the documents containing the details of the inquiry preceding the entry of François and Jean into the Order have not been found, either in Paris or in Valetta.

12. AOM, Arch. 3566.

13. BN, DB, 362, fols. 2–3.

14. See BN, Cabinet d'Hozier, 189, fol. 3: in the margin of the passage where this contract is reproduced, someone has written: "this act is a fake."

15. AN, MC, 6, 32; this is also found transcribed in the insinuations of the Châtelet of Paris, AN, Y, 106, fol. 59.

16. Note that this gift was not the first transaction that Louis and his cousin had enacted jointly; see AN, MC, VI, 15, 29 January 1544, for an exchange between the two.

17. The goldsmiths were part of the *six corps*, the richest and most influential corporations in the city of Paris during the *ancien régime*.

18. Note that in the two documents cited in this chapter, n. 15, the notarial document and his insinuation at the Châtelet of Paris, Louis is designated in the first as "*écuyer*," while in the second his name is preceded by "*noble homme maistre*." In both cases, the title attributed to Étienne Victor is "*Honorable homme*."

19. AN, MC, VI, 15, 27 June 1545. Maréchal, according to P. Richelet, *Dictionnaire françois* (Geneva, 1700) was "an artisan who makes wheel rims, coulters, and ploughshares, who shoes horses and is their doctor." Again,

note an interesting document in which was found the following: "Étienne Victor, goldsmith: a lease to him of a forge on the pont au Change, by Germain Rebours, *avocat au parlement*," AN, MC, 122, 41, 30 May 1543.

20. AN, Y, 106, fol. 59, gift of 22 May 1565, registered after the gift of Louis Huault.

21. The faculty is not specified.

22. See Genealogical Table 2.

23. In the communal archives of Azay-le-Rideau there are no surviving parish registers prior to 1594. In Register I, which commences at this date, there are several Huaults, but it is impossible to establish any sort of connection with the Paris Huaults. In the departmental archives of Indre-et-Loire (E972), I have consulted the tax roll of the parish of Azay for the year 1519; there are several Huaults and several Victors there, but there was no way of knowing the family ties between these persons, much less their relationship with the Huaults and Victors of Paris.

24. This was the chancery attached to the parlement of Paris; also in Paris was the Grand Chancery, which operated under the direct responsibility of the chancellor of the realm.

25. Lapeyre and Scheurer, *Les notaires et secrétaires du roi*, vol. 1, entry 639, Thomas Thiuost; entry 330, Pierre Huault.

26. Richelet in his *Dictionnaire françois* defined "clerc" as "he who, being in the office of a notary or a procurator or some other professional man, makes copies of acts, so as to train himself to become, one day, capable of his master's functions."

27. Lapeyre and Scheurer, *Les notaires et secrétaires du roi*, and AN, MC, XIX, 12, 9 November 1497: sale of a seigneurie by Madeleine Badouiller, widow of Thomas Thioust. See this chapter, n. 32.

28. The date he acquired this office is unknown. See Lapeyre and Scheurer, *Les notaires et secrétaires du roi*, 165; several facts are given there, but not the date of the acquisition.

29. BN, PO, 1542, fol. 3.

30. F. Bluche and P. Durye, *L'anoblissement par charges avant 1789*, 2 vols (Paris: Les Cahiers nobles II, nos. 23 and 24, 1963).

31. This passage is taken from G. Brunet et al., eds., *Mémoires-journaux de Pierre de l'Estoile*, "Journal de Henri III, 1574–1580" (Paris, 1875), 1: 116ff. A daughter of Huault de Montmagny had married a Bragelongne in 1573. The Hennequins were related to the Huaults de Vayres through the Hacquevilles. A "pasquil," according to Richelet, was "a kind of satire. Its subjects were individuals whose conduct was being criticized." I found this reference in H. Michaud, *La grande chancellerie et les écritures royales au seizième siècle (1515–1589)* (Paris: PUF, 1967), 169.

32. This is the commonest spelling of this surname; but Badovilliers [with or without the final s] is often what is found in signatures at the start of the sixteenth century; also seen is Badouiller.

33. BN, Cabinet d'Hozier, 23. He later acquired the office of master registrar in the *chambre des comptes*.

34. BN, *Mss frs*, 32 588, 630: copy of the parish registers of Saint-Jean-en-Grève. Isabeau Le Brest was the widow of Dreux Anjorrant. An interesting study could be made of this Anjorrant family, whose social ascent paralleled that of the Huaults, to whom they had numerous ties. See this chapter, n. 136.

35. AOM, Arch. 2926. Here Isabeau's parents are given as Sebastien Le Brest, seigneur of Bayne, and Jeanne de Chambly.

36. BN, Cabinet d'Hozier, 193, fol. 4.

37. This information is taken from B. Guenée, *Catalogues des gens de justice de Senlis et de leurs familles, 1480–1550*, typewritten supplementary thesis, 183–188; BN, PO, 2626; extracts from family books, BN, DB, 598, fols. 114–120.

38. BN, DB, 362, fols. 2ff. (the third degree of the genealogy) gives the date of 17 September 1527. The engagement ceremony took place in June in the church of Saint-Jean-en-Grève; BN, *Mss frs*, 32 588, 632.

39. BN, DB, 598, fols. 114–120.

40. See Chapter 3, para. 1 and 2.

41. The guardianship account gives no indication of the value of the two largest components, i.e., the two principal land holdings. See this chapter, n. 42. In the case of Montmagny, it was a seigneurie; in that of Montreuil it is not certain, though there is constant reference to "the Seigneur of Montreuil."

42. AN, MC, VI, 15, 1 September 1545; the guardianship had begun on 19 September 1534.

43. Now a part of the canton of Saint-Ouen.

44. The rue des Blancs Manteaux is in the Marais; the rue de la Grande Truanderie is not far away, close to the Halles and the church of Saint-Eustache.

45. Reference in the gift of 19 May 1565, AN, MC, VI, 32. I found no indication of the extent or the value of these lands.

46. No detail is given, apart from the silverware. Note the abbreviations: L= livres, S=sols, D=deniers.

47. It is an important Parisian metro station.

48. BN, DB, 362, 2ff: entry on Pierre Huault in the genealogy; it is stated there that he did homage for it on 24 April 1527. In a marginal note of BN, Nouveau d'Hozier, 189, fol. 2 (repeated in Cabinet d'Hozier, 193) the

following has been added: "It was only in 1526 that he took over the *mairie*, land and seigneurie of Montmagny provisionally, and he gave faith and homage to Montmorency on 8 July 1532."

49. Montmorency is now a *sous-préfecture* of the department of Val d'Oise, situated about four kilometres northwest of Montmagny.

50. See this chapter, n. 48.

51. In 1984, the eighth centenary of this foundation was celebrated in the town of Montmagny. A booklet entitled *Montmagny: Huit siècles d'histoire* was published at Deuil-la-Barre on this occasion. Saint Thomas of Canterbury is also the patron of the oldest parish in the town of Montmagny, Québec. See this chapter, n. 48.

52. Two tombstones, Adrien (d. 1699) and his son Armand (d. 1676).

53. In 1709 there numbered 101 hearths, about 400 persons. See G. Poisson, *Évocation du grand Paris*, vol. 2, "La banlieue nord-ouest" (Paris: Éd. de Minuit, 1960), 495ff.

54. AD, Val d'Oise, *Minutes des notaires de Montmagny*, passim.

55. It can also be mentioned that Pierre Huault was church warden at Saint-Jean-en-Grève; see reference in AN, MC, VI, 21, 25 February 1550. It was undoubtedly he who arranged the purchase of a crypt for him and his family in the same church, AN, MC, VI, 52, 5 May 1575.

56. BN, PO, 1542, fol. 10.

57. He thus died relatively old for the time, considering that he was born between 1499 and 1509.

58. AN, MC, VI, passim.

59. BN, PO, 1542, fol. 3.

60. BN, Cabinet d'Hozier, 193, fol. 3.

61. M. Marion, *Dictionnaire des institutions de la France aux XVIIe et XVIIIe siècles* (Paris: Picard, 1923), article on the *bureau des pauvres*.

62. AN, MC, VI, 35, 18 August 1566. For the father, see n. 56.

63. Ibid., 40, 9 March 1569: allusion to the marriage of 1564.

64. BN, DB, 36. He was designated as baron of Vayres; but Vayres was certainly not a barony at this time. Note that this is Vayres-sur-Essonne, south of Paris, toward Étampes. The evolution of this family (see the extensive dossier in BN, DB, 343) bore some resemblance to that of the Huaults. Philippe's great-grandfather, Jean de Hacqueville (a little place in Eure) had been a cloth merchant and bourgeois of Paris; a great-uncle, also a merchant, had been an *échevin*; among Philippe's cousins (she was of the fourth generation after Jean) there appear a *maître des comptes*, a *secrétaire du roi*, and a *conseiller au parlement*, who later was a *président des requêtes* of the Palais. Above all, keep in mind that this prolific family gave the Huaults access to an important network of alliances, a few of which are:

the Hennequins, the Du Dracs, the de Fictes, the Bocharts, the Courtins; and most especially the families intimately bound up in the movement of the Counter Reformation: the Avrillots, the Rentys, the Brularts, and the Tronsons.

65. See M. Etchechoury, *Les maîtres des requêtes de l'hôtel du roi (1553–1589)* (Paris: École des Chartes, 1991), 231ff.

66. AN, MC, VI, 40, contract of marriage, 7 September 1559.

67. Canons regular as opposed to secular canons, who assist the bishop but are not subject to a rule.

68. This act does not appear in the minutes held in Study VI, but there is an allusion to it in a transaction between his two brothers, dated 25 February 1551, AN, MC, VI, 21. The Order had been given 2,400 livres.

69. AN, MC, VI, 15, 1 October.

70. F. Bonnard, *Histoire de l'abbaye royale et de l'ordre des chanoines réguliers de St-Victor de Paris* (Paris, 1904), 2: 285. It is not known how long he remained parish priest.

71. Bonnard, *Histoire de l'abbaye royale*, 45, n. 1.

72. BN, *Mss latins*, 14 456.

73. This is my translation of the "*Ordinarium.*" At the beginning of the manuscript cited in this chapter, n. 72, is found the following: "*Incipit prologus in ordinarium divini officii Sti Victoris pariensis:*" ("[Here] begins the prologue for the book of rules of the Divine Office of Saint Victor of Paris").

74. *Ordinarium*, 238, where it says: "*Hic liber est Sti Victoris quem scripsit Frater Claudius Huault, quondam prior de Valle Jocosa.*" ("Here is the book of Saint Victor, written by Brother Claude Huault, erstwhile prior of Vaujours.") In this passage it is not quite certain that the reference is being made to the *Ordinarium*. It could be an allusion to the rules of the Abbey.

75. The title which is seen most often in AN, MC, VI. Note that he never took the title of *écuyer*.

76. AN, MC, VI, 1 October 1545, account of guardianship, in which he was said to be twenty-five years old.

77. BN, Carrés d'Hozier, 345, fols. 136ff. According to the date on his tombstone in Saint-Jean-en-Grève, he died on 10 November 1576. Note the coincidence: he lived fifty-six years, his son, the first Charles, fifty-seven years, his grandson (the chevalier) fifty-six years.

78. AN, MC, VI, 15, 1 October 1545, reference in the account of guardianship.

79. Did the first Charles also go there? There is no indication.

80. AN, P, 2308, 127. He succeeded to this office after Simon Machaut.

81. See Marion, *Dictionnaire des institutions*.

82. Reference in AN, MC, VI, 79, inventory of 17 December 1577 – the first of the papers that appear there.

83. The payments of the sum were spread out between 23 July 1547 and 31 May 1550, AN, MC, VI, 79. Later the sum of 6,000 livres, coming from an aunt, Catherine de Billon, was added. See AN, MC, VI, 27, 25 July 1559.

84. He died before 26 April 1544, on which date Guillaume Bohier was given the office of the late Jean de Billon. *Catalogue des actes de François I* (Paris: Archives nationales, 1882–1908), 4: 601.

85. See BN, PO, 351, fol. 17: act of 5 August 1562: Louis Huault de Montmagny, quittance as executor of the will of *noble Damoiselle* Catherine Lescuyer, widow of *noble homme maître* Jean de Billon, *conseiller du roi et maître ordinaire en sa chambre des comptes*. See also the two entries (62 and 63) contained in Lapeyre and Scheurer, *Les notaires et secrétaires du roi*, vol. 1. To prepare an exhaustive genealogy of this family would have required a long and exhaustive study, which I have not been able to undertake.

86. *DBF*.

87. AN, MC, CXXI, 12, 31 January 1648.

88. BN, DB, 97, fol. 1.

89. *DBF*.

90. AN, MC, VI, 79, inventory of 17 December 1577, and MC, III, 151, 9 September 1578, distribution of effects.

91. From 1557 on, this title no longer appears on notarial documents.

92. Around Messy and Saint-Soupplets, in the vicinity of Meaux.

93. AN, MC, VI, 32 and 33; numerous acts for the year 1565 – they could make a very interesting study.

94. AN, MC, VI, 35, contract of 2 November 1566.

95. Ibid., 44.

96. Ibid., 48.

97. BN, PO, 1542, fols. 266ff., printed genealogy.

98. AN, MC, VI, 58, 22 January 1578.

99. He was received on 16 June 1579, BN, Carrés d'Hozier 345, fols. 139v–140, Cabinet d'Hozier, 193, fol. 3.

100. "Avec bonne et deue equipage," he served under the Duc de Longueville and the Sr de la Noue, according to what the proofs of nobility of Malta said in 1622. AOM, Arch. 2926. See also BN, Carrés d'Hozier, 345.

101. BN, Cabinet d'Hozier, 193, fol. 3v; Carrés d'Hozier, 345, fols. 139v–140.

102. They were judges in the first instance of the cases concerning the officers of the king's household, the king's secretary, etc. They were sovereign judges of the cases that were sent to them by the king's council (before which they had to bring them back), or those concerning the publishing and printing trades, Marion, *Dictionnaire des institutions*.

103. A. Bonvallet, "Le bureau des finances de la généralité de Poitiers," *Mémoires de la société des antiquaires de l'Ouest*, 4 (1883): 137–400 passim; 205.

104. The genealogies created within the family have turned this modest commission, which they date to 16 January 1599, into a commission as intendant, and this has been repeated by later historians.

105. A. Barbier, "Les intendants de province et les commissaires royaux en Poitou," *Mémoires de la société des antiquaires de l'Ouest* 26 (1902): 360–62. The author has reproduced two ordinances issued by the two commissioners, dated 10 March and 22 May 1599, 540ff.

106. BN, Collection Dupuy, 837, fols. 144–147, 159 vers. A study was published in 1877 by René Kerviler, *Nicolas Bourbon (1574–1644): Étude sur sa vie et sur ses travaux* (Paris: Librairie de H. Menu, 1877); the author devotes two pages to the study of this poem, but says nothing about Charles de Montmagny, who was being taken to task here by Nicolas Bourbon.

107. *DBF*, Nicolas Bourbon article.

108. Allusion to the Roman grammarian and poet Valerius Cato, at the end of the Republic, who also taught rhetoric. Also note that this seems to be a play on words; "secretioribus consiliis" and the "secretaries" of the king – the *maîtres des requêtes* were even more "secret" (closer to the "secrets" of the king?) than the king's own secretaries.

109. In 1620 he entered the Oratorians. He was received into the *Académie française*. At the end of his life he directed a literary circle at the Oratory of the rue Saint-Honoré See both Kerviler, *Nicolas Bourbon* and the *DBF* article.

110. The fee in question was called "le droit de landit"; it was an honorarium which the students paid to their professors at the opening of the Landit fair held 11–24 June each year at Saint-Denis.

111. Between 21 February 1604, AN, MC, LXXXVIII, 21 and 14 September 1606, AN, MC, LXVII, 86, when he used the new title.

112. AN, MC, CXVII, 481, 20 September 1618.

113. AN, MC, LI, 125, 20 May 1619.

114. Marion, *Dictionnaire des institutions* sets the value of such offices at 150,000 livres in 1665; probably 90,000 livres in 1610.

115. It was a specialty of the local soil. AD, Val d'Oise, *Minutes des notaires de Montmagny*, passim.

116. AN, MC, VI, 64, 23 February 1581. See Map 1.

117. AN, MC, XIX, 341, 27 March 1600.

118. I have not found the contracts of purchase, but there is reference to it in later documents. See Chapter 2.

119. See L. Mirot, "Les origines de l'hôtel de Sully," *Bull. Soc. de l'Hist. de Paris et de l'île de France*, 38 (Paris: Champion, 1911); G. Douillard, *Les origines de*

l'Hôtel de Sully (ca. 1985): MS available from the Centre de documentation of the Hôtel de Sully; also H. Ballon, *The Paris of Henri IV: Architecture and Urbanism* (New York, NY: The Architectural History Foundation, 1991), 57ff.

120. Roughly 100 feet by 78 feet, or 32 metres by 27.
121. AN, MC, CXVII, 473, 1 March 1611.
122. AN, MC, VI, 58, 22 January 1578.
123. A little town close to Reims toward Épernay.
124. It seems, though it is not absolutely certain, that all Antoinette's sisters married before her. One was already dead.
125. AN, Y, 126, fol. 338v, insinuation at the Châtelet, 27 February 1585. The notary was Thomas Fourniet [?], named as clerk substitute for the notary of Jouy-le-Chatel (Seine-et-Marne).
126. See for example the Hacqueville-Broé marriage: "they have in good faith made, and make, the following treaty, agreements and conventions of the marriage," AN, MC, LXXIII, 231, 9 August 1597.
127. BN, DB, 241.
128. See the numerous notes on the Du Drac family contained in the book by F. Autrand, *Naissance d'un grand corps d'État: Les gens du parlement de Paris, 1345–1454* (Paris: Publications de la Sorbonne, 1981). According to this work, it was one of the families which contributed most, through their alliances, to the formation of the "great family networks" which assured "the formation of the parlementary milieu." See the second part of the work, 43ff. The statement in BN, DB, 241, that Barthélemy Du Drac, *trésorier des guerres*, was a "Picard gentleman" makes no sense. See also a very interesting work, S. Charton-Le Clech, *Chancellerie et culture au XVIe siècle (Les notaires et secrétaires du roi de 1515 à 1547)* (Toulouse: P.U. Mirail, 1993), which contains numerous facts about the Du Dracs and their allies. As I observe later in this chapter, n. 136, a very interesting study could be made from all these elements.
129. Autrand, *Naissance*, 63–65.
130. *DBF*, a very short article. He died in 1473.
131. BN, *Mss frs*, 32 946, 8: elected in 1486, re-elected in 1488.
132. Two seigneuries are mentioned for the Du Dracs, Ay and Mareuil-sur-Ay. Ay is in the department of the Marne; there is a Mareuil-en-Brie in the same department, eighteen kilometres from Épernay. Possibly the place called Mareuil was a seigneurie dependent on the viscounty of Ay.
133. Numerous references in AN, series Y, starting with Y, 86, 1532. Also, numerous acts in the study MC, LXVIII, among others, starting in 1555.
134. See for example his will in AN, MC, VIII, 74, 27 February 1548.
135. See *DBF*, article on the Du Dracs, and O. Dresch, "Les couvents des Minimes à Paris," 2 vols (PhD thesis, l'École des Chartes, 1966), 1: 60.

The village of Chaillot is near the present-day Chaillot Palace, place du Trocadéro. A work which I was unable to consult is J. de Launay, *Une Sainte parisienne au XVIIe siècle, Marie Du Drac et sa famille* (Vannes, 1908).

136. The limits of this study prevented me from spending time on the familial links and alliances which united these families. Of the numerous connections I shall only mention a few examples. Around 1490 Marguerite Du Drac married Louis Anjorrant. Pierre Huault's second wife (in his 1516 marriage) was the widow of Dreux Anjorrant. In 1578, Antoinette Huault married Jean Anjorrant. The cycle, if I may call it that, continued into the seventeenth century – on 17 September 1606 Jean Du Drac married his daughter Charlotte to Charles Faucon, AN, MC, LXVIII, 86.

137. BN DB, 28, the beginning of the genealogy. Note that this Bochart family also entered the Robe at this time, and it would shine there throughout the *ancien régime*; one of its members was Intendant of New France at the end of the seventeenth century.

138. The archdeacon had been important in the medieval diocese, as assistant to the bishop. From the fifteenth century on, archdeacon was simply an honorary dignity. The apostolic proto notary held an office attached to the pontifical court of Rome, an office that was purchasable until 1624.

139. AN, MC, LI, 178.

140. S. Charton-LeClech, *Chancellerie et culture*, 225. I have already mentioned the damage which his decision caused him.

141. AN, Y, 94, fol. 204v, 4 February 1549.

142. AN, MC, CXVII, 474, fol. 747, 21 December 1611. In BN, DB, 557 he is further named as *maître en la chambre des comptes*, but this is unlikely. Charton-Le Clech, *Chancellerie et culture*, says that he was an alderman of Paris; but he does not appear in the list found in BN, *Mss frs*, 32 946.

143. AN, DB, 557. In this dossier, Jacques Rappouel, father of Thomas, was turned into an *écuyer* and *lieutenant-général* at Melun, and his wife Jeanne Olivier was supposed to have been a sister of the chancellor of this name.

144. BN, PO, 2435. The parchment, dated 19 November 1490, seems authentic; he is identified in this act as the son of Denis Rappouel, bourgeois residing at Melun, and Marguerite Grandine.

145. This surname is sometimes spelt Rapoil or Rapouel.

146. AN, MC, VI, 71, 16 October 1554.

147. Charton-Le Clech, *Chancellerie et culture*, 158ff.

148. The present-day rue de Braque, right by the *Archives nationales*. See Map 1.

149. AN, Y, 94, fol. 206v, 4 February 1549.

150. On the grand priory, see Chapter 4.

151. Charton-Le Clech, *Chancellerie et culture*, 158ff.

152. Ibid., 48.

153. AN, MC, VIII, 74, 27 February 1548.

154. A community founded in 1226 to aid repentant women; it was established in the fifteenth century on the rue Saint-Denis in Paris.

155. BN, PO, 2435, fol. 10.

156. Jean (IV) Du Drac.

157. Jean (II) Du Drac.

158. "To be received as a knight of Malta one must have the proofs of a legitimacy and a nobility of at least a hundred years for each of the eight quarterings, and these must be produced by authentic titles, and a family tree," AOM, libr. 767, n.d.

Chapter 2

1. AN, MC, LI, 140, 19 December 1623. The analysis of the contract and of its results will be taken up at length in Chapter 4.

2. This is the first time that he is seen signing a document, and in a very fine hand, as "the chevalier Huault de Montmagny."

3. The expression used here seems to signify the religious vows of poverty, chastity, and obedience. But we must note that, as has already been said, the word "Religion" also meant, at this time, the Order of Malta.

4. See Chap. 4.

5. More information concerning this relationship is contained in the discussion related to Louis Huault later in this chapter.

6. BN, DB, 241, fol. 40v.

7. BN, *Mss frs*, 32 588, 102, 111, 117, 126, 131.

8. BN, N.a.f. 784, fol. 326v. Baptism of Adrien in Saint-Nicolas-des-Champs.

9. BN, *Mss frs*, 32 591.

10. AN, MC, CXVII, 473, 1 March 1611.

11. Ibid., 23 March 1611.

12. It should be noted, however, that Charles and his brother Adrien must by then have begun to attend the college of La Flèche. Thus they only resided in Paris for a few months in the year; there was doubtless need for less space. The return to the hôtel seems to have taken place in 1615, some months after the marriage of Louis which took place in October 1614. In any event, the lease to Langlois and Morel ended in 1615.

13. AN, MC, CXVII, 474, fol. 233, April 1612: Claude, Jean and Geneviève Anjorrant "lease to X ... a house standing beside a house belonging to the

said sieurs and Damoiselle, lessors, in which Madame de Montmagny is presently residing, and on the other side, the tennis court of Tabarin."

14. AN, MC, CXVII, 474, fol. 356, 28 May 1612: a minor transaction of 45 livres.

15. Ibid., 478, fol. 609, 28 October 1615.

16. Ibid., 477, fol. 441, 1 October 1614.

17. Ibid., 477, fol. 681, early November.

18. Ibid., 481, 10 February 1618.

19. In the minutes of Study CXVII only one act is found in which she concerns herself with her lands: on 7 November 1615 she cedes "the cutting and clipping" of brushwood on her seigneurie of Vignolles in Brie, AN, MC, CXVII, 480, fol. 628.

20. AN, MC, XCI, 71.

21. AN, MC, CVII, 112.

22. This orphanage, created in 1534, stood at the end of the rue du Grand Chantier, which was a continuation of the rue du Chaulme (now the rue des Archives). It was situated not far from the Temple, less than 200 metres from the rue de Braque.

23. Her name was already engraved on a stone behind the high altar of Saint-Jean-en-Grève church. After those of Pierre Huault and Isabeau Le Brest, of Louis Huault and Claire de Billon, and of Charles Huault, was written: "Antoinette Du Drac, his wife, Lady of La Baillie and of Vignolles, who died ... [blank]." It was Louis Huault who went to the church and arranged for this inscription to be transcribed by his notary; AN, MC, CXVII, 476, 5 November 1613.

24. BN, DB, 362, fol. 15.

25. None of the notarial acts that I have been able to find includes this reference.

26. The first was that of "contrôleur général de la cavalerie légère au département de deçà les Monts," bought on 2 February 1624, AN, MC, LI, 141; in 1626 and 1628 he did not have any title in the documents that I have been able to see. In two contracts of 29 June 1631, he was designated as: "conseiller du roi, controleur général de l'extraordinaire des guerres," AN, MC, LI, 162; but in September of the same year no title appears after his name, and the same goes for 1633. Then in 1636, in the power of attorney which his brother Charles gave him, he was called "Controller General of the Light Cavalry," AN, MC, LI, 285, 16 March. There was no further reference in later years, according to my research.

27. From 1619 to 1646, when he was in Paris, he lodged with his brother Louis on the rue Saint-Antoine; at the Hôtel de Baillet; on the rue des Barres; on the rue du Chaulme; on the rue Saint-Avoye; on the rue du Bourg-Tibourg;

on the rue Sainte-Croix de la Bretonnerie; and after 1646, on the rue des Blancs Manteaux; the rue du Chaulme; the rue Chapon; and the rue de Moussy.

28. AN, MC, LI, 146, 5 October 1625.
29. Ibid., 141, 2 February 1624.
30. Ibid., 146, 5 October 1625.
31. Ibid., 125, 18 May 1619.
32. Ibid.
33. AN, MC, LI, 247, 22 December 1655. At the time of the distribution of 20 May 1619 it was valued at 93,000 livres, LI, 125.
34. "Fort caduque." According to Richelet, *Dictionnaire françois*, caduque meant "old, ill, and broken."
35. AN, MC, LXXXVIII, 188, 6 July 1663.
36. Ibid., 186 and 187.
37. AN, Y 203, fol. 37.
38. AN, MC, LXXXVIII, 188, 6 July 1663.
39. If the donor died soon, it would be the recipients who would profit; in the contrary circumstance, it would be the donor.
40. There is no other reference to the identity of the persons involved in this, nor to the date on which this pension began.
41. "To his nephew de Cartigny [he gives] all his books so that they may help his children to study."
42. According to the *Dictionnaire de l'Académie française* (Paris, 1765), a *chaise roulante* is "a two-wheeled vehicle drawn by a horse in harness."
43. See later in this chapter for more details of Louis's will.
44. AN, MC, LXXXVIII, 21.
45. 18,000 livres on the eve of the wedding, and 12,000 livres on the feast of Saint-Remy, 1 October. The two quittances are added at the bottom of the contract.
46. According to La Chesnaye-Desbois, *Dictionnaire*, their nobility dated to before 1350; but this dictionary, as I have already said, is not very reliable.
47. The place name Gouy is very common in Hainault and Artois. See H. Hasquin, ed., *Communes de Belgique: Dictionnaire d'histoire et de géographie administrative*, 4 vols (n.p.: Renaissance du Livre, [1981–1983]).
48. AN, MC, LXXXVIII, 21, 21 February 1604.
49. AN, MC, CVII, 109, 12 January 1615.
50. BN, DB, 326, item 16: "Provisions of the captaincy of the town of Crépy in Laonnais, 14 February 1581, to Michel de Gouy, governor of La Fère, in consideration of his noteworthy services."
51. AN, MC, CXVII, 477, 5 October 1614. It is in BN, DB, 326 that allusion is made to services rendered to the king, item 11, "Provisions of the

government of the château of Pierrefonds given by the king on 8 May 1594 to Anne-Antoine de Gouy, in place of the said Sr d'Arcy his father, as recompense for the proofs that he has given of his fidelity in the reduction of this place"; item 10, "Commission to hold the charge of conseiller d'Estat given by the king on 12 May 1614 to Anne-Antoine de Gouy in consideration of the noteworthy services that he had rendered to His Majesty in the great and important affairs entrusted to him."

52. AN, MC, CVII, 109, 12 January 1615, the will.
53. See Chapter 1.
54. AN, MC, XXIII, 106 (July 21 1603).
55. AN, MC, XX, 276 (July 3 1651).
56. Around 1570 Gaspard de Vignacourt married Madeleine de Gouy, Michel's sister; it is not certain that this was the Vignacourt line which gave the Order of Malta two Grand Masters in the seventeenth century. Vignacourt is a small place situated in the neighbourhood of Amiens.
57. BN, DB, 326, fol. 3: "Preuves de noblesse de Delle Marie-Françoise-Louise de Gouy d'Arsy pour être reçue dans la communauté des filles demoiselles de la maison de Saint- Louis ...," dated September 1697.
58. See DBF, three articles about the Gouys d'Arsy.
59. BN, Mss frs, 32 588, 126.
60. BN, DB, 362, fols. 2ff., genealogy.
61. Ibid.
62. AN, M, 436, item 17.
63. See, for example, D. Dessert, "Finances et société au XVIIᵉ siècle: à propos de la chambre de Justice de 1661," Annales E.S.C. 4 (1974): 847–882.
64. AN, MC, LXXV, 13, 15 April 1624.
65. DBF.
66. "Il faut souffrir la faim, & coucher sur la dure; eust-on plus de tresors que n'en perdit Galet N'avoir en sa maison ni meubles ni valet," N. Boileau-Despréaux, Satires: édition critique, avec introduction et commentaire, A. Cahen, ed. (Paris: Droz, 1932), 103–4. Tallemant des Réaux also speaks about Gallet in his Historiettes, in a paragraph which he devotes to "gamblers." See A. Adam, ed., Historiettes de Tallemant des Réaux (Paris: Gallimard, 1961, Collection Bibliothèque de la Pléiade), 2: 751–2.
67. R. Prévost, Le Paris des Québécois (Montréal: Libre Expression, 1989), 71.
68. In the deed of sale of the hôtel, he was said to be residing on the rue des Barres. See this chapter, n. 64. He had been there for some time, since in the account of guardianship which he gave to his brother Charles on 11 June 1622, he was declared to be residing there, AN, MC, LI, 136. It is not impossible that this house had a connection with the Lottin family. In November 1614 Guillaume Lottin, seigneur de Charny, was said to be living on the rue des Barres, AN, MC, CXVII, 477, 24 November. Besides,

during the *ancien régime* there was on the rue des Barres a house that went under the name of Hôtel de Charny. See J. Hillairet, *Connaissance du vieux Paris* (Paris: Éd. Gonthier, 1981), 1: 63. Charny was the Lottin family's principal seigneurie.

69. AN, MC, LI, 147.

70. AN, MC, LI, 176, 10 February 1635.

71. He transferred three annuities for this purpose. AN, MC, LI, 176, 27 January 1635.

72. AN, MC, LI, 262, 26 February 1646, article 94 of the inventory of his papers.

73. AN, MC, XXX, 27, 30 December 1643.

74. See this chapter, n.72, article 93 of the inventory of his papers.

75. AN, MC, LI, 216.

76. Ibid. 5 February.

77. AN, MC, LI, 262.

78. Ibid., 216.

79. Payment in three stages: 50,000 livres before a year, 30,000 before eighteen months, 27,000 before two years. The receipts for these payments have not been found.

80. In the documents of 18 and 20 May 1619, the date of the distribution of the goods of the first Charles and his wife, the following figures are recorded: for Montmagny, 66,000 livres; for a third of Messy, 30,000 livres. AN, MC, LI, 125. Of La Baillie and Goyencourt there are no details; but these were small seigneuries. Undoubtedly his seigneurial properties could be valued at 110,000 livres.

81. See the beginning of this chapter.

82. AN, MC, CXVII, 477, 5 October 1614.

83. AN, MC, XXVI, 31, 10 January 1613. Note the dowry of 120,000 livres which Marie Goussault brought into her marriage with Nicolas Lottin, Catherine's brother. AN, MC, LI, 192, 7 January 1639.

84. The information from BN, DB, 407 can be verified by notarial acts, one of which is the marriage contract of Robert Lottin and Louise Hurault. AN, MC, XIX, 48, 20 June 1519.

85. La Chesnaye-Desbois, *Dictionnaire*, Lottin entry. In the same work it is stated that the family originated in Beauce, not Bruges, BN, DB, 407.

86. This is Charny, Seine-et-Marne, commune of Claye-Souilly, arrondissement of Meaux.

87. See M. Lucas, *L'ancien site de Vaux-le-Vicomte* (Le-Mée-sur-Seine: Amatteis, 1988). Theoretically, 16,630 écus = 49,890 livres.

88. AN, MC, XXX, 24, 1 February 1640. The price was 6,000 livres in annual annuities.

89. See inventory of Isabelle Lottin, wife of François de Lauson, AN, MC, XXVI, 39, 17 September 1601.
90. *DCB*.
91. J.C. Dubé, *Les intendants de la Nouvelle-France* (Montréal: Fides, 1987), 280ff.
92. *DCB*.
93. Ibid.
94. Archives départementales du Val d'Oise (hereafter ADVO): parish registers of Montmagny.
95. See above, paragraph 4.
96. ADVO, notary of Montmagny, 14 September 1678; see also ibid., 30 September 1696.
97. AN, MC, XX, 276, 3 July 1651.
98. His brother, also named Nicolas, was the celebrated philosopher (1638–1715), a disciple of Descartes. He entered the Oratory.
99. ADVO, notaries of Montmagny, testament, 23 May 1699.
100. ADVO, 26 August 1699.
101. BN, DB, 362. The statement found there that Jacques Huault was a captain in the cavalry has not been confirmed by any document, notarial or other. It was also declared there that the parents of Julle de "Magis," whom he married in 1654, were Joseph de Magis, a Florentine noble, and Thérèse Paléologue, of the city of Lucca.
102. The location of these two fiefs has not been found.
103. BN, *Mss frs*, 32 591, 272.
104. AOM, Arch. 463, fol. 24, 7 June 1631. At this age, a young man could go to Malta and serve as a page to the Grand Master, in a sort of pre-novitiate. See the painting by Caravaggio of the Grand Master Alof de Wignacourt, accompanied by a page.
105. AN, MC, XXX, 27, 11 February, 13 April, and 30 April 1643.
106. Locality unknown.
107. Reference in AN, MC, LI, 216, 5 February 1646.
108. AN, MC, CX, 151, 23 March 1664; the vendor was the Verthamon family.
109. AN, MC, LXXV, 376, inventory of 11 June 1691.
110. The Bassanos were a family of Italian painters in the sixteenth and seventeenth centuries.
111. Pente, "a band which hangs around the canopy of a bed, on top of the curtains," *Dictionnaire de l'Academie françoise*, 1765.
112. AN, MC, LXXV, 376, 28 June 1691, deposit of an act of 11 April 1679.
113. AN, MC, LXXV, 377, 27 July 1691.
114. She was baptized at Saint-Paul on 27 August 1618, BN, *Mss frs*, 32 591, 256.

115. AN, MC, XIX, 414, 24 December 1637.
116. Arch. communales of Montmagny, parish registers for this date.
117. Baptized at Saint-Gervais on 4 December 1622, BN, *Mss frs,* 32 838, 189.
118. Baptized in Saint-Jean-en-Grève on 5 August 1629, BN, *Mss frs,* 32 588, 343.
119. AN, MC, LI, 219, 1 March 1647.
120. The distribution of her father's assests (he had died the previous year) had not been settled at the time of her marriage.
121. A congregation founded by César du Bus in 1592 in Provence, approved by Rome in 1597. The principal task of these priests (who became religious after 1659) was the instruction of children in catechism.
122. AN, MC, XX, 154, 19 September 1656.
123. Ibid., in the margin: 13 September 1671.
124. BN, PO, 2473; DB, 564; DB, 362.
125. BN, DB, 362.
126. Ibid., 21 February 1660; DB, 333 (Guérin); it was stated that the contract was passed before Dreüe and Billecocq, notaries at Roye.
127. BN, DB, 362.
128. Ibid. It was said that she was still alive in 1716, thus making her 87 years old.
129. AN, MC, LXXV, 437, 26 January 1699.
130. BN, DB, 362. In this document he is said to have been born in 1632.
131. Ibid., information to be taken with reservation.

Chapter 3

1. AN, MC, LI, 136, 11 June 1622. See the transcription of part of this act in the appendix to this chapter.
2. Normally, the duration of studies at the college was eight years. Since Charles finished in 1618, he should have started in 1610. But there is no evidence to confirm this supposition.
3. It is not known which college he attended.
4. Possibly the Faculty of Orléans, attendance at which seems to have been a family tradition.
5. See Chapter 1.
6. AOM, Arch. 2926. Note that it is likely that Charles Huault was born not in Montmagny but in Paris.
7. Arch. communales of Montmagny (*mairie* of Montmagny), parish registers. Louis had also been a godfather, on 15 August 1612. Catherine Lottin, his wife, was godmother on 18 July 1616. Unfortunately, there are serious gaps

in these registers, e.g., one that goes from December 1589 to January 1611. Note the expression, "*écuyer* to our lord the king" – the godfather (or his mother) wanted to impress the peasant family whom he was honouring by a high-sounding title, which, as is known, did not correspond to anything real.

8.   M. Motley, *Becoming a French Aristocrat: The Education of the Court Nobility 1580–1715* (Princeton: Princeton University Press, 1990). The study applies first and foremost to the court nobility, but there is good reason to believe that the families of the *grande robe* – the Du Dracs, and the Huaults as they became with the first Charles – would have modelled themselves on this pattern.

9.   Ibid., 52.

10. AN, MC, LI, 216, 5 February 1646. See Chapter 2.

11. He was canonized in 1665.

12. AN, MC, XXIV, 501, 6 July 1667. See Chapter 2.

13. Pierre de Bérulle (1575–1629) founded a society of priests, the Oratory (1611). Named cardinal in 1627, he exercised great influence; he was one of Saint Vincent de Paul's mentors. Jean Huault de Vayres had married Anne de Piedefer (see Chapter 1, Table 6); and there had been two marriages between Piedefers and Bérulles in the sixteenth century.

14. Barbe Avrillot (1566–1618) married Pierre Acarie. Once widowed, she entered the Carmel that she herself had founded. A double connection with the Huault family; Barbe Avrillot was the daughter of Nicolas, and niece of Marie Du Drac (who had married Jacques Avrillot). She married Pierre Acarie, son of Simon and of Marguerite Lottin, great-aunt of Catherine Lottin, wife of Louis Huault (the chevalier's brother).

15. See the article devoted to him in L. Campeau, SJ, ed., *Monumenta Novae Franciae*, 8 vols to date (Québec: Les Presses de l'Université Laval, and Montréal: Bellarmin) (hereafter *MNF*), III, 836. He was born in 1570, and died in 1652. In 1590, he entered the Society. He was rector of the college of La Flèche from 1606 to 1616. Note that the *Relations* refer to him often, especially after the year 1636.

16. See Chapter 1.

17. Their college in Orléans was founded in 1617.

18. He had expelled them from a part of France at the end of 1594, after their condemnation by the parlements of Paris, Rouen, and Dijon. They were accused of having incited Jean Châtel to regicide. This man, who had studied with them, attempted in 1594 to kill Henry IV, who had just made his entry into Paris.

19. In his original plan, law and medicine would also be taught at La Flèche.

20. On the college of La Flèche see J. Clère, *Histoire de l'école de La Flèche* (La Flèche, 1854); P. Delattre, ed., *L'établissment des jésuites en France, 1540–1940* (Enghien: Institut supérieur de théologie, 1952), 2: 904–5.; C. de Rochemonteix, *Un collège des jésuites aux XVIIe et XVIIIe siècles: le collège de Henri IV de La Flèche*, 4 vols (Le Mans, 1889).

21. Delattre, *L'établissment*, 906.

22. The eight years were disposed as follows: sixth, fifth, fourth, third, second, rhetoric, mathematics, philosophy.

23. 300,000 livres were attributed to the college, 165,000 of which were for the church and the buildings.

24. M.-M. Compère and D. Julia, *Les collèges français, 16e– 18e siècles* (Paris: CNRS, 1988), 2: 381.

25. It would reopen on 20 August 1610.

26. From the 1540s, and until 1599, date of the definitive edition of the *Ratio Studiorum.*

27. F. de Dainville, *Naissance de l'humanisme moderne* (Paris: Beauchesne, 1940), 278. I have used this work essentially to study the teaching methods developed by the Jesuits. See as well a collection of articles by F. de Dainville, *L'éducation des jésuites (XVIe–XVIIIe siècles)* (Paris: Minuit, 1978).

28. Ibid., 73. A difficult expression to translate.

29. Ibid., 290ff: paragraph entitled "culture des élites."

30. Ibid., 312. See also, on the subject of the egalitarianism that reigned in Jesuit colleges, the reflections of Descartes cited in this chapter, n. 40.

31. De Rochemonteix, *Un collège des jésuites*, 2: 216–7.

32. De Dainville, *Naissance*, 256.

33. Ibid., 152–3.

34. Ibid., 279–80.

35. These were kinds of production co-operatives, autonomous in their administration, and inspired in their management and their government by Christian principles.

36. *DCB.*

37. See Chapters 5 to 8.

38. *DCB.*

39. *DBF.*

40. Cited in Delattre, *L'établissment*, 2: 913–4.

41. M.C. Daveluy, *La Société de Notre-Dame de Montréal, 1639–1663* (Montréal: Fides, 1965), 95–103.

42. See Chapter 7.

43. *DBF.*

44. See Chapter 7.

45. F. Gaston-Chéreau, "Pages de la vie de collège (La Flèche, 1611–1616)," *Mélanges Felix Grat* (Paris, 1949), 2: 413–443.
46. His father, Claude Thévenin, took the name of his estate of La Roche, situated not far from Montaigu in the Vendée; the name became La Roche-Thévenin.
47. Gaston-Chéreau, "Pages de la vie," 414 n. 2.
48. See Chapter 9.
49. See Chapters 5 to 8.
50. AN, MC, CVII, 112, 1 September 1618. See Chapter 2.
51. See Chapter 1. There is no information as to where Charles, the father of the chevalier and Louis, his brother, made their studies.
52. AN, MC, LI, 146, 11 June 1622. See the appendix to this chapter. Charles Huault left for Orléans on 1 May 1619, and returned on 25 March 1620. In other passages of the same document there is reference to the stay that Adrien Huault made there simultaneously.
53. See Chapter 2, n. 26.
54. Their father, his four brothers-in-law, their brother Louis; only Anne-Antoine de Gouy, their sister Charlotte's husband, was not a magistrate.
55. S. Guenée, *Histoire des universités françaises des origines à la Révolution* (Paris: Picard, 1970). Note that for a period of time in the fifteenth century there was a faculty of medicine and a school of surgery at the University of Orléans.
56. V. Verger, ed., *Histoire des universités en France* (Toulouse: Privat, 1986), 175–6.
57. *DBF.*
58. Ibid.
59. Ibid.
60. Recent confirmation of this fame can be found in two articles that appeared in *Le Monde* of 25 June 1993, by J.F. Augereau: "Le théorème de Fermat enfin démontré?" and "Le triomphe de l'inaccessible."
61. He occupied a lodging in one of the houses on the rue Saint-Antoine. See the account of guardianship in the appendix to this chapter. What was he doing? A mystery.
62. See Table 6, showing the employment of his time between 1618 and 1622.
63. See the account of guardianship in this chapter, n. 61.
64. Ibid.
65. See J. Bousquet, *Recherches sur les peintres à Rome au XVIIᵉ siècle* (Montpellier: Alpha, 1980), 24, for the example of Étienne Pasquier (1529–1615), humanist and historian.
66. Cited in ibid., 25.

67. De Dainville, *Naissance*, 76.

68. Ibid., 25.

69. M. de Montaigne, *Journal de voyage en Italie*, C. Dedeyan, ed. (Paris: Les Belles Lettres, 1946).

70. BN, coll. Clairambault 841. This manuscript was published in 1982 by Michel Bideaux, *Voyages d'Italie 1605* (Geneva: Slatkine, 1982), with an interesting introduction and copious notes.

71. BN, coll. Clairambault 1006. This text was published in 2001 by the C.I.R.V.I. of Moncalier, Italy, under the title: *Florisel de Claveson, voyages d'Italie (1608–1609)*. This edition was prepared by J.-C. Dubé (introduction, notes, setting-up of the text).

72. *Voyage du Levant du Sr de Stochove, seignr de Ste Catherine*, 2nd ed. (Brussels, 1650); there was a third edition in 1652. In 1664 there appeared in Rouen: "Le Voyage d'Italie et du Levant de MM. Fermanel, Fauvel, sieur d'Oudeauville, Baudouin de Launay et de Stochove, sieur de Ste-Catherine, contenant la description des royaumes, provinces, vies, moeurs, actions, tant des Italiens, que des Turcs, Juifs, Grecs, Arabes, Mores, Nègres et autres nations."

73. For the moment I have left aside the artists who came to perform, or complete, their apprenticeship in Italy. See this chapter, nn. 65, 74, 88.

74. A very interesting book is L. Schudt, *Italienreisen im 17. und 18. Jahrhundert* (Vienna, 1959).

75. There is evidence of a pilgrimage there from the fourteenth century, and it was highly in vogue in the fifteenth century. In about 1430 a basilica was erected around the famous house; this was a fortified church, because of the proximity of the Adriatic and the need to be protected from enemy incursions. In the seventeenth century Loretto was the most popular sanctuary in Christianity – the voyage to Jerusalem being dangerous because of the risk, among others, of privateers.

76. Y. Bercé, *Le roi caché: Sauveurs et imposteurs. Mythes politiques populaires dans l'Europe moderne* (Paris: Fayard, 1990), 234–5.

77. A pilgrimage much followed in the Middle Ages and up to this day. For the period concerning us, remember that in 1602 Marie de' Medici went there to give thanks for the birth of Louis XIII. Louis later went there several times with his wife Anne of Austria, to beseech the Virgin to give them an heir.

78. See *DCB* and the entry about him in *MNF*, 3: 837. It was in 1673 that the Jesuit founded the Huron mission of Notre-Dame de Lorette, not far from Québec City. He was a very interesting person. In his youth he sought refuge in Italy after a series of pranks. Following a sermon that moved him, he entered (in 1632) the Jesuit novitiate in Rome. René Latourelle

S.J. has just brought out a biography of Father Chaumonot: *Compagnon des Martyrs canadiens: Pierre-Joseph-Marie Chaumonot* (Montréal: Bellarmin, 1998).

79. Gaston-Chéreau, "Pages de la vie," 417, 422. The book appeared first in Latin, *Laurentanae historiae libri quinque* (Rome, 1597); it was later translated into Italian, Spanish, and French. The French translation appeared in Paris in 1600 under the following title: *L'histoire mémorable de Nostre-Dame de Lorette*.

80. A. Baillet, *La Vie de Monsieur Des-Cartes* (1691), cited in C. Adam and P. Tannery, *Oeuvres de Descartes* (Paris: Vrin 1966, re-edited), 10: 186.

81. Saint Peter, Saint Paul, Saint John Lateran, and Saint Mary Major.

82. J. Delumeau, *Vie économique et sociale de Rome dans la seconde moitié du XVIe siècle* (Paris: De Boccard 1958), 1: 174–5.

83. Delumeau, *Vie économique*, 151–2.

84. There were also exchanges between intellectuals; the limits of this work do not permit me to address these, but I will mention two notable French savants of the seventeenth century who had numerous contacts with Italy: Peiresc (1580–1637), who was Galileo's pupil at Padua, and Gabriel Naudé (1600–1653) – the latter almost a contemporary of Montmagny. Naudé studied medicine at Padua and was librarian for two Roman cardinals, before being taken back by Richelieu and Mazarin.

85. One example: *Ludovici de montiosii Gallus Romae Hospes ubi multa antiquorum monumenta explicantur* ... (RomÆ, apud J.O.S. Marinum, 1585), five parts in one volume, part 4 (engraved plates); his French name was L. de Montjosieu. See Delumeau, *Vie économique*, 167–8.

86. The site of Cuma, east of Naples, preserves the traces of an ancient city founded by the Greeks about 750 BC. One can still see a grotto which is said to have been the Sybil's retreat. The Sybil was a woman who claimed to be inspired by God, and who predicted the future. For the reference to Claveson see this chapter, n. 71.

87. See the works cited in this chapter, nn. 65, 74.

88. A beautiful exhibition was devoted to him at the Grand Palais, in Paris, from 9 November 1990 to 11 February 1991. See the article by J. Bousquet, "Documents sur le séjour de Simon Vouet à Rome," in *Mélanges d'archéologie et d'histoire* (Paris: De Boccard, 1952) 64: 287–300.

89. His search for models among the lower classes caused scandal.

90. Pursued by Roman justice, Caravaggio found refuge in Malta, where he spent more than a year.

91. Delumeau, *Vie économique*, plate 9. This painting can be seen in the church of Sant' Agostino in Rome.

92. Delumeau, *Vie économique*, 187.

93. Florisel de Claveson wrote that he had attended an audience and a papal Mass, in the company of the Duke of Nevers. See this chapter, n. 71.

94. This is what the testimony of the composers of the *Relations* would have us understand. See Chapters 5 to 8.

95. M. de Montaigne, *Journal de Voyage*, F. Garavini ed. (Paris: Gallimard, 1983), 231.

96. He was born in February 1602, a few months after Montmagny.

97. See F. Billacois, *Le duel dans la société français des XVIᵉ et XVIIᵉ siècles: essai de psychosociologie historique* (Paris: Éditions de l'École des hautes études en sciences sociales, 1986).

98. The battle of Rocroi took place on 18 May 1643.

Chapter 4

1. The date mentioned in AN, MC, LI, 140, 19 February 1623.

2. AN, MM 43, 17 July 1651.

3. See Table 13, in the appendix to Chapter 2.

4. See the Introduction and n. 7 in it for a discussion of the Baroque age.

5. F. Billacois, *Le duel.*

6. C. Morrisson, *Les croisades*, 5th ed. (Paris: PUF, 1988, Collection "Que sais-je?").

7. Of this person, only his first name, Gérard, and his work are known. Neither his birthplace – Martigues, close to Aix-en-Provence, or Scala, close to Amalfi? – nor his birthdate have been determined. He died on 30 September 1120. See the very short entry in A. Baudrillart et al. eds., *Dictionnaire d'histoire et de géographie ecclésiastique* (Paris: Letouzey et Ané, 1984).

8. See J.-C. Poutiers, *Rhodes et ses chevaliers, 1306–1523: Approche historique et archéologique* (Lebanon: Imprimerie catholique sal Araya, 1989).

9. Poutiers, *Rhodes et ses chevaliers*, 64. The Knights were able to carry away their archives, library, and relics.

10. A complete contrast with the luxuriance of Rhodes. Note, however, what the official document, dated 15 March 1530, contains: "We have ceded and freely given to the said very reverend Grand Master of the said religious Order of Saint John of Jerusalem, as fief noble, free and frank, the castles, places and islands of Tripoli, Malta and Gozo and all their territories and jurisdictions ... " It was impossible to hold on to Tripoli, which fell into the hands of the Berbers in 1547. See C.E. Engel, *Histoire de l'Ordre de Malte* (Geneva: Nagel, 1968), 167, for the official document, and 185–87 for other details concerning Tripoli.

11. There is debate regarding the provenance of the present-day population –
     Phoenicia, Carthage, Italy? See Engel, *Histoire*, 175; also J. Godechot,
     Histoire de Malte, 3rd ed. (Paris: PUF, 1981, Collection "Que sais-je?"). The
     Maltese language closely resembles Arabic (the island was occupied by
     the Arabs from 870 to 1091), but it is written in Latin letters.

12. In 1622, there were 41,000 inhabitants, according to M. Miège, *Histoire
     de Malte* (Paris, 1841), vol. 2 (pages on the administration of Alof de
     Wignacourt).

13. But it was not in theory an absolute power; the Grand Master had to submit
     to the decisions of the general council, which, however, met only rarely.

14. Auvergne, France, and Provence for France; Castille and Aragon for Spain
     and Portugal; Germany, Italy, and England.

15. The Temple was the seat of the grand priory of France. The Temple
     was a vast enclosure north of the Marais in Paris, containing several
     residences and a church (the Temple), which had previously belonged to
     the Templars. The Knights of Saint John of Jerusalem inherited it in 1312,
     after the suppression of the "Order of Knights of the Army of the Temple"
     (the official name of the Templars).

16. See in this regard the interesting article by J.F. Grima, "The Maintenance
     of the Order's Galley-Squadron (1600–1650)," in *Melita Historica* 7 (1977), 2:
     145–56. During the grand mastership of Antoine de Paule (1623–1636), the
     maintenance of the Order's six galleys cost somewhat more than 125,000
     scudi, almost half of the total revenue of the Order, which was around
     270,000 scudi.

17. "Hostes nostrae fidei" – this was the formula which is encountered, for
     example, in the permissions which the Grand Master gave to those who
     were authorized to go privateering.

18. "Servant of the poor of Christ and guardian of the hospital of
     Jerusalem."

19. Poverty, chastity, and obedience, as pertained to all religious in the
     Church.

20. Justice, strength, prudence, and temperance.

21. See Chapter 9 for a further discussion of this person.

22. In the town of Filerimos, situated not far from Rhodes, the capital city of
     the island of the same name, was the church of the Virgin of All Graces,
     which sheltered within its walls an icon, the object of great veneration.
     This devotion was adopted by the Knights. See Poutiers, *Rhodes et ses
     chevaliers*, 269–70.

23. Reference in the act of guardianship, AN, MC, LI, 11 June 1622.

24. Claude Anjorrant was the son of Jean, *maître des requêtes*, and of Antoinette
     Huault, Charles's aunt; his brother had been a Knight of Malta from 1613.

Note that Charles had signed the marriage contract of Claude Anjorrant with Marguerite Feydeau de Brou, AN, MC, XII, 48, 7 April 1619.

25. Richelet, *Dictionnaire françois*.
26. See this chapter, n. 23.
27. If one adds 6,469L, 10S, 6D (the money given) to 1,633L 6S 8D (pension paid) and 300L (the money given for the completion of his studies at La Flèche (see Chapter 3) it amounts to 8,402L, 17S, 2D; but as all the expenses in the account of the guardianship are said to come to 8,578L, 11S, 8D, there remains 175L, 1S, 6D, of which no reference is made. Could it be money given to his brother to defray the expenses occasioned by his presence in his house when he was in Paris? Who can say?
28. AN, MC, LI, 125, 20 May 1619.
29. Messy-en-Brie, near Meaux.
30. See Chapter 2.
31. According to Marion, *Dictionnaire des institutions*, the greffe was the depository where all the acts of a jurisdiction were held. The office of greffier became purchasable in 1521.
32. AN, MC, LI, 125, 20 May 1619.
33. AOM, Arch. 2926, repeated in BN, Carrés d'Hozier 345
34. AOM, Arch. 3566.
35. A dignity, as previously mentioned, which was recompense for services, above all military services, to the king.
36. "d'or au dragon de sinople, armé couronné et lampassé de gueule."
37. See Chapter 1.
38. Reference in AN, MC, LI, 140, 19 February 1623.
39. AOM, Libr. 315, 278.
40. Abbé R. de Vertot, *Histoire des chevaliers hospitaliers de Saint-Jean de Jérusalem*, 6 vols (Paris, 1754), 5: 175.
41. De Vertot, *Histoire*, 177.
42. AOM, Arch. 461, 6.
43. Malta possesses a collection of notarial archives in very good condition, and there still exist very useful repertories of the period.
44. For example, the important contract which Charles signed with his brothers and sister on 19 December 1623 must have been discussed over several days by the parties concerned, AN, MC, LI, 140, 19 December 1623.
45. I have had to qualify some dates as thereabouts [ca.] for the period between May 1628 and July 1631 as precise dates are missing.
46. See AOM, Arch. 58, fols. 312ff: letter from Montmagny, 29 April 1650, to the Grand Master: he declares that he is short one of the four prescribed caravans; in fact, he had performed five, but apparently two must have

been cut short. See also AOM, Arch. 117, 14 May 1650. In principle, a caravan was supposed to last six months.

47. There is a rich literature on the corso. See a recent study, P. Crowhurst, "'Guerre de Course' et 'privateering,' vers une étude comparative," in *Guerre et Paix, 1660–1815* (Vincennes: Service historique de la Marine, 1987), 311–322.

48. Several interesting studies on Maltese privateering have appeared recently. The ones which have been most useful to me are: R.E. Cavaliero, "The Decline of the Maltese Corso in the 18th Century: A Study of Maritime History," *Melita Historica* 2 (1965), 4: 224ff; P. Cassar, "The Maltese Corsairs and the Order of St. John of Jerusalem," *The Catholic Historical Review* 46 (July, 1960), 2: 137ff; P. Earle, *Corsairs of Malta and Barbary* (London, 1970); and three works by M. Fontenay, "L'empire ottoman et le risque corsaire au XVIIe siècle," *RHMC* 32 (1985): 185ff; "Corsaires de la foi ou rentiers du sol? Les chevaliers de Malte dans le 'corso méditerranéen' au XVIIe siècle," *RHMC* 35 (1988): 361ff, and "La course dans l'économie méditerranéenne au XVIIe siècle," *AESC* 43 (1988): 1321ff.

49. See n. 48 above, especially Fontenay's 1985 article.

50. The use of an expression in Italian is explained by the fact that the grand admiral was chosen from among the chevaliers born in Italy. It refers to the armament of ships.

51. See Fontenay, "L'empire ottoman."

52. Earle, *Corsairs,* speaks of "staple."

53. Godechot claims that there were 10,000 slaves in Malta at the start of the eighteenth century, *Histoire de Malte,* 51.

54. The island only produced 50 per cent of its food requirements in the seventeenth century, and 30 per cent in the eighteenth. Sometimes, at a moment of extreme need, the authorities forced a foreign vessel that was passing by to sell them its cargo of grain.

55. AN, MC, LI, 140.

56. He ratified this agreement on his return to Paris in February 1624; this ratification is added to the contract indicated in n. 55 above.

57. AN, MC, LI, 125, addendum to the distribution of 20 May 1619.

58. No details (date, route, incidents) have been found regarding the caravans in which Montmagny took part. In addition to the account which I use here, and as a point of comparison, I have been able to analyze another (which remains unpublished) left by the chevalier de Villages. See AOM Libr. 480.

59. J.B. de Luppé du Garrané, *Mémoires et caravanes,* published in Paris in 1865.

60. It is likely that his name, Luppé, is taken from the commune in the Gers now called Luppé-Violles. About Garrané there is nothing.

61. A duration falling well short of the six months that a caravan usually lasted.
62. Brigantin: "a vessel of deep draught which moves with sails and oars." A. Furetière, *Dictionnaire universel* (La Haye, 1690; reprint, Paris: Le Robert 1978)
63. Chaloupe: "a small vessel designed for the service of larger ships, used for short trips." Furetière, *Dictionnaire*.
64. The scudo, the currency of Malta at the time, was the equivalent of 2½ French livres.
65. In 1622 he participated in the campaign against La Rochelle.
66. I have not exhausted the subject; there are numerous other interesting details to draw from this account.
67. But a ruin that was only relative, since the Order would not have abandoned one of its members to his fate.
68. AOM, Arch. 461.
69. AN, MC, LI, 147, 31 January 1626.
70. His presence in Marseille is attested to in AD, Bouches-du-Rhône, 360E, 62, notary F. Baldouyn, 16 March 1626.
71. AN, MC, LI, 152, 18 May 1628. This is what is found in this document: "Furthermore, the said chevalier declares that beside the payment of the said pension (3,600L for two years, 1626 and 1627) the said Srs de Montmagny and de Messy have lent him, for the purpose of the fitting out, which he has already undertaken, of a vessel in the city of Marseille, the sum of 640L 8S." The first two payments of that sum had been made on 8 June 1627 (3,109L, 7S, 6D). Note that there is reference here only of outfitting the vessel; but according to the information found in Malta, it seems that the vessel belonged to him.
72. Notarial Archives of Malta (hereafter ANM) 476, v. 18, notary P. Vella, passim from 17 August 1626. Note the mix of Italian (San Giovanni) and Latin, which was current at that time in Maltese notarial documents.
73. ANM 488, v. 48, notary A. Sceberras, passim from 8 January 1627.
74. ANM 476, v. 19, fol. 155, notary P. Vella.
75. See A. Joyau, *Belain d'Esnambuc* (Paris: E. Bellenand, 1950), 53. In 1627 d'Esnambuc bought one in Le Havre for 4,000 livres, but it had already served.
76. "A round, high-sided vessel, used in war for privateering: it is also intended for the service of large ships." Furetière, *Dictionnaire*. It will take on a different meaning in the eighteenth and nineteenth centuries. In Latin it is *pittacium*, in Italian *petaccio*, and in Spanish *pataje*.
77. The word *patache* may be of Arab origin: "batas" signifying "boat with two masts."

78. Between 100 and 140 feet (about 36 metres).
79. Information taken from a conversation in 1990 with Joseph Muscat, a Maltese expert in questions of maritime history.
80. ANM 476, v. 18, notary P. Vella.
81. This is the formula generally found in the contracts. See ANM 476, v. 18, notary P. Vella.
82. See this chapter, n. 71.
83. AOM, Arch. 462, fols. 292–3.
84. ANM 476, v. 18, fol. 717, notary P. Vella.
85. The reimbursement appears at the end, or in the margin, of the document which contains the loan itself.
86. ANM 476, v. 18, fol. 559, notary P. Vella. The terms employed are as follows: "Charles has received from noble seigneurs Louis and Adrien de Montmagny, absent, who have jointly made the loan, 800 scudi, to respond amicably to the demands [that he has made of them], both out of friendship for him, and without any desire for great profits, but only to render him service." Note that this was added to the sum of 4,652 livres, 10 sols lent on 8 June. See this chapter, n. 71.
87. U.M. Ubaldini, *La Marina del Soverano Militare Ordine di San Giovanni di Gerusalemme di Rodi e di Malta* (Roma: Regionale Editrice, 1971), 364ff.
88. Ubaldini, *La Marina*.
89. ANM 488, v. 48, fol. 488v, notary A. Sceberras.
90. Most of the acts were passed this time before A. Sceberras, ANM 488, v. 48–49 passim. There was also one before L. Grima, ANM 309, v. 25, 4 March; twelve before P. Vella, ANM 476, v. 18, fol. 277ff; one before P.P. Vincella ANM 480, v. 6, 18 March; and one before L. Dello Re, ANM 228, v. 8, 1 April.
91. ANM 488, v. 49, fol. 848, 30 March, notary Sceberras.
92. Ibid., 3 April. He had sold another for 100 scudi, ANM 476, v. 19, 30 January, notary P. Vella, and two others on 10 February, ANM 172, v. 21, fol. 493v, notary T. Cauchi.
93. ANM 476, v. 19, 19 August 1627, notary P. Vella.
94. ANM 488, v. 49, 1 April, notary A. Sceberras. He was called Janettino Fornaccia.
95. ANM 488, v. 49, 5 April, notary A. Sceberras, act. On 13 April he was said to be absent.
96. A man of letters given a pension to write the history of the sovereign, an office created under Catherine de' Medici; see Marion, *Dictionnaire des institutions*.
97. Plus three others posthumously; three remain as manuscripts. See the article about him in the *DBF*.

98. Page 959. Note that the first edition of this book dates from 1617; the second does not appear in the catalogue of the BnF.

99. Note the very interesting shipboard journal of an English captain who left his country at the beginning of January 1628, to return at the beginning of February 1629. He travelled the Mediterranean. Sir Kenelm Digby, *Journal of a Voyage into the Mediterranean* (London: Johnson Reprint 1968).

100. ANM 478, v. 21, notary P. Vella.

101. "Ad multum illrem [illustrem] Dnum [dominum] Carolum de Montmagnii."

102. "Cum sua non parum prudentia et virtute."

103. It is amusing to note that the word "avarié" is of Arab origin. It was first adopted by the Genoese as "avara"; the Arab "avar" means "defect."

104. ANM 488, v. 48, fol. 612, notary A. Sceberras.

105. Moreri, *Le Grand dictionnaire*, Huault entry. See the text reproduced at the beginning of the Introduction.

106. Under what influence? No doubt the family's.

107. He even adds that he "commanded" them in 1630. There is no mention of that in the Maltese documents that I have been able to consult.

108. Ubaldini, *La Marina*, 366; B. Dal Pozzo, *Historia della Sacra Religione Militare di San Giovanni Gerosolimitani detta di Malta* (Verona, 1703), 762.

109. Caramussel: "a Turkish vessel with a very high stern." Furetière, *Dictionnaire*.

110. This according to Dal Pozzo. See this chapter, n. 108.

111. AN, MC, XXX, 14, 15 September 1631. I cannot identify what is meant by "his people," other knights? servants? friends?

112. Ibid.

113. AN, MC, LI, 152, 18 March 1628: "... and 342 livres, also from his funds and according to his order, being on the back of a letter of exchange belonging to the said chevalier, dated at Rome on 2 [?] October [?] 1627."

114. See n. 113 above.

115. ANM 488, 48, fol. 612, notary A. Sceberras.

116. AN, MC, LI, 152, 18 March 1628.

117. ANM 478, 21, notary P. Vella. See this chapter, nn. 100–02.

118. Reference in AN, MC XXX 14, 15 September 1631.

119. See the names of the notaries referenced in this chapter, n. 90.

120. AN, MC, XXX, 14, 15 September 1631.

121. Ibid.

122. AN, MC, VI, 120, 30 July 1633.

123. A comparison can perhaps be made with the three Coligny brothers in the sixteenth century, Oder, Gaspard, and François. See C.E. Engel, *L'amiral de Coligny* (Geneva: Labor et Fides, 1967).

124. See Chapter 2.
125. L. de La Roque, *Catalogue des chevaliers de Malte* (Supplement to the *Bulletin héraldique*, February 1890).
126. Twenty months at least.
127. ANM 476, 26, notary P. Vella, 19 April and 15 May 1634.
128. AOM, Arch. 464, fol. 42v, 11 June 1634.
129. Grand Master of Navigation and Commerce, one of Richelieu's titles.
130. P. Varillon, "L'ordre de Malte, pépinière de marins français," *Revue des deux mondes* (1957), 672ff.
131. L. Guérin, *Les marins illustres de la France* (Paris, 1844); twelve of the thirty-one whom he mentioned were members of the Order of Malta.
132. See the reference to the chevalier Paul at the end of the Introduction.
133. C.-M. de La Roncière, *Histoire de la marine française* (Paris: Plon, Nourrit, 1899), 2: 432. See also R. Lacour-Gayet, *La marine militaire sous Louis XIII et Louis XIV*, vol. 1, *Richelieu et Mazarin* (Paris: Champion, 1911).
134. *DBF.*
135. A. Jal, *Dictionnaire critique de biographie et d'histoire* (Paris, 1867).
136. *DCB.*
137. La Roncière, *Histoire*, 394.
138. L.A. Boiteux, *Richelieu, grand maître de la navigation et du commerce* (Paris: Ozanne, 1954).
139. He was received as a Knight of Malta in 1584. According to T. Guérin, *From the Crusades to Quebec* (Montréal, 1949): 16, he was the Grand Master's ambassador to the king of France.
140. La Roncière, *Histoire*, 604ff.
141. L. Deschamps, *Un colonisateur au temps de Richelieu. Isaac de Razilly* (Paris, 1887). See also La Roncière, *Histoire*, 489ff. This memoir has been published in *Revue de géographie* 19 (1886): 374–83 and 453–64.
142. See DBF.
143. Several authors make this claim, but it has not yet been possible to find confirmation of it in the archives. See Guérin, *From the Crusades*, 69; Roy, "M. de Montmagny," 1: 111, and the reference he makes to L.E. Bois, *Le chevalier Noël Brulart de Sillery* (Québec, 1871). The only indication (but it is not altogether explicit) is in *MNF*, 3: 474: in a letter, the directors of the Company of New France speak of "our associate," in referring to Montmagny.
144. The popular revolts that accompanied the rise in taxes caused by this war have been studied by several historians.
145. See J. Favier, *Paris au XVe siècle* (Paris: Hachette diffusion, 1974, Collection "Nouvelle histoire de Paris"); there is a very instructive map on page 21: "La ville aux cent clochers."

146. See the lengthy citation in Chapter 3.
147. Even today the people of Malta will tell you outright that it was the Knights who made Malta and Valetta.
148. See a very interesting book, P. Matvejevitch, *Bréviaire méditerranéen*, trans. 1992 (Paris: Fayard, 1992).

Chapter 5

1. See F. Braudel, *La Méditerranée et le monde méditerranéen à l'époque de Philippe II*, 2 vols (Paris: A. Colin, 1966).
2. Braudel, *La Méditerranée*, 1: 227.
3. Acts of the Apostles, chapters 27 and 28. He spent the winter of 60–61 there, before resuming his journey to Rome. A bay named Saint Paul recalls this shipwreck; furthermore, several churches are consecrated to the memory of the apostle, whose cult is still very much alive on the island.
4. R.C. Harris, *Atlas historique du Canada*, vol. 1, "Des origines à 1800" (Montréal: PUM, 1987), plates 17 and 17A.
5. *MNF*, 3: 646. For the *Relations*, I used the edition prepared by L. Campeau, S.J., and published in the *MNF*: vol. 2, "Établissement à Québec (1614–1643)," which contains the *Relations* of 1633 and 1634 (Québec: PUL, 1979); vol. 3, "Fondation de la mission huronne (1635–1637)" (Québec: PUL, 1987); vol. 4 (1638–1640) (Québec: PUL, 1989), vol. 5 (1641–1643) (Québec: PUL, 1990); vol. 6 (1644–1646) (Québec: PUL, 1992). For the subsequent years I used R.G. Thwaites, *The Jesuit Relations and Allied Documents*, 73 vols (Cleveland: Burrows Bros, 1896–1901), (hereafter RJ).
6. Possibly Lake Saint Charles; though L. Campeau thinks that it is Lake Saint Joseph.
7. A very fine exhibition, "Suleiman the Magnificent," took place in Paris, in the Grand Palais, from 15 February to 14 March 1990 – a superbly illustrated catalogue.
8. See Chapter 4.
9. AOM, Arch. 58, fols. 312–312v. Letter from Montmagny to the Grand Master, 29 April 1650.
10. AN, AC, E 225, 6 May 1645.
11. *MNF*, 4: 207.
12. See Marion, *Dictionnaire des Institutions* entry for "gouverneur."
13. *MNF*, 4: 494. Note how Richelet, in his *Dictionnaire françois* defined the term moderator as "one who rules, governs and moderates [God is the supreme moderator in all things]."
14. *MNF*, 4: 496. "Royal prefect" – obviously a throw-back to Roman history and the "prefect" who administered a province of the empire.

15. See this chapter, n. 10.
16. See this chapter, n. 4.
17. B. Trigger and D. Jenness, among others.
18. M. Trudel, L. Campeau, and L.-P. Desrosiers, among others.
19. Even to the very end, e.g., the famous *bailli* of Suffren (1729–1788).
20. See La Roncière, *Histoire*, vol. 4; R. Lacour-Gayet, *La marine militaire sous Louis XIII et Louis XIV*, vol. 1, *Richelieu et Mazarin* (Paris: Champion, 1911).
21. See the catalogue cited in n. 24.
22. *DBF*, several pages about the Forbin family.
23. See Chapter 4 and the *DCB*.
24. They do not appear in La Roque, *Catalogue*. There are no proofs of nobility in the pertinent series either in Malta or in France. L. Campeau, who has examined all the documents relating to New France at this time, says nothing about the status of Brasdefer. Most Canadian historians assume that he belonged to the Order.
25. BN, DB, 130.
26. James Bradford?
27. The first "paper" mentioned in the post-mortem inventory of Jean de Brasdefer (24 November 1616) in AN, MC, LI, 120. Also see AN, Y, 124, fol. 191v. The dowry was 1,200 écus.
28. Richelet, *Dictionnaire françois*, said that *vivres*, used in connection with the army, meant victuals for the soldiers and all other army personnel.
29. AN, MC, CXXII, 1575, fol. 61.
30. See this chapter, n. 27.
31. *DCB*.
32. *MNF*, 3: 254.
33. Ibid.: 682.
34. Archives du séminaire de Québec (hereafter ASQ), fonds Faribault 5, 8, 9, 13, 27.
35. Ibid., doc. 17.
36. Ibid., doc. 19, for 20 April 1639; doc. 33 for 4 May 1642. Also note that in the collection "Paroisse de Québec" at the ASQ, in 1642 (perhaps at the moment of his departure from Canada) he appears among the benefactors of the church of Notre-Dame de la Recouvrance; he had given "a robe of beaver pelt with which we bought the two pieces of tapestry that surround the altar."
37. AOM, Arch. 461, fol. 10. Note that he does not appear in La Rocque's catalogue. See this chapter, n. 24.
38. See *DCB*, article about Brehaut [sic] Delisle, Achille (Antoine-Louis?) and its references.

39. See BN, DB, 131; also see N.C.B. de Bréhant, *Généalogie de la maison de Bréhant* (Paris, 1867).

40. Official letter from the pope, or apostolic letter, in the form of a brief, which is to say that it concerns an individual affair of private concern. AOM, Arch. 464, fols. 262v, 263. The caravan completed by the chevalier is mentioned here.

41. BN, DB 131, fol. 105; he was in command of the frigate *Marie du Croizic.*

42. In the genealogy contained both in the MSS of the BN and in the history of the Bréhant de Lisle family (see this chapter, n. 39), Antoine-Louis appears as his father's successor. He married (date uncertain) Marie Le Brun, by whom he had five children. Note that his older brother died without heirs.

43. *MNF,* 3: 484. He does not appear in La Rocque's catalogue. See this chapter, n. 24. Searches in the Cabinet des Titres also failed to turn up anything.

44. *MNF,* 3: 78, 79.

45. Ibid.: 82.

46. Le Picart, Hennequin, and Avrillot.

47. See several articles in the *DBF.*

48. See L.E. Bois, *Études et recherches biographiques sur le chevalier Noël Brulart de Sillery* (Québec, 1855).

49. *DBF.*

50. AN, MC, LI, 190.

51. See *MNF,* 2: 558ff and 3: 835, biographical entry.

52. E. Mannier, *Les commanderies du grand prieuré de France* (Brionne: Gérard Montfort, 1987), 319–20.

53. See this chapter, n. 48; also *MNF,* 3: 480ff and 514ff.

54. M. Trudel, *Histoire de la Nouvelle-France,* tome III, *La seigneurie des Cent-Associés,* vol. 1, *Les événements,* 142–3 (Montréal: Fides, 1979); also vol. 2, *La société* (1983); tome II, *Le comptoir (1604–1627)* (1963). Hereafter cited: M.T., x (for the tome) and x (for the volume, if necessary).

55. See Chapter 9.

56. AN, AC, E 225.

57. *Édits, ordonnances royaux, déclarations et arrêts du conseil d'État du roi concernant le Canada,* 3 vols (Québec, 1854–6) 1: 7. (Hereafter *E.O.*)

58. *DCB.*

59. M.T., III, 2: 15–6.

60. The first Frenchman to have become established definitively in Québec. See *DCB.*

61. *DCB.*

62. It is impossible to give precise numbers for this period. See A. Delâge, *Le pays renversé: Amérindiens et Européens du Nord-Est – 1600–1664* (Montréal: Boréal, 1991) 54–5, and the *Atlas historique du Canada,* 1: plate 18.

63. M.T., III, 1: 144.
64. Though it must be remarked that some of the priests and brothers were working in Huronia. See *MNF,* 3: 305–6.
65. See D. Deslandres, "Le modèle français d'intégration socio-religieuse, 1600–1650: Les missions intérieures et les premières missions canadiennes" (PhD thesis, University of Montréal, 1991).
66. Franciscan friars, reformed in the sixteenth century.
67. *DCB.*
68. Father Gabriel Sagard, *Le Grand Voyage au pays des Hurons ... avec un dictionnaire de la langue huronne* (Paris, 1632).
69. G. Sagard, *Histoire du Canada et voyages que les Frères Mineurs Récollets y ont faicts pour la Conversion des Infidèles* (Paris, 1636).
70. See J. Lacouture, *Jésuites,* vol. 1, "Les conquérants" (Paris: Seuil, 1991).
71. See the thesis cited in this chapter, n. 65. It has an interesting appendix: "Liste des auteurs d'Indipetae de la province de France et la destination qu'ils demandaient." (Indipetae: requests to be sent to America.)
72. See Chapter 6.
73. See A. Beaulieu, *Convertir les fils de Caïn: Jésuites et Amérindiens nomades en Nouvelle-France 1632–1642* (Québec: Nuit Blanche Éditeur, 1990).
74. M.T., III, 2: 422.
75. *DCB.*
76. Ibid.
77. Ibid.
78. Ibid.
79. Ibid.
80. M.T., III, 2: 95.
81. *DCB* and M.T., III, 2: 260.
82. *MNF,* 3: 186ff.
83. Ibid.
84. Richelet, *Dictionnaire françois,* gave leste as "propre en habits." No doubt his lieutenant was there, plus some military officers, and the Repentignys.
85. *MNF,* 3: 229.
86. Ibid., 3: 281.
87. Ibid., 3: 282ff.
88. In fact, they had barely enough for their own defence.
89. See Furetière's *Dictionnaire,* "On dit aussi qu'un esprit est massif quand il est pesant, grossier et stupide."
90. Note that the choice of Adam was not one of the best – a very rare occurrence for the Jesuits sent to Canada. This man, though highly intelligent, was periodically afflicted by bouts of paranoia. Vimont obtained his recall in 1641. See *MNF,* 2: 799.

91. The parish of Saint-Gervais.
92. *DCB*. See also this chapter, n. 97.
93. *DCB*.
94. *MNF,* 2, biographical entry.
95. Ibid.
96. They had come as domestics in 1633; later they asked to enter the Society. They had begun their novitiate in France.
97. Pierre Chastelain, S.J., *Affectus amantis Christum Jesum seu exercitium erga Dominum Jesum pro tota hebdomeda* (auctore P. Pietro Chastelain, Parisiis, apud D. Bechet, 1648).
98. *MNF,* 3: 253.
99. See the *DCB* articles about them.
100. The word "gentlemen" used by the Jesuit does not imply a great and ancient nobility; the great-grandfather of Pierre Legardeur had been ennobled in 1510. See *Bulletin des recherches historiques* (1947): 167; one of the sons of the great-grandfather was *lieutenant criminel* to the *bailliage* and *siège presidial* of Caen, a minor position in the magistracy. Pierre and his brother Charles, who came to Canada, seem to have been sailors by profession.
101. *MNF,* 3: 190.
102. *DBF*.
103. *MNF,* 3: 250.
104. Ibid., 192.
105. A seigneurie close to Abbeville. This rent had been promised by the marquis in 1627, but its delivery had been delayed.
106. *MNF,* 3: 23–4.
107. Ibid., 191. Father Campeau does not think that this was Noël Brulart.
108. Ibid., 194.
109. Ibid., 52.
110. Ibid., 198.
111. Ibid.
112. "Marri" meant "faché" according to Richelet, *Dictionnaire françois*.
113. *MNF,* 3: 218–21.
114. Ibid., 3: 270.
115. Ibid., 3: 239.
116. "Pseudo-religious" for Le Jeune; today's ethnologists and historians of religion think differently.
117. *MNF,* 3: 269, 244. Le Jeune says "this devil or Manitou."
118. Ibid., 3: 208.
119. Ibid., 3: 305; see also 230, 291ff.
120. Ibid., 3: 128ff.

121. Frequent references in *MNF*, 3, of the admiral of the fleet, Charles Duplessis-Bochart, and commissioner Francois Derré de Gand, among others.
122. Ibid., 3: 238–9.
123. Ibid., 3: 205–6. The title of the chapter is "Of the Present State of New France, on the Great Saint Lawrence River."
124. See M.T., III, 130–1.
125. *MNF*, 3: 261.
126. Were these readers real or fictitious? This may simply have been a literary device.
127. *MNF*, 3: 251–2.
128. Ibid., 3: 255.
129. Ibid., 3: 266–7.
130. The first commission naming him to his post has not been found. In a document dated 15 January 1636 he is designated as "governor." See M.T., III, 1: 142. It is possible that he had already been chosen – at the end of 1635 – but that the official letters were, perhaps, issued to him later.
131. The first volumes of the *Relations*, and what Champlain and Sagard had published.
132. AN, AC, LI, 285.
133. *MNF*, 3: 151 n. 4.
134. Ibid., 3: 148–9.
135. Ibid., 249–50.
136. Ibid., 640–1.
137. It was later called the Richelieu River.
138. Montmagny had a map of the region made up by Jean Bourdon. See *MNF*, 3: 655 n. 29.

Chapter 6

1. *RJ*, 27: 272.
2. *DCB*, article about Jérôme Lalemant.
3. Io: great; Onont: mountain.
4. *RJ*, 27: 280.
5. *MNF*, 3: 657. Le Jeune went on: "I made Monsieur de Montmagny, our governor, laugh heartily when I communicated this letter to him" (the letter which contained these remarks).
6. *MNF*, 4: 307.
7. Lacking the correspondence, I am reduced to using indirect sources.
8. I should mention here a work which was brought to my attention shortly before I submitted the copy of my book to the editor. It is J. Axtell, *The*

Contest of Cultures in Colonial North America: The Invasion Within (New York: Oxford University Press, 1985) – a very interesting book, which helps us to comprehend, particularly from a cultural point of view, all that is represented by the encounter of two civilizations as different from each other as the European and the Amerindian. The first part of the book is devoted to New France in the seventeenth century.

9. AN, AC, E, 225, 6 May 1645.
10. *MNF*, 3: 77.
11. Ibid.
12. This name covers the tribes scattered through the east of Canada and having cultural – and above all linguistic – affinities. The French of Québec were in contact principally with the Montagnais, who lived along the north bank of the Saint Lawrence from Québec to Sept-Îles, and the Algonquin, established along the Ottawa River between Montréal and the Île aux Allumettes.
13. In the middle of the continent – more precisely, in the Great Lakes region – the languages sometimes called "Iroquoian" were predominant. The two principal families of tribes were the Iroquois and the Huron.
14. See, among others, L.P. Desrosiers, *Iroquoisie*, vol. 1 (Montréal: Fides, 1947), the only volume to have appeared.
15. A word used by the Jesuits; see for example *RJ*, 16: 52. There are also references to "contagious illnesses." See *RJ*, 25: 104, 106.
16. *MNF*, 3: 643.
17. Ibid., 3: 573–4.
18. Hence, a Montagnais.
19. *MNF*, 3: 648.
20. Ibid., 3: 657.
21. Ibid., 3: 650.
22. Ibid., 3: 658–9.
23. Neither Champlain nor Montmagny believed that firearms should be distributed to the Amerindian allies. See the ordinance of the latter, dated 9 July 1644, which forbade "the selling, giving, trading and exchanging of arquebuses, pistols and other firearms, powder and lead, with savages, whether Christian or non-Christian." P.G. Roy, *Ordonnances, commissions des gouverneurs et intendants de la Nouvelle-France, Compagnie des Cent-Associés, 1636–1706* (Beauceville, L'Eclaireur, 1924), 1: 5–6.
24. *MNF*, 3: 660–1.
25. Ibid., 3: 668.
26. A word that appears frequently in the *Relations*.
27. *MNF*, 4: 82–3.
28. Ibid., 4: 279.

29. Ibid., 4: 567.
30. Ibid., 4: 266–7.
31. Ibid., 4: 269–70.
32. Ibid., 4: 581–2.
33. Ibid., 4: 556.
34. Ibid., 4: 268.
35. Ibid., 4: 371.
36. Ibid., 4: 284.
37. In the eastern part of Canada the native peoples were nomads: the Algonquin, who came to the French posts (Tadoussac, Québec, and Trois-Rivières) to sell furs and to buy European goods. "Reducing" them meant encouraging them to come and settle in villages where they would learn to live as Europeans. The Huron were a different case; they were semi-sedentary, which is to say that they lived ten or fifteen years in one place and then, when the returns from their farming fell off, went to live elsewhere. They were no longer nomads. But even with them the Jesuits established a sort of "reduction," with the village of Sainte-Marie that, by means of the services that it offered and the development of European techniques, could offer them more stability and improve their quality of life, as well as making them more open to the reception of the gospel.
38. *MNF,* 3: 669.
39. *MNF,* 4: 174. For Father Le Mercier see *DBF;* he drew up the *Relation* of the Hurons in 1637 and 1638.
40. Desrosiers, *Iroquoisie,* 35.
41. *DCB.*
42. *MNF,* 4: 208, 455–457.
43. Ibid., 4: 564.
44. Ibid., 4: 750.
45. Ibid., 4: 568.
46. Ibid. The title of Chapter 3 is as follows: "The Savages Reassemble at St. Joseph after the Epidemic, Elect Several Captains, and Show Their Zeal for the Faith."
47. See A. Jamet, *Les Annales de l'Hôtel-Dieu de Québec, 1636–1716* (Québec: Hôtel-Dieu, 1939), 29; and H.R. Casgrain, *Histoire de l'Hôtel-Dieu de Québec* (Québec, 1878), 102 and passim.
48. *MNF,* 3: 475.
49. Ibid., 3: 366.
50. Ibid., 3: 234–5.
51. Ibid., 4: 656.
52. See a short summary in R.C. Harris, ed., *Atlas historique du Canada,* (Montréal: PUM, 1987), 1: plate 35. B. Trigger, *Les enfants d'Aataensic: L'histoire du peuple huron* (Montréal: Libre Expression, 1991).

53. Trigger, *Les enfants d'Aataensic*, 568.
54. *MNF*, 4: 120.
55. Trigger, *Les enfants d'Aataensic*, 577.
56. See the works mentioned in this chapter n. 47.
57. *MNF*, 4: 351, 281–2.
58. Ibid., 4: 627–8.
59. *DCB*.
60. *MNF*, 3: 587.
61. *DCB*.
62. *MNF*, 3: 562.
63. Cited in N.E. Dionne, *Le séminaire de Notre-Dame des Anges* (Montréal, 1890), 76.
64. Richelet, *Dictionnaire françois*; it meant the second meaning of séminaire, which was "a sort of college where the Canons of Saint Augustine boarded lodgers and taught school."
65. *MNF*, 4: 304.
66. Ibid., 4: 610–11.
67. Ibid., 4: 612
68. Ibid., 4: 623.
69. Ibid., 4: 90.
70. Ibid., 4: 116.
71. Ibid., 4: 123.
72. Ibid., 4: 125.
73. Ibid., 4: 333.
74. Ibid., 4: 554–5.
75. Ibid., 4: 364.
76. Ibid., 4: 364 n. 8, commentary of L. Campeau.
77. *MNF*, 3: 529 n. 12.
78. Ibid., 3: n. 5: "The seminaries for children have already had a beginning. Guillaume Huboust and his wife Marie Rollet are keeping some little girls." See *DCB* article about Marie Rollet.
79. *MNF*, 3: 531.
80. *DCB*, article about J.R. Poncet de la Rivière.
81. There is an abundant literature on these two women. See *DCB* articles about M.-M. de Chauvigny de La Peltrie, and Marie Guyart (whose religious name was Marie de l'Incarnation). See also F. Deroy-Pineau, *Marie de l'Incarnation, femme d'affaires, mystique, mère de la Nouvelle-France* (Paris: Laffont, 1989) and *Madeleine de La Peltrie: amazone du nouveau monde (Alençon 1603–Québec 1671)* (Montréal: Bellarmin, 1992).
82. *MNF*, 4: 280.
83. Ibid., 4: 636–7.

84. Richelet, *Dictionnaire françois*, civility was "a discipline which teaches how to do and say only things that are respectable and appropriate in daily life."
85. *MNF*, 3: 572.
86. See *DCB* article about Champlain, and Desrosiers, *Iroquoisie*.
87. *DCB*.
88. Ibid.
89. Desrosiers, *Iroquoisie*, 121. See 125–6 for the letter to Richelieu.
90. *DCB*.
91. Desrosiers, *Iroquoisie*, 141.
92. Ibid., 171.
93. Ibid., 149.
94. *MNF*, 3: 340–1.
95. Ibid., 3: 278–9.
96. Desrosiers, *Iroquoisie*, 171.
97. *MNF*, 3: 662–3.
98. Ibid., 4: 387. See *DCB* article about Taratouan.
99. Ibid., 4: 220, 387.
100. Ibid., 404; Desrosiers, *Iroquoisie*, 202.
101. Desrosiers, *Iroquoisie*, 193–4.
102. *MNF*, 4: 291.
103. Ibid., 4: 653; see also Desrosiers, *Iroquoisie*, 206–7.
104. Desrosiers, *Iroquoisie*, 211.
105. Ibid.
106. Ibid., 297.
107. Ibid., 212–3 and *MNF*, 5: 124–5.
108. Desrosiers, *Iroquoisie*, 214–5; *MNF*, 5: 129–30.
109. Desrosiers, *Iroquoisie*, 219.
110. *MNF*, 3: 42, 44–5.
111. Ibid., 3: 459.
112. Desrosiers, *Iroquoisie*, 239.
113. Ibid., 229.
114. See Chapter 7.
115. Desrosiers, *Iroquoisie*, 243.
116. Ibid., 244.
117. See *MNF*, 3: 378–9, 766–7, 780–1; *RJ*, 26: 180–1; Desrosiers, *Iroquoisie*, 244–5.
118. *DCB*; see also the biographical entry in *MNF*, 4.
119. Desrosiers, *Iroquoisie*, 247–8.
120. *MNF*, 5: 277.
121. Desrosiers, *Iroquoisie*, 248–9.

122. *MNF*, 5: 469.
123. Ibid., 5: 471. The term used here is "larron," "one who steals and makes away with another's goods without being seen." Richelet, *Dictionnaire françois*.
124. *RJ*, 26: 174.
125. *MNF*, 5: 758; Desrosiers, *Iroquoisie*, 265.
126. *MNF*, 5: 758.
127. Ibid., 5: 759–60.
128. Ibid., 5: 764–5.
129. Ibid.
130. Ibid., 5: 764.
131. Ibid., 5: 642.
132. Desrosiers, *Iroquoisie*, 280. He suggests that they were experiencing some difficulties in their relations with their Dutch allies.
133. *RJ*, 26: 34–5.
134. Desrosiers, *Iroquoisie*, 281–2.
135. *DCB*.
136. *RJ*, 26: 44–5.
137. Ibid., 26: 42–3; Desrosiers, *Iroquoisie*, 288–9.
138. *RJ*, 26: 58.
139. *Le Journal des jésuites* (hereafter *JJ*), published by C.H. Laverdière and H.R. Casgrain (Montréal, 1892), 9.
140. *RJ*, 27: 220–1.
141. Ibid., 28: 228–9.
142. Desrosiers, *Iroquoisie*, 301.
143. Ibid., 304.
144. *RJ*, 28: 248–9. See also *DCB*.
145. Desrosiers, *Iroquoisie*, 313.
146. Ibid., 315. One of the ambassadors declared that she "was all ready to be delivered, and that if the Huron entered into peace, she would return with them if she wished; that if not, they would keep her as a child raised by the hand of the French, to prepare their food when they [the French] returned to their country."
147. Desrosiers, *Iroquoisie*, 317.
148. Ibid.
149. Ibid.
150. The Mohawk tribe was, in fact, the tribe situated closest to the territories inhabited by the French.
151. *JJ*, 26–29, mentioned on 8 January 1646.
152. Desrosiers, *Iroquoisie*, 323; the author asks himself several questions, for which he can find no response.

153. *MNF*, 5: 655–6. Five chapters out of fourteen in the *Relation* for this year.
154. Ibid., 5: 655 n. 2.
155. Ibid., 5:663.
156. Ibid., 5: 691–2.
157. Ibid., 5: 679–80. The whole chapter deals with this subject.
158. *RJ*, 26: 74.
159. H.R. Casgrain, *Histoire de l'Hôtel-Dieu*, 120–1.
160. *MNF*, 5: 727.
161. Ibid., 5: 725–6, 733–4.
162. A tribe living on the Connecticut River, allied to the Mohawk. See *MNF*, 5: 55, 81.
163. *MNF*, 5: 113.
164. *RJ*, 26: 18–9.
165. It has been reproduced in Daveluy, La société de Notre-Dame. The title is "Les veritables motifs de Messieurs et Dames de la Societe de Nostre Dame de Monreal pour la conversion des Sauvages en la nouvelle France."
166. *MNF*, 5: 441–2.
167. Ibid., 5: 100–01.
168. Ibid., 5: 428.
169. Ibid., 5: 655 n. 4.
170. Deroy-Pineau, *Madeleine de La Peltrie*.
171. *MNF*, 5: 651–2.
172. Ibid., 5: 431.
173. Ibid., 5: 356, 434–5.
174. Ibid., 5: 654.
175. Ibid., 5: 411.
176. Ibid., 5: 153–4.
177. For the place he occupies in the *Relations*, see *RJ*, vols 25–36 passim.
178. *RJ*, 28: 270.
179. Ibid., 28: 290.
180. Ibid., 28: 290–1.
181. Ibid., 30: 226–7.
182. Richelet, *Dictionnaire françois*, "conjure" meant "to conspire, to decide on something fatal to some person. To cabal, and join together against someone."
183. Did the Mohawk attribute the cause of their misfortunes that summer (sickness, for example) to the presence of the coffer? Or was this merely a pretext for their change of policy?
184. *RJ*, 31: 110–11.
185. Ibid., 31: 116.
186. Ibid., 30: 228, 230.

187. Ibid., 33: 80–1.
188. Ibid., 30: 230.
189. *MNF*, 5: 835, biographical entry. See also *DCB*, article on Simon Pieskaret, Algonquin chief of the Pessoua.
190. *RJ*, 31: 170.
191. Ibid., 32: 22.
192. Ibid., 33: 70, 72.
193. Ibid., 33: 124.
194. Ibid., 33: 126–7.
195. Trigger, *Les enfants d'Aataensic*, 735.
196. *RJ*, 32: 178.
197. Ibid., 32: 184.
198. Ibid., 32: 186.
199. Trigger, *Les enfants d'Aataensic*, 739–40.
200. *RJ*, 33: 258.
201. Trigger, *Les enfants d'Aataensic*, 737–8.
202. Ibid., 740.
203. *RJ*, 32: 172.
204. Trigger, *Les enfants d'Aataensic*, 742.
205. *RJ*, 32: 178.
206. Ibid., 28: 266.
207. Ibid., 28: 268–9.
208. Ibid., 30: 218.
209. Ibid., 31: 138–9.
210. Ibid., 31: 208, *RJ*, 32: 282–3.
211. Ibid., 32: 286.
212. Ibid.
213. Ibid., 32: 204.
214. Ibid., 31: 164.
215. *DBF*, article about Marie Guénet, reference to Jeanne de Sainte-Marie, who arrived in 1640.
216. Casgrain, *Histoire de l'Hôtel-Dieu*, 149.
217. *DCB*.
218. *RJ*, 32: 166, 212–3.
219. Ibid., 32: 214.
220. Ibid., 32: 232.
221. See *DCB*. In principle, each Ursuline convent had its own constitution; she had some drawn up for the Québec convent, adapted to the realities of New France.
222. Charlevoix suggests that Montmagny had some reservations about Father Jogues: "Nevertheless, whatever repugnance he felt in exposing to the caprices of a fickle people a man who had been so much abused by

them that they could never be regarded favourably, he agreed to keep his promise." P. de Charlevoix, SJ, *Histoire et description générale de la Nouvelle-France* (Paris, 1744, reprint ed., 1976), 269–70.

223. Charlevoix, *Histoire et description*, 233, 246–7.
224. *Collection de manuscrits relatifs à l'histoire de la Nouvelle-France*, vol. 1 (Québec, 1883), 112–13. Here are the words of Champlain: "All that is needed is a hundred and twenty men, lightly armed to escape the arrows, together with two or three thousand warriors at our side; in a year we could gain absolute mastery of all these people, bringing them the necessary order; and that will increase the practice of religion and an incredible commerce." At the end of the text someone has put the date 15 August 1635; the historians whose works I have been able to consult place the date at 1633.
225. *Rapport des Archives de la province de Québec pour 1930–1931*, 41–2.

Chapter 7

1.   AN, AC, E, 225.
2.   *MNF*, 4: 265.
3.   BN, Carrés d'Hozier 345, 10 March 1642.
4.   The *Compagnie des Îles d'Amérique*, see Chapter 9.
5.   J.B. Du Tertre, *Histoire générale des Antilles habitées par les Français*, 3 vols (Paris: Édition et Diffusion de la Culture Antillaise, reprinted 1978), 1: 139.
6.   *MNF*, 5: 643.
7.   Ibid., 5: 380.
8.   Ibid., 3: 2534.
9.   "Qui peuvent avoir connaissance de": who have the necessary competence.
10.   *RJ*, 28: 170.
11.   L. Campeau, *Les Cent-Associés et le peuplement de la Nouvelle-France (1633–1663)* (Montréal: Bellarmin, 1974), 31.
12.   *JJ*, 62.
13.   *Ordonnances, commissions des gouverneurs et intendans de la Nouvelle-France Compagnie des Cent-Associés 1636–1706* (Beauceville: L'Éclaireur, 1924), 1: 8–9.
14.   M.T., III, 2: 258.
15.   *JJ*, 23. See the cases (eight in Québec during Montmagny's time there) cited in M. T., III, 2: 453–455, and an interesting analysis, 426. These cases, which were the only ones he found, do not appear to him to be an exhaustive list. Chevalet: "a type of wooden horse with a sloping back, on

which soldiers in garrison are set when they have committed some fault, while attaching cannon balls or some such things to their feet." Richelet, *Dictionnaire françois*.

16. *JJ*, 23, 106.
17. See this chapter, n. 8.
18. *DCB*.
19. M.T., II, 344–5, 10 March 1626.
20. *DCB*.
21. M.T., III, 2: 151–2.
22. M.T., III, 2: 98.
23. 15 January 1635, P.G. Roy, *Inventaire des concessions en fief et seigneurie, fois et hommages et aveux et dénombrements conservés aux Archives de la Province de Québec* (Beauceville, 1927–1929), 1: 50 (hereafter *ICFS*).
24. Ibid., 141, 160.
25. Ibid., 142–3.
26. Ibid., 155.
27. Ibid., 180–1.
28. *MNF*, 4: 16–7.
29. Ibid., 4: 199.
30. *ICFS*, 1: 175.
31. Ibid., 1: 230, 234.
32. Ibid., 1: 238.
33. Ibid., 1: 269.
34. Ibid., 1: 233, 245.
35. L. Lavallée, *La Prairie en Nouvelle-France, 1647–1760* (Montréal: McGill-Queen's, 1993), 50.
36. *ICFS*, 1: .228.
37. *MNF*, 4: 16–7.
38. Ibid., 4: 254–5.
39. *JJ*, 54.
40. A. Cambray, *Robert Giffard, premier seigneur de Beauport et les origines de la Nouvelle-France* (Cap de la Madeleine, 1932), 73–4.
41. M. Trudel, *Les débuts du régime seigneurial au Canada* (Montréal: Fides, 1974), 134.
42. M.T., III, 2: 20.
43. Trudel, *Les débuts*, 138.
44. Ibid., 94–5.
45. Does this mean a farm, or a half-and-half sharing (métayage) between the proprietor and the tenants?
46. Trudel, *Les débuts*, 116.
47. *MNF*, III, 252.

48. *ICFS*, 1: 270.
49. Ibid., 1: 271.
50. *MNF*, III, 224.
51. Ibid., 251–2.
52. See the very fine study of A. Charbonneau, Y. Desloges, M. Lafrance, *Québec, ville fortifiée du XVIIe au XIXe siècle* (Québec: Edition du Pélican, 1982), especially 22–24, 331–334. There is a very instructive illustration, "Reconstitution du plan rayonnant de Québec, 1636 et 1644," 332.
53. Ibid., 331.
54. See Q. Hughes, *The Building of Malta, 1530–1795* (Malta: Progress Press, 1986).
55. Richelet, *Dictionnaire françois*, defined "roture" as describing heritages which are not held nobly but on payment of *cens* and rent and other common duties.
56. Trudel, *Les débuts*, 85 n. 17.
57. Campeau, *Les Cent-Associés*, 21.
58. Trudel, *Les débuts*, 81.
59. *DCB*.
60. *MNF*, 4: 204, 456–7.
61. Campeau, *Les Cent-Associés*, 23.
62. Trudel, *Les débuts*, 235.
63. Campeau, *Les Cent-Associés*, 47.
64. Richelet, *Dictionnaire françois*.
65. Campeau, *Les Cent-Associés*, 48–9.
66. *JJ*, 8.
67. *ICFS*, 201.
68. *JJ*, 12.
69. *ICFS*, 201–2.
70. A. Béchard, *Histoire de l'Île-aux-Grues et des îles voisines* (Arthabaskville: Imprimerie de "La Bataille," 1902).
71. Campeau, *Les Cent-Associés*, 29; M.T., III, 2: 327; where it is said (without giving the date) that the cattle were worth 1,590 livres.
72. *JJ*, 60.
73. Trudel, *Les débuts*, 104 n. 4.
74. *ICFS*, 202.
75. This is the second sense of the word "mortmain."
76. AN, MC, LI, 241.
77. Trudel, *Les débuts*, 140.
78. *Ordonnances, commissions*, 1: 1.
79. *MNF*, 4: 75–6.
80. Not only for the sick, but for the nuns and the employees.

81. Richelet, *Dictionnaire françois*, "hops" was "a sort of herb flourishing in August and September, and which had the virtue of purifying and refreshing the blood."
82. *Ordonnances, commissions*, 1: 1–2.
83. Ibid., 1: 8–9. He did not hesitate, when necessary, to pass laws to protect lands under cultivation – already noted is the ordinance which he published to protect sown fields from animals.
84. M.T., III, 1: 231.
85. *MNF*, 3: 249–50.
86. Ibid., 3: 260–1.
87. Ibid., 3: 642.
88. For example, in the dress, or in the ceremony of profession. See Chapter 9.
89. See M. Buhagiar, *The Iconography of the Maltese Islands, 1400–1900* (Valletta: Progress Press, 1987). All the arts, and particularly painting, were profoundly influenced by Italian artists in the sixteenth and seventeenth centuries.
90. *MNF*, 4: 632.
91. Gospel of John, 13: 2–15.
92. A feast which falls on the Thursday following Trinity Sunday; in 1646, 31 May.
93. *JJ*, 47, 31 May 1646.
94. Poele: the canopy under which the Blessed Sacrament was carried to the sick and in processions. *Dictionnaire de l'Académie françoise.*
95. *MNF*, 4: 85.
96. Ibid., 3: 533–4.
97. Ibid., 3: 534–5.
98. P.G. Roy, *La ville de Québec sous le Régime français* (Québec: R. Paradis, 1930), 1: 83.
99. That is to say, lit by candles.
100. Richelet, *Dictionnaire françois*, "serpenteau" was "a sort of flying firework which snaked around in the air." And he added: "Anyone wishing to see beautiful and agreeable *serpenteaux* needed only to go to see the Saint John's fires which were lit every year in Paris on the Place de la Grève." The Place de la Grève was situated close to the hôtel where Montmagny was born.
101. Furetière, *Dictionnaire universel*, a "fusée" was "a piece of firework which rose into the air and which was shot off for amusement during public celebrations. There were flying fusées and running fusées ... A fusée of stars was one which had a number of balls of gunpowder that when they caught fire resembled stars. A fusée of serpenteaux is a large fusée which contains a number of little ones.

102. Ibid., trompe, in architectural terms, is a sort of vault very cunningly fashioned, the crown of which is in the air and seemingly supported by nothing.
103. Probably Jacques Gourdeau de Beaulieu; see *DCB* article about Eléanore de Grandmaison.
104. *JJ*, 38, and 80 for 1647.
105. The Order of Saint John of Jerusalem.
106. *JJ*, 53–4.
107. Ibid., 60–1.
108. *MNF,* 4: 83. He had been canonized in 1622, the same year as Saint Ignatius.
109. *JJ*, 16.
110. Ibid., 96.
111. Every 100 years to start with, then every twenty-five years.
112. *JJ*, 18–19.
113. From the purse of the *Communauté des Habitants*, it seems. See a similar gift, *JJ*, 77, "at the beginning of this month [February 1647] Monsieur the Governor gave me an order to receive a hundred livres at the store, to be employed in good works."
114. *JJ*, 22.
115. *MNF*, 4: 127.
116. R. Laurentin, *Le voeu de Louis XIII: Passé ou avenir de la France* (Paris: F.-X. Guibert 1988), passim.
117. *MNF,* 4: 266–7.
118. Furetière, *Dictionnaire universel.*
119. *MNF*, 3: 652–3.
120. Ibid., 4: 270; see also passim in *JJ.*
121. *JJ*, 20, Christmas, 1645.
122. See Chapter 3.
123. De Rochemonteix, *Un collège des jésuites*, 1: 216.
124. Which can be translated as "the royal cortège" or "The triumphal procession of royalty."
125. First king of Jerusalem, in 1099, at the time of the First Crusade.
126. A Muslim amazon loved by a crusader.
127. See Chapter 6, n. 33.
128. *JJ*, 75.
129. Ibid., 166. The reference is to the *Scide* [sic] of Corneille.
130. Jamet, *Les Annales de l'Hôtel-Dieu*, 19.
131. *DCB*, article about Robert Giffard. His daughter, Marie-Françoise, entered the community of the hospital sisters; as a dowry he gave a quarter of the seigneurie of Saint-Gabriel.
132. Jamet, *Les Annales de l'Hôtel-Dieu*, 70.

133. G. Oury, ed., *Marie de l'Incarnation, Ursuline (1599–1672), Correspondance* (Solesmes, Abbaye Saint-Pierre, 1971), 168.
134. Ibid., 224.
135. See *MNF*, 5: 827–8 for a short biography. See also Daveluy, *La société de Notre-Dame de Montréal* (Montréal: Fides, 1965), 95–6.
136. Pierre Chevrier, baron of Fancamp, *MNF*, 5: 103.
137. G. Lanctot, *Montréal sous Maisonneuve, 1642–1665* (Montréal: Beauchemin, 1966), 243–4.
138. He was captain of the expedition before becoming governor of Montréal.
139. The same man who had housed the nuns of the Hôtel-Dieu. See *DCB*.
140. M. Trudel, *Initiation à la Nouvelle-France* (Montréal: Holt, Rinehart and Winston, 1968), 56.
141. *MNF*, 5: 447.
142. Jamet, *Les Annales de l'Hôtel-Dieu*, 36.
143. Ibid.
144. This was 15 October, *MNF*, 5: 443.
145. G. Lanctot, *Montréal*, 252.
146. *MNF*, 5: 443–4.
147. L.-P. Desrosiers, *Paul de Chomedey, sieur de Maisonneuve* (Montréal: Fides, [1967]), 50.
148. *DCB*, article about Chomedey de Maisonneuve.
149. G. Lanctot, *Montréal*, 50.
150. See Campeau, *Les Cent-Associés*; M.T., III, 1: 55–6.
151. The *Relation* of 1636, *RJ*, 9: 168–9, mentioned that "some persons with an eye to their business" sent over to France pieces of wood prepared by them. Trudel thinks that this refers in the first place to Robert Giffard, M.T., III, 2: 144.
152. M.T., III, 1: 144.
153. Ibid., 1: 151–2.
154. Ibid., 1: 164.
155. L. Campeau, *Les finances publiques de la Nouvelle-France sous les Cent-Associés, 1632–1665* (Montréal: Bellarmin, 1975), 192.
156. *RJ*, 23: 268.
157. M.T., III, 1: 167.
158. *JJ*, 3.
159. See *DCB*.
160. M.T., III, 1: 170.
161. Campeau, *Les Cent-Associés*.
162. It exacted a symbolic rent of 1,000 beaver pelts.
163. M.T., III, 1: 171.

164. Campeau, *Les Cent-Associés*, 68–9.
165. Ibid., 65.
166. Campeau, *Les Cent-Associés*,71.
167. Ibid., 77, 80.
168. Ibid., 77.
169. Note, for the autumn of 1646, the shipwreck mentioned in *JJ*, 88: "This same day (21 November 1646) the confirmed news arrived of the worst disaster that has yet befallen Canada, namely the loss or break-up of the brigantine which was going from Québec to Trois-Rivières, in which was a good part of what was necessary for the store and the inhabitants of Trois-Rivières; we lost a great deal there, but the principal loss was of 9 men."
170. *RJ*, 27: 88.
171. *Ordonnances, commissions*, 6.
172. Ibid., 7.
173. *JJ*, 13.
174. Posted at Québec on 26 November. *JJ*, 15.
175. *Ordonnances, commissions*, 6–7.
176. Campeau, *Les Cent-Associés*, 77.
177. *JJ*, 13.
178. Ibid., 91.
179. Ibid., 90.
180. *Ordonnances, commissions*, 7.
181. *JJ*, 30–1.
182. *DCB*.
183. See *DCB* article about Louis Maheut (born in 1650), René's son.
184. *DCB*.
185. Campeau, *Les Cent-Associés*, 79.
186. M.T., III, 2: 299–300.
187. *JJ*, 67.
188. Campeau, *Les Cent-Associés*, 82.
189. M.T., III, 1: 188.
190. Campeau, *Les Cent-Associés*, 83–4.
191. *JJ*, 90.
192. Ibid., 92.
193. Ibid., 93.
194. Ibid., 95.
195. Campeau, *Les Cent-Associés*, 88.
196. *JJ*, 90. Trudel sees these "habitants" as those of the *Communauté des Habitants*, M.T., III, 2: 324.
197. F. Dollier de Casson, *Histoire du Montréal, 1642–1672*, New edition, M. Trudel and M. Baboyant (Ville Lasalle, QC: Hurtubise HMH, 1992)

198. Charlevoix, *Histoire et description*, 282.

Chapter 8

1. *JJ*, 115.
2. *DCB*. He returned to New France in the summer of 1646, only to leave again at once.
3. *JJ*, 95, 21 October 1647.
4. RJ, 32: 130.
5. It would be interesting to know to what the author was referring: quitting a post that he greatly loved? Did it displease him to leave his seigneurie? We shall never know.
6. *DCB*.
7. See this chapter, n. 10.
8. *JJ*, 117.
9. M. Laugaa, ed., *Voyage dans la Lune (L'Autre Monde ou les Empires de la Lune)* (Paris: Garnier-Flammarion, 1970), 10. The extract is found on page 34.
10. M.T., III, 192–3.
11. François de Chavigny de Berchereau, Robert Giffard, and Jean-Paul Godefroy.
12. *DCB*
13. *JJ*, 116.
14. Ibid., 111.
15. *DCB*, article about Louis d'Ailleboust.
16. The first birth in an immigrant family took place on 21 November 1648. See Y. Landry, ed., *Pour le Christ et le roi: La vie au temps des premiers Montréalais* (Montréal: Libre Expression, 1992), 311.
17. Ibid.
18. M.T., III, 2: 150, 189.
19. Ibid., 2: 152.
20. Ibid., 2: 81.
21. *JJ*, 44.
22. M.T., III, 2: 88–9, 146–7.
23. *JJ*, 101.
24. It is still in the main portal of the Château Frontenac, a large hotel built on the site at the end of the nineteenth century. (See illustration, 194)
25. R. Pichette, J.J. Lussier, "Armorial des Chevaliers de Malte français en terre d'Amérique," *Revue de l'Université d'Ottawa* (jan.–mar.) (1976): 42.
26. M.T., III, 2: 410.
27. Ibid., 2: 16–19.

28. Ibid., 2: 81.
29. Ibid., 2: 84.
30. First in dignity, following a tradition which goes back to the high Middle Ages.
31. M.T., III, 2: 410.
32. Ibid., 2: 430.
33. Ibid., 1: 174–5, and 2: 343–4.
34. *DCB*.
35. Ibid.
36. M.T., III, 1: 174–5, 2: 578–9.
37. Among the notables of 1648 the only ones who were not joined to this complex by family or marriage ties were Jean Bourdon, Charles Sevestre, and François Chauvigny de Berchereau.
38. *JJ*, 109–10.
39. M.T. III, 2: 419–20.
40. Ibid., 2: 425–6.
41. Ibid., 2: 506–7.
42. Ibid., 2: 405–6.
43. Ibid., 2: 416–17.
44. Angélique Faure (d. 1662) had been the wife of Claude de Bullion (1580–1640), who was one of Marie de' Medici's trusted servants; he also had Richelieu's confidence; in 1632 he was named *surintendant des finances*. He possessed a considerable fortune; it is claimed that in 1622 he enjoyed an annual income of 60,000 écus. *DBF*.
45. *RJ*, 32: 130–132.
46. See this chapter, nn. 68 and following.
47. M.T., III, 2: 409.
48. Richelet, *Dictionnaire français*, "ténèbres" was the divine office said in the Roman Church at four or five o'clock in the evening on Wednesday, Holy Thursday and Good Friday, to remind Christians that about two hours after Jesus Christ was crucified, darkness covered all the earth.
49. *JJ*, 105.
50. Ibid., 119.
51. Ibid., 107.
52. Ibid., 112.
53. Richelet, *Dictionnaire français*, catechism was instruction given on some point of the 'Religion.'
54. *JJ*, 101–2.
55. Ibid., 1067.
56. Richelet, *Dictionnaire français*.
57. *JJ*, 116.

58. *RJ*, 33: 48–9.
59. Ibid., 32: 126.
60. Ibid., 32: 146.
61. Ibid., 32: 224.
62. M.T., III, 2: 382.
63. Ibid., 2: 377–8.
64. *DCB*.
65. Ibid.
66. Ibid.
67. *RJ*, 32: 282. By "bars" the Jesuit here means courts of justice, and by "Louvres," the courts of sovereigns or princes.
68. 1634–1648.
·69. *RJ*, 33: 58: "Relation de ce qui s'est passé en la mission des Pères de la Compagnie de Jésus aux Hurons pays de la Nouvelle-France envoyée au P. Estienne Charlet, provincial ... ."
70. *RJ*, 32: 184.
71. Ibid., 32: 178.
72. Lake Huron.
73. *RJ*, 33: 253–4.
74. Ibid., 33: 257.
75. See Chapter 6.
76. *RJ*, 33: 230.
77. Ibid., 33: 234.
78. Ibid.
79. The position of Samuel de Champlain, founder of Québec and New France, was in certain respects very different from that of Montmagny. Through the years he was lieutenant to the lieutenant general or to the viceroy of Canada. After 1627, with the establishment of the Company, he was commandant at Québec; then, after 1629, but in actual fact from 1 March 1633, he was commandant of New France in the absence of Richelieu. Without the title, he exercised the function of lieutenant general and governor. As his health was declining, it was decided at the end of 1635, even before his death was known, to replace him. But in fact, as the key figure in the foundation of New France, he had a standing comparable to no other.
80. His friend, Henri Lebret, to whom he had entrusted its publication, decided to take out the passages that bothered his conscience. See Laugaa, *Voyage*; see this chapter, n. 9.
81. *Dictionnaire de l'Académie française*, "subtle, fine, slight."
82. F. Lachèvre, ed., *Les oeuvres libertines de Cyrano de Bergerac* (Geneva: Slatkine, 1968), 10. (Hereafter Lachèvre, ed., *Les oeuvres*).

83. Hercule de Rohan, duc de Montbazon, ca 1568–1654, lieutenant general and governor of the city of Paris and of the Île-de-France.
84. In Lachèvre, ed., *Les oeuvres*, Cyrano's text is preceded by a copious entry on his life and some facts about his family.
85. 1576–1643. See *DBF*.
86. It was a short phrase in his play *La mort d'Agrippine*: "Let us strike, there is the enemy" [hostie, or host, being used in the sense of the Latin word *hostis*]; it provoked an outcry in the audience.
87. A beam fell on his head.
88. See J. Delumeau, *Une histoire du paradis*, vol. 1, *Le jardin des délices* (Paris: Fayard, 1992).
89. Lachèvre, ed., *Les oeuvres*, 70.
90. Ibid., 11.
91. Ibid., 13.
92. Ibid., 13–14.
93. In fact, Aristotle had maintained that the sun was a perfect star. When, by means of his famous looking glass, Galileo discovered flaws on the sun's surface, it was thought in Roman circles that his instrument was defective, since it showed up impossible imperfections.
94. Lachèvre, ed., *Les oeuvres*, 14.
95. Ibid., 16.
96. Ibid., 15.
97. Ibid., 19.
98. Ibid.
99. Ibid., 100.
100. Ibid., 101.
101. R. Pintard, *Les libertins érudits de la première moitié du XVIIe siècle* (Paris: Boivin, 1943).
102. Claudius Ptolemy (ca 90–ca. 168), Greek astronomer, mathematician, geographer.
103. Tycho Brahe (1546–1601), Danish astronomer.
104. Lachèvre, ed., *Les oeuvres*, 11.
105. R. Ferland, *Les Relations des Jésuites: un art de la persuasion. Procédés de rhétorique et fonction conative dans les Relations du père Paul Le Jeune* (Québec: Les Éditions de la Huit, 1992), 13, n. 17.
106. Pintard, *Les libertins*, 138, 303.
107. Ibid., 357, 511.
108. One example, among others, drawn from *RJ*, 28: 223: "On the evening of the 8th [of August 1646] there appeared the boat of Captain Paullet and the flyboat of Monsieur de la Tour [Charles de Saint-Étienne de la Tour] who came to take refuge here; they arrived here the following morning; there was a salute for Sieur de la Tour and his children; he was lodged

at the fort and Monsieur the Governor gave him precedence on the first day. He [La Tour] accepted for the first day, and then refused it, as he should."

Chapter 9

1. La Roncière, *Histoire de la marine française* (Paris: Plon, 1920), 5: 226. See a more recent work: P. Pluchon, *Histoire de la colonisation française* (Paris: Fayard, 1991), 71, the beginning of a paragraph entitled "Richelieu colonial: grands projets, maigres bilans." Two works by N.M. Crouse are of interest on these questions: *The French Struggle for the West Indies, 1665–1713* (London: Frank Cass, 1996), and *French Pioneers in the West Indies 1624–1664* (New York: Octagon Books, 1977). Perhaps the reaction of Poincy, who will be studied next, should be connected to contemporary events in Acadia and the squabbles between Menou d'Aulnay and Saint-Étienne de La Tour (see *DCB*). I cannot tell if they had an effect on Poincy, but they help to show that a similar situation could have developed in the Antilles.
2. *DBF*.
3. Ibid.
4. A. Joyau, *Belain d'Esnambuc* (Paris: Bellenand, 1950), 15. Most of the information used here on the beginnings of Saint Christopher come from this study. See also a very short article on Belain in the *DBF*.
5. The temperature varies between 26 and 31 degrees Celsius. The Caribs had baptized it Liamauga, "the fertile island."
6. See the recent work on the Carib Indians by P. Boucher, *Cannibal Encounters, Europe and Island Caribs, 1492–1763* (Baltimore: Johns Hopkins University Press, 1992).
7. Sixty-eight square miles, about 176 square kilometres.
8. See C.C. Goslinga, *The Dutch in the Caribbean and on the Wild Coast, 1580–1680* (Gainesville: University of Florida Press, 1971).
9. Joyau, *Belain*, 53.
10. Ibid., 61; see 56 for the French *recrue*.
11. Ibid., 61–2.
12. See A. Martineau and L.P. May, *Trois siècles d'histoire antillaise* (Paris: Leroux, 1935), 20–1. At the beginning of this book there is a useful chronology of the colonial history of Saint Christopher.
13. Martineau and May, *Trois siècles*, 22.
14. Joyau, *Belain*, 112–118.
15. Ibid., 131.

16. *DBF*, article about Du Parquet (Jacques Dyel).
17. Joyau, *Belain*, 170–1.
18. P. Cultru, "Colonisation d'autrefois: Le commandeur de Poincy à Saint-Christophe," *Revue d'histoire des colonies françaises* (1915): 342. By his household is meant his officers, his workers, and his slaves.
19. Du Tertre, *Histoire générale*, 1: 540.
20. Ibid., 1: 139.
21. P. Cultru, "Colonisation d'autrefois," 353–4.
22. These genealogical details were given to me by Mrs. Gouyon-Guillaume, who is preparing a work on Commander de Poincy.
23. AN, MC, XCVI, 285bis and ter: "Titres de la famille de Messieurs Lonvilliers Poincy," item 17, acquisition, on 14 February 1550, of the seigneurie of Poincy, in exchange for two others.
24. La Roque, *Catalogue*.
25. AN, MC, XCVI, 285bis, item 39.
26. AOM, Arch. 445, fol. 326.
27. AN, MC, XCVI, 285bis, item 44.
28. M. Baudier, *Inventaire de l'histoire des Turcs* (Paris, 1631), 703–4.
29. AOM, Arch. 457, fols. 266–7.
30. It was not undertaken due to lack of time, because doubtless a careful survey of the notaries of Malta for the years 1610 on might discover some evidence of his privateering activity.
31. AOM, 459, on 21 March 1619. See also AN, MC, XCVI, 285bis, item 48. This was a commandery of little value, situated south of Paris, not far from Sens.
32. E. Mannier, *Les commanderies du Grand Prieuré de France* (Brionne: Gérard Montfort, 1987), 604–5.
33. AN, MM, 42, passim. In April 1634 he presided at the examination of the proofs of nobility of Charles Luillier; the Luilliers appear in the kinship of the Huaults.
34. AOM, Arch. 109, fol. 245.
35. AOM, Arch. 1549, correspondence 164, 4 January 1634. The Grand Master hoped that he would speak to the Cardinal of a certain affair (the controversial candidacy of the chevalier de Saint-Simon to a commandery).
36. M.T., III, 1: 428. The author adds that Poincy stayed briefly in Acadia (though he does not say when) before going to the Antilles.
37. La Roncière, *Histoire*, 5: 227–8. Note that the title of squadron chief was temporary at this time; it applied to a specific mission.
38. M. Vergé-Franceschi, *Marine et éducation sous l'Ancien Régime* (Paris: CNRS, 1991), 91.

39. La Roncière, *Histoire*, See P. Grillon, ed., *Papiers de Richelieu* (Paris: Pedone 1977), vol. 2 (1628), 273 with references also on 92, 93, 95, and vol. 3 (1629), 278.

40. *Lettres, instructions diplomatiques et papiers d'État du cardinal de Richelieu* (Paris, 1863), 5: 997.

41. *DBF.*

42. Cultru, "Colonisation d'autrefois," 301; BN, N.a.f. 9318, fol. 70.

43. Du Tertre, *Histoire générale*, 1: 138.

44. See Chapters 5–8.

45. La Roncière, *Histoire*, 4: 664, 20 February 1639.

46. E.C. Wilkie, "'Une bibliothèque bien fournie':The Earliest Known Caribbean Library," *Libraries and Culture* 25 (Spring 1990), 2: 171–193; see also D.F. Allen, "The Social and Religious World of a Knight of Malta in the Caribbean, ca. 1632–1660," in *Malta, A Case Study in International Currents* (Malta, 1991), 147–157.

47. Du Tertre, *Histoire générale*, 1: 159–60.

48. Ibid., 1: 145–6.

49. Ibid., 1: 165–6.

50. Ibid., 1: 172–3.

51. La Chesnaye-Desbois, *Dictionnaire*. For the gossip around this nomination see (in addition to the following note), *Mémoires de Nicolas Goulas* (Paris, 1879), 2: 216–7.

52. Tallement des Réaux, *Historiettes*, 2: 859.

53. S. Daney, *Histoire de la Martinique, depuis la colonisation jusqu'en 1815* (Fort-de-France 1963, original ed. 1846), 36; he does not give his source.

54. For what follows, see P. Cultru, art.cit., 322–3; and Du Tertre, *Histoire générale*, 1: 258–9.

55. BN, N.a.f. 9318, fol. 147v.

56. BN, *Mss frs*, 18593, at 22 August 1645.

57. Cultru, "Colonisation d'autrefois," 323–4.

58. *DBF*, Charles Houel (ca. 1615–1682), governor of Guadeloupe from 1643.

59. BN, Clairambault 951, fols. 95–6, 25 February 1647.

60. BN, N.a.f. 9318, fol. 153v.

61. BN, N.a.f. 9318, fol. 151v.

62. Du Tertre, *Histoire générale*, 1: 298.

63. AN, MC, XCVI, 285ter, item 89.

64. Du Tertre, *Histoire générale*, 1: 259.

65. See La Chesnaye-Desbois, *Dictionnaire*, Knight of Malta in 1605; military career in the service of the king of France until 1646, then the Grand Master's ambassador and Grand Prior of France.

66. AOM, Arch. 258, fol. 206–7.
67. See this chapter, n. 61.
68. The château close to Basseterre, the farm to Cayonne.
69. AOM, Arch. 2111, fol. 694v. In reality the false news arose from the fact that Thomas Warner, the governor of the English part of Saint Christopher, died on 10 March of that year. See *Dictionary of National Biography* (London, 1899).
70. Ibid.
71. AOM, Arch. 58, fols. 308–9. This is a signed letter.
72. AOM, Arch. 1554, 31 January 1650, letter from the Grand Master to Souvré.
73. Gabriel de La Haye Coulonces, who had entered the Order in 1637.
74. AOM, Arch. 258, fol. 209v; see also Arch. 1554, for the same date.
75. AOM, Arch. 1554.
76. AOM, Arch. 258, fols. 208–9.
77. "It is said figuratively that a man who has the office, the benefice, the succession of another, has his *dépouille* (spoils). The *dépouille* of a Knight of Malta belongs to the Order." *Dictionnaire de l'Académie française.*
78. AN, MC, LXXXVIII, 122bis, 24 May 1645. The complete bundle is filled with loans to individuals: the Grand Master was permitted to borrow up to 180,000 livres.
79. This referred to Crete, where the Venetians had been since the beginning of the thirteenth century – they had settled there shortly after the fourth Crusade (1202–1204). In 1645, the Turks began its conquest, which was only completed in 1669 with the fall of Candia [today Heraklion].
80. Poincy's sister, Charlotte de Lonvilliers, married Florimond des Vergers in 1592; see J. Petitjean-Roget, "Les titres de noblesse des Vergers de Sannois," *Annales des Antilles* (1958), 6: 66–88.
81. AOM, Arch. 58, fol. 312, letter of 29 April 1650.
82. Pichette and Lussier, "Armorial," 53; they speak of a priory, not a commandery, for Acadia.
83. AOM, Arch. 1554, letter to Souvré of 27 July 1650.
84. AOM, Arch. 59, fols. 315–16.
85. AOM, Arch. 1554, 13 June 1650.
86. AN, MC, XCVI, 285ter, item 90.
87. Ibid.
88. AOM, Arch. 1554.
89. Ibid.
90. There is a reference in the contract of 24 May; see the following note.
91. AN, MC, LXXXVIII, 286, 24 May 1651.

92. Of this sum of 120,000 livres, 10,000 were paid immediately; the rest was to be remitted in installments before the end of 1654.
93. AN, MC, XCVI, 285ter, item 92.
94. Du Tertre, *Histoire générale*, 1: 375. Poincy had to pay 90,000 livres to Thoisy, as damages for the expenses which the latter had to incur in coming to the Antilles. There was an exchange of letters, the tone of which was cordial. To all appearances, the affair was on the way to being settled.
95. AN, MC, LXXXVIII, 148, 13 March 1652, he rented out a lodging which had been placed at his disposal when another knight had left it; he was said to be living on the rue des Blancs Manteaux.
96. AN, MC, XX, 3 July 1651.
97. AN, MC, LI, 235, 16 March 1652.
98. AOM, Arch. 58, fol. 303v, letter of 29 April 1650.
99. AOM, Arch. 1554, 13 June 1650, letter to Delbene. See also Arch. 117, 16 May 1650, and Arch. 473, fol. 313, apostolic letter from the pope of 13 July 1650; and fol. 8v, letter from the pope dated 11 August 1650.
100. AN, MM, 43.
101. AOM, Arch. 455.
102. For lack of any indication from him or from other persons, I resort to hypotheses. Scruple? It does not seem likely. Humility? This is more plausible – traces of this tendency to humility are found in his correspondence; or perhaps a high idea of the religious life?
103. F. Ducaud-Bourget, *La spiritualité de l'Ordre de Malte, 1099–1963* (Paris: La Carraque, 1955), 223.
104. *Gazette de France* (Paris, 1651), 743.
105. AN, MM 43.
106. AOM, Arch. 473, fol. 36. The amount of 1,000 livres to be taken from the commandery of "Castres" – no doubt Caestre, close to Dunkirk. See Mannier, *Les commanderies*, 692.
107. See this chapter, n. 95.
108. Several historians, relying on the word of the abbé de Vertot, have claimed that upon his return from Canada, Montmagny became receiver for the Grand Priory of France. I have found no reference to this title, either in the notarial acts or in the documents of the Order of Malta.
109. AOM, Arch. 58, fol. 320ff, 4 January 1652.
110. I have not been able to discover the identity of this Monsieur de Thou. Doubtless he belonged to the well-known family of Parisian parlementarians of this name, who had ties to the Huault–Du Drac network, through the Sanguins and the Allegrains. At Montmagny's request, the Grand Master repaid him by giving him the "right to wear the cross of gold as a mark of affiliation and aggregation to our Order";

he asked Delbene, the receiver of the Grand Priory of France, to give him a gold chain. AOM, Arch. 1554 (September 25 1652).

111. AOM, Arch. 1554, reference in a letter of 23 June 1652.

112. Ibid., 12 February 1652: despatch to Souvré; letter to Montmagny.

113. It is curious that nobody in the Order, apart from Montmagny, wished to be involved in this. De Thou was a laymen. Was the commander's reputation so bad within the Order?

114. AOM, Arch. 259, fols. 33vff.

115. AOM, Arch. 1554, fols. 55ff.

116. AOM, Arch. 259, following the official instructions.

117. AN, MC, LXXXVIII, 150, 1 January 1652 to Brother Jean de Haudesens; and LI, 237, 11 January 1652 to Adrien Huault.

118. Mentioned in the post-mortem inventory, AN, MC, LXXXVIII, 164, 22 December 1657; not found.

119. No information had been found on this man.

120. AN, MC, LXXXVIII, 165, 13 March 1658, account between Adrien Huault and the receiver of the Grand Priory; reference to these two dates in the document.

121. Du Tertre, *Histoire générale*, 1: 424–5.

122. 29 August and 2 October 1655 and 7 May 1656, mentioned in AN, MC, LXXXVIII, 165, 13 March 1658.

123. AOM, Arch. 6437, 11 August 1653.

124. AOM, Arch. 1555.

125. Ibid.

126. La Roncière, *Histoire*, 5: 229.

127. AN, MC, XCVI, 285ter, item 99.

128. AN, MC, XCVI, 285ter, item 97.

129. AOM, Arch. 1554, 16 April 1654.

130. P. Pelleprat, *Relation des missions des Pères de la Compagnie de Jésus, dans les Îles et dans la terre ferme de l'Amérique méridionale* (Paris, 1655), second part (unpaginated).

131. A little island north of Haiti, which he had conquered some years before. He had also occupied the little islands of Sainte-Croix, Saint-Martin, and Saint-Barthélemy, all of which depended on Saint-Christophe.

132. AOM, Arch. 1554, 8 October 1654.

133. He had entered the Order of Malta in 1631.

134. BN, Moreau 841, fol. 112.

135. Pelleprat, *Relation des missions*, 16.

136. AN, MC, LXXXVIII, 164, 22 December 1657. For the citation by Du Tertre, see this chapter, n. 121.

137. See this chapter, n. 68.

138. AOM, Arch. 476, 12 March 1659. What makes me suspect Montmagny's intervention is the reference in a document dated 2 March 1659 (ibid., fol. 12) of a brief from the pope in Mesnager's favour, dated 5 November 1657, and thus shortly after Montmagny's death.

139. AOM, Arch. 1214, 13 July 1666.

140. Mannier, *Les commanderies*, 89.

141. To Louis-Théandre, Sieur de Lotbinière, his wife Elisabeth, and another couple. See Chapter 7.

142. Reference in the account of 1658, AN, MC, LXXXVIIII, 165, 13 March 1658.

143. AN, MC, LI, 541, 9 September 1656.

144. Reference in the account of 1658, see this chapter, n. 142.

145. Reference, ibid.

146. AN, MC, LXXXVIII, 164.

147. The rule which required that 80 per cent of a chevalier's goods should come to the Order, and that he could dispose of the remaining 20 per cent, would have proved embarrassing in this case. In Malta, however, I found the following disposition for Brother Charles Huault de Montmagny, "licentiam disponendi de suis patrimonialibus tam in vita quam in mortis articulo dummodo [sit] in forma ..." AOM, Arch. 473, 30 March 1652.

148. See this chapter, n. 142.

149. See Chapter 4.

150. Jean-Paul de Lascaris (d. 1657); Martin de Redin (d. 1660); Annet de Clermont (d. 1660); Raphael Cotoner (d. 1663); Nicolas Cotoner (elected 1663, d. 1680).

151. AOM, Arch. 260, fols. 22ff.

152. Mannier, *Les commanderies*, 74. In 1668 he was granted the commandery of Slype in Belgium.

153. See *Biographie universelle ancienne et moderne* (Paris: Michaud Frères, 1825). Articles on Saint François de Sales and his nephew, the Knight of Malta.

154. In 1650 he took back from them a part of the city which they had just conquered. For Crete, see this chapter, n. 79.

155. Du Tertre, *Histoire générale*, 1: 544.

156. AN, M 1001; AOM, Arch. 1556, about 10 September 1658.

157. AOM, Arch. 1556, 3 April 1659.

158. AE, Amérique 4, fol. 539. See also Boucher, *Cannibal Encounters*, 60–1.

159. Those of Saint-Christophe, Nevis, Monserrat, and Antigua.

160. Du Tertre, *Histoire générale*, 1: 540.

161. AOM, Arch. 1214, 6 February 1662.

162. Ibid.; Arch. 6437, 16 December 1660.

163. AOM, Arch 1557, February 1662.

164. AOM, Arch. 6437, 21 August 1662.
165. AOM, Arch. 1214, March 1663, and Arch. 261.
166. AOM, Arch. 6437, 3 March 1665.
167. AN, MC, LXXXVIII, 195; copy in AOM, Arch. 261, 29 September 1665.
168. Pécule: "all the goods that one has acquired by his cares and by his work." Richelet, *Dictionnaire françois*.
169. See this chapter, n. 77.
170. AOM, Arch. 1214, 21 November 1665.
171. Ibid., 10 December 1665.
172. Ibid., 15 January 1665.
173. Cultru, "Colonisation d'autrefois."
174. AOM, Arch. 261, 15 February 1666.
175. J.L. Bourgeon, *Les Colbert avant Colbert* (Paris: PUF, 1973).
176. AOM, Arch. 1214, 6 March and 25 May 1668.
177. Mannier, *Les commanderies*, 719–20.
178. These dates and these numbers appear in the margins of the contract of sale, AN, MC, LXXXVIII, 195, 10 August 1665.

By way of a conclusion

1. AOM, Arch. 2926.
2. BN, DB, 362, the Huaults of Bernay, "the only survivors of the name of Huault of Vayres and of Montmagny ... in 1714" had themselves adopted the following motto: "*Me virtus, non praeda trahit*" which can be translated as "It is virtue that distinguishes me from the others, not the lure of gain."
3. AOM, Arch. 2926. See also La Chesnaye-Desbois, *Dictionnaire*, at the end of the Huault entry.
4. In 1984 the town of Montmagny, situated close to Paris, celebrated the eighth centenary of the foundation of the parish of Saint Thomas. A little brochure entitled *Montmagny, huit siècles d'histoire* was published on this occasion; on the cover page there appeared the coat of arms of the town, which is thus described: "D'or à une fasce d'azur chargée de trois molettes d'éperon du champ, accompagnées de trois groupes de coquerelles de gueules, bordure de gueules, chargées de huit pivoines d'argent." A motto accompanies the arms: "*Acta, non verba*," which can be translated as "Acts, not just words."
5. Translation of the heraldic language: on a gold background, a horizontal band of blue, in which appear three gold stars with six points pierced in the centre [representing the spurs that knights wore on their boots]. Around

the central band, three bouquets, two above, one below, each composed of three stylized hazelnuts, one upright, the others on their side.

6. Translation of the heraldic language: on a gold background, a winged dragon of green, with claws, tongue and crown of red.

7. BN, *Mss frs*, 23 981, 5 October 1642, letter to Mathieu de Goussaincourt. AOM, Arch. 58, letters of 26 November 1649 (fols. 308ff.); 29 April (fols. 320–1); 6 May 1650 (fols. 314–5); and 4 January 1652 (fols. 320–1). These letters are signed. A letter, of which the original has been lost, was published in part by L.E. Bois in *Études et recherches biographiques sur le chevalier Noël Brulart de Sillery* (Québec, 1855), 10–11; it probably dates from September 1637. Campeau has reproduced the two letters, that of Noël Brulart and that of Montmagny, in *MNF*, 3: 480–1 and 514–5.

Glossary

Aveu et dénombrement: Description of the goods and dues related to a fief upon change of ownership.

Caravan: Involvement of a Knight of Malta in an expedition organized by his order against the Turks in the Eastern Mediterranean. He was supposed to take part in four of these if he wished to *commanderie* (a land which had been conceded to the order in his country).

Chambre des comptes: Chamber of accounts, a body charged with controlling the public funds.

Chambre du roi: A section of the royal court; persons who are in charge of the private life of the royal family, such as the *valets de chambre* or the *valets de garde-robe du roi*.

Châtelet: Tribunal of the *prevots* and *vicontés* of Paris, subordinate to the parliament. The most important court of justice of Paris.

Chevalier: Knight; a title given to the high nobility.

Commissaire des guerres: Commissioner for military affairs. A *commissaire* is a person to whom the king concedes, by letter of commission, a function which is removable. Thus a *commissaire* is not, like an *officier*, the owner of his charge.

Conseil d'état et privé: Council of State, supervising the justice and the administration of the government. Its members are entitled *conseillers d'État*.

Conseiller du roi: a title given to most office-holders working in some part of the government.

Corso: The Italian word for a privateering expedition; in French, "course."

Cour des aides: The court with jurisdiction over a number of cases relating to taxes, not only the "aides" or indirect taxes.

Echevin: Alderman, member of a town council.

Écuyer: Squire; a title that can be used by any noble, following his name and before the name of his *seigneurie*.

Engagé: Man recruited to work in a colony. He is "engaged" for thirty-six months (engagés were often called "trente-six mois"); after which he is allowed to settle in the colony, either in a *seigneurie* or in a town.

Grand Conseil: Court of law chaired by the chancellor, and dealing, among other things, with disagreements among the sovereign courts.

Greffier: Registrar or clerk of a court; the man whom the court employs to receive, send, and store judgments.

Lettre de cachet: A sealed letter sent by the king concerning a particular case, and linked most of the time to an order for exile or imprisonment.

Lieutenant / maître particulier des eaux et forêts: Officer in charge of a jurisdiction concerned with waters and forests. These jurisdictions are called *grand maîtrises* or *maîtrises particulières*, the latter depending on the former.

Maître des comptes: Official in charge of supervising, for a financial jurisdiction, certain transactions; the most important magistrate in the *Chambre des comptes*.

Maître des requêtes: Magistrate of high rank, recruited in the sovereign courts to conduct investigations throughout the country; often called to become an *intendant*.

Maréchal de camp: Before the 1670s, an army officer in charge of organizing the lodging of an army during a campaign.

Parlement: Court of justice, but with some administrative and political powers. The most important is the parlement of Paris; there are thirteen parlements in the provinces.

Président à mortier: A judge of the *Grand Chambre* of the Paris parlement.

Requêtes du Palais: Sector of the parlements charged with supervising certain special cases.

Robe: See robin.

Robin: Person belonging to the legal profession (la "robe") as a lawyer or a magistrate.

Roture: Absence of nobility, commoner status.

"Savonette à vilain": Soap that washes away the taint of non-nobility; a metaphor for the purchase by a commoner of a title. The expression was coined by the Duke of Saint-Simon (1675–1755) in his memoirs, but the practice developed much earlier in time.

Secrétaire du roi: Originally an office holder charged with signing the letters sent out by the chancery. But in fact, most of the time, a title given to a good civil servant, bringing with it certain advantages, the most important of which is ennoblement.

Seigneur de ...: A man who possesses a seigneurie, who can claim the title of "'N' seigneur de 'XX'" (name of the place).

Surintendant des finances: The *Surintendant* is the man who is in charge of the financial administration of the kingdom. This charge disappears after the departure of Fouquet.

Taille: The most important direct tax, calculated on personal possessions.

Vicomte: Holder of a viscounty.

N.B. A good reference book on this subject is: Roland Mousnier, *The Institutions of France under the Absolute Monarchy, 1598–1789, Society and State*, translated by Brian Pearce (Chicago: U. of Chicago Press 1979), 2 volumes. At the end of each volume there is a very good glossary.

Bibliography

I - Manuscripts

A. Paris
  1. Bibliothèque nationale de France.
     a. Cabinet des titres.

        Concerning the Huault Family: Pièces originales (abbrev. P.O.) 1542, Cabinet d'Hozier (Cab. H.) 193, Dossiers bleus (D.B.) 362, Carrés d'Hozier (Car. H.) 345, Nouveaux d'Hozier (Nouv. H.) 189.

        Concerning the Du Drac Family: P.O. 1036, D.B. 241, Cab. H. 122, Car. H. 231.

        Concerning the families in alliance: Anjorrant, D.B. 24, Car. H. 10; Arbaleste, D.B. 28; Avrillot, Nouv. H. 19; Barrillon, D.B. 58; de Beauvais, D.B. 77; de Billon, P.O. 351; D.B. 97, Car. H., 94; Cuvier, D.B. 228, Car. H. 218, Cab. H. 116; Faucon, D.B. 261, Car. H. 246, Cab. H. 135; de Ficte, D.B. 269, Car. H. 256; de Gouy, D.B. 326; Hacqueville, D.B. 343; Lauson, D.B. 386; Le Brest, D.B. 132; Lescuyer, D.B. 391; Lottin, D.B. 407, Car. H. 392; Petremol, Cab. H. 276; Piedefer, D.B. 522; Rappouel, D.B. 527, Cab. H. 285, P.O. 2435; Ribier. D.B. 564, P.O. 2473; Sevin, D.B. 614.

        Concerning other families: Malebranche, D.B. 417; Poincy, P.O. 1744, Nouv. H. 213; Thomé, D.B. 632; Wignacourt, D.B. 668.

     b. Other series.

        French manuscripts (Mss frs):
        4826, 16738, 18593, 24974; 23981 (letter by Charles Huault de Montmagny).

Transcriptions of Parisian parish registers: 32 588 (Saint-Jean-en-Grève), 32 591 (Saint-Paul), 32 838 (Saint-Gervais); 32 946 (list of provosts of merchants and aldermen of Paris).

New French acquisitions (N.a.f.)
784 (copy of the parish register of Saint-Nicolas-des-Champs) 9281, 9318, 9319, 9323.

Latin manuscripts 14 456 (Saint-Victor Abbey).

Various collections:
Cinq Cents de Colbert 45; Clairambault 381, 841, 951, 1006; Dupuy 837 (poem written in 1600, incriminating Charles Huault, the chevalier's father); Moreau 841; Morel de Thoisy 445.

2. Archives nationales (AN) (National Archives of France)
   a. Minutier central (MC).

Most important notarial offices (systematic research for certain years, in offices VI and LI) and selected studies in XXIV, XXVI, XXX, LXVIII, LXXV, LXXXV, LXXXVIII, XCVII, CVII, CXXII.

Other offices where acts were found: III, IV, VIII, XII, XIV, XVI, XIX, XX, XXIX, XL, XLII, LIII, LIV, LXX, LXXIII, XCI, CV, CVIII, CX, CXV, CXVIII, CXXI; note an important file on the Lonvilliers de Poincy in XCVI, 285 bis and ter.

   b. Other series.

M and MM, important series for the Order of Malta: meetings of the Grand Prieuré de France, proofs of nobility; methodically studied.

O^1 7 (1652), commission of Lieutenant General of Saint-Christophe (in the absence of the governor) for Charles Huault de Montmagny.

P 2308.

S 1025 (1611), sale by the Huault de Montmagny family of a property in Paris to the king.

Y, methodical study of this series for the Huault et Du Drac families.

    c.   Archives des colonies (AC).

Relative gaps for the years 1635–1648. We pulled out information from the following numbers: C 10 B, 1; E, 191, 225 (extension in 1645 of Montmagny's term as governor of Québec); F 3, 52.

  3.   Affaires étrangères (AE).

Memoirs and documents, America, 4 (17th century): numerous documents about the American colonies.

Political correspondance, England, v. 42 (concerning Saint-Christophe).

B.   Other depositories in France
  1.   Archives départementales du Val d'Oise (ADVO).

Parish registers of Saint-Thomas de Montmagny, contents from 1692 to 1714.

Offices of the notaries of the city of Montmagny: contents from 1635 (start of the series) to 1657; 1661, 1677 to 1680, 1687 to 1690; surveys from 1690 to 1696; contents from 1697 to 1702; 1707, 1708, 1710.

Series B contains no interesting data.

  2.   Montmagny town hall: parish registers, contents from 1550 to 1707.

  3.   Archives départementales d'Indre-et-Loire (ADIL).

E 972, tax roll of the Azay-le-Rideau parish, 1519.

4. Archives communales d'Azay-le-Rideau: parish registers, contents from 1594 to 1619.

    P.S. in 3 and 4, these documents contain numerous mentions of Huault and Victor families, but it was not possible to uncover the ties they had with the Huaults and Victors of Paris.

5. Archives départementales des Bouches-du-Rhône (Marseille).

    A reference (from a Parisian document) to Notary F. Baldouyn, (E360,62) was used. Surveys done on other years in the same office were not informative; neither were other tests done in other notaries' offices.

C. Malta
    1. Archives of the Order of Malta (AOM) at the National Library of Malta (in Valletta).

        a. Archives (Arch.). Systematic research in various series for the years 1622 to 1636 and 1648 to 1666. Selected studies were held from 1605 to 1621 (regarding Philippe de Lonvilliers de Poincy) and for the years 1636 to 1648. References were found in the following registers: 58, 111, 112, 117, 256, 258, 259 to 261, 460 to 477, 966, 1200, 1214, 1554 to 1557, 1707, 1720, 1722, 1724, 1768, 2111, 2226, 2234, 6402, 6437, 6475. Note the proofs of nobility for Charles Huault de Montmagny, 2926, and for Alexandre Huault de Vayres, 3566.

        b. Library (libr.) Cxxv, 315, 413, 480.

    2. Notarial Archives of Valletta.

        The offices of the notaries of Malta were systematically researched for the years 1622 to 1636. Pietro Vella was the most important. Many things were found in the offices of the following notaries: Lucciano Dello Re, Ambrosio Sceberras. Some details were collected in the offices of Aloysius Fallun, Antonio Abela, Thomas Cauchi, Pietro Paulo Vincella.

    3. Tribunale Armamentorum, part of the National Archives of Malta: disputes over the outfitting of boats. Research found nothing.

D. Canada
1.   Archives des Ursulines de la Ville de Québec.

    1.1.1.: 1, 2, 3, 5.
    1.1.2.: 1.
    1. A4: 1 to 4.

2.   Archives nationales du Québec (at Québec City).

    P 1 000, 50, 994, manuscripts concerning Louis Huault and the Lottin family.

    Notarial offices for the years 1636 to 1648 were searched: M. Piraube, J. Guitet, G. Tronquet, P. Vachon, H. Bancheron, L. Barmen, C. Lacoustre.

3.   Archives du Séminaire de Québec (ASQ).

    Documents held there (essentially in the Faribault collection) concern the internal administration of the colony.

II – Published Sources

Les Annales de l'Hôtel-Dieu de Québec. Edited by Dom Albert Jamet. Québec City, 1939.

Baudier, M. *Inventaire de l'histoire des Turcs*. Paris, 1631.

Bideau, M., ed. *Voyage d'Italie (1605)*. Geneva: Slatkine, 1982. (The author of this account remains anonymous.)

Bouchard, Jean-Jacques. *Un Parisien à Rome et à Naples en 1632*. Paris: Éditions L. Marcheix, 1896.

Cyrano de Bergerac, Savinien. *Voyage dans la Lune (L'Autre Monde ou les Empires de la Lune)*. Edited by M. Laugaa. Paris: Garnier-Flammarion, 1970.

—— *L'autre Monde*. Edited by F. Lachèvre. Geneva: Slatkine, 1968. (The original Lachèvre edition: ca 1921).

Digby, Kenelm. *Journal of a Voyage into the Mediterranean*. London: Honson Reprint, 1968 (trip taken in 1628–1629).

Dollier de Casson, François. *Histoire de Montréal*. Edited by M. Trudel and M. Baboyant. Montréal: HMH, 1992.

Du Tertre, Jean-Baptiste. *Histoire générale des Antilles habitées par les Français.* Paris, 1978, 4 v.

Édits, ordonnances royaux, déclarations et arrêts du conseil d'État du roi concernant le Canada. Québec City, 1854–1856, 3 v.

Inventaire des concessions en fief et seigneurie, fois et hommages, aveux et dénombrements, conservés aux Archives de la Province de Québec. Edited by P.G. Roy. Beauceville: L'Éclaireur, 1927–1929, 6 v.

The Jesuit Relations and Allied Documents. Edited by R.G. Thwaites. Cleveland, 1896–1901, 73 v.

L'Estoile, Pierre de. *Mémoires-journaux.* Edited by G. Brunet et al., vol. I, Journal de Henri III, 1574–1580. Paris, 1975.

Le Journal des Jésuites. Edited by C.H. Laverdière and H.R. Casgrain. Montréal, 1892.

Luppé du Garrané, J.B. *Mémoires et caravanes.* Paris, 1865.

Montaigne, Michel de. *Journal de voyage en Italie.* Edited by C. Dedeyan. Paris: Les Belles Lettres, 1946.

Monumenta Novae Franciae. Edited by L. Campeau, s.j. from vol. II (1616–1634), Québec City: PUL, 1969, to vol. VI, (1644–1646), published in 1992 in Montréal by Éditions Bellarmin. These works contain a critical edition of the *Relations.*

Ordonnances, commissions des gouverneurs et intendants de la Nouvelle-France. Beauceville: L'Éclaireur, Vol. I, 1924.

Pelleprat, P. *Relation des missions des Pères de la Compagnie de Jésus dans les Îles et dans la terre ferme de l'Amérique méridionale.* Paris, 1655.

Pouget, P. *Instructions sur les principaux devoirs des chevaliers de Malte.* Paris, 1712.

Provins, P. Pacifique de. *Brève relation du voyage des Îles de l'Amérique.* Assisi: Collegio S. Lorenzo, 1939.

Richelieu, Armand Jean Du Plessis, Cardinal de. *Lettres, instructions diplomatiques et papiers d'Etat du cardinal de Richelieu.* Edited by D.L. M. d'Avenel. Paris, 1855–1876, 8 v.

—— *Les papiers de Richelieu, Section politique intérieure, correspondance et papiers d'État.* Edited by P. Grillon. Paris: A. Pedone, from 1975, 6 v. published.

Roy, P.G. *Inventaire des concessions en fiefs et seigneuries, fois et hommages et aveux et dénombrements conservés aux Archives de la Province de Québec.* Beauceville, 1927, v. I.

Stochove. *Voyage du Levant du Sr de Stochove, seignr de Ste-Catherine.* Brussels, 1650 (2nd ed.).

Tallemant des Réaux, Gédéon. *Historiettes.* Edited by A. Adam. Paris: Gallimard, 1960, 2 v. (Bibliothèque de la Pléiade).

III -Dictionaries

Biographie universelle ancienne et moderne. Paris: chez Michaud frères, from 1811.

Dictionnaire biographique du Canada, v. I (1000 to 1700). Québec City: PUL, 1966.

Dictionnaire de biographie française (DBF). Paris, from 1933, (ongoing).

Dictionnaire de l'Académie française. Paris, 1765, 2 v.

Dictionnaire d'histoire et de géographie ecclésiastiques. Paris: Letouzey et Ané, from 1912.

Furetière, A. *Dictionnaire universel*. Paris: Dict. Le Robert, 1978 (reprint), 3 v.

Hasquin, H., ed. *Communes de Belgique, Dictionnaire d'histoire et de géographie administrative*, n. p., Renaissance du Livre, 1981–1983, 4 v.

Jal, A. *Dictionnaire critique de biographie et d'histoire*. Paris, 1867.

La Chesnaye-Desbois, F. A. Aubert de. *Dictionnaire de la noblesse*. Paris, 1863–1876, 3rd ed. 19 v.

Marion, M. *Dictionnaire des institutions de la France aux XVIIe et XVIIIe siècles*. Paris: Picard, 1923.

Moreri, L. *Le Grand Dictionnaire Historique ou le Mélange de l'histoire sacrée et profane*. Paris, 1756, 10 v.

Richelet, P. *Dictionnaire François*. Geneva, 1700.

Taillemite, E. *Dictionnaire des marins français*. Paris: Éditions maritimes et d'Outre-mer, 1982.

IV -Other Works

A.   France during the Old Regime

Alcover, M. *La pensée philosophique et scientifique de Cyrano de Bergerac*. Geneva: Droz, 1970.

Autrand, F. *Naissance d'un grand corps de l'Etat, Les gens du Parlement de Paris, 1345–1454*. Paris: Publications de la Sorbonne, 1981.

Ballon, H. *The Paris of Henri IV, Architecture and Urbanism*. New York: The Architectural History Foundation, 1991.

Barbier, A. "Les intendants de province et les commissaires royaux en Poitou." In *Mémoires de la société des antiquaires de l'Ouest*, t. XXVI, 1902.

Bergin, J. *L'ascension de Richelieu*. Paris: Payot, 1994 (translation).

Bluche, F. and P. Durye. *L'anoblissement par charges avant 1789*, n.p., 1962, 2 v. (Les Cahiers nobles, no. 23 and 24).

Boiteux, L.A. *Richelieu, grand-maître de la navigation et du commerce.* Paris: Ozanne, 1955.

Bonnard, R. *Histoire de l'abbaye royale et de l'ordre des chanoines réguliers de St-Victor de Paris.* Paris, 1902, 2 v.

Bonvallet, A. "Le bureau des finances de la généralité de Poitiers." In *Mémoires de la société des antiquaires de l'Ouest,* t. VI, 137–400, 1883.

Brasart, G. "La Vie des écoliers au XVIe siècle d'après deux comptes de tutelle." In *Bibliothèque d'humanisme et Renaissance,* t. VII, 273–281, 1945.

Braudel, F. *La Méditerranée et le monde méditerranéen à l'époque de Philippe II.* Paris: A. Colin, 1966 (2nd ed.), 2 v.

Bréhant, N.C.B. *Généalogie de la maison de Bréhant,* Paris, 1867.

Brinbinet, J.E. *Histoire de l'Université de lois d'Orléans.* Paris and Orléans, 1853.

Charton-Le Clech, S. *Chancellerie et culture au XVIe siècle : Les notaires et secrétaires du roi de 1515 à 1547.* Toulouse: Presses universitaires du Mirail, 1993.

Chère, J. *Histoire de l'école de La Flèche,* La Flèche, 1854.

Compère, M.M. and D. Julia. *Les collèges français, 16e – 18e siècle.* Paris: CNRS, 1988.

Dainville, F. de. *L'éducation des jésuites (XVIe – XVIIIe siècles).* Paris: Minuit, 1978.

—— *Naissance de l'humanisme moderne.* Paris: Beauchesne, 1940.

Delattre, P., ed. *L'établissement des jésuites en France, 1540–1940.* Enghien: Institut supérieur de théologie, 1949–1957, 5 v.

Delumeau, J. *Une histoire du paradis,* t. I, *Le Jardin des délices.* Paris: Fayard, 1992.

—— *Vie économique et sociale de Rome dans la seconde moitié du XVIe siècle.* Paris: De Boccard, 1957, 2 v.

Descimon, R. *Qui étaient les Seize? Mythes et réalités de la Ligue parisienne (1585–1594).* Paris: Klincksieck, 1983.

Douillard, G. *Les origines de l'Hôtel de Sully.* (ca. 1985, typewritten at the documentation centre at the Hôtel de Sully in Paris.)

Dresch, O. "Les couvents des minimes à Paris." Thesis, École des Chartes, 1966, 2 v.

Etchechoury, M. *Les maîtres des requêtes de l'Hôtel du roi sous les derniers Valois (1553–1589).* Paris: École des Chartes, 1991.

Fraguier, L. de. *Une famille parisienne (la famille de Fraguier).* Paris, 1963.

Garrison, F. *Histoire des institutions publiques et des faits sociaux*. Paris: Les cours de droit, 1969, 3 v.

Gaston-Chéreau, F. "Pages de la vie de collège (La Flèche, 1611–1616)." In *Mélanges Félix Grat*, 413–443. Paris, 1949, t. II.

Guénée, S. *Bibliographie d'histoire des universités françaises des origines à la Révolution. Université d'Orléans*. Paris: A. and J. Picard, 1970.

Guérin, L. *Les marins illustres de la France*. Paris, 1844.

Hillairet, J. *Connaissance du vieux Paris*. Paris: Éditions Gonthier, 1981, 3 v.

Kerviler, R. *Nicolas Bourbon (1574–1644): Étude sur sa vie et sur ses travaux*. Paris: Librairie H. Menu, 1877.

La Roncière, C. de. *Histoire de la marine française*. Paris: Plon, Nourrit et Cie, 1899ff, 6 v.

Lacour-Gayet, R. *La marine militaire sous Louis XIII et Louis XIV*, t. I, *Richelieu et Mazarin*. Paris: Champion, 1911.

Lacouture, J. *Jésuites*, t. I, *Les conquérants*. Paris: Seuil, 1991.

Lapeyre, A. and R. Scheurer. *Les notaires et secrétaires du roi sous les règnes de Louis XI, Charles VIII et Louis XII (1461–1515)*. Paris: BN, 1978, 2 v.

Lebeuf, J. *Histoire de la ville et de tout le diocèse de Paris*. Paris, 1863–1870, 4 v.

Masson, P. *Histoire du commerce français dans le Levant au XVIIe siècle*. Paris, 1886.

Michaud, H. *La grande chancellerie et les écritures royales au XVIe siècle*. Paris: PUF, 1967.

Mirot, L. "Les origines de l'hôtel de Sully." In *Bulletin de la Société de l'histoire de Paris et de l'Île-de-France* 38 (1911).

Motley, M. *Becoming a French Aristocrat: The Education of the Court Nobility, 1580–1715*. Princeton, NJ: Princeton University Press, 1990.

Pintard, R. *Les libertins érudits de la première moitié du XVIIe siècle*. Paris: Boivin, 1943.

Poisson, G. *Evocation du grand Paris*, t. 2, *La banlieue Nord-Ouest*. Paris: Les Éditions de Minuit, 1960.

Rochemonteix, C. de. *Un collège de jésuites aux XVIIe et XVIIIe siècles: le collège de Henri IV de la Flèche*. Le Mans, 1889, 4 v.

Schudt, L. *Italienreisen im 17. und 18. Jahrhundert*. Vienna, 1959.

Tessereau, A. *Histoire chronologique de la grande Chancellerie de France*. Paris, 1710.

Verger, F., ed. *Histoire des universités en France*. Toulouse: Privat, 1986.

B.   New France and other French Cultures

Axtell, J. *The Contest of Cultures in Colonial North America: The Invasion Within*. Oxford: Oxford University Press, 1985.

Beaulieu, A. *Convertir les fils de Cain, Jésuites et Amérindiens nomades en Nouvelle-France, 1632–1642*. Québec City: Nuit blanche, 1990.

Béchard, A. *Histoire de l'île-aux-Oies et des îles voisines*. Arthabaskaville: Impr. La Bataille, 1902.

Blet, H. *Histoire de la colonisation française*, v. I. Paris: Arthaud, 1946.

Bois, L.E. *Études et recherches biographiques sur le chevalier Noël Brulart de Sillery*. Québec City, 1855.

Boucher, P. *Cannibal encounters, Europeans and Island Caribs, 1492–1763*. Baltimore: Johns Hopkins University Press, 1992.

Cambray, A. *Robert Giffard, premier seigneur de Beauport et les origines de la Nouvelle-France*. Cap-de-la-Madeleine, 1932.

Campeau, L. *La mission des jésuites chez les Hurons*. Montréal: Bellarmin, 1987.

——*Les Cent-Associés et le peuplement de la Nouvelle-France (1633–1663)*. Montréal: Bellarmin, 1974.

—— *Les finances publiques de la Nouvelle-France sous le régime français, 1632–1665*. Montréal: Bellarmin, 1975.

Charbonneau, A., Y. Desloges, and M. Lafrance. *Québec, ville fortifiée du XVIIe au XIXe siècle*. Québec City: Éditions du Pélican, 1982.

Crouse, N.M. *The French Struggle for the East Indies, 1665–1713*. London: Frank Cass, 1966.

Cultru, P. "Colonisation d'autrefois. Le commandeur de Poincy à Saint-Christophe." In *Revue de l'histoire des colonies françaises*, 289ff, 1915.

Dampierre, J. de. *Essai sur les sources de l'histoire des Antilles françaises, 1492–1664*. Paris: Picard, 1907.

Daney, S. *Histoire de la Martinique, depuis la colonisation jusqu'en 1815*. Fort-de-France, 1963 (original edition, 1846).

Daveluy, M.-C. *La Société de Notre-Dame de Montréal, 1639–1663*. Montréal: Fides, 1965.

Delâge, D. *Le pays renversé, Amérindiens et Européens en Amérique du Nord-Est, 1600–1664*. Montréal: Boréal, 1991.

Deroy-Pineau, F. *Marie de l'Incarnation, femme d'affaires, mystique, mère de la Nouvelle-France*. Paris: Laffont, 1989.

—— *Madeleine de La Peltrie, Amazone du Nouveau Monde*. Montréal: Bellarmin, 1992.

Deschamps, L. *Un colonisateur au temps de Richelieu, Isaac de Razilly*. Paris, 1887.

Deslandres, D. Le modèle français d'intégration socio-religieuse, 1600–1650: Les missions intérieures et les premières missions canadiennes. Doctoral thesis, University of Montréal, 1991 (typewritten).

Desrosiers, L.-P. *Iroquoisie 1534–1646*. Montréal: Institut d'Histoire de l'Amérique Française, 1947, t. I, (only volume published).

Dionne, N.E. *Le séminaire de Notre-Dame des Anges*. Montréal, 1890.

Ferland, R. *Les Relations des jésuites: un art de la persuasion. Procédés de rhétorique et fonction conative dans les Relations du Père Paul Lejeune.* Québec City: Les éditions de la Huit, 1992.

Goslinga, C.C. *The Dutch in the Caribbean and on the Wildcoast, 1580–1680.* Gainsville: University of Florida Press, 1971.

Harris, R.C., ed. *Atlas historique du Canada*, t. I, *Des origines à 1800.* Montréal: PUM, 1987.

Joyau, A. *Belain d'Esnambuc*. Paris: Bellenand, 1950.

Lanctot, G. *Montréal sous Maisonneuve, 1642–1665.* Montréal: Beauchemin, 1966.

Landry, Y., ed. *Pour le Christ et le Roi, La vie au temps des premiers Montréalais*. Montréal: Libre expression, 1992.

Lavallée, L. *La Prairie en Nouvelle-France, 1647–1760.* Montréal: McGill Queens University Press, 1993.

Martineau, A. and L.-P. May. *Trois siècles d'histoire antillaise*. Paris: Librairie Leroux, 1935.

Petitjean-Roget, J. "Les titres de noblesse des Vergers de Sannois." In *Annales des Antilles*, no. 6 (1958): 66ff.

Pluchon, P. *Histoire de la colonisation française*. Paris: Fayard, t. I, 1991.

Rennard, J. *Histoire religieuse des Antilles françaises des origines à 1914, d'après des documents inédits*. Paris: Larose, 1954.

Roberts, A. *The French in the West Indies*. New York: Cooper Square, 1971.

Roy, J.E. "M. de Montmagny." In *La Nouvelle-France*, t. V, I, (his administration), 105–121, and 161–173; II, (his character), 417–428 and 520–530, 1906.

Roy, P.-G. *La ville de Québec sous le Régime français*. Québec City: R. Paradis, 1930.

Trigger, B. *Les enfants d'Aataentsic, L'histoire du peuple huron*. Montréal: Libre expression, 1991.

Trudel, M. *Les débuts du régime seigneurial au Canada*. Montréal: Fides, 1974.

——*Histoire de la Nouvelle-France*, t. II, *Le comptoir (1604–1627)*. Montréal: Fides, 1966; t. III, v. 1, *Les événements*, 1979, v. 2, *La société*, 1983.

—— *Montréal, la formation d'une société, 1642–1663*. Montréal: Fides, 1976.

Wilkie, E.C. "Une bibliothèque bien fournie: The Earliest Known Caribbean Library." In *Libraries and Culture* 25, no. 2 (1990).

C.   The Order of Malta

Allen, D.F. "The Social and Religious World of a Knight of Malta in the Caribbean, c. 1632–1660." In *Malta, A Case Study in International Cross Currents*, 147–167. Malta, 1991.

Bernaby, A.A. "Cavalieri di Malta in Canada (1636–1682)." In *Archivo storico di Malta*, 53–57, v. X, 1938–1939.

Buhagiar, M. *The Iconography of the Maltese Islands, 1400–1900*. Valletta: Progress Press, 1987.

Cassar, P. "The Maltese Corsairs and the Order of Malta." In *Catholic Historical Review* XLVI (July 1960): 137–156.

Cavalliero, R.E. "The decline of the Maltese Corso in the 18th Century, a case study of maritime history." In *Melita Historica* 224ff, 1956.

Dal Pozzo, B. *Historia della Sacra Religione Militare di San Giovanni Gerosolimitano*, 2 v. Verona, 1703–1715.

Ducaud-Bourget, F. *La spiritualité de l'ordre de Malte (1099–1963)*. Paris: La Caraque, n.d.

Earle, P. *Corsairs of Malta and Barbary*. London: Sidgwick and Jackson, 1970.

Engel, C.-L. *Histoire de l'Ordre de Malte*. Geneva: Nagel, 1968.

Fontenay, M. "Corsaires de la foi ou rentiers du sol? Les chevaliers de Malte dans le 'corso' méditerranéen au XVIIe siècle." In *RHMC* 35(1988): 361 *ff*.

—— "La course dans l'économie méditerranéenne au XVIIe siècle." In *AESC* 43 (1988): 321 *ff*.

—— "L'empire ottoman et le risque corsaire au XVIIe siècle." In *RHMC* 32 (1985): 185*ff*.

Gangneux, G. "Société nobiliaire et Ordre de Malte." In *Cahiers d'histoire* 20, no 3 (1975): 347ff.

Godechot, J. *Histoire de Malte*. Paris: PUF, 1981 (3rd ed., collection "Que sais-je?").

Grima, J.F. "The maintenance of the Order's Galley Squadron (1600–1650)." In *Melita Historica* 1977, 145 *ff*.

Guérin, T. *From the Crusades to Quebec, the Knights of Malta in the New World*. Montréal: Palm Publishers, 1949.

Hughes, Q. *The Building of Malta, 1530–1795*. Valletta: Progress Press, 1986.

Jurien de La Gravière. *Les chevaliers de Malte et la marine de Philippe II.* Paris, 1887, 2 v.

Labignette, J.E. "Les chevaliers de Malte dans l'histoire du Canada." In *Bulletin des Recherches historiques* 68 (1966): 7 *ff.*

La Roque, L. de. *Catalogue des chevaliers de Malte.* Supplement to the *Bulletin Héraldique*, February 1890.

Macpherson, D.D. *De Poincy and the Order of St. John in the New World.* London, 1949 (Library Committee Order of St. John of Jerusalem, Historical pamphlet, no. 9).

Mannier, E. *Ordre de Malte, Les commanderies du grand prieuré de France.* Brionne: Gérard Montfort, 1987.

Miège, M. *Histoire de Malte.* Paris, 1841, 2 v.

Pichette, R. and J.-J. Lussiser. "Armorial des Chevaliers de Malte français en terre d'Amérique." In *Revue de l'Université d'Ottawa* 1976: 40 *ff.*

Poutiers, J.-C. *Rhodes et ses chevaliers, 1306–1523.* Lebanon: Imprimerie catholique sal Araya, 1989.

Roy, J.-E. *L'ordre de Malte en Amérique.* Québec City, 1888.

Ubaldini, U. M. *La marina del soverano militare ordine di San Giovanni di Gerusalemme, di Rodi e di Malta.* Rome: Regionale editrice, 1971.

Varillon, P. "L'ordre de Malte, pépinière de marins français." In *Revue des deux mondes*, 1957: 672ff.

Verane, L. and G.-M.-J. Chassin. *Le chevalier Paul.* Paris: Renaissance du Livre, 1931.

Vertot, R. Aubert de. *Histoire des chevaliers hospitaliers de Saint-Jean de Jérusalem.* Paris: 1753, 6 v.

Index